THE DANCE OF FREEDOM

NUMBER NINETEEN

*Jack and Doris Smothers Series
in Texas History, Life, and Culture*

The Dance of Freedom

TEXAS AFRICAN AMERICANS DURING RECONSTRUCTION

Barry A. Crouch

Edited by Larry Madaras

Foreword by Arnoldo de León

UNIVERSITY OF TEXAS PRESS
Austin

"'Unmanacling' Texas Reconstruction: A Twenty-Year Perspective" originally appeared in *Southwestern Historical Quarterly* 93 (January 1990): 275–302.

"Reconstructing Black Families: Perspectives from the Texas Freedmen's Bureau Records" (with Larry Madaras) originally appeared in *Prologue: Journal of the National Archives* 18 (Summer 1986): 109–122.

"Black Dreams and White Justice" originally appeared in *Prologue: Journal of the National Archives* 6 (Winter 1974): 255–265.

"Seeking Equality: Houston Black Women during Reconstruction" originally appeared in *Black Dixie: Afro-Texas History and Culture in Houston,* ed. Howard Beeth and Cary D. Wintz (College Station: Texas A&M University Press, 1992): 54–73.

"A Spirit of Lawlessness: White Violence, Texas Blacks, 1865–1868" originally appeared in *Journal of Social History* 18 (December 1984): 217–232.

"Crisis in Color: Racial Separation in Texas during Reconstruction" (with L. J. Schultz) originally appeared in *Civil War History* 16 (March 1970): 37–49.

"'All the Vile Passions': The Texas Black Code of 1866" originally appeared in *Southwestern Historical Quarterly* 97 (July 1993): 13–34.

"The Fetters of Justice: Black Texans and the Penitentiary during Reconstruction" originally appeared in *Prologue: Journal of the National Archives* 28 (Fall 1996): 183–193.

"Guardian of the Freedpeople: Texas Freedmen's Bureau Agents and the Black Community" originally appeared in *Southern Studies* 3 (Fall 1992): 185–201.

"Hesitant Recognition: Texas Black Politicians, 1865–1900" originally appeared in *East Texas Historical Journal* 31 (Spring 1993): 41–58.

"Self-Determination and Local Black Leaders in Texas" originally appeared in *Phylon* 39 (December 1978): 344–355.

"A Political Education: George T. Ruby and the Texas Freedmen's Bureau" originally appeared in *Houston Review* 18, no. 2 (1996): 144–156.

LIBRARY OF CONGRESS
CATALOGING-IN-PUBLICATION DATA

Crouch, Barry A., 1941–
  The dance of freedom : Texas African Americans during Reconstruction / Barry A. Crouch ; edited by Larry Madaras ; foreword by Arnoldo de León. — 1st ed.
    p.   cm. — (Jack and Doris Smothers series in Texas history, life, and culture; no. 19)
  Includes bibliographical references and index.
  ISBN-13: 978-0-292-71463-2 (cloth : alk. paper)
  ISBN-10: 0-292-71463-7 (cloth : alk. paper)
  ISBN-13: 978-0-292-71487-8 (paper : alk. paper)
  ISBN-10: 0-292-71487-4 (paper : alk. paper)
  1. African Americans—Texas—History—19th century.   2. African Americans—Texas—Social conditions—19th century.   3. African Americans—Civil rights—Texas—History—19th century.   4. African Americans—Texas—Politics and government—19th century.   5. Freedmen—Texas—History—19th century.   6. Reconstruction (U.S. history, 1865–1877)—Texas.   7. Texas—Social conditions—19th century.   8. Racism—Texas—History—19th century.   9. Texas—Race relations—History—19th century.   10. Texas Politics and government—1865–1950.   I. Madaras, Larry.   II. Title.
  E185.93.T4C75   2007
  976.4'00496073—dc22   2006023207

CONTENTS

FOREWORD

From Barry A. Crouch, I learned that persons could be paid for something they would do for free. Crouch taught at Angelo State University during the last years of the 1960s, when I was attending there as an undergraduate. He prized teaching, whether at Angelo State or the several other universities where he worked. Equally dear to him were research and writing. After his classroom duties ended, he would spend hours working on his dissertation or preparing articles for publication. His passion infected me, and over the years I've come to marvel that the academy pays me as a professor for working at something I would do for sheer personal and intellectual gratification.

Mr. Crouch was no older than twenty-eight in 1969, when I enrolled in his class titled The Era of the Civil War and Reconstruction. I was twenty-four, just two years out of the military, and pursuing, at most, a BA in history so I could have a life better than the one I had left behind as the son of South Texas farm laborers. The quality of instruction at small colleges, I have found over the years, matches that at any name university, and that judgment certainly applied to Crouch's abilities. To me, at least, he was a captivating lecturer (I am told he was equally stimulating when signing at Gallaudet College (now Gallaudet University), where he spent the greater portion of his career) who did more than narrate the historical events that led to the Civil War and laid the groundwork for Reconstruction. He vigorously denounced the tradition, originating in the works of William Archibald Dunning, that depicted white southerners as helpless victims of Radical Republicans and made villains of the freedmen, scalawags, and carpetbaggers. More exciting to me were his digressions into the field of research, about which he spoke with equal zeal. The way he told it, historians had a duty and responsibility not only to teach, but also to dedicate themselves to research. The title of "scholar" was not to be used generically just because a person held a PhD, he commented. Scholars were those who searched for historical truths in archival documents and whose work we read in the classroom. A PhD was the license to write and to legitimately claim the title of "historian." As an example of a historian's tome, he would hold up a book titled *White over Black: American Attitudes toward the Negro, 1550–1812,* written by Winthrop D. Jordan, a brilliant historian of that period.

In keeping with his views on scholarship, Crouch required an extensive research assignment in that class I took under him in 1969. He wanted it to be fifty pages, I seem to recall, and to be based on primary documents. It was a formidable undertaking for anyone, but Crouch had an uncanny ability to detect seriousness of purpose in his students, and he took time to mentor me on the secrets of the craft. By the time I finished the course, he had "discovered" me, identifying me as one with high prospects for a career in the history profession. I do not think I disappointed him, for he remarked many years later that he had "discovered" others, but that none could match my scholarly record.

In 1970 both Crouch and I left Angelo State. He finished his dissertation that year and accepted a postdoctoral fellowship from the National Endowment for the Humanities to study at Howard University in Washington, D.C. I had received a fellowship to attend Texas Christian University (TCU) at the same time, and enrolled in TCU's PhD program, majoring in Latin American history (though my field of specialty was, and has been, Chicano history). Our parting in 1970 did not signal an end to our friendship; for the next thirty years we remained fast friends. In fact, Barry (it took me awhile to move away from addressing him as "Mr. Crouch") continued to monitor my progress in graduate school, writing to me at least once a month (and at times more frequently), encouraging me to stay on track and assuring me that I had chosen a noble profession. He insisted that I call him collect should I run into problems, and I believe I must have taken him up on his offer once or twice during those down days that pervade graduate-school life. He visited us in Fort Worth when research brought him to Texas, and he would take us out to dinner, a special treat for a family on a graduate student's austere budget. As I approached the dissertation-writing stage, I sought his counsel on doing something along the lines of Winthrop Jordan's work on African Americans, and he encouraged me to proceed as intended. The result was my dissertation, "White Racial Attitudes toward Mexicans in Texas, 1821–1900" (TCU, 1974), which the University of Texas Press published in 1983 under the memory. It was not the only book I so dedicated. My very first one, *The Tejano Community, 1836–1900*, had acknowledged the deep debt I owed him. How small these tributes seem for a person who led me into a career that richly compensates me for doing something I do not regard as work at all.

Arnoldo De León
Angelo State University

title *They Called Them Greasers: Anglo Attitudes toward Mexicans in Texas, 1821–1900*.

After finishing at TCU, I returned to Angelo State. Common interests kept us corresponding and visiting. We would exchange copies of our publications (his on slavery in general, but on Texas Reconstruction in particular), and we would mail each other manuscripts for input and editing. Annually we would get together at the Texas State Historical Association (TSHA) conference, if not at some other historical meeting, and make a point of having lengthy discussions over breakfast or dinner. He never failed to express pride in my accomplishments, and I never stopped feeling that if it had not been for Barry, I would probably have gone through life as an unfulfilled public-school teacher.

The name of Barry A. Crouch and the topic of Reconstruction Texas became almost synonymous for thirty years after he arrived in the East; his only competitors were people like Carl Moneyhon, James Smallwood, and Randolph B. Campbell. His reputation rested on his use of the National Archives (where he was in "researcher's heaven," he would say) as his main source, his masterful command of the secondary literature, and a narrative style of writing that offered proof of interpretation instead of a reliance on theory. His works provoked discussion and debate in journal articles, and his writings constituted the center of any Reconstruction debate. He was ever ready to give a helping hand with a manuscript, and his critique of the Reconstruction chapter in *The History of Texas* (which I wrote with Robert A. Calvert) proved valuable. In all three editions of the book, we thank him for his assistance.

By the mid-1980s, and certainly by the 1990s, he was considered a "senior statesman" of Texas history. At the annual conferences of the TSHA, both young scholars and old hands would want to visit with the master. The scene around him at times resembled a class of eager students wanting to hear more from their favorite professor. After the day ended, the gatherings retreated to the cocktail lounge at the hotel, where the shop-talk continued. Upon my recommendation, the TSHA in 1995 inducted Crouch as a fellow of the association in recognition of his immense contributions to Texas historical studies.

Like other of his Texas friends, I saw Barry Crouch just a few days before he passed away in March 2002. He had made the long flight from Washington, D.C., to Corpus Christi, Texas, to participate in the yearly TSHA conference and to get together with his Texas colleagues. I published another of my books in the fall of that year and dedicated it to his

ACKNOWLEDGMENTS

There are a number of debts owed to friends and colleagues. Thanks to Jim Smallwood and Carl Moneyhon, who suggested which of Barry's seminal articles to include and how to arrange them. Donaly Brice of the Texas State Archives provided me with copies of some of Barry's articles that I had failed to locate and introduced me to Barry's friends at the Texas State Historical Association. Charles Sparlin of Victoria College, a longtime chair of the History Department, convinced the library there to accept Crouch's entire collection of papers, notes, books, and articles on the 1850–1880 period. At the TSHA meeting, I tried to fill in for Barry at the restaurant and bar, but this was akin to George Selkirk taking Babe Ruth's place in Yankee Stadium in right field in 1935. My final thanks go to Jennifer Crouch, Barry's daughter; to Lynn Wilder, who typed the entire manuscript; to Bill Bishel of the University of Texas Press, who supported the project from its inception to its near completion; and to Lynne Chapman, also of the University of Texas Press, who completed the task.

Finally, two people were indispensable for the shape of the final product. Copy editor Kip Keller not only reworked and corrected the tables in Chapter 5, but also caught more misspellings and grammatical errors than my tenth-grade English teacher. Thanks also go to my magnificent lifetime companion, Maggie Cullen, whom I met in the same NEH seminar (on race and ethnicity at Columbia University in 1977–1978) at which I became friends with Barry Crouch.

INTRODUCTION

Barry Alan Crouch died suddenly on March 13, 2002, at his home in Riverdale, Maryland, after a short bout with cancer. He was sixty-one. He was born in Glendale, California, on February 26, 1941, with his twin brother, Robert. Most of his childhood was spent in Syracuse, Kansas, and later in Norwood, Colorado, where he became a football and basketball star and still holds the school record for the most points scored in one basketball game. Barry went to Mesa State College in Grand Junction and graduated from Western State College of Colorado in Gunnison with a bachelor's degree. Quickly he earned his master's degree at the University of Wyoming and his doctorate at the University of New Mexico in 1970.

While still working on his PhD, Barry embarked upon a series of academic teaching jobs and fellowships that kept him on the move for more than a decade. From 1967 to 1970 he taught at Angelo State University in San Angelo, Texas, where he inspired one of his students, the well-known scholar Arnoldo De León, to become a historian. From 1970 to 1971 he studied at Howard University on an NEH postdoctoral fellowship in black American historical studies. He spent the 1972–1973 academic year at the University of Maryland working as an assistant editor on the Booker T. Washington papers. From 1974 to 1979 he taught at Bowie State College in Bowie, Maryland. Finally, in 1980 he became an assistant professor of history at Gallaudet College (now Gallaudet University) in Washington, D.C., where he spent the next twenty-one years as a teacher and scholar. Along the way, he received a half dozen research and study grants from the National Endowment for the Humanities.

Barry was a prodigious researcher. During his career he turned out three dozen journal articles, almost as many book reviews, and three monographs (two coauthored). Three more books, including this collection of his articles, will be published posthumously. His career spanned a variety of interests that always resulted in a publication. His earliest article, on New Mexico senator Dennis Chavez and FDR's court-packing bill, came from his master's thesis. Two journal articles on the conservative reformer Amos A. Lawrence were drawn from his dissertation. Two articles, one comparing the American slave South and ancient Rome and one comparing different slave societies in Latin America, were based upon research in NEH seminars. During his career at Gallaudet, he used primary sources to write several articles on deaf history, and was coauthor (with John Vickery Van Cleve) of the field's major history, *A Place of Their Own: Creating the Deaf Community in America*.

Barry's major contributions to American history, however, lay in two fields: Reconstruction Texas and the bandits of the Wild West. Probably because of his first teaching assignment at Angelo State, Barry developed a lifelong interest in Texas history. Along with Randolph Campbell, James Smallwood, Carl Moneyhon, and a handful of other scholars, Barry began in the 1970s to undo the racist Dunning school interpretation of Reconstruction Texas, which had prevailed since Charles Ramsdell's 1910 monograph, *Reconstruction in Texas*. Barry mined the Freedman's Bureau Records on Texas for a dozen journal articles over a twenty-year period, and in 1992 the University of Texas Press published his monograph *The Freedman's Bureau and Black Texans*. For years, scholars such as Herbert Gutman and Eric Foner relied on conversations with Barry and on dozens of his journal articles for research that went into their major books about the slave family and Reconstruction. It is well known that Barry was one of the earliest practitioners of social history written from the bottom up, his conclusions drawn from prodigious and time-consuming research in Record Group 105 of the Texas Freedman's Bureau. In 1992 David Donald wrote a full-page review of *The Freedman's Bureau and Black Texans* in the Sunday *New York Times Book Review,* an honor rarely accorded historical monographs. The book broke new ground in Reconstruction history, and as Professor Donald remarked, the "episodes in Texas Reconstruction history that Mr. Crouch relates perhaps do more than broad generalizations to explain why the Freedman's Bureau failed, and how we lost the peace after the Civil War."

In his last years, Barry became interested in the bandits who roamed the South during and after the Reconstruction era. His biography *Cullen Montgomery Baker: Reconstruction Desperado,* written with Donaly E. Brice, besides serving as a case study and revisionist treatment of an outlaw, removed the romantic image of these bandits, which continually emerges in the pop literature, television shows, and even documentaries about this era. A second book, *Murder and Mayhem: The War of Reconstruction in Texas,* cowritten with James M. Smallwood and Larry Peacock, was published after Barry's death and reverses the lost-cause mythology surrounding the Lee-Peacock feud. His last book, *The Governor's Hounds: The Texas State Police, 1870–1873,* also coauthored with Donaly E. Brice, reverses the Dunning school mythology and presents a positive view of the work performed by the state police during Reconstruction.

Before he died, Barry was forced to abandon two projects that were to cap his career: (1) a full-scale treatment of Reconstruction in Texas and (2) a revisionist biography of John Wesley Hardin. Two friends and colleagues have, or will have, completed their own works in these areas. Carl H. Moneyhon has written *Texas after the Civil War: The Struggle of Reconstruction,* a modern revisionist synthesis that replaces Ramsdell's as the major interpretation of Texas Reconstruction, and James M. Smallwood is at work on a revisionist treatment of John Wesley Hardin and other Texas outlaws.

The following dozen articles constitute the core of Crouch's work on Texas Reconstruction. Part I sets the tone by analyzing the shift in Texas Reconstruction historiography, away from the typical Dunning School interpretation. Part II demonstrates the speed at which former slaves tried to reconstitute their families at the end of the war, and how they attempted to achieve fairness in the labor contracts they negotiated with their former slave masters. Part III documents the enormous amount of violence perpetrated against the freedmen in their attempts to attain their political and racial rights. This section contains a pathbreaking essay (Chapter Eight) on how the criminal justice system functioned from the bottom up rather than from the top down, as "penal slavery became one method by which the disgruntled losers in the war punished their former chattels." Part IV analyzes the work of Texas Freedmen's Bureau agents, and their achievements under the most trying circumstances. The article in Chapter Nine was developed more fully in Crouch's 1992 monograph *The Freedmen's Bureau and Black Texans* (University of Texas Press). Less well known are the articles on Texas black politicians.

These essays, written over a twenty-six-year period, are conveniently collected here to provide a comprehensive picture of the many facets of Texas Reconstruction.

Larry Madaras
Professor Emeritus
Howard Community College

THE DANCE OF FREEDOM

PART I *Historiography*

One   "UNMANACLING" TEXAS
     RECONSTRUCTION
     A Twenty-Year Perspective

Reconstruction historiography has gone through three discernible phases: the Dunning, the revisionist, and the postrevisionist. The oldest interpretation stressed the South's unfortunate experience with Reconstruction, espousing the view that Radicals had forced full citizenship rights for blacks upon a conquered Southern society. The revisionist argument concentrated upon the successes of the era and the significant contributions made by Afro-Americans; it destroyed the idea that reconstruction was a time of economic rape and plunder. The postrevisionist reaction has stressed the conservatism of national and state legislators and the programs that they enacted. Additionally, the latter school has emphasized the importance of class as opposed to race. Reconstruction really changed little, the postrevisionists argue, leaving black Southerners in a precarious condition.[1]

In the past two decades Texas Reconstruction scholarship has generated a substantial body of secondary works. Significantly, this new historiography has challenged most historical perceptions and interpretations of the postwar years; most notably, revisionist studies have questioned the classic Dunning school position articulated for Presidential Reconstruction by Charles W. Ramsdell and for the Radical Republican years by William C. Nunn. Although the historiography of Texas during Reconstruction went through similar changes, revisionist works were never fully incorporated into the few general surveys of the state, and the recent appearance of various studies suggests that Reconstruction writing is entering a postrevisionist phase.[2]

Up to a score of years ago [i.e., around 1970], the body of Texas Reconstruction works was composed of a general study of the Presidential Reconstruction years (Ramsdell), one survey of the Republican years (Nunn), a wide-ranging monograph of the prewar and postwar years that basically accepted the two previous interpretations (Wallace), and a handful of other essays. Generally based upon a limited array of sources (many times, conservative newspaper accounts), these studies discussed controversial topics such as the Freedmen's Bureau, the two state constitutions of 1866 and 1869, the law, economics, and a few other related issues, such as the Republican Party and to a lesser extent the state police. All were portrayed in a baneful light. Blacks were almost totally neglected.[3]

In the last major reassessment of Texas Reconstruction historiography, Edgar P. Sneed in 1969 discredited past interpretations of the postwar years, asserting that Texas historians writing about the postbellum era had "confused sympathy with judgment" and thought it their "duty" to record and convey "folk experience, wisdom, and myth." In 1974 James A. Baggett, who has written about the birth and growth of the state's Republican Party, agreed with this observation, contending that "unfortunately, Texas has been plagued by a retelling of the standard unrevised version of Reconstruction. Taking the torch of traditionalism from earlier writers, and unrestrained by historical revisionism," he continues, "contemporary historians have proceeded to further stereotype the state's post–Civil War era." Time changed little in the writing of Reconstruction Texas, Baggett concludes, as "each generation has not rewritten its history, but has merely reworded that of its fathers." Another writer, Merline Pitre, asserts that the writings of Texas Reconstruction have been "left to the not very tender mercies of Bourbons, or at least to Bourbon sympathizers."[4]

A different day was dawning for Lone Star State postwar history almost at the same time that Sneed analyzed the current state of Texas Reconstruction historiography. A spate of theses, dissertations, articles, monographs, and books appeared in the two decades after 1969. The presence of this significant amount of fresh material calls for revisiting Texas Reconstruction historiography. At least four major areas intimately connected with the state Reconstruction process need reevaluation: the United States Army and the Freedmen's Bureau; politics (mostly the Republican Party); life within the black and white communities; and the county and urban studies.

THE ARMY AND THE
FREEDMEN'S BUREAU

While earlier writers neglected the Texas occupation army and the Texas Freedmen's Bureau, both these groups have now become major topics of attention. The army and its operations were a unique

American occurrence during the Reconstruction era; thus, the subject has generated controversial historical perspectives. William L. Richter and Robert W. Shook are the main antagonists on the significance of the military's presence, but additional writings supplement these scholars' contributions.[5] These studies ask how much influence the army asserted in the social and political spheres. Richter in his many works staunchly maintains that Texans were hostile to military rule (as were all Americans) but that military commanders and Republican Party leaders were deeply committed to assuring Republican ascendancy in the state. Thus, the "army alone was responsible for the Radical success in 1869," he observes, "and every knowledgeable Texan knew it."[6]

The army's intrusion into everyday life, according to Richter, was continued by the Republicans when they created the state police and resurrected the state militia. Throughout his work, Richter (a postrevisionist) displays a strong affinity for the conservative whites, sides with James W. Throckmorton against Gen. Philip Sheridan, and deplores the idea of army occupation. In spite of his charge that the army engaged in "political manipulation," Richter does concede the revisionists' contention that the "army generally conducted itself well in Texas."[7] Richter, as did Ramsdell before him, indicates that the occupation army was a problem because of the psychological and cultural impact it exerted upon the state and its citizens.

Shook (a revisionist) dissents from Richter's ideas. He argues that "military occupation in both extent and ramifications has been highly exaggerated." In fact, there were so few troops stationed in the state that the situation precluded "adequate law enforcement and social-political reform." The records, Shook writes, "offer little support for the theory that occupation of Texas following the Civil War involved general abuse of the residents of the state, subversion of their constitutional rights, or even a concerted attempt to reform [the] social structure." The years of military-directed government in Texas, he concludes, were "so unusual to the American experience that reaction to the process was destined to become a historiographical issue."[8]

The debate over the army's influence on Reconstruction politics involves disagreement over numbers, location of troops, and degree of intrusion into civilian affairs and politics. For example, Richter's figures for the number of troops periodically stationed in the Lone Star State are consistently higher than Shook's. Richter, agreeing that "the army's physical strength was usually minimal," would further argue that the small size of the army is irrelevant because military influence, through aiding and assisting the Republican Party, extended far beyond numbers. Moreover, in "situations of potential violence the blue uniform seemed generally to provoke, not to restrain, armed resistance."[9] Thus, Richter blames the military for much of the violence, whereas Shook points to civilian provocation of the military and of the general violence that permeated Texas during the entire Reconstruction era.

The other major federal agency involved in Texas Reconstruction, the Bureau of Refugees, Freedmen, and Abandoned Lands, commonly referred to as the Freedmen's Bureau, is similarly a major issue in the historiographical battleground. The interpretations relating to the bureau are as sharply divided as those concerning the army. In 1952, Claude Elliott concluded, on the basis of newspaper accounts, that "during the approximate five years of the Bureau's existence in Texas it achieved little success except possibly in its educational work." Swayed by the then prevalent Dunning tradition, Elliott dismissed the reasons for the murder of blacks as trivial, even though the bureau reports suggested violence abounded. He viewed the bureau assistant commissioners as "pathetically ignorant" of their "wards" and of "the true situation" in the Lone Star State. Whether this is Elliott's interpretation of the bureau or an idea funneled through the eyes of extremely hostile newspaper editors appears uncertain. Elliott does imply that the newspapers were justified in their views because "blunder after blunder of petty officers of the bureau had been largely responsible for this" state of affairs. Moreover, the bureau's "fundamental partiality for the negro and a snobbish disdain for the interests of the white man" led to this "critical opposition."[10] Unfortunately we learn little or nothing about the agents, bureau policy (except for education), or any other significant services that this agency initiated and that would provoke such hatred from local whites, except an endeavor to treat blacks as equals.

Recent scholarship has seriously revised Elliott's negative portrait of the Texas Freedmen's Bureau. For example, Cecil Harper, Jr., in a yet unpublished paper, provides the most intensive analysis that has ever been done on the Texas bureau agents. Harper finds that 202 men served as subassistant commissioners during the bureau's relatively brief Texas tenure, so the turnover rate was indeed rapid. One-half served five months or less, and another seventy-three (36 percent) were on the job for less than three months. Over 62 percent (127) of the bureau agents were active army officers, and seventy-five (37 percent) came from the civilian ranks. Of sixty agents on which Harper has been able to gather biographical information, thirty-eight originated from states that remained loyal to the Union. Further, twenty-five had lived in Texas before the war. These civilians claimed longer average bureau service (a little over a year) than did their military counterparts. Only four agents were arrested for crimes committed while serving the bureau, and Harper concludes that "on the whole," Texas bureau agents were "men of ability and integrity."[11]

Studies of the bureau on the local level reinforce Harper's overall evaluation of the bureau in Texas. In essays on two bureau agents who supervised counties in northeastern Texas, James M. Smallwood found these agents (who incidentally were killed in the line of duty) to have been "scrupulously honest and conscientious in performing" their duties. Crouch, surveying the agents who served the Smith County area and its environs, concluded that the subassistant commissioners "believed in their job," felt strongly about the bureau, and attempted to make black freedom "a partial reality" through their efforts to aid black education.[12]

Between 1865 and 1870, according to Alton S. Hornsby, black educational endeavors were a "series of 'ups and downs,'" but the combined bureau and black effort bequeathed a large nucleus of literate blacks, the foundation for a system of higher education, and a local structure the state could build on if it so desired. This is borne out by the facts. When bureau activities in Texas were suspended, Hornsby notes (and Smallwood confirms), 66 schools, 3,248 pupils, and 63 teachers (27 blacks and 36 whites) had made use of the bureau's operations (quite significantly, blacks themselves owned 43 schools). In 1865, Hornsby writes, the situation was "chaotic," but by 1870 matters had reversed themselves because the bureau had, "to a considerable degree, brought order out of chaos." Smallwood largely agrees but adds the rejoinder that "progress developed more slowly than supporters of blacks desired."[13] Until a lengthier and more thorough study of black education and the bureau appears, Hornsby's and Smallwood's favorable appraisal of the bureau's educational efforts seems eminently fair.

POLITICS

Revisionist writings have changed the political landscape considerably from the Dunning tradition of Ramsdell and Nunn. Newer and extensive reinterpretations of Presidential Reconstruction, the conservative backlash, the brief ascendancy of the Republicans, the role of black politicians, and the army's influence upon the Republican Party's efforts to rule the state have demonstrated nuances that need to be considered. More sources have given us a different perspective on the relationship of black and white Republican leaders and the factionalism that rent the party. There has been considerable attention paid to the railroad question and how the opposing parties responded to railroad politics. In brief, Reconstruction Texas is now largely unrecognizable from the way past interpretations depicted it.

Postwar Texas Reconstruction politics began with a transplanted Alabamian, Andrew Jackson Hamilton, who was appointed provisional governor by Andrew Johnson. He has escaped definitive categorization by historians perhaps because of his change in party affiliation before the war. Hamilton saw his mission as provisional governor as threefold: to stabilize the state, to use patronage in a nonproscriptive manner, and to promote elections at the earliest possible moment. Offering "quality leadership," according to Allan C. Ashcraft, Hamilton met "head on, the problem of the newly freed Negro, and he approached the much deeper problem of race relations." Richard Moore, an unquestioned revisionist, adds to Ashcraft's portrait by declaring that Hamilton's "practical interpretation of his role, in reality, conformed more to the reconstruction theories of the radical Republicans than to those of President Johnson."[14]

Hamilton's elected successor, the conservative Democrat James W. Throckmorton, resented congressional Reconstruction laws and continually obstructed efforts by the army and the bureau to enforce them. Because of his actions, he was removed by the military. The only biography of the irascible individual, a hero to the Dunningites, is now over five decades old. More recently, Richter comes to Throckmorton's defense in the governor's running feud with the military. Richter is impressed by Throckmorton's "skillful use of civil power to subordinate the army to many of his demands." Again, Shook is on the opposite side, maintaining that "by disposition and action," Throckmorton "unconsciously aided the Radical Republican cause and invited his own dismissal." Owens is more critical, stating that Throckmorton's "staunch defense of a lawless people as law-abiding, his incessant quarreling with the military and Freedmen's Bureau, his recommendations to the legislature on the frontier situation and the Thirteenth and Fourteenth Amendments exacerbated tensions." By constantly importuning and insisting upon "his own philosophy of power," Owens contends, Throckmorton "infuriated and baffled the military officers with whom he had to work." He never relinquished the idea that "voluntary restoration" was possible.[15]

The other major civilian figure during this period was E. M. Pease, an antebellum Texas governor who was a witness or participant in every significant happening in Texas history "from the Anglo-American revolt against Mexico to the early post-reconstruction era." Pease, who served twenty-six months as provisional governor, was, according to his most recent biographer, Roger Allen Griffin, sympathetic to the Republicans, though he was clearly a moderate, since "radicalism was not consistent with" his "character." He brought to the "office the same willingness for work and intelligent common sense that had characterized his prewar governorships."[16]

Even with much new material available, Griffin admits that "it is still difficult to evaluate his role in reconstruction." Although it angered the Radicals, Pease effectively solved the ab initio controversy (by annulling all state laws that aided the Confederacy) with the military's assistance. [In brief, the ab initio controversy concerned whether secession was illegal from the beginning ("ab initio") or only as a result of the outcome of the war. Logically, ruling secession illegal ab initio would have entailed annulling all government acts in Texas from 1861 to 1866.] At first, Pease did not favor giving blacks the right to vote, but later reversed his stand because he saw the importance of the freedmen to the Republican Party. Moreover, Griffin notes that Pease and Hamilton were the closest of friends, though the former "lacked" the latter's "speaking ability and the qualities of leadership." Pease generally supported whatever position Hamilton assumed on a particular issue. He opposed dividing the state and aided in attempting to get a railroad line to Austin. There is no evidence, however, that Pease was involved in wrongdoing. Generally, Pease was progressive in his outlook, advocating a state educational system, a policy of minimally penalizing the ex-rebels, and a platform of promoting legal equality for blacks.[17]

Through the efforts of Carl H. Moneyhon and James A. Baggett (both revisionists but with different perspectives), major explorations of the Republican Party, its components, and leaders have also appeared in the past two decades. Both drastically revise the previous interpretations of Republican achievements, approaches toward change, and motivation for actions.[18] It is difficult enough to understand the rise, success, and decline of the Republicans, but the party's early factionalism makes the task even more of a chore. One problem concerns labels: almost every writer who has investigated Texas Reconstruction has a particular name for the two wings of the party (for our purposes, Moderate and Radical will suffice). The main question is why did factionalism emerge.

Republicans believed they "must rubb [*sic*] out and begin anew" and attempted this in the 1868 Reconstruction constitutional convention. The conflict over race became obvious as the Moderates opposed ab initio, the division of the state, and the extension of comprehensive black rights. The Radicals favored annulment, division of the state, black equality and suffrage, public schools, and ex–Confederate disfranchisement. But, as Betty J. Sandlin (a revisionist) concludes, "despite all of the time spent on Radical objectives, moderation triumphed, which in itself made the Texas Convention unique." The constitution's flaws included legislating "too much, establish[ing] salaries and *per diems,* creating a poor county court system," and leaving "county government inadequate, . . . in places unpolished." Still, the constitution's strengths overrode its faults by providing the "basis for a good educational system," establishing a "truly outstanding judicial system above the county level," embodying the legislature with enough power, and laying the "foundation for a strong executive department on a very broad basis." To the Republican Congress, the 1869 document came "closer" to an "ideal Constitution than any other state" in the South. This achievement, in Sandlin's assessment, should be credited to the Moderate leadership.[19]

Once the Republicans assumed power in 1870 they moved hastily to implement their philosophy. In a special legislative session, "one of the most controversial, dramatic, and despised legislatures ever assembled in the state," writes Baggett, the Republicans in one hundred days, and without extravagance, "instituted centralized law enforcement, internal improvements, civil rights legislation, and free schools." Taxation, which was increased to pay for Republican programs, has been studied, and state money was not misused or wasted, since "by far the greatest percentage of revenue flowed to law enforcement, education, and frontier defense."[20] Recent historians have now examined in detail Republican motives in relation to education and law enforcement, overturning older mistaken interpretations.

The Republicans, in an 1871 comprehensive education law, attempted to establish a common school system for the Lone Star State. Attacked by previous historians of Texas Reconstruction as "alien" to the individualistic nature of white Texans, the plan was seen as being too centralized and as imposing a heavy tax burden upon state citizens. Neither charge is true, as Moneyhon has recently pointed out. To be sure, private schools (mostly Catholic) did complain about the idea of "teacher certification" and the "ban on sectarian instruction," but it was the Democrats who were responsible for eliminating the Republican ideas about education. "The system created by the Republicans," writes Moneyhon, was "rejected because one political party, the Democratic party, decided to use the schools and the taxes they necessitated to attack their opponents." He concludes that the 1873 Democratic "overthrow of the [Republican-created] public school system" had "disastrous consequences both for education and for society as a whole."[21]

Even the Texas state police, which has "traditionally been regarded as one of the more unsavory aspects of Radical rule," has been reexamined. Although Richter would maintain that the state police were simply an extension of military rule, Ann Patton Baenziger contends that, "while not above criticism," they were a "worthwhile agency created for a legitimate purpose" and were "far more successful and well-received" than historians have suggested. In fact, once the conservatives assumed power, the resurrected Texas Rangers performed many of the duties of the state police, and several former members of the latter group achieved "enviable reputations" with the Rangers.[22]

Another controversial subject among past and present Texas Reconstruction historians is railroad politics. Revisionist writers have downplayed the power of the railroads. Mark W. Summers has pointed out that Texas railroads found Edmund J. Davis a "doughty opponent" when they sought relief from their prewar obligations. Real "ideological disagreement" occurred over the railroad issue: the Radicals, on the one hand, encouraged new lines to be developed by loyal northern interests, whereas Moderate Republicans and Democrats supported the other established roads with ties to secession and the Confederacy. In 1870 matters reached a temporary impasse when, in the famous quorum-breaking incident, thirteen senators were arrested for attempting to block a vote on providing financial subsidies to the railroads. The "evidence suggests," writes John M. Brockman, that is was the fault of the thirteen "who violated democratic procedures" and not the Radicals' "disregard for the democratic process," as almost all Texas Reconstruction historians have charged in past writing.[23]

The leader of the Republican Party, Edmund J. Davis, had a long and successful career in Texas history. He too has been rehabilitated by revisionist historians. "Because of the controversial nature of his gubernatorial administration," argues Ronald N. Gray in a recent biography, "few Texas leaders, if any, have been more abused and castigated." The charges include "fiscal irresponsibility, unwarranted centralization of the state government, the despotic exercise of executive authority, and an incessant drive for self-aggrandizement." His biographer concludes that "some of his policies, especially those dealing with law and order, public schools, and railroads, proved beneficial."[24]

Although the Davis administration has been charged with being "arrogant, extravagant, and corrupt," the facts do not generally support such a thesis. Among the best summaries of what the Radical Republicans attempted and accomplished is the overview of Richard R. Moore. "An impartial view of the Davis administration leads to a very different conclusion," writes Moore. State government costs did triple under Davis, but Texas was larger in population and territory, the frontier was more extensive, and much of the financial burden came from the Throckmorton people, who concentrated on frontier defense.[25]

If the Radicals had some influence in making changes in Texas, and this is debatable, such changes did not extend to the national arena. Republicans were able to dominate the Texas congressional delegation for only eighteen months before the Democrats gained the majority. But even the Radicals demonstrated an overriding concern for "amnesty and the removal of political disabilities" for the ex-secessionists. Philip J. Avillo, Jr., remarks that "their failure to match this concern for the former secessionists with similar sentiments for the plight of the freedmen unwittingly revealed the shallowness of their radicalism." The radical Texas congressmen "tragically" ignored black pleas "for civil rights while in Congress and the dream of the Texas blacks for equality remained just that, a dream." Moreover, as Terry L. Seip notes, Texas "prided itself for being the first southern state to return a solidly Democratic delegation to the House; four of the six Texans had held slaves and five had served in the Confederate army." This only confirmed how tenuous the Republican hold was on the Lone Star State.[26]

Our knowledge of Texas politics has also been expanded by some of the revisionist articles about the less important political figures. Dale A. Somers, summarizing the career of the scalawag James P. Newcomb, stated that "men become Radicals for reasons much more admirable and more complex than those ordinarily assigned by the staunchly southern historians who have applauded the moves of Democrats and Moderate Republicans and hissed the activities of the Radicals." Although dismissed by Ramsdell as a "spoilsman," Newcomb was a significant driving force among the Republicans in their rise to power, in certain ways a political wizard. Others, like the fabulous Tom Ochiltree, were more moderate in their outlook and attempted to find ways to heal the party's schisms. This "world[-]renowned raconteur," who was a conservative Republican, advocated "fair treatment" for blacks but disapproved of the policies followed by the Davis administration. A Hamilton supporter, Ochiltree, who later served in Congress, expressed admiration for the national party but had mostly contempt for state Republican leaders. After Reconstruction he advised various presidents concerning Texas patronage and assisted Norris Wright Cuney, the black political leader, in getting an appointment.[27]

Three biographies have treated Conservative Democrats. One focuses upon Sul Ross, who played a minor role in politics during the immediate postwar years because of disfranchisement and voluntary withdrawal from the political arena. After Reconstruction, Ross became very active in Democratic state politics. Another prominent figure, Ashbel Smith, a member of the Eleventh Legislature, has received attention. Smith opposed the Fourteenth Amendment and generally condemned the "unbearable" policies of Davis's governorship. His long and distinguished career brought a certain continuity to Texas politics since he participated in the war for independence, the Civil War and Reconstruction, and the redemption of the Lone Star State. Samuel Bell Maxey, a United States senator after Reconstruction, was a leading opponent of the Republicans, though he did not always agree with his own party leaders like Throckmorton.[28]

Also neglected in the past were blacks, the group that composed the Republic party's major constituency. Very little is known about black state and county leaders, probably because blacks never became major administrative officials, nor were they elected to Congress, as occurred in several other states. The only two black state senators in the nineteenth century, George T. Ruby and Matt Gaines, have received the bulk of attention. Moneyhon claims that Ruby (one of the state's few carpetbaggers) "envisioned a comprehensive program of education, economic development, and legal protection," continually condemned "violence against blacks," and reasserted the "blacks' claim to basic civil rights." Gaines, almost the exact opposite in personality, was, according to Ann Patton Malone, outspoken and developed "a critical, emotional, and apocalyptic style in politics."[29] Both these individuals have been thoroughly investigated by scholars.

A compilation of what is presently known about state, local, and community black political impresarios comes from a recent work by Merline Pitre. Although Texas black politicians have received increasing historical attention, Pitre notes, "we still do not know very much about these black legislators who served the state from 1868 to 1898." Pitre attempts a comprehensive portrait of these assemblymen, writing that these individuals "did not differ markedly from the most of those they sought to lead." The average lawmaker had been born a slave, was dark complected, and was the son of an "uprooted slave immigrant." During the Civil War he was probably a runaway rather than a soldier. Of the forty-one (in actuality there were forty-two) blacks she identifies as serving in the legislature in the latter third of the nineteenth century, one had completed college, six had either attended or finished a normal school, three had managed elementary grades, twenty-seven had a "rudimentary education," and only four had never received some form of schooling. Emerging from the lower middle class, these legislators tended to be wealthier and more skilled "than the overwhelming majority of freedmen." The difference in social origin and distance between the leaders and the masses was never as great in Texas, she concludes, "as that which existed in Louisiana and South Carolina, where the leadership consisted of a disproportionately high number of mulatto and well-educated blacks with considerable property."[30]

More recently Alwyn Barr has provided a model for future scholars to follow in an analysis of the fourteen blacks (twelve in the House and two in the Senate) who served in the Twelfth Texas Legislature (1870). Composing 12 percent of the total legislative number (120), they "reflected a striking diversity" of backgrounds. All but possibly one were from outside the state. They were generally skilled, and three-fourths held some form of property. Black legislators unanimously tended to support protection from violence, education, and frontier defense. Although not as unified on economic issues, they did emphasize rights for laborers.[31]

In spite of this promising work, what is needed are more essays and even book-length treatments of black Reconstruction Texas politics. More importantly, essays (on the order of Moneyhon's on Ruby and Malone's on Gaines) focusing upon some of the less well-known state black elected officials are imperative. For now, we must sadly agree with Malone, who observes that "not enough reliable research has been done on all the individual black legislators of Texas to provide the necessary information for a composite biography." In the lesser political offices, those who occupied positions are barely known and should become part of a composite picture of black leaders who integrated themselves into the Texas political arena.[32]

Yes, there does not seem to be a great deal of difference between white and black Republican leadership. Although whites descended from a different economic background, the overall similarities of the two groups are rather remarkable. Unfortunately, no such precise study of whites exists for the Twelfth Legislature as Barr has done for blacks, and thus a true comparison is quite impossible. The white dissimilarities are slight, and in spite of the racial attitudes and behavior of the Republican Moderates, it was essential, if they wanted their success to endure, for them to work together with all other party members, which clearly included blacks. In

recent years John Pressley Carrier's synthesis has been modified in various degrees by several writers.[33] We now know that white Moderates and
Radicals split over legislation regarding blacks and railroads, with the former leaning toward the Democratic camp.

One of the most important developments in the past two decades in
Texas Reconstruction historiography is that black Texans have begun to
receive the attention they have long deserved. The major work for the immediate postbellum period is unquestionably James M. Smallwood's *Time
of Hope, Time of Despair.* Smallwood seeks to survey the Reconstruction
black community in its entirety. Providing background on slavery, the
beginnings of freedom, economics, education, churches, and the concept
of self-help, Smallwood also explains how Texas blacks began to develop a
community and involve themselves in the political arena. His conclusions
"differ markedly from those advanced by traditionalists, while tending to
agree with the main outlines of revisionism." Faced with violence and hostility, newly freed black Texans tested their freedom in a variety of ways,
reunited and rebuilt their families, established the church as the "central
institution," fought to better themselves economically and educationally,
used government agencies, initiated self-help programs to aid the community in general, and founded newspapers. Politics brought forth additional challenges and conflicts, particularly through the concept of white
supremacy. "For the Negroes," Smallwood concludes, "Reconstruction
had been a time of hope, but it became a time of despair."[34]

Interestingly, historians have discerned social stratification emerging in
the postwar years within the black community. Less than 1 percent composed an upper class; this group included businessmen, large farm owners,
government officials, ministers, and teachers. A more perceptible middle
class consisted of domestic servants who worked for wealthy whites (their
"status rested on psychological as well as material factors"), artisans, shop-
keepers, and small landowners. According to Smallwood, a "virtual social
revolution began after Emancipation," when blacks "gained control over
primary institutions" such as the family, schools, and churches. Nevertheless, the majority in the Texas black community remained on the bottom
rung of the economic ladder.[35]

Indeed most blacks (approximately 80 percent) worked the land in
some form. Although one of the strongest desires among blacks was to
own property, most had little or no money to purchase land, and the
Freedmen's Bureau had no confiscated property for blacks to buy. Some
did advance on the economic scale, and perhaps 20 percent eventually
purchased their own land. Approximately the same percentage applied

to black ownership in urban areas. In the early 1880s, 25 percent of black households in a specific Houston ward were owner-occupied, according to Cary D. Wintz, as were about 14 percent in San Antonio. Most, however, became fastened to the sharecropping or renting system (peonage) of the agricultural South. By the end of Reconstruction, Smallwood concludes, a "large majority of rural blacks, denied the opportunity to become landowners by the discriminatory homestead law, by Anglos who refused to sell them land, and by inability to secure credit, could only remain tenants with their well being determined by the whim of landlords." Whites intended to "ensure the perpetuation of caste." Despite these several restrictions, some occupational and geographical mobility among black workers in Texas did occur.[36]

According to recent writing, blacks sought equal treatment through the law despite the turmoil of Reconstruction. Donald G. Nieman has suggested what enfranchisement and political power meant to blacks in relation to the criminal justice system. Focusing upon Washington County, Nieman found that blacks constituted the "vast majority" of the Republican party's "rank and file," though they did not win a "share of county offices equal to their" population percentage. Moreover, "black jurors did not adhere to white norms that sanctioned the use of violence to avenge personal insults and defend one's honor. Instead, they used their authority to deter intraracial violence and to preserve order and stability within the black community." Thus, "black political influence did make the criminal justice system more responsible to the freed people in numerous important ways."[37]

The major obstacle confronting Texas blacks in their attempt at independence and advancement was the widespread brutality directed at them by the white population. Although it has been charged by the Dunningites that "Radical Reconstruction brought in its train an epidemic of unparalleled violence and lawlessness," new research discounts this as a distortion. Although disagreeing about certain particulars, recent investigations portray a society psychologically devastated by the outcome of the war. The writings of Smallwood, Crouch, and Cantrell, partially challenged by Richter, suggest fresh directions about the motivations behind these incidents. Smallwood emphasizes the desire to maintain white supremacy, though he avoids any analytical assessment of social, economic, or political motives for violence.[38]

Partly disagreeing with Smallwood and arguing that "politically motivated violence against blacks" has been overemphasized, Crouch sees racial conflicts arising from a wide array of economic and social causes. He estimates that *1 percent* of all black males between the ages of fifteen and forty-five were killed between 1865 and 1868. Gregg Cantrell believes that Smallwood and Crouch are correct in avoiding the "pitfalls of a mono-causal explanation" and finds that the violence was "in fact an expression of hostility to political conditions" and "closely associated with political developments." By asserting "himself or herself in a variety of ways," the former slave was the "most available symbol of the South's defeat and of Northern 'aggression,' and thus served as a convenient scapegoat." Richter paints a less bleak picture than the previous three authors, all of whom obviously fall into the revisionist mold.[39]

Along with new perspectives on violence during Reconstruction in Texas came investigations of race relations. As early as 1970, Texas race-relations research took a new path. Building upon Joel Williamson's thesis that segregation began immediately after the war and that it did not wait until its strange emergence legally in the 1890s, Crouch and L. J. Schultz indicated that Texas followed this pattern. Additional work has confirmed this idea. These customary structures, embodied in law and culturally dic-tated, remained in place until the twentieth century. Segregation quickly surfaced in education, and even the Freedmen's Bureau did not enforce integration. Blacks were confined to specific sections in most towns, sub-jected to vagrancy statutes, and segregated on transportation facilities. Ra-cial separation and subjugation, according to these two authors, was a "basic fact of life during the years 1865 to 1877."[40]

COUNTY AND URBAN STUDIES

Among the more exciting developments in Texas postwar historiography is the trend toward focusing upon specific areas, namely, counties. Randolph B. Campbell is the major purveyor of this approach, having studied the 1850–1880 history of Harrison County. Surveying the area's economic structure, Campbell finds that commercial activity re-mained limited within Harrison County during the time under study, though diversification and specialization with each passing decade did oc-cur. Some urbanization did take place, and the county had excellent rail connections with other areas, but it "remained primarily agricultural in 1880 with self-professed farmers and farm laborers constituting 65% of all household heads."[41]

Campbell's theme is clear. Traumatic as the Civil War and Reconstruc-tion were, the same planter group (though suffering more "severe dislo-

cations" than the "population in general") came to control the county
economically and politically when the Union soldiers left and the county
had been redeemed from the Reconstructionists. "Investigations of central
Virginia, the Alabama black belt, and East Texas all point toward the same
general conclusions," he writes, "elite landholding-slaveholding groups in
plantation areas of the antebellum South such as Harrison County were
highly stable geographically and socially during the years from 1850 to
1870 and beyond." Additional studies of Brownsville (where "antebellum
machine politics and ethnic prejudices survived") and Smith County tend
to support Campbell's thesis.[42]

A brief comparison between Harrison County and an urban area like
San Antonio serves to remind us of the amount of work that needs to
be done on the economic aspects of Texas Reconstruction. According
to Alwyn Barr's study of geographical and occupational mobility in San
Antonio, blacks and Mexican Americans composed the majority of the
manual laborers in the Alamo City, whereas European immigrants made
up the largest percentage of skilled workers and also had more individuals
in the proprietorial, managerial, and professional categories. San Antonio
statistics, concludes Barr, "lend support for the idea that most Americans
remained in the same occupational class throughout their lives, but that
more showed upward rather than downward mobility in the manual labor
class." These percentages are quite close to what Campbell found for Harrison County.[43]

In addition to the efforts of Campbell and others, there have been recent explorations into the social and cultural activities of the white population. John A. Edwards has undertaken the task of unearthing the recreative activities of whites amidst conflict and Reconstruction. Studying
the home and family, the church, schools, social clubs and associations,
and recreational and leisure pursuits, Edwards concludes that "life may
have been more pleasant and rewarding for Texans living in rural areas
or in small communities than we have traditionally believed." The size
and structure of the family remained unchanged, provided stability, and
"acted as a haven amidst other changes." Churches and schools also gave
coherence to the "Texas social scene." Clubs and organizations enhanced
the variety of social life for rural Texans. Finally, Edwards concludes that
Southern antebellum civilization did not erode in Texas after the war.
"There is little evidence of a waning in antebellum social and cultural patterns," he writes, "in this western-most southern state."[44]

Like the Texas black community, Texas whites demand penetrating economic and cultural analyses. Campbell has pointed the direction for such works in his pioneering county assessment. Unfortunately, Texas still does not have a major work concentrating solely upon the economic sphere during the Reconstruction years. A published monograph on the topic seems paramount for a further understanding of the relationship between politics and the economic process. In addition, these two themes need to be tied to Texas blacks and whites and their influence on social and cultural activities. It is now time for a thoroughgoing evaluation of the economic system and cultural patterns during the postwar era.

CONCLUSION

The "unmanacling" of Texas Reconstruction historiography is only in the nascent stage. Since 1969, when Sneed evaluated the condition of the subject, much has been written. The newer works indicate that historians are taking fresh directions and offering significant reinterpretations of postwar Texas. The army and the Freedmen's Bureau and their related activities, for example, are now the focus of controversial interpretations between revisionists and postrevisionists. The Republican Party, its black and white leaders, and its ideological and legislative program are the subject of numerous writings that have dramatically changed the party's image from that reflected in older viewpoints. Even the Conservatives/Democrats have received some probing analyses, clearly demonstrating they were not the "heroes" so characterized by the Dunning school. Black Texans and their economic status, as well as their families, religion, and community structure, are now being subjected to the kind of assessment they should have received long ago; these newer studies demonstrate that older stereotyped notions of the freedmen were largely inaccurate. In addition, fields of inquiry now deal with violence, race relations, segregation, the law, and criminal justice. For the white population, county history has been used to note personal economic and demographic persistence and the relative lack of change for the years before, during, and after the Civil War. Moreover, geographic and occupational mobility, plus social and cultural affairs, have gained the attention of historians.

Many areas remain, however, that require further and in-depth investigations. Although a steady stream of works has appeared in the past two decades, there are lacunae that merit careful and thoughtful consideration. For example, the Freedmen's Bureau records need to be further utilized.

Recent essays appraising these Texas sources point to a host of possibilities for further research. These materials have much to tell about the early years of Texas Reconstruction.[45]

Moreover, various political, social, cultural, and economic themes are ripe for exploration. The Conservatives/Democrats and others who opposed the Republicans need to be scrutinized more carefully at both the county and state level. How the Tejanos interacted with blacks and the entire state political process are further avenues for research. Now perhaps the most neglected group in Texas Reconstruction writings is women. We know very little about their role, their legal and occupational status, their beliefs, or their response to what was occurring in Reconstruction Texas. Indeed, the whole question of family history and the effects of the turbulent postwar years upon this institution surely demand more attention than it has received. This is largely fallow ground in the Reconstruction pasture.[46]

Although Texas was still largely rural during the Reconstruction years, the beginnings of urban growth and development started even before the war. The major centers like Houston, Galveston, and San Antonio have been covered in newer works, but we still need to know more about how urbanization related to Reconstruction political, social, and cultural events. In addition, the problems that cities had to confront, such as ravaging epidemics, are necessary investigative fields that require more attention, since it was here that the army and the Freedmen's Bureau concentrated their activities. Still unclear is the interaction of the urban denizens with the federal presence and how their relationship helped shape the attitudes of those who governed the state.[47]

Despite the writings that have revised Texas Reconstruction history, the materials have been only partially integrated into the national historiographical arena (there are a few superb exceptions), but, more surprisingly, they have not become part of the broader state historical record. Why they have not been incorporated into state history is somewhat perplexing, particularly with so much new information and so many changed perspectives. Old myths are difficult to dislodge, and this remains true in Texas history textbooks that cover this era. They have not kept abreast of the more recent writings on the postwar years, preferring to maintain older discredited interpretations. Occasionally they provide a cursory glance at the new work, but there is not a sustained commitment to incorporating these ideas into the overall picture. This conflict between the old and the new becomes apparent as more anthologies of Texas history appear, challenging what has previously been written.[48]

While historians of Texas history have been steadily revising the old Dunning model of Reconstruction, readings available to the general public still convey the old story of military dominance and Radical misrule. The new material, whatever its historiographical school or background, clearly demonstrates that this was not the case. The scenario has been "radically" revised, and now other factors have to be considered and pondered. All this poignantly suggests that Texas still remains a fertile field for the enterprising Reconstruction scholar.

Even after two decades of stirring in the Reconstruction historiographical arena, scholars still need to give Texas additional attention. Many positive signs are on the horizon that this is now occurring. In the past twenty years interpretations of Texas Reconstruction have spanned the historiographical spectrum, hovering on the fringes of the new but clinging tenaciously to the old. Recent writings, whatever their orientation, make it obvious that the former perception of this dark and bloody ground are, for the most part, no longer valid. It is now time to build upon this foundation and rewrite Texas Reconstruction history.

NOTES

1. Michael Perman, *Emancipation and Reconstruction, 1862–1879* (Arlington Heights, Ill.: Harlan Davidson, 1987), 2–4; John Harelson Hosmer, "William A. Dunning: 'The Greatest Historian,'" *Mid-America: An Historical Review* 68 (Apr.–July, 1986): 57–78; Philip Muller, "Look Back without Anger: A Reappraisal of William A. Dunning," *Journal of American History* 61 (Sept. 1974): 325–338; Larry Kincaid, "Victims of Circumstance: An Interpretation of Changing Attitudes toward Republican Policy Makers and Reconstruction," *Journal of American History* 57 (June 1970): 48–66; Michael Les Benedict, "Preserving the Constitution: The Conservative Basis of Radical Reconstruction," *Journal of American History* 61 (June 1974): 65–90; Armstead L. Robinson, "Beyond the Realm of Social Consensus: New Meanings of Reconstruction for American History," *Journal of American History* 68 (Sept. 1981): 276–297; Richard O. Curry, "The Civil War and Reconstruction, 1861–1877: A Critical Overview of Recent Trends and Interpretations," *Civil War History* 20 (Sept. 1974): 215–228. Perman writes that the divergent explanations "are all permeated by a tone of recrimination and blame," 3. To him, the "central question is not why Reconstruction failed but whether it had any chance of succeeding in the first place," 4. A brilliant summary of all the changing perspectives is Eric Foner, *Reconstruction: America's Unfinished Revolution, 1863–1877* (New York: Harper & Row, 1988), xix–xxvii. For analysis, see C. Vann Woodward, "Unfinished Business," *New York Review of Books* 35 (May 12, 1988), 22–24, 26–27.

2. Charles William Ramsdell, *Reconstruction in Texas* (New York: Columbia Univ. Press, 1910); W. C. Nunn, *Texas under the Carpetbaggers* (Austin: Univ. of Texas Press, 1962). On Ramsdell, see James Payne Sutton, "Texas Historiography in the Twentieth Century: A study of Eugene C. Barker, Charles W. Ramsdell and Walter P. Webb" (PhD diss., Univ. of Denver, 1972). Especially useful for analysis are three works by Eric Foner: "The New View of Reconstruction," *American Heritage* 34 (Oct. / Nov. 1983): 11; "Reconstruction Revisited," *Reviews in American History* 10 (Dec. 1982): 82–100; and *Nothing but Freedom: Emancipation and Its Legacy* (Baton Rouge: Louisiana State Univ. Press, 1983). Two excellent recent surveys of Reconstruction historiography are John Hope Franklin, "Mirror for Americans: A Century of Reconstruction History," *American Historical Review* 85 (Feb. 1980): 1–14; and LaWanda Cox, "From Emancipation to Segregation: National Policy and Southern Blacks," in *Interpreting Southern History: Historiographical Essays in Honor of Sanford W. Higginbotham,* ed. John B. Boles and Evelyn Thomas Nolen (Baton Rouge: Louisiana State Univ. Press, 1987), 199–253. A work that surveys several Southern states during this era but completely ignores Texas is Otto H. Olsen, ed., *Reconstruction and Redemption in the South* (Baton Rouge: Louisiana State Univ. Press, 1980). In *Reconstruction: America's Unfinished Revolution,* Foner successfully weaves Texas into the national Reconstruction context. His many observations about Reconstruction Texas are careful and splendid at the same time.

3. Ernest Wallace, *Texas in Turmoil: The Saga of Texas, 1849–1875* (Austin, Tex.: Steck-Vaughn, 1965).

4. Edgar P. Sneed, "A Historiography of Reconstruction in Texas: Some Myths and Problems," *Southwestern Historical Quarterly* 72 (Apr. 1969): 436 (1st quotation), 437 (2nd and 3rd quotations), 440, 443, 446; James A. Baggett, "Birth of the Texas Republican Party," *Southwestern Historical Quarterly* 78 (July 1974): 1 (4th quotation), 2 (5th quotation); Merline Pitre, "A Note on the Historiography of Blacks in the Reconstruction of Texas," *Journal of Negro History* 66 (Winter 1981–1982): 340 (6th quotation). Sneed cites most of the relevant secondary material up to the time of his article. They are cited herein when necessary for the historiographical argument. In the same volume of *Southwestern Historical Quarterly* (72 [Apr. 1969]) containing Sneed's article, see Dale A. Somers, "James P. Newcomb: The Making of a Radical," 449–469, and Ann Patton Baenziger, "The Texas State Police during Reconstruction: A Reexamination," 470–491, both of which demonstrate that Texas Reconstruction historiography was taking a turn from the past; a similar tendency was indicated somewhat earlier in William T. Field, Jr., "The Texas State Police, 1870–1873," *Texas Military History* 5 (Fall 1965): 136–138. A good survey of general Reconstruction historiography up to the time Sneed published his essay is Vernon L. Wharton, "Reconstruction," in *Writing Southern History: Essays in Historiography in Honor of Fletcher M. Green,* ed. Arthur S. Link and Rembert W. Patrick (Baton Rouge: Louisiana State Univ. Press, 1965), 295–315. Two other historiographical updates are in James M. Smallwood, "Black Texans during Re-

construction, 1865–1874" (PhD diss., Texas Tech Univ., 1974), 1–30, and Nora Estelle Owens, "Presidential Reconstruction in Texas: A Case Study" (PhD diss., Auburn Univ., 1983), 1–21. The most recent survey, which provides much bibliographical information, is Ralph A. Wooster, "The Civil War and Reconstruction in Texas," in *A Guide to the History of Texas,* ed. Light Townsend Cummins and Alvin R. Bailey, Jr. (New York: Greenwood, 1988), 37–50, though some of the newer works elude his scope.

5. For the final military skirmishes and the initial occupation activities, see Robert L. Kerby, *Kirby Smith's Confederacy: The Trans-Mississippi South, 1863–1865* (New York: Columbia Univ. Press, 1972); Tony E. Duty, "The Home Front— McLellan County in the Civil War," *Texana* 12, no. 3 (1974): 197–238; and Max S. Lale, "The Military Occupation of Marshall, Texas, by the 8th Illinois Volunteer Infantry, U.S.A.," *Military History of Texas and the Southwest* 13, no. 3 (1976): 39–47.

6. William L. Richter, *The Army in Texas during Reconstruction, 1865–1870* (College Station: Texas A&M Univ. Press, 1987), 187 (quotation). Two reviews that seriously question Richter's interpretation are Cecil Harper, Jr., in *Locus* 1 (Fall 1988), 95–96, and Carl H. Moneyhon in *Southwestern Historical Quarterly* 92 (Oct. 1988): 377–379.

7. Richter, *Army in Texas,* 187–188 (quotations). Richter's articles include "Spread-Eagle Eccentricities: Military-Civilian Relations in Reconstruction Texas," *Texana* 8, no. 4 (1970): 311–327; "Outside My Profession: The Army and Civil Affairs in Texas Reconstruction," *Military History of Texas and the Southwest* 9, no. 1 (1970): 5–21; "The Army and the Negro during Texas Reconstruction, 1865–1870," *East Texas Historical Journal* 10 (Spring 1972): 7–19; "Texas Politics and the United States Army, 1866–1867," *Military History of Texas and the Southwest* 10, no. 3 (1972): 159–186; "'We Must Rubb Out and Begin Anew': The Army and the Republican Party in Texas Reconstruction, 1867–1870," *Civil War History* 19 (Dec. 1973): 334–352; "The Brenham Fire of 1866: A Texas Reconstruction Atrocity," *Louisiana Studies* 14 (Fall 1975): 287–314; "Tyrant and Reformer: General Griffin Reconstructs Texas, 1865–66," *Prologue: Journal of the National Archives* 10 (Winter 1978): 225–241; "'It Is Best to Go in Strong Handed': The Army and the Republican Party in Texas Reconstruction, 1865–1866," *Arizona and the West* 27 (Summer 1985): 113–142; "'Devil Take Them All': Military Rule in Texas, 1862–1870," *Southern Studies* 25 (Spring 1986): 5–30; "General Phil Sheridan, the Historians, and Reconstruction," *Civil War History* 33 (June 1987): 131–154; and what started it all, "The Army in Texas during Reconstruction, 1865–1870" (PhD diss., Louisiana State Univ., 1970).

8. Robert W. Shook, "Federal Occupation and Administration of Texas, 1865–1870" (PhD diss., North Texas State Univ., 1970): 10 (2nd quotation), 486 (4th quotation), 488–489 (3rd quotation); Shook, "Military Activities in Victoria, 1865–1866," *Texana* 3 (Winter 1965): 351 (1st quotation). A good summary of his ideas is "The Federal Military in Texas, 1865–1870," *Texas Military History* 6

(Spring 1967): 3–53. Shook also has a relevant discussion of the army's place in Texas Reconstruction historiography in "Federal Occupation," 1–12.

9. Richter, *Army in Texas,* 189 (quotations). His other works simply confirm this belief. For the numbers, see Richter, "The Army in Texas" (diss.), 294; Shook, "Federal Occupation," 220–223; Shook, "Federal Military in Texas," 46–53. For a comparison with other states, see James A. Sefton, *The United States Army and Reconstruction, 1865–1877* (Baton Rouge: Louisiana State Univ. Press, 1967), 261–262, which also has considerable material concerning the Lone Star State; Joseph G. Dawson III, "General Phil Sheridan and Military Reconstruction in Louisiana," *Civil War History* 24 (June 1978): 133–151; and Joseph G. Dawson III, *Army Generals and Reconstruction: Louisiana, 1862–1877* (Baton Rouge: Louisiana State Univ. Press, 1982). In addition, Richter's and Shook's attitudes about one specific individual, George Armstrong Custer, can be further compared in William L. Richter, "'A Better Time Is in Store for Us': An Analysis of the Reconstruction Attitudes of George Armstrong Custer," *Military History of Texas and the Southwest* 11, no. 1 (1973): 31–50; and Robert W. Shook, "Custer's Texas Command," *Military History of Texas and the Southwest* 9, no. 1 (1971): 49–54. For another perspective, see John M. Carroll, comp. and ed., *Custer in Texas: An Interrupted Narrative* (New York: Sol Lewis, 1975).

10. Claude Elliott, "The Freedmen's Bureau in Texas," *Southwestern Historical Quarterly* 56 (July 1952), 3 (3rd quotation), 6n14, 7 (2nd and 4th quotations), 22 (5th–7th quotations), 24 (1st quotation). Richter considers Elliott's piece the "standard study of the bureau," (*Army in Texas,* 210n6). This is no longer true. For Texas bureau-military relations and evaluation, see Richter, *Army in Texas,* 39; Richter, "The Army and the Negro," 7–19; and Shook, "Federal Occupation," 171, 239–289 (especially 239–240 and 261), 486. Richter has been much influenced by Lonnie Sinclair, "The Freedmen's Bureau in Texas: The Assistant Commissioners and the Negro" (unpub. paper submitted to the Institute of Southern History, Johns Hopkins Univ., 1969), of which I have not seen a copy. An older and a newer national study that have much relevant Texas material are George R. Bentley, *A History of the Freedmen's Bureau* (Philadelphia: Univ. of Pennsylvania Press, 1955), and William S. McFeely, *Yankee Stepfather: General O. O. Howard and the Freedmen* (New Haven, Conn.: Yale Univ. Press, 1968).

11. Cecil Harper, Jr., "Freedmen's Bureau Agents in Texas: A Profile" (paper presented at the Texas State Historical Association annual meeting, Galveston, 1987), 4–11,12 (quotations). For additional confirmation, see James Smallwood, "The Freedmen's Bureau Reconsidered: Local Agents and the Black Community," *Texana* 11, no. 4 (1973): 309–320; Smallwood, "Charles E. Culver, a Reconstruction Agent in Texas: The Work of Local Freedmen's Bureau Agents and the Black Community," *Civil War History* 27 (Dec. 1981): 350–361; Smallwood, *Time of Hope, Time of Despair: Black Texans during Reconstruction* (Port Washington, N.Y.: Kennikat Press, 1981), 25–42; Barry A. Crouch, "The Freedmen's Bureau and the 30th Sub-District in Texas: Smith County and Its Environs During Reconstruc-

tion," *Chronicles of Smith County, Texas* 11 (Spring 1972): 15–30; and Barry A. Crouch, ed., "View from Within: Letters of Gregory Garrett, Freedmen's Bureau Agent," *Chronicles of Smith County, Texas* 12 (Winter 1973): 13–28.

12. Smallwood, "Freedmen's Bureau Reconsidered," 317 (1st quotation); Smallwood, "Charles Culver," 350–361; Crouch, "30th Sub-District," 27 (2nd and 3rd quotations); Crouch, "View from Within," 13–28. Smallwood's account of William G. Kirkman's death in "Freedmen's Bureau Reconsidered" is erroneous. For a study that concludes, on incredibly weak archival evidence, that the Texas bureau failed in its social welfare function, see Ira C. Colby, "The Freedmen's Bureau in Texas and Its Impact on the Emerging Social Welfare System and Black-White Social Relations" (PhD diss., Univ. of Pennsylvania, 1984).

13. Alton Hornsby, Jr., "The Freedmen's Bureau Schools in Texas, 1865–1870," *Southwestern Historical Quarterly* 76 (Apr. 1973): 398, 399 (1st quotation), 416, 417 (2nd and 3rd quotations); Hornsby, "Negro Education in Texas, 1865–1917," (master's thesis, Univ. of Texas at Austin, 1962), 166–170; Crouch, "30th Sub-District," 20; Smallwood, *Time of Hope,* 72 (4th quotation), 89; Smallwood, "Early 'Freedom Schools': Black Self-Help and Education in Reconstruction-Texas: A Case Study," *Negro History Bulletin* 41 (Jan.–Feb. 1978): 790; Smallwood, "Black Education in Reconstruction Texas: The Contributions of the Freedmen's Bureau and Benevolent Societies," *East Texas Historical Journal* 19, no. 1 (1981): 17. It should be noted that Hornsby's conclusions are not based upon archival material but on published bureau reports. See also Elliott, "Freedmen's Bureau in Texas," 24; Crouch, "30th Sub-District," 20; and Lawrence D. Rice, *The Negro in Texas, 1874–1900* (Baton Rouge: Louisiana State Univ. Press, 1971), 209–215. Also worth consulting are Henry Allen Bullock, *A History of Negro Education in the South from 1619 to the Present* (Cambridge, Mass.: Harvard Univ. Press, 1967); Robert C. Morris, *Reading, 'Riting, and Reconstruction: The Education of the Freedmen in the South, 1861–1870* (Chicago: Univ. of Chicago Press, 1981); and William Preston Vaughn, *Schools for All: The Blacks and Public Education in the South, 1865–1877* (Lexington: Univ. Press of Kentucky, 1974). It seems to me there is enough material to warrant a separate monograph on black education during Texas Reconstruction. For a comparison with another oppressed class, see Kenneth L. Stewart and Arnoldo De León, "Literacy among *Inmigrantes* in Texas, 1850–1900," *Latin American Research Review* 20, no. 3 (1985): 180–187. For the development of higher education during this era, see Michael R. Heintze, *Private Black Colleges in Texas, 1865–1954* (College Station: Texas A&M Univ. Press, 1985), 3–46; Lloyd K. Thompson, "The Origins and Development of Black Religious Colleges in East Texas" (PhD diss., North Texas State Univ., 1976); Alton Hornsby, Jr., "The 'Colored Branch University' Issue in Texas—Prelude to *Sweatt vs. Painter,*" *Journal of Negro History* 61 (Jan. 1976): 51–60; and Pitre, "The Evolution of a Black University in Texas," *Western Journal of Black Studies* 3 (Fall 1979): 216–223.

14. Allan C. Ashcraft, "Texas in Defeat: The Early Phase of A. J. Hamilton's

Provisional Governorship of Texas, June 17, 1865 to February 7, 1866," *Texas Military History* 8, no. 4 (1970): 215 (1st and 2nd quotations); Ashcraft, "Texas, 1860–1866: The Lone Star State in the Civil War" (PhD diss., Columbia Univ., 1960); Richard Moore, "Radical Reconstruction: The Texas Choice," *East Texas Historical Journal* 16, no. 1 (1978): 17 (3rd quotation). Of extreme importance are Michael Perman, *Reunion without Compromise: The South and Reconstruction, 1865–1868* (Cambridge: Cambridge Univ. Press, 1973), 42, 64, 116–117; Dan T. Carter, *When the War Was Over: The Failure of Self-Reconstruction in the South, 1865–1867* (Baton Rouge: Louisiana State Univ. Press, 1985), 25–27, 32, 255–256; and Owens, "Presidential Reconstruction in Texas," 512. A new biography of Hamilton and an interpretive work on Texas Presidential Reconstruction is sorely needed.

15. Claude Elliott, *Leathercoat: The Life History of a Texas Patriot* (San Antonio: Standard Printing Co., 1938); Richter, *Army in Texas,* 95 (1st quotation); Shook, "Federal Occupation and Administration," 161, 162 (2nd quotation); Owens, "Presidential Reconstruction in Texas," 510 (3rd–5th quotations). For explications of Throckmorton's stance, see Richter, "General Phil Sheridan," 147–151; James Martin, ed., "The Lamentations of a Whig: James Throckmorton Writes a Letter," *Civil War History* 31 (June 1985): 163–170; Michael Perman, "The South and Congress's Reconstruction Policy, 1866–67," *Journal of American Studies* 4 (Feb. 1971): 183–194; and Perman, *Reunion without Compromise,* 26, 29–30, 42, 78, 192, 236, 253–254, 273–274, 294, 301–304, 314. Perman extends his original analysis in *The Road to Redemption: Southern Politics, 1869–1879* (Chapel Hill: Univ. of North Carolina Press, 1984), 3–131. Michael Les Benedict, *A Compromise of Principle: Congressional Republicans and Reconstruction, 1863–1869* (New York: Norton, 1974), 212, 251–252, 290, 311, 322, 427; John Conger McGraw, "The Texas Constitution of 1866" (PhD diss., Texas Technological College, 1950), 270; James Alan Marten, "Drawing the Line: Dissent and Disloyalty in Texas, 1856 to 1874" (PhD diss., Univ. of Texas at Austin, 1986), to be published by University Press of Kentucky. Theodore Brantner Wilson, *The Black Codes of the South* (Tuscaloosa: Univ. of Alabama Press, 1965), 108 (footnote quotations), 109–111, claims the 1866 Texas legislators were "paragons of discretion" when they enacted the Black Codes, giving black Texans "more specific guarantees" than any other Southern state. This is misleading, however, when one really notices the loopholes in the law, which was poorly drawn, and gave whites an enormous advantage in their dealings with blacks.

16. Roger Allen Griffin, "Connecticut Yankee in Texas: A Biography of Elisha Marshall Pease" (PhD diss., Univ. of Texas at Austin, 1973), v (1st quotation), 225–227, 233–234, 242 (3rd quotation), 243 (2nd quotation). Worth considering is Robert J. Franzetti, "Elisha Marshall Pease and Reconstruction" (master's thesis, Southwest Texas State Univ., 1970).

17. Griffin, "Connecticut Yankee in Texas," v, 225–227, 228 (2nd quotation), 233–234, 243, 242, 271 (1st quotation).

18. Carl H. Moneyhon, *Republicanism in Reconstruction Texas* (Austin: Univ. of Texas Press, 1980), 195–196; Baggett, "Birth of the Texas Republican Party," 3, 8, 11, 17–19; Baggett, "The Rise and Fall of the Texas Radicals, 1867–1883" (PhD diss., North Texas State Univ., 1972), 211, 213; Baggett, "Origins of Early Texas Republican Party Leadership," *Journal of Southern History* 40 (Aug. 1974): 441–451.

19. Richter, "'Rubb Out and Begin Anew,'" 334 (1st quotation), 335–352; Baggett, "Birth of the Texas Republican Party," 3, 8, 11, 17–19; Baggett, "Texas Radicals," 211, 213; Baggett, "Republican Party Leadership," 441–454; Moneyhon, Republicanism in Texas, 195–196; Betty Jeffus Sandlin, "The Texas Reconstruction Constitutional Convention of 1868–1869" (PhD diss., Texas Tech Univ., 1970), 213 (3rd quotation), 214 (4th–6th quotations), 236 (2nd quotation), 237 (7th and 8th quotations). See also Kenneth Ray Bain, "The Changing Basis of the Republican Party, 1865–1870" (master's thesis, North Texas State Univ., 1970). For background, see Walter L. Buenger, *Secession and the Union in Texas* (Austin: Univ. of Texas Press, 1984). For the ethnic influence on Republicanism, see Terry G. Jordan, "The German Settlement of Texas after 1865," *Southwestern Historical Quarterly* 73 (Oct. 1969): 193–212; and Jordan, "A Century and a Half of Ethnic Change in Texas, 1836–1986," *Southwestern Historical Quarterly* 89 (Apr. 1986): 385–422. For a more precise analysis of the Republican party and its components than it is possible to elaborate upon here, see Robert Shook, "Toward a List of Reconstruction Loyalists," *Southwestern Historical Quarterly* 76 (Jan. 1973): 315–320; Richard L. Hume, "The 'Black and Tan' Constitutional Conventions of 1867–1869 in Ten Former Confederate States: A Study of Their Membership" (PhD diss., Univ. of Washington, 1969), 637–653; and Peter Kolchin, "Scalawags, Carpetbaggers, and Reconstruction: A Quantitative Look at Southern Congressional Politics, 1868–1872," *Journal of Southern History* 45 (Feb. 1979): 63–76. For an in-depth look at the division question, see Ernest Wallace, *The Howling of the Coyotes: Reconstruction Efforts to Divide Texas* (College Station: Texas A&M Univ. Press, 1972), which clearly leans toward older interpretations.

20. James A. Baggett, "Beginnings of Radical Rule in Texas: The Special Legislative Session of 1870," *Southwestern Journal of Social Education* 2 (Spring–Summer, 1972), 37.

21. Carl H. Moneyhon, "Public Education and Texas Reconstruction Politics, 1871–1874," *Southwestern Historical Quarterly* 92 (Jan. 1989): 293, 394 (1st quotation), 399 (2nd and 3rd quotations), 400, 415, (4th–6th quotations). Moneyhon confirms that taxes were not burdensome. The per capita rate was one of the lowest in the nation, and proportionately may have been the lowest in the entire country (406–408).

22. Baenziger, "Texas State Police," 470 (1st–3rd quotations), 490 (5th quotation), 491 (4th quotation). Richter, *Army in Texas,* 193, concludes that previous analyses overlook the state police's "basic purpose," which was to "handle not merely the soldiers' police duties but their political functions as well, including po-

licing the polls and protecting Republican voters, blacks, and loyal men in general from coercion and intimidation." An older theory is that the militia was created not to reduce lawlessness, but for Republican political protection; see Otis A. Singletary, "The Texas Militia during Reconstruction," *Southwestern Historical Quarterly* 60 (July 1956): 23–25. A more recent discussion is in Allan Robert Purcell, "The History of the Texas Militia, 1835–1903" (PhD diss., Univ. of Texas at Austin, 1981).

23. Mark W. Summers, *Railroads, Reconstruction, and the Gospel of Prosperity: Aid under the Radical Republicans, 1865–1877* (Princeton, N.J.: Princeton Univ. Press, 1984), 151 (1st quotation), 152, 242, 243 (2nd quotation), 245; John M. Brockman, "Railroads, Radicals, and the Militia Bill: A New Interpretation of the Quorum-Breaking Incident of 1870," *Southwestern Historical Quarterly* 88 (Oct. 1979): 119, 120 (4th–6th quotations); Brockman, "Railroads, Radicals, and Democrats: A Study in Texas Politics, 1865–1900" (PhD diss., Univ. of Texas at Austin, 1975), 27, 52, 307. In addition, see Carolyn P. Odom, "Radical Reconstruction and Railroads in Texas" (master's thesis, Southern Methodist Univ., 1972). For a city rivalry that created further political problems, see Vera L. Dugas, "A Duel with Railroads: Houston vs. Galveston, 1866–1881," *East Texas Historical Journal* 2 (Oct. 1964): 118–127; and John S. Garner, "The Saga of a Railroad Town: Calvert, Texas (1868–1918)," *Southwestern Historical Quarterly* 85 (Oct. 1981): 139–160. For the involvement of Texas congressmen and railroads, see Terry L. Seip, *The South Returns to Congress: Men, Economic Measures, and Intersectional Relationships, 1868–1879* (Baton Rouge: Louisiana State Univ. Press, 1983), 219–268. Older interpretations are expressed in Ramsdell, *Reconstruction in Texas*, 216–217, and Wallace, *Texas in Turmoil*, 205–206.

24. Ronald N. Gray, "Edmund J. Davis: Radical Republican and Reconstruction Governor of Texas" (PhD diss., Texas Tech Univ., 1976), ii (1st and 2nd quotations), 440, 442 (3rd quotation). See also William T. Hooper, Jr., "Governor Edmund J. Davis, Ezra Cornell, and the A&M College of Texas," *Southwestern Historical Quarterly* 78 (Jan. 1975): 307–312, which claims that Davis was a "strong and conscientious executive who was accustomed to making his own decisions and who was determined to obtain every possible benefit for his state" (312).

25. Richard R. Moore, "Reconstruction," in *The Texas Heritage,* ed. Ben Proctor and Archie P. McDonald (St. Louis, Mo.: Forum Press, 1980), 101 (1st and 2nd quotations), 102. Another relatively balanced perspective is Ralph A. Wooster, "Statehood, War, and Reconstruction," in *Texas: A Sesquicentennial Celebration,* ed. Donald W. Whisenhunt, 114–120 (Austin: Eakin Press, 1984). For local Republican developments, see David Ryan Smith, "Reconstruction and Republicanism in Grayson, Fannin, and Lamar Counties, Texas, 1865–1873" (master's thesis, Univ. of Texas at Austin, 1979); John T. Carrier, "The Era of Reconstruction, 1865–1875," in *Tyler and Smith County, Texas: An Historical Survey,* ed. Robert W. Glover (Marceline, Mo.: Walsworth Publishing Co., 1976), 57–79; James Robert Crews, "Reconstruction in Brownsville, Texas" (master's thesis, Texas Tech Univ.,

1969); and A. C. Greene, "The Durable Society: Austin in the Reconstruction," *Southwestern Historical Quarterly* 72 (Apr. 1969): 492–506. For a newer perspective on county officials, see Randolph B. Campbell, "Grassroots Reconstruction: The Personnel of County Government in Texas, 1865–1876" (paper presented to the Southern Historical Association meeting, New Orleans, 1987).

26. Philip J. Avillo, Jr., "Phantom Radicals: Texas Republicans in Congress, 1870–1873," *Southwestern Historical Quarterly* 77 (Apr. 1974): 439 (1st and 2nd quotations), 444 (3rd and 4th quotations); Avillo, "Slave State Republicans in Congress, 1861–1877" (PhD diss., Univ. of Arizona, 1975); Seip, *South Returns to Congress,* 188. Seip also explores various economic issues and money questions. See also Janice Carol Hood, "Brotherly Hate: A Quantitative Study of Southern Reconstruction Congressmen, 1867–1877" (PhD diss., Washington State Univ., 1974). The congressmen discussed by Avillo include Edward Degener, George W. Whitmore, William T. Clark, James W. Flanagan, and Morgan C. Hamilton.

27. Somers, "James P. Newcomb," 468 (1st quotation), 449–469; Ramsdell, *Reconstruction in Texas,* 286n (2nd quotation), 287n; Claude H. Hall, "The Fabulous Tom Ochiltree: Promoter, Politician, and Raconteur," *Southwestern Historical Quarterly* 71 (Jan. 1968): 347 (3rd quotation), 359 (4th quotation), 356n37. The life of a Republican merchant banker who split with the Radicals is recounted in Marilyn McAdams Sibley, *George W. Brackenridge: Maverick Philanthropist* (Austin: Univ. of Texas Press, 1973), 72–105. See also Jane Lynn Scarborough, "George W. Paschal: Texas Unionist and Scalawag Jurisprudent" (PhD diss., Rice Univ., 1972). For local leaders, see Paul D. Casdorph, "Some Early Republicans of Smith County, Texas," *Chronicles of Smith County, Texas* 7 (Fall 1968): 1–7; James Smallwood, "Mr. Republican: Silas D. Wood," *Chronicles of Smith County, Texas* 9 (Spring 1970): 1–7.

28. Judith Ann Benner, *Sul Ross: Soldier, Statesman, Educator* (College Station: Texas A&M Univ. Press, 1983), 115–123; Elizabeth Silverthorne, *Ashbel Smith of Texas: Pioneer, Patriot, Statesman, 1805–1886* (College Station: Texas A&M Univ. Press, 1982), 160–179, 180 (quotation), 181–185; Louise Horton, *Samuel Bell Maxey: A Biography* (Austin: Univ. of Texas Press, 1974), 46–69. For background on other Conservatives/Democrats, see Mary Whatley Clarke, *David G. Burnet* (Austin: Pemberton Press, 1969); John Moretta, "William Pitt Ballinger: Public Servant, Private Pragmatist" (PhD diss., Rice Univ., 1987); and Max S. Lale, "Robert W. Loughery: Rebel Editor," *East Texas Historical Journal* 21, no. 2 (1983): 3–15.

29. Carl H. Moneyhon, "George T. Ruby and the Politics of Expediency in Texas," in *Southern Black Leaders of the Reconstruction Era,* ed. Howard N. Rabinowitz (Chicago: Univ. of Illinois Press, 1982), 363–370 (1st quotation), 371–385, 386 (2nd and 3rd quotations), 387–392; Ann Patton Malone, "Matt Gaines: Reconstruction Politician," in *Black Leaders: Texans for Their Times,* ed. Alwyn Barr and Robert A. Calvert (Austin: Texas State Historical Association, 1981), 57 (4th quotation), 73. For additional material on Ruby that confirms Moneyhon's

perceptions, see Randall B. Woods, "George T. Ruby: A Black Militant in the White House Business Community," *Red River Valley Historical Review* 1 (Autumn 1974): 269–280; James Smallwood, "G. T. Ruby: Galveston's Black Carpetbagger in Reconstruction Texas," *Houston Review* 5 (Winter 1983): 24–33; Barry A. Crouch, "Self-Determination and Local Black Leaders in Texas," *Phylon* 39 (Dec. 1978): 344–355. The background for black political participation is delineated in Lamar L. Kirven, "A Century of Warfare: Black Texans" (PhD diss., Indiana Univ., 1974), 1–37.

30. Merline Pitre, *Through Many Dangers, Toils, and Snares: The Black Leadership of Texas, 1868–1900* (Austin: Eakin Press, 1985), 4 (1st quotation), 199 (2nd and 3rd quotations), and 200 (4th–6th quotations). The title on the book jacket and that on the title page are different. For a long critique, see Crouch, "A Savvy Group: Texas Black Politicians, 1865–1900" (unpublished manuscript), 1–37. See also Richard L. Hume, "Negro Delegates to the State Constitutional Conventions of 1867–69," in Rabinowitz, *Southern Black Leaders of the Reconstruction Era,* 129–154.

31. Alwyn Barr, "Black Legislators of Reconstruction Texas," *Civil War History* 32 (Dec. 1986): 340–341, 342 (quotation), 343–351.

32. Malone, "Matt Gaines," 56 (quotation), 64–65. For some local observations, see Crouch, "Self-Determination and Local Black Leaders," 344–355; Crouch, "Savvy Group," 1–37; and Pitre, *Through Many Dangers,* 75. A local piece that has no scholarly pretensions is the Rev. Jacob Fontaine III, with Gene Burd, *Jacob Fontaine: From Slavery to the Greatness of the Pulpit, the Press, and Public Service . . .: A Legacy of Church, Campus, and Community* (Austin: Eakin Press, 1983). Fontaine appears in the Bureau records, was a local leader among Austin blacks, and briefly edited a newspaper.

33. John Pressley Carrier, "A Political History of Texas during the Reconstruction, 1865–1874," (PhD diss., Vanderbilt Univ., 1971), 104, 166, 248, 404, 524–525.

34. Smallwood, *Time of Hope,* 111–117, 159 (1st quotation), 163 (3rd quotation); Smallwood, "Black Texans during Reconstruction: First Freedom," *East Texas Historical Journal* 14, no. 1 (Spring 1976): 9–23; Smallwood, "Emancipation and the Black Family: A Case Study in Texas," *Social Science Quarterly,* 57 (Mar. 1977): 849–857; Smallwood, "From Slavery to Freedom: Smith County's Black Community in 1870; A Statistical Overview," *Chronicles of Smith County, Texas* 18 (Summer 1979): 58–61; Smallwood, "Texas," in *The Black Press in the South, 1865–1979,* ed. Henry Lewis Suggs (Westport, Conn.: Greenwood, 1983), 357–377; Smallwood, *A Century of Achievement: Blacks in Cooke County, Texas* (Gainesville, Tex.: American Revolution Bicentennial Committee, 1975), and his short account *The Struggle for Equality: Blacks in Texas,* Texas History Series (Boston: American Press, 1983). An overview can be found in Alwyn Barr, *Black Texans: A History of Negroes in Texas, 1528–1971* (Austin: Jenkins, 1973), 30–111, and Roland C. Hayes, "Blacks in Texas," in Whisenhunt, *Sesquicentennial Celebra-*

tion, 327–337. The literature on black Texans is surveyed in Alwyn Barr, "Black Texans," in Cummins and Bailey, *History of Texas,* 107–121. An amateur effort is Doris Hollis Pemberton, *Juneteenth at Comanche Crossing* (Austin: Eakin Press, 1983), 53–87. Slavery and the legalities surrounding its demise are recounted in Randolph B. Campbell, *An Empire for Slavery: The Peculiar Institution in Texas, 1821–1865* (Baton Rouge: Louisiana State Univ. Press, 1989); Campbell, "Slave Hiring in Texas," *American Historical Review* 93 (Feb. 1988): 107–114; Campbell, "The End of Slavery in Texas: A Research Note," *Southwestern Historical Quarterly* 88 (July 1984): 71–80. A weak and very outdated survey is Jesse Dorsett, "Blacks in Reconstruction Texas, 1865–1877" (PhD diss., Texas Christian Univ., 1981). An important study that encompasses Texas and discusses the evolving nature of the slave's status during the war is Armstead L. Robinson, "'Day of Jubilo': Civil War and the Demise of Slavery in the Mississippi Valley, 1861–1865" (PhD diss., Univ. of Rochester, 1977). Splendid general works that contain much information about Texas are Leon F. Litwack, *Been in the Storm So Long: The Aftermath of Slavery* (New York: Knopf, 1979), and Foner, *Reconstruction: America's Unfinished Revolution.* Also important are Randolph B. Campbell, "The Slave Family in Antebellum Texas," in *The American Family,* Victoria College Social Sciences Symposium, 1988 (Victoria, Tex.: Victoria College Press, 1988), 1–28; Barry A. Crouch and Larry Madaras, "Reconstructing Black Families: Perspectives from the Texas Freedmen's Bureau Records," *Prologue: Journal of the National Archives* 18 (Summer 1986): 109–122, reprinted in *Our Family, Our Town: Essays on Family and Local History Sources in the National Archives,* comp. Timothy Walch (Washington, D.C.: National Archives and Records Administration, 1987), 156–167; and Charles William Grose, "Black Newspapers in Texas, 1868–1970" (PhD diss., Univ. of Texas at Austin, 1972), 45–46, 55–56, 74.

35. Smallwood, *Time of Hope,* 110 (1st quotation), 127 (2nd and 3rd quotations).

36. James Smallwood, "Perpetuation of Caste: Black Agricultural Workers in Reconstruction Texas," *Mid-America: An Historical Review* 61 (Jan. 1979): 5, 23; Smallwood, *Time of Hope,* 43–66, 67 (quotations); Claude F. Oubre, *Forty Acres and a Mule: The Freedmen's Bureau and Black Land Ownership* (Baton Rouge: Louisiana State Univ. Press, 1978), 37. For black urban migration and other black economic activities, see Alwyn Barr, "Black Migration into Southwestern Cities, 1865–1900," in *Essays on Southern History Written in Honor of Barnes F. Lathrop,* ed. Gary W. Gallagher (Austin: General Libraries, Univ. of Texas at Austin, 1980), 17–38; Kenneth W. Porter, "Negro Labor in the Western Cattle Industry, 1866–1900," *Labor History* 10 (Summer 1969): 346–374. For other variations, see William Cohen, "Negro Involuntary Servitude in the South, 1865–1970: A Preliminary Analysis," *Journal of Southern History* 42 (Feb. 1976): 31–60; Robert A. Calvert, "Nineteenth-Century Farmers, Cotton, and Prosperity," *Southwestern Historical Quarterly* 73 (Apr. 1970): 509–521; Calvert, ed., "The Freedmen and Agricultural Prosperity," *Southwestern Historical Quarterly* 76 (Apr. 1973): 461–471;

L. Tuffly Ellis, "The Revolutionizing of the Texas Cotton Trade, 1865–1885," *Southwestern Historical Quarterly* 73 (Apr. 1970): 478–508; and William Warren Rogers, ed., "'I Am Tired Writeing': A Georgia Farmer Reports on Texas in 1871," *Southwestern Historical Quarterly* 87 (Oct. 1983): 183–188. Occupational and geographical mobility can be followed in William Cohen, "Black Immobility and Free Labor: The Freedmen's Bureau and the Relocation of Black Labor, 1865–1868," *Civil War History* 30 (Sept. 1984): 225; Cary D. Wintz, "Blacks," in *The Ethnic Groups of Houston,* ed. Fred R. von der Mehden (Houston: Rice Univ. Studies, 1984), 16–19; Robert D. Bullard, *Invisible Houston: The Black Experience in Boom and Bust* (College Station: Texas A&M Univ. Press, 1987); and Alwyn Barr, "Occupational and Geographic Mobility in San Antonio, 1870–1900," *Social Science Quarterly* 51 (Sept. 1970): 398–399, 400n9, 402.

37. Donald G. Nieman, "Black Political Power and Criminal Justice: Washington County, Texas, 1865–1884," *Journal of Southern History* 55 (Aug. 1989): 394 (1st and 2nd quotations), 395 (3rd quotation), 396–399, 401–403, 406, 416–417 (4th quotation), 419 (5th quotation), 420. Other legal aspects are treated in Barry A. Crouch, "Black Dreams and White Justice," *Prologue: Journal of the National Archives* 6 (Winter 1974): 255–265; Nieman, *To Set the Law in Motion: The Freedmen's Bureau and the Legal Rights of Blacks, 1865–1868* (Millwood, N.Y.: KTO Press, 1979); and Eric Foner, "Rights and the Constitution in Black Life during the Civil War and Reconstruction," *Journal of American History* 74 (Dec. 1987): 863–883.

38. Sneed, "Historiography of Reconstruction," 43 (quotation); Smallwood, *Time of Hope,* 33–34, 57, 61, 81, 128–158.

39. Barry A. Crouch, "A Spirit of Lawlessness: White Violence, Texas Blacks, 1865–1868," *Journal of Social History* 18 (Winter 1984): 217–220, 221 (1st quotation), 222–232; Crouch, "To Destroy Their Own: White Violence against Texas Whites" (paper presented at the Organization of American Historians convention, Cincinnati, 1983); Crouch, "Women and Children Too: White Violence, Texas Black Women and Children, 1865–1868" (paper presented at the Fourth Citadel Conference on the South, Charleston, 1985); Gregg Cantrell, "Racial Violence and Reconstruction Politics in Texas, 1867–1868," *Southwestern Historical Quarterly* 93 (Jan. 1990): 337 (2nd–4th quotations), 355 (5th and 6th quotations). He has been influenced by the psychological interpretation of George C. Rable, *But There Was No Peace: The Role of Violence in the Politics of Reconstruction* (Athens: Univ. of Georgia Press, 1984); Richter, *Army in Texas,* 143–144, 152. For additional information on the Texas Klan, see Allen W. Trelease, *White Terror: The Ku Klux Klan Conspiracy and Southern Reconstruction* (New York: Harper & Row, 1971), 137–148. For a precise delineation of some of the characteristics that promoted violence, see Billy D. Ledbetter, "White Texans' Attitudes Toward the Political Equality of Negroes, 1865–1870," *Phylon* 40 (Sept. 1979): 253–263. See also Charles V. Keener, "Racial Turmoil in Texas, 1865–1874" (master's thesis, North Texas State Univ., 1971).

40. Barry A. Crouch and L. J. Schultz, "Crisis in Color: Racial Separation in Texas during Reconstruction," *Civil War History* 16 (Mar. 1970): 37–48, 49 (quotation); Thomas W. Kremm, "Race Relations in Texas, 1865 to 1870" (master's thesis, Univ. of Houston, 1970); Bruce A. Glasrud, "Jim Crow's Emergence in Texas," *American Studies* 15 (Spring 1974): 47–60. In addition, see Joel Williamson, *After Slavery: The Negro in South Carolina during Reconstruction, 1861–1867* (Chapel Hill: Univ. of North Carolina Press, 1965), 274–299; Williamson, ed., *The Origins of Segregation* (Lexington, Ky.: Heath, 1968); C. Vann Woodward, *The Strange Career of Jim Crow,* 4th ed. (New York: Oxford Univ. Press, 1985); Woodward, "The Strange Career of a Historical Controversy," in C. Vann Woodward, *American Counterpoint: Slavery and Racism in the North-South Dialogue* (Boston: Little, Brown, 1971), 234–260; Howard N. Rabinowitz, *Race Relations in the Urban South, 1865–1890* (New York: Oxford Univ. Press, 1978), 182; David Herbert Donald, "A Generation of Defeat," in *From the Old South to the New: Essays on the Transitional South,* ed. Walter J. Fraser, Jr., and Winfred B. Moore (Westport, Conn.: Greenwood, 1981), 3–20; Stephen J. Riegel, "The Persistent Career of Jim Crow: Lower Federal Courts and the 'Separate but Equal' Doctrine, 1865–1896," *American Journal of Legal History* 28 (Jan. 1984): 17–40.

41. Randolph B. Campbell, *A Southern Community in Crisis: Harrison County, Texas, 1850–1880* (Austin: Texas State Historical Association, 1983), 368, 371–372, 375 (quotation), 379; Carrier, "Political History of Texas," 408.

42. Randolph B. Campbell, "Population Persistence and Social Change in Nineteenth-Century Texas: Harrison County, 1850–1880," *Journal of Southern History* 48 (May 1982): 193, 195 (1st and 2nd quotations); Campbell, *Southern Community in Crisis,* 377, 380–381, 390–391, 394 (3rd quotation), 394–395 (4th quotation). His other supporting works are "Slaveholding in Harrison County, 1850–1860: A Statistical Profile," *East Texas Historical Journal* 11 (Spring 1973): 18–27; "Human Property: The Negro Slave in Harrison County, 1850–1860," *Southwestern Historical Quarterly* 76 (Apr. 1973): 384–396; "The Productivity of Slave Labor in East Texas: A Research Note," *Louisiana Studies* 13 (Summer 1974): 154–172; "Planters and Plain Folk: Harrison County, Texas, as a Test Case, 1850–1860," *Journal of Southern History* 40 (Aug. 1974): 369–398; "Local Archives as a Source of Slave Prices: Harrison County, Texas, as a Test Case," *Historian* 36 (Aug. 1974): 660–669; "Political Conflict Within the Southern Consensus: Harrison County, Texas, 1850–1880," *Civil War History* 26 (Sept. 1980): 218–239; and Randolph B. Campbell and Richard G. Lowe, *Wealth and Power in Antebellum Texas* (College Station: Texas A&M Univ. Press, 1977). Another worthwhile comparison for considering the persistence of wealth is Ralph A. Wooster, "Wealthy Texans, 1860," *Southwestern Historical Quarterly* 71 (Oct. 1967): 163–180; Wooster, "Wealthy Texans, 1870," *Southwestern Historical Quarterly* 74 (July 1970): 24–35; and Wooster, "Wealthy Southerners on the Eve of the Civil War," in Gallagher, *Essays on Southern History,* 133–159. For other locales, see Crews, "Reconstruction in Brownsville," 114 (5th quotation); Carrier, "Era of Reconstruction," 57–

79. Two good comparisons for Campbell's methodology are Orville Vernon Burton, *In My Father's House Are Many Mansions: Family and Community in Edgefield, South Carolina* (Chapel Hill: Univ. of North Carolina Press, 1985), and Robert C. Krenzer, *Kinship and Neighborhood in a Southern Community: Orange County, North Carolina, 1849–1881* (Knoxville: Univ. of Tennessee Press, 1987). Worth considering, if only for local flavor, is Traylor Russell, *Carpetbaggers, Scalawags, and Others* (Waco, Tex.: Texian Press, 1973).

43. Barr, "Occupational and Geographic Mobility," 399–400, 402, 403 (quotation). An adequate overview is Larry Earl Adams, "Economic Development in Texas during Reconstruction" (PhD diss., North Texas State Univ., 1980). For immigrants who became involved in farming, see Winston Lee Kinsey, "The Immigrant in Texas Agriculture during Reconstruction," *Agricultural History* 52 (Jan. 1979): 125–141.

44. John Austin Edwards, "Social and Cultural Activities of Texans during Civil War and Reconstruction, 1861–1873" (PhD diss., Texas Tech Univ., 1985), 5–7, 324 (1st quotation), 325 (2nd quotation), 327 (3rd quotation), 331, 333 (4th quotation). See also Willard B. Robinson, "Houses of Worship in Nineteenth-Century Texas," *Southwestern Historical Quarterly* 85 (Jan. 1982): 235–298, and William G. Harper, "A Short History of the Texas Blue Laws" (master's thesis, Texas Tech Univ., 1973). The life of the Hardin family during the Civil War and Reconstruction can be traced through Camilla Davis Trammell, *Seven Pines: Its Occupants and Their Letters, 1825–1872* (Houston: C. D. Trammell; dist. by Southern Methodist Univ. Press [Dallas], 1986).

45. Barry A. Crouch, "Hidden Sources of Black History: The Texas Freedmen's Bureau Records as a Case Study," *Southwestern Historical Quarterly* 83 (Jan. 1980): 211–226; Crouch, "Freedmen's Bureau Records: Texas, a Case Study," in *Afro-American History: Sources for Research,* ed. Robert L. Clarke, 764–794 (Washington, D.C.: Howard Univ. Press, 1981); Crouch and Madaras, "Reconstructing Black Families," 109–122; Smallwood, *Time of Hope,* 196.

46. Arnoldo De León, *The Tejano Community, 1836–1900* (Albuquerque: Univ. of New Mexico Press, 1982); De León, *They Called Them Greasers: Anglo Attitudes toward Mexicans in Texas, 1821–1900* (Austin: Univ. of Texas Press, 1983), 87–102. A brief summary of Texas women is in Fane Downs, "Texas Women at Work," in Whisenhunt, *Sesquicentennial Celebration,* 209–325. A bibliographic survey of Texas women is in Ann Patton Malone, "Women in Texas History," in Cummins and Bailey, *History of Texas,* 123–136. See also Suzanne D. Lebsock, "Radical Reconstruction and the Property Rights of Southern Women," *Journal of Southern History* 43 (May 1977): 195–216; Bettye Ann Showers Key, "Women of Texas Cattle Ranches, 1870–1915" (master's thesis, Univ. of Texas at Arlington, 1971); Kathleen Elizabeth Lazarou, "Concealed Under Petticoats: Married Women's Property and the Law of Texas, 1840–1913" (PhD diss., Rice Univ., 1980); Elizabeth York Enstam, "The Frontier Woman as City Worker: Women's Occupations in Dallas, Texas, 1856–1880," *East Texas Historical Journal* 18 (Spring

1980): 12–28; Sandra L. Myres, *Westering Women and the Frontier Experience, 1800–1915* (Albuquerque: Univ. of New Mexico Press, 1982); Myres, ed., "A Woman's View of the Texas Frontier, 1874: The Diary of Emily K. Andrews," *Southwestern Historical Quarterly* 86 (July 1982): 49–80; David C. Humphrey, "Prostitution and Public Policy in Austin, Texas, 1870–1915," *Southwestern Historical Quarterly* 86 (Apr. 1983): 473–516; Ann Patton Malone, *Women on the Texas Frontier: A Cross-Cultural Perspective* (El Paso: Texas Western Press, Univ. of Texas at El Paso, 1983); and Randolph Campbell, "Family History from Local Records: A Case Study from Nineteenth-Century Texas," *East Texas Historical Journal* 19, no. 2 (1981): 13–26.

47. Kenneth W. Wheeler, *To Wear a City's Crown: The Beginnings of Urban Growth in Texas, 1836–1865* (Cambridge, Mass.: Harvard Univ. Press, 1968); Harold L. Platt, "Urban Public Services and Private Enterprise: Aspects of the Legal and Economic History of Houston, Texas, 1865–1905" (PhD diss., Rice Univ., 1974); David G. McComb, *Houston: A History,* rev. ed. (Austin: Univ. of Texas Press, 1981), 38–64; McComb, *Galveston: A History* (Austin: Univ. of Texas Press, 1986), 84–120; William Foster Fleming, "San Antonio: The History of a Military City, 1865–1880" (PhD diss., Univ. of Pennsylvania, 1963; Arthur James Mayer, "San Antonio, Frontier Entrepot" (PhD diss., Univ. of Texas at Austin, 1976); Michael Quinley Hooks, "The Struggle for Dominance: Urban Rivalry in North Texas, 1870–1910" (PhD diss., Texas Tech Univ., 1979); Kathleen Davis, "Year of Crucifixion: Galveston, Texas," *Texana* 8, no. 2 (1970): 140–153. For an unusual perspective, see W. R. Young III, "A Capital View: Photography in Austin, Texas, after the Civil War," *Journal of the West* 26 (Apr. 1987): 52–62.

48. Those who perpetuate older stereotypes are T. R. Fehrenbach, *Lone Star: A History of Texas and the Texans* (New York: Macmillan, 1968), 393–432; Seymour V. Conner, *Texas: A History* (New York: Crowell, 1971), 212–248; Joe B. Frantz, *Texas: A Bicentennial History* (New York: Norton, 1976), 115–125; and Rupert Norval Richardson, Ernest Wallace, and Adrian N. Anderson, *Texas: The Lone Star State,* 4th ed. (Englewood Cliffs, N.J.: Prentice-Hall, 1981), 244–267. A new general history is sorely needed.

POSTSCRIPT TO PART I

In the past sixteen years, a number of important general histories of Texas with up-to-date interpretations have been published. These include Robert A. Calvert, Arnoldo De León, and Gregg Cantrell, *The History of Texas,* 3rd ed. (Harlan Davidson, 2000); Randolph B. Campbell, *Gone to Texas: A History of the Lone Star State* (Oxford, 2003); Jesus F. de la Teja, Paula Marks, and Ron Tyler, *Texas: Crossroads of North America* (Houghton Mifflin, 2005). See also the readings in *Major Problems in Texas History: Documents and Essays,* edited by Sam W. Haynes and Cory D. Wintz (Houghton Mifflin, 2002), and *The Human Tradition in Texas,* edited by Ty Cashion and Jesus F. de la Teja (Scholarly Resources, 2001).

The two standard works on Texas Reconstruction, written by Charles Ramsdell and W. C. Nunn before the explosion of the revisionist literature of the 1960s, have been replaced by Carl H. Moneyhon, *Texas after the Civil War: The Struggle of Reconstruction* (Texas A&M Univ. Press, 2004), a carefully balanced, well-written, and up-to-date synthesis, which should be sought out by the current reader of Crouch's essays. See also the carefully researched county studies of Randolph B. Campbell in *Grass-Roots Reconstruction in Texas, 1865–1880* (Louisiana State Univ. Press, 1997).

PART II *Freedom*

Two

RECONSTRUCTING
BLACK FAMILIES

Perspectives from the Texas Freedmen's Bureau Records

BARRY A. CROUCH AND LARRY MADARAS

Emancipation provided many former slaves with the opportunity to reunite families that had been torn apart during the period of bondage. Numerous problems arose because of the past social relationships of the ex-slaves, which now had to be resolved in the turbulent era of Reconstruction. The National Archives houses a number of excellent sources that enable us to document the family turmoil that came with freedom. This essay examines some of the information available at the archives from the Bureau of Refugees, Freedmen, and Abandoned Lands, Record Group 105, which will aid family and local history researchers in documenting the Afro-American family during the Reconstruction era. What follows is a short history of the Freedmen's Bureau records as a major source of black family history, an explication of the information in the Freedmen's Bureau records using Texas as a case study, and a concluding note on the general use of these records.

In March 1865, a month before the Civil War ended, Congress created the Bureau of Refugees, Freedmen, and Abandoned Lands, commonly known as the Freedmen's Bureau. Established under the War Department for one year, the bureau had as its original goal the care and well-being of thousands of white and black Southerners whose lives had been uprooted by the war. With branches located in every ex-Confederate state, the bureau provided a variety of services for its constituents. These included schools and hospitals, the distribution of rations, legal aid, information and assistance in relocation to other countries or states, and negotiations of contracts with employers.

The bureau received the name Freedmen's Bureau because it primarily ministered to the needs of former slaves. Southern whites avoided the agency for two reasons. First, poor whites would have to concede that blacks were their social equals if both groups used the bureau. This was something the white community was unwilling to admit. Second, President Andrew Johnson had begun to pardon the former rebels and allow them to reoccupy their lands. This meant the bureau had little land to redistribute. Whites either did not need the other services that the bureau offered or were too embarrassed to use them.

Until the late 1950s, historians generally portrayed the Freedmen's Bureau as a political instrument of the Radical Republicans. As a result, they sympathized with the white Southerners who hated the bureau. Since it was directed by the military primarily to aid the former slaves, the bureau served as a constant reminder that the Confederacy had lost the war. Critics were quick to point out any corruption that occurred in the agency. Northern and Democratic newspapers magnified its problems through countless editorials. Nineteenth-century Americans who believed in a minimal role for government were even more hostile than twentieth-century Americans to the notion of "welfare." Finally, when Congress overrode President Johnson's veto and extended the life of the agency, the bureau came to be seen as one of the tools with which the Radicals persecuted the South.[1]

Revisionist writers, who reject the racial biases of traditional historians, also view the Freedmen's Bureau in an unfavorable light. Instead of portraying the bureau as the political arm of the corrupt Radicals, the revisionists believe the bureau did not go far enough in aiding the newly freed blacks. The bureau failed to reach its potential because it was underfinanced by Congress, unsupported by the white American public, and undermined by the agency's own high-level officials, who believed the complaints of white Southerners that the bureau was doing too much to help the ex-slaves. In the words of Forrest Wood, "it appears that the white South could have lived with a corrupt Bureau, but it could not live with a humanitarian one."[2]

The authors of this paper reject the negative views of the Freedmen's Bureau presented in the works of both the traditional and revisionist historians. Most of the histories of the bureau take an administrative approach and discuss policies set in motion by the national commissioner in Washington, D.C., the assistant commissioner there, and the assistant commissioners who were assigned to each of the former Confederate states. If one studies the bureau from a "bottom up" perspective, as the authors of this paper have done, a more favorable impression is formed concerning the work that the bureau performed.

Record Group 105 in the National Archives contains an abundance of letters and reports written by the state commissioners and local agents. This material demonstrates not only how national, state, and local agents

worked with the black community, but also how the
with the bureau to solve their immediate problem
for each ex-Confederate state vary in size and qua
upon the number of ex-slaves in the state and the
occupation.

The Texas records are only of medium size (17,
compared with the large collection of bureau recorus
Louisiana, or Mississippi. The Texas records, although comprising a smaller
quantity of manuscripts, do not suffer from a lack of quality, and the local
material is amazingly informative. Supplemental information can be found
in the records of the national administrative offices and divisions of the bureau in the same record group. The army materials in Record Group 393
complement those of the Freedmen's Bureau, since the two groups often
worked together and many bureau officers came from the army.[3]

The records of the bureau contain thousands of cases relevant to the in-
ner workings of black communities across the South in the first five years
after the Civil War. Combined with other manuscript source materials, the
Freedmen's Bureau records provide a composite picture of how the ex-
slaves began their adjustment to freedom, what some of their conceptions
were about the society in which they lived, and how they responded to the
social values of their communities. These are exceptional papers, for they
include both a cross-section of white attitudes about the black family and
materials written by the freedmen themselves. They demonstrate, among
other things, that the burdens of freedom were never easy and that many
times the issues were bewildering to a largely illiterate people. How the
freedmen began this long struggle of adjustment and how the controlling
white majority reacted to their actions are clearly delineated in this invaluable collection.

For Texas, the records constitute the major source of information about
race relations and the concerns of the state's black community during the
early postwar years. Texas bureau agents were sympathetic to aiding Texas
blacks in the reunification of families torn asunder by slavery, in assuring
fair treatment for children apprenticed to former slaveholders, and in attempting to protect women and children from abuse in both the white and
black communities.

The Civil War ended in April 1865, but the first bureau agents did not
arrive in Texas until early September. The agency expanded its operations as quickly as possible. A large portion of the Texas bureau's records
covers the early Reconstruction process in such large towns as Houston
and Galveston. Less information is available about the eastern portion of

—which is equal in size to Mississippi and Alabama combined— e few bureau agents were immediately available to cover the entire tate. The Texas bureau completed its operations in 1868.

Texas slaves were officially declared free on June 19, 1865. When the newly established bureau sent its agents into Texas, many blacks asked for help in reuniting their families. The records indicate that Texas blacks used whatever resources were at hand to gain information about family members separated for many years. Often the hopes of the former slaves were dashed. Julia Shephard, for example, wanted to obtain her children and sister from their former owner, who was also their father. As in so many other instances, the outcome never became part of the record.[4]

Julia Washington, a Houston black woman, had been brought to Texas by a slave trader when the war came. Her husband had last been heard of in Springfield, West Virginia, and her two children, John and Ida, who had also been sold, were allegedly in the same vicinity. Mrs. Washington was well situated in the city, had a good position paying fine wages, and desired that her family join her. She wrote to West Virginia several times but never received a reply. As a last resort, she turned to the Freedmen's Bureau, which was equally unsuccessful in locating them.[5]

Aged black folk aware of where their children lived expressed a deep desire to spend their remaining days with them. Aunt Rachel, a ninety-three-year-old Houstonian in good health, enlisted the aid of a white city teacher, Julia B. Nelson, hopeful that she could get back to Charleston, where her only daughter lived. Both women were attempting to raise money for the trip. Nelson wrote that if Aunt Rachel could "only get started first, she would be okay." The records do not reveal whether Aunt Rachel returned to Charleston. More successful was a "very feeble" octogenarian, Isaac Thompson, who wanted to return to Linden, Alabama, where he had four children who would care for him. The bureau first sent Thompson to the hospital, and then paid his transportation to Alabama.[6]

The Freedmen's Bureau received numerous inquiries from outside the state from black parents who were anxious to ascertain where their children had been taken in Texas. James Kelley, a Chicot County, Arkansas, black man, made a painstaking search for his three offspring. In this case the efforts were rewarded, for he found them living with a Baptist preacher on the Horne plantation, six miles south of Waco. From Madison, Arkansas, came the plea of Coleman, a black man over fifty, a porter at McCarty's Hotel and a "worthy old man," who reported that four of his five children were abducted from a plantation near Jefferson City, Missouri, by bushwhackers in August 1864. They were supposedly removed to Arkansas or possibly northern Texas. It was virtually impossible to find children who had been forcibly removed in similar circumstances, and Coleman's luck was no better.[7]

From mid-1865 until the 1870s, black parents attempted to locate or reclaim children who had been left on plantations, forcibly separated from them by sale, or detained unlawfully by a former master. Harry Pope and Sarah Timsy of Cherokee County, Texas, requested that a provost marshall issue an order to the sheriff of the county and deliver to them their five children: Chaley Jane, two; Henry, seventeen; Eddy, fourteen; and the twins Chuff and Lucy, twelve. The children had been taken and force was used to retain them. "Our children does not want to stay with ther [sic] former owner," the parents pleaded, and prayed that their "petition be granted" for their return. In another case, John E. Chisholm, former owner, spirited away the four children of Washington Ake shortly after federal troops invaded Texas. The children, according to the parents, had no desire to go with Chisholm, and neither Ake nor his wife gave their assent.[8] As is often the case, the records do not indicate the outcome.

From all over Texas, black heads of families sought information, aid, or any type of help the Freedmen's Bureau could provide. According to the records, most of the requests came from black women, but black men were concerned with locating their offspring as well. Blacks, of course, did not rely solely on the bureau. They searched individually, and at other times demanded concrete proof so that if they started on a long journey, they would not be thwarted in reclaiming their children by hostile whites. In certain cases the bureau agreed to pay transportation expenses, as in the example of Charity Watley. She lived in Galveston, and her three children were seven miles outside of Marlin, Texas, which was approximately four hundred miles away.[9]

Distances in Texas were often so immense that black parents had neither the money nor the means to make the required journeys. When this situation arose, they turned to the black community or to the bureau for assistance. Betsey Webster attempted to locate two sons who had last resided in Georgia: Hubbard Leonard, thirty or forty years old, and William Leonard, twenty-two. The Freedmen's Bureau was willing to pay the Leonard sons' transportation to the Lone Star State, but there is no indication they were ever found.[10]

A number of young black adults, according to bureau records, attempted to locate their parents. Sometimes they were successful, like twenty-year-old Eliza Finnick, originally sold in Maryland as a young teenager in 1860 before being taken to Louisiana and Texas. Her parents lived in Charles

County, Maryland, and she was able to trace them. Eliza Finnick was also encouraged by the fact that her grandfather, a free black, had left some valuable property and that Finnick's mother, Henny Adams, held some money for her, which she had promised to keep until Finnick came of age.[11]

Both Flora Hewes and Adeline Strouder, Galveston black women, were anxious to find their parents and other blood relatives in Wainsborough (Burke County), Georgia, and Louisville, Kentucky, respectively. In Austin, Mary Riggs resorted to the Freedmen's Bureau to learn if her mother, Matilda Riggs, still resided in Lexington, Kentucky. In these cases, none of the women succeeded in finding the whereabouts of their families.[12] As long as there was an institution or an individual to aid them, blacks continued to search, no matter how minimal the chances. For children whose parents were not located, however, the system posed obstacles.

Too often young children were not found by their parents, or the parents were dead, and the Texas black community simply did not have the money to support them. Just how many orphan children there were in Texas in 1865 will never be known with certainty, but the number was undoubtedly large. In the closing months of 1865 former slave owners and county courts were beginning to wonder what to do in these types of cases. In San Marcos a white planter had nine "orphans" among his ex-slaves. Some of the mothers had remarried, and "others were not able to support and take care of [their children]." The blacks were getting ready to disperse, making the farmer "shudder at the thought of the suffering that must initially follow." He was willing to care for them "through sympathy" if he was given the "power to retain them from their mothers who have no home or means of support for them." In Washington County the chief justice's office had been apprenticing or binding out children so they would have "good comfortable homes" and "receive some education." The office was satisfied that it was acting properly under Texas law and that it could "select homes that will do justice to these children."[13]

The vast correspondence in the Texas bureau's files between the agents and ex-slaves reveals the concern of the black community that children apprenticed to former slaveholders be treated fairly. Throughout Texas, county officials and military personnel began to bind out children as soon as Union forces took control of the state. If the children's parents could not immediately be found or if it was ascertained that the youngsters were orphans, they were usually apprenticed to a planter, who saw them as a cheap source of labor, or to a white person with whom they had formerly lived. The standard procedure was for the county court to give at least ten days public notice. Then, if no one came forward to challenge the action, the child was "legally" apprenticed.

Blacks correctly perceived that the apprenticeship system established throughout the South after the war was another form of slavery. Freedmen were at an enormous disadvantage simply because most of them were illiterate. Unless some sympathetic individual apprised them of the workings of the apprenticeship system, they were at the mercy not only of the law but also of white society in general.[14] As a result, blacks constantly urged the Freedmen's Bureau to void the apprenticeship agreements and restore the children to adoptive and "fictive" kin.

Almost every volume or box in the Freedmen's Bureau papers for Texas contains material on apprenticing. These records document clashes between blacks and whites over the issue of binding out children, a controversy that continued throughout the early years of Texas Reconstruction. In many instances the former slaves were anxious to care for these orphans and were "clamorous" in their desire to see that the children were not left to the mercy of whites. But many white officials disagreed, believing the freedmen wanted to "carry them over the country where they have nothing to support and maintain" them. In the view of the officials, the children would clearly be much worse off with black protectors than if they were taken care of by good white families.[15]

In 1866 the Texas legislature enacted an apprenticing statute without regard to race. But it was quite clear to both black and white observers that the new law was to be used almost solely in regard to black children. One disgusted Freedmen's Bureau agent wrote that its aim was to "enslave the rising generation (in particular) of the freedmen in a worse condition of slavery than they have ever been." And another argued that the parents "(when able) are the most natural guardians of their own children."[16]

Blacks did not stand idly by. Quite often they succeeded in overturning what they considered to be illegal apprenticeship agreements. Sandy Mingoe, a Boston black, learned that his grandchild, Julia, had been bound without his consent to Edward Runnels after Runnels had forcibly taken the child from him. Mingoe made application to revoke the apprenticeship. As a result, the child was returned to her grandfather and an order was given to the chief justice of the county to cancel the bond that Runnels had given to fulfill the contract. Far to the south, in Galveston, Solomon Riley obtained his daughter, Louisa, who was being held by a widow outside Seguin, Texas. In Austin, Toby, the son of Nellie Thompson, was returned to his mother through the intervention of the Freedmen's Bureau. On occasion blacks used community information and support from relatives to negate an apprenticing arrangement. With the assistance of kin, Clara Rives of Austin reclaimed her son, and James Buck and Nancy Moss retrieved Lucinda and Kinchey, who had been indentured to a white woman.[17]

Blacks sometimes did apprentice their children because the parent or parents needed the income. When a black child was hired out to a white person, the adults made sure, if at all possible, that the agreement was fair and equitable. Such was the case of Lew Lewis of Columbia, Texas, who worked out an agreement for his son Gabriel with E. Burchard. Lewis's terms were specific and demanding, quite sufficient to protect his son. Burchard could employ Gabriel if he paid $12 currency a month and accepted the responsibility for boarding and schooling him. Lewis wished a guarantee to this effect, and he also retained the right to take his son away whenever he saw fit. Lewis's objective was quite clear: to bind Burchard within the details outlined or be able to exact double wages for the work performed by his son. The contract, moreover, was approved by a provost marshall. Although the terms were quite detailed, Burchard agreed to them, and Lewis rested somewhat easier in the knowledge he had done all that was humanly possible to guarantee the maximum amount of protection for Gabriel. Probably most blacks were not able to be so careful in legally guarding their children as Lew Lewis, but wherever possible they took measures to protect their offspring.[18]

Blacks also worried about making sure children were well treated and not taken advantage of by either their own or whites. Lee Russell declared that he had seen Mr. and Mrs. Sam Ellington of Williamson County "shamefully beat" a black girl and that the "neighbors all talk about the way she is used." Josiah Coleman reported that two children, a boy and a girl, bound to William D. Patten of Austin, a white man, were abused, and that the girl had come to him "for protection." In other cases, the evidence of child abuse was indisputable. Two black women, Ellen Jones and Mary Lewis, stated that a Mrs. Roberts mistreated a black girl named Mary, who was around twelve years of age. Mary was summoned to the office and "showed [the bureau agent] her marks and wished to be taken away."[19]

The local Texas bureau records indicate that the black community demonstrated a sense of their new rights as freedmen by their willingness to use the bureau's courts to deal with problems between members of their own community. Blacks insisted upon bringing to light and prosecuting child abuse not only by whites but also by other blacks. Howard, a black man, charged Ham Serell, also black, before the bureau court with "unmercifully" beating Howard's daughter and refusing to pay for her hire. Serell, however, was found not guilty. In Ryan, Texas, Martha Gee complained that Berry Hodges cruelly whipped her six-month-old granddaughter. Hodges pleaded guilty and was sentenced to three days hard labor in the guardhouse. In Galveston, Isiah Lemmons declared that Mahalia A. Morris abused and beat her adopted child. Morris was warned, and gave the bureau assurances that the child would be well treated in the future. When it appeared that the disciplining of children might turn into child abuse, blacks carefully watched the individuals involved.[20]

Blacks, moreover, reported to the bureau against their own folks when other transgressions were particularly severe. These concerned sexual indictments of one form or another. Fathers, especially, attempted to protect their daughters. Wesley Henderson complained that Newton Collins, who was married, had seduced his daughter Celeste. Henderson could not confirm her pregnancy when he made the charge, so the bureau was of little help. The agent advised the irate father to "wait and see the result." In another case, George Watrous stated that Stephen slept with his daughter, Georgianna, and wished to live with her. Stephen, who was already married, denied the charge. In this particular instance nothing came of the allegation.[21]

The Texas black community also had their own internecine quarrels on behalf of children. Many women from Austin to Houston brought suits against their husbands and lovers for nonsupport of themselves and their children. Sara Tinsely, in Gonzales, stated that Elias Brown was the father of her fifteen-month-old child. After hearing the case, the bureau decided that Brown was the father, and when Brown refused to take the baby and support it, the bureau ordered him to pay Tinsely a $10 settlement and $2 a month and to clothe the infant until "he saw proper to take the child and support it." Martha Pelham brought charges against Steward Hamilton, who was the father of her daughter's child. Hamilton had promised to support them but had not done anything. There was also a $10 doctor's bill due because the infant had been ill. In bureau court, Hamilton agreed to pay the medical bill and to take the child and raise it in a "proper manner," but Mary Pelham refused to surrender her daughter. Other cases in a similar vein were settled in like fashion.[22]

Nonsupport of children was but one of several internal crises that racked the Texas black community. The bureau records are sprinkled with cases too numerous to elaborate in this article. There were clashes when a sister had been willed to a certain individual, when both parents claimed a child, and when blacks took children and promised to return them but did not.

There were runaways, stolen children, debts for delivering children, the unlawful keeping of adopted children, and two young men claiming the same boy as a brother.[23]

A persistent problem involved black men who had fathered children during slavery and then were sold away, leaving the mothers to raise and support them. During Reconstruction the fathers appeared, desiring to take the children away so they could reap the proceeds from their labor. In most cases of this nature, the bureau and other courts held the father had no right to the children, but they were also governed by the character of the parents and the wishes of the children. In Meridian, Lucie Williams had to take Mark Walker to court to retain her offspring. They had lived together during slavery, but afterward she cared for the children. When they became old enough to pick cotton, however, Walker desired to have them. He was unsuccessful in his rather mercenary attempt to exploit their labor.[24]

Texas blacks rose to the occasion in caring for orphan children when circumstances either warranted or required it. When Jack Talbot's wife died in June 1867, she had charge of two orphan children. When Talbot admitted that he was not able to keep them, Jacob Fountain, a leader of the Austin black community, agreed to care for them. Jackson McKinney, did the same thing for Abraham, an orphan freedboy from Huntsville. The following case clearly demonstrates the close ties, feelings of affection, and independent spirit of Texas blacks in taking care of their own. Cesar Kennedy and Mary McGee of Bastrop County had lived together as husband and wife for a year during slavery. A child was born of the union, but Kennedy was later sold. Both eventually remarried; Kennedy admitted that he had no right to the child and did not claim him. But when Kennedy learned that Mary was having a very hard time supporting the boy and her other family, Kennedy assumed the responsibility of supporting, educating, and raising the young man in a proper way. In another case, two children in Liberty were orphaned when their mother died during a smallpox epidemic, and Liberty blacks came forward to care for them.[25] Both incidents are strong reminders that blacks had deep attachments to children, no matter to whom they belonged. This general characteristic was perhaps a carryover from practices made necessary under the institution of slavery.

Among other things, the bureau records confirm that Texas blacks frequently turned to the bureau for assistance. They did so for two particular reasons. First, the bureau, because it was spread throughout the South, had a communications network that reached into isolated areas and made it possible to gain information that simply was not otherwise obtainable for the vast majority of ex-slaves. Second, the bureau, because of its ties to the federal government, was supported by national law, and served as a buffer for the black community against the often hostile legal and judicial decisions of local and state officials. This is not to argue that bureau agents were consistently sympathetic or always made the right decision when the interests of former slaves were at stake. It merely suggests that blacks "used" the bureau in myriad ways. The tremendous number of cases involving the freedmen in the Texas records and those of other southern states attests to that fact.

These cases indicate that the Freedmen's Bureau papers are a valuable source for historians interested in writing about the Afro-American family during Reconstruction. Most Reconstruction scholars are aware that microfilm copies of some of the Freedmen's Bureau records have been deposited in federal records centers across the nation so that these vital documents will be more accessible to historians. While the papers of the national and state Freedmen's Bureau offices are immensely valuable, they often focus on administrative problems that have little direct relevance to blacks. The most penetrating insights into the Afro-American community are frequently found in the manuscripts of the local agents. Many of these papers, such as correspondence between local citizens—black and white—and the agents, are not duplicated in the microfilm project and therefore are available only in the National Archives.[26]

Fortunately, scholars who do not have immediate access to the bureau's files at the National Archives will be able to sample its rich holdings on black history in a multivolume work entitled *Freedom and Southern Society: A Documentary Record, 1861–1867.* Funded by the National Historical Publications and Records Commission and by the University of Maryland, this documentary is being edited (and given lengthy introductions) by a team of scholars led by Ira Berlin. The first volume to appear, which is the second in the planned series, deals with the black military experience during the Civil War. Other volumes will follow. "Reflecting editorial interest in a *social* history of emancipation," the editors assert, "*Freedom* is organized thematically, following the process of emancipation." These manuscripts are "central to the transition from slavery to freedom." In future volumes the "transformation of black life that followed the conclusion of armed conflict" will be the central focus.[27] Even after this project is completed, however, it will still be necessary for scholars of Afro-American history to consult the local files of the Bureau of Refugees, Freedmen, and Abandoned Lands in Record Group 105 of the National Archives.

The Freedmen's Bureau records are unique. Through the use of the local materials in the Texas bureau records, this paper has demonstrated the concerns of the black community for civil rights, a stable family life, the security of their children, justice, and independence. Although many of the conceptions are filtered through white perspectives, the beliefs and behavior of the ex-slaves are apparent at every stage of the Reconstruction era. Used cautiously and with other supporting evidence, these materials point to the fact that Reconstruction was a "great experiment" in which Southern blacks actively participated. Just as importantly, these records reach across generations to researchers interested in learning more about black family life and local history.

NOTES

1. The best and most complete explication of these ideas is George R. Bentley, *A History of the Freedmen's Bureau* (Philadelphia: Univ. of Pennsylvania Press, 1955). After thirty years, this is still the only major overview of the bureau based upon manuscripts. Claude A. Elliot's essay on the Texas bureau is written in the same vein, but with more vengeance; see "The Freedmen's Bureau in Texas," *Southwestern Historical Quarterly* 56 (1952): 1–24.

2. Forrest G. Wood, *The Era of Reconstruction, 1863–1877* (Arlington Heights, Ill.: Harlan Davidson, 1975), 27. The strongest argument for the bureau having failed to reach its potential is William S. McFeely, *Yankee Stepfather: General O. O. Howard and the Freedmen* (New York: Norton, 1968). A more sympathetic portrait is Herman Belz, *Emancipation and Equal Rights: Politics and Constitutionalism in the Civil War Era* (New York: Norton, 1978).

3. Barry A. Crouch, "Hidden Sources of Black History: The Texas Freedmen's Bureau Records as a Case Study," *Southwestern Historical Quarterly* 83 (Jan. 1980): 211–226, and "Freedmen's Bureau Records: Texas, a Case Study," in *Afro-American History: Sources for Research,* Robert L. Clarke, ed., 74–94 (Washington, D.C.: Howard Univ. Press, 1981). For the army, see James E. Sefton, *The United States Army and Reconstruction, 1865–1877* (Baton Rouge: Louisiana Univ. Press, 1967); Joseph G. Dawson, III, *Army Generals and Reconstruction: Louisiana, 1862–1877* (Baton Rouge: Louisiana Univ. Press, 1982); and for Texas, see Robert W. Shook, "Federal Occupation and Administration of Texas, 1865–1870" (PhD diss., North Texas State Univ., 1970); William Lee Richter, "The Army in Texas during Reconstruction, 1865–1870" (PhD diss., Louisiana State Univ., 1970).

4. Samuel Canby to agent, Bryan, [Tex.], Aug. 8, 1867, Records of the Bureau of Freedmen, Refugees, and Abandoned Lands, Texas, Record Group (RG) 105, National Archives (NA), vol. 57, 101. Unless otherwise noted, all references are to the Texas bureau records, RG 105, NA. See also Crouch, "Hidden Sources of

Black History," 214. A description of these local bureau materials can be found in Elaine Everly, comp., "Preliminary Inventory of the Records of Field Offices of the Bureau of Refugees, Freedmen, and Abandoned Lands," RG 105; Elaine Everly and Willna Pacheli, comps., "Records of the Field Offices of the Freedmen's Brach, Office of the Adjutant General, 1872–78" (mimeographed; Part 3 of 3 parts, National Archives and General Services Administration, 1973–1974). Examples of work based on local agent's records are Crouch, "The Freedmen's Bureau and the 30th Sub-District in Texas: Smith County and Its Environs during Reconstruction," *Chronicles of Smith County, Texas* 11 (Spring 1972): 15–30; Crouch, ed., "View from Within: Letters of Gregory Barrett, Freedmen's Bureau Agent," *Chronicles of Smith County, Texas* 12 (Winter 1973): 13–26; James Smallwood, "The Freedmen's Bureau Reconsidered: Local Agents and the Black Community," *Texana* 11 (Spring 1973): 309–320; James Smallwood, *Time of Hope, Time of Despair: Black Texans during Reconstruction* (Port Washington, N.Y.: Kennikat Press, 1981).

5. Statement of Julia Washington, Apr. 10, 1867, vol. 96, n.p.; Abner Doubleday to agent, Springfield, W.V., Apr. 11, 1867, D-14, box 42.

6. Julia B. Nelson to Louis W. Stevenson, Oct. 30, 1869, box 42; Statement of Isaac Thompson, Feb. 14, 1867, vol. 96, n.p.

7. G. W. S. Benson to agent, Waco, [Tex.], Nov. 7, 1867, vol. 165, 62; endorsement, Charles Haughn, Apr. 11, 1868, vol. 165, 63; Benson to Haughn, Nov. 7, 1867, vol. 166, 26; endorsement, Haughn, Apr. 11, 1868, vol. 116, 27; John Tyler to agent, Napoleon, Ark., Apr. 22, 1867, box 5, Arkansas; endorsement, J. C. Predmore, May 14, 1867, box 5, Arkansas.

8. Harry Pope and Sarah Timsy to A. J. Hamilton, n.d., 1865, governor's correspondence, A. J. Hamilton (Texas State Library, Austin), hereafter cited as Hamilton Papers); C. E. Culver to J. T. Kirman, Aug. 31, 1867, vol. 86, 35.

9. W. H. Sinclair to A. P. Delano, Apr. 17, 1866, vol. 4, 191.

10. Edgar M. Gregory to Rufus Saxton, Sept. 19, 1865, vol. 4, 5.

11. W. H. Sinclair to E. M. Gregory, May 20, 1867, box 42.

12. Statement of Flora Hewes, Apr. 15, 1867, vol. 96, n.p.; Statement of Adeline Strouder, Apr. 13, 1867, vol. 96, n.p.; James Oakes to agent, Lexington, Ky., Apr. 6, 1868, vol. 49, 157.

13. L. Dixon to A. J. Hamilton, Nov. 27, 1865, Hamilton Papers; O. H. P. Garrett to Hamilton, Dec. 11, 1865, ibid.

14. A. G. Haskins to W. G. Kirkman, July 9, 1867, vol. 66, 6–7.

15. For an example of this, see Garrett to Hamilton, Dec. 11, 1865, Hamilton Papers. Additional material on apprenticing is in John P. Carrier, "The Era of Reconstruction, 1865–1875," in *Tyler and Smith County, Texas: An Historical Survey,* ed. Robert W. Glover (Marceline, Mo.: Walsworth Publishing Co., 1976), 65–66; "Book of Indentures to Bonds of Apprenticing, 1867–1870" (University Archives, James G. Gee Library, East Texas State Univ. [Commerce]).

16. A. H. Mayer to Henry A. Ellis, Nov. 24, 1866, vol. 120, 43–44; W. G.

Kirkman to Charles Garretson, Oct. 31, 1867, vol. 67, 96; Theodore Brantner Wilson, *The Black Codes of the South* (Tuscaloosa: Univ. of Alabama Press, 1965), 110–111; Smallwood, *Time of Hope,* 54–58. For a comparison with other states, see Donald G. Nieman, *To Set the Law in Motion: The Freedmen's Bureau and the Legal Rights of Blacks, 1865–1868* (Millwood, N.Y.: KTO Press, 1979), 76–82, 137–138, 199; Richard Paul Fuke, "A Reform Mentality: Federal Policy toward Black Marylanders, 1864–1868," *Civil War History* 22 (Sept. 1976): 222–226; Rebecca Scott, "The Battle over the Child: Child Apprenticeship and the Freedmen's Bureau in North Carolina," *Prologue: Journal of the National Archives* 10 (Summer 1978): 101–113.

17. W. G. Kirkman to Edward Runnels, Nov. 5, 1867, vol. 69, 4; *Sandy Mingoe v. Edward Runnels,* Nov. 11, 1867, vol. 70, 12; Statement of Solomon Riley, Mar. 26, 1867, vol. 96, n.p.; Byron Porter to George Glasscock, Jan. 21, 1867, vol. 46, n.p.

18. Complaints and Memo of Business, June 20, 1867, vol. 52, 11; W. G. Kirkman, Circular No. [?], Jan 6., 1867, vol. 70, 12; Statement of Solomon Riley, Mar. 26, 1867, vol. 96, n.p.; Byron Porter to George Glasscock, Jan 21, 1867, vol. 46, n.p.

19. Complaints and Memo of Business, Aug. 9, 1867, vol. 52, 32, 29, 34; *Thomas Glascow v. Busley,* May 9, 1868, vol. 75, 49; J. A. A. Robinson to agent, Huntsville, [Tex.], Nov. 12, 1867, vol. 110, 29; endorsement, Joseph A. Mower, Oct. 30, 1867; endorsement, James P. Butler, Dec. 19, 1867.

20. *Howard v. Hamp Serell,* Aug. 15, 1866, vol. 131, 1; *Martha Gee v. Berry Hodges,* Aug. 27, 1866, vol. 58, 10–11; *Isiah Lemmons v. Mahalia A. Morris,* Mar. 1867, vol. 96, n.p.; *Mary Jane Chapman v. Ann Saunders,* Apr. 22, 1867, vol. 96, n.p.

21. *Parry Lee v. Patrick Gibben,* Mar. 27, 1868, vol. 75, 42; Complaints and Memo of Business, June 8, 1867, vol. 52, 7; *George Watrous v. Stephen,* May 3, 1867, vol. 51, 77–78.

22. *Sara Tinsley v. Elias Brown,* Aug. 18, 1866, vol. 131, 3; Complaints and Memo of Business, June 4, 1867, vol. 52, 4; June 7, 1867, vol. 52, 7; June 11, 1867, vol. 52, 9; Oct. 31, 1867, vol. 52, 59; *Juliann Stevens v. Durke Woodall,* Sept. 15, 1868, vol. 108, 194–195.

23. These types of difficulties appear in almost every agent's records in Texas, RG 105, NA.

24. *Minnie Qualls v. Samuel Handy,* June 23, 1867, vol. 96, n.p.; *George Brown v. Former Wife,* Oct. 16, 1867, vol. 96, n.p.; Byron Porter to agent, San Antonio, Oct. 20, 1866, vol. 48, 106–107; Chauncey C. Moore to assistant commissioner, Louisiana, Sept. 15, 1865, vol. 4, 3; *William Smith v. Eliza Smith,* May 15, 1867, vol. 131, n.p.; *Doney Hamilton v. Caroline Flash,* Aug. 25, 1868, vol. 108, 176–177; *Mary Ann Holmes v. J. Tooke,* Mar. 30, 1868, vol. 75, 40; *Clara Parker v. Louisa Hutt,* Aug. 19, 1868, vol. 108, 170–171; *Jim McSween v. Alfred Reddick,* Dec. 25, 1867,

vol. 54, 28–29; J. P. Richardson to S. C. Plummer, May 29, 1867, vol. 49, 17; *Lucie William v. Mark Walker,* n.d., vol. 138, 88–89.

25. Complaints and Memo of Business, June 28, 1867, vol. 52, 14; James C. Devine, order no. [?], Oct. 12, 1866, vol. 110, 12; J. P. Richardson to Byron Porter, June 10, 1867, vol. 49, 30; Complaints and Memo of Business, June 10, 1867, vol. 52, 8; A. H. Mayer to W. H. Sinclair, Aug. 28, 1868, vol. 121, 2–3; Mayer to J. B. Kiddoo, Aug. 31, 1868, vol. 121, 6.

26. Three valuable publications from the National Archives and Records Service in Washington, D.C.: *Black Studies: A Select Catalog of National Archives Microfilm Publications* (1984), 19–81; *Records of the Assistant Commissioner for the State of Texas, Bureau of Refugees, Freedmen, and Abandoned Lands, 1865–1869* (1973), microfilm publication M-821; *Records of the Superintendent of Education for the State of Texas, Bureau of Refugees, Freedmen, and Abandoned Lands, 1865–1870* (1973), microfilm publication M-822.

27. Ira Berlin, Joseph P. Reidy, and Leslie S. Rowland, eds., *Freedom: A Documentary History of Emancipation, 1861–1876,* series 2: *The Black Military Experience* (New York: Cambridge Univ. Press, 1982), xxi; I. Berlin, Barbara J. Fields, J. P. Reidy, and L. S. Rowland, "Writing *Freedom*'s History," *Prologue: Journal of the National Archives* 14 (Fall 1982): 129–139; LaWanda Cox, "From Great White Men to Blacks Emerging from Bondage, with Innovations in Documentary Editing," *Reviews in American History* 12 (1984): 31–39.

Three

BLACK DREAMS AND
          WHITE JUSTICE

T he prevailing system of law during the antebellum
years was something that was both special and unique to white and black
southerners. To whites, it was a practical tool and an institution for maintaining a stable society based on slavery. To the slaves, it was a system with
which they had little formal contact but which surrounded their very be-
ings with its regulations. Because the bondsmen were considered both
persons and property, they were never entirely outside the law.[1]

Following emancipation, millions of black Americans encountered for
the first time legal and social relationships that assumed they were equal
with other Americans before the law. Given the status of the South's "peculiar institution" and the relative swiftness with which emancipation was
achieved in the aftermath of four years of savage civil war, even social sci-
entists as sympathetic as W. E. B. Du Bois assumed that the former slaves'
experience with the law hampered the North's efforts to establish the
freedpeople securely in their new status. Du Bois wondered, for example,
whether blacks "showed any signs of a disposition to learn better things" in
a hostile environment, thereby implying that the former slaves' ignorance
would be a difficult burden to overcome.[2] To what extent, however, may
we assume that the cultural deprivation experienced by slaves undermined
the freedpeople's efforts to build a viable way of life? To what extent does
the evidence reveal or fail to reveal that the former slaves brought with
them ideas of justice; of domestic and community obligations; of business,
labor, and other contractual responsibilities—all necessary to participate
fully in the society that was emerging from the ashes of the war?

An intensive analysis of the blacks' legal response to white society and
justice during the early Reconstruction years should tell us much about
the cultural autonomy that they had developed under slavery and its potential suitability to the new order. A positive answer to these questions
would render obsolete many popular and scholarly notions concerning

the nature and scope of white dominion over slave society and of the black man's capacity to function adequately in a formally free society. By focusing on black communities in Texas and on their interaction with the Freedmen's Bureau courts, we hope to suggest that substantial modifica tion of the conventional wisdom is necessary.

The first extensive contact that emancipated blacks had with the law and the judicial process came during the year after the Civil War. The Bureau of Refugees, Freedmen, and Abandoned Lands, commonly known as the Freedmen's Bureau, was created March 3, 1865, assigned to the War Department, and "committed" to "control of all subjects relating to refu- gees and freedmen from rebel states, or from any district or county within the territory embraced in the operations of the army, under such rules and regulations as may be prescribed by the head of the bureau and approved by the President." [3]

Texas provides a clear perspective on blacks' perception of justice under the law. Moreover, it affords a good opportunity to assess the intentions of the bureau. Bureau operations in the Lone Star State were delayed until September 1865, when Assistant Commissioner Edgar M. Gregory arrived. During the interim, the army attempted to secure a measure of equality for blacks. Maj. Gen. Gordon Granger, head of the occupation forces, declared publicly that all the slaves were free and that freedom involved "an absolute equality of personal rights and rights of property between former masters and slaves, and the connection heretofore exist- ing between them becomes that between employer and hired labor." The freedmen, however, were counseled that they would not be "allowed to collect at military posts," nor would they be supported in "idleness either there or elsewhere." Later the scope of this order was enlarged, stating that for the present freedmen were to work under contracts that would be reviewed upon the arrival of bureau agents, when permanent disposition of the labor force would be made. Nor were blacks allowed to travel on public roads or assemble without passes from their employers. [4]

After Commissioner Gregory arrived in Texas, he issued his own cir- cular, outlining the rights of blacks and informing local bureau agents that they would adjudicate all cases of civil officers' failing to give the freed- men "impartial justice." Planters were to accord the former bondsmen all the rights of free men, and the lash, or corporal punishment, was to give way to "law and moral power." Anything, including the pass system, that conflicted with the rights and liberties of the blacks was declared null and void. [5] The problem now became one of space and time. It was important that bureau agents be strategically located so that the maximum number of freedpeople would have access to bureau courts for redress of their grievances. In spite of this precaution, agents and bureau courts were more available to Negroes in the larger towns than to those scattered in rural areas. Between 1866 and the bureau's termination in 1868, Texas agents operating as mediators heard hundreds of cases, encompassing every aspect of black life. Most of the cases during the courts' early stages, however, involved problems concerning labor contracts and the blacks' efforts to receive their fair share of wages or crops. For the most part, these cases reveal that the freedpeople had a well-developed sense of business enterprise and understood the nature and purpose of contracts.

Napoleon Easely, for example, complained that his white employer, T. P. Washington, was feeding the mule teams out of the crop that had just been grown. At Easely's insistence, the bureau agent examined the contract. It clearly showed that Washington was bound to furnish the feed himself.[6] The business acumen displayed by the former slave in this contractual relationship indicated that he knew precisely what its terms were and how and where he was being cheated; he knew the business in which he was engaged and the means necessary to assure its success. Blacks were equally assertive in contracting with employers of their own choosing. Richard Cole, a white planter in Liberty, charged that four blacks, two men and two women, had violated their contract by leaving his plantation and finding work elsewhere. Cole asked that they be returned to his place to work out their unexpired terms. His allegation told only part of the story, however. The four freedpeople had good reason for leaving him and proved that he had violated the contract by using violence and threats of death against them. The contract was therefore canceled, and they were allowed to seek new employment.[7]

In a similar situation freedman Lewis Jones was restrained by R. B. Heath from finding another employer. Jones realized that his rights as a free laborer were being violated and sought recourse in the bureau courts. Heath was enjoined to pay Jones for his labor, and he was permitted to seek a new employer.[8] Like many other Texas blacks, Jones recognized that a black had to be able to select his own employer if he were to attain independence and equality. Jones's case demonstrates that blacks understood the labor system and sought to establish their own way of life and cultural patterns within the context of a free-labor market.

Not all cases were as simple and straightforward as that of Lewis Jones. Nevertheless, blacks continued to demonstrate a high degree of perspicacity in interpreting the nature of their contractual relationships with whites. In Seguin, freedman Samuel Morgan believed that he had been cheated out of his share of a cotton crop he raised in 1867. Morgan had made a special contract with Patrick Lyons, a white planter, under which he claimed that he was to receive two-thirds of the crop, as well as wages for extra labor in clearing the land. The case came to trial on June 1, 1868, with both parties represented by attorneys.[9]

Allegedly, the agreement provided that Lyons would rent Morgan forty-five acres of good tillable land and furnish a yoke of oxen and a beef, and Morgan would raise corn and cotton for shares. However, only the corn was fairly divided, Morgan claimed. Lyons sold the cotton, amounting to 1,320 pounds, at eight cents a pound, receiving $105.60. Less $10.50 taken out for ginning, two-thirds, or $63.40, was due Morgan. But Lyons produced accounts against the freedman for bagging and necessaries in the amount of $46, leaving a balance of $17.40. Morgan then proved that the land was not in tillable condition and that he had been about to seek another position when Lyons agreed to pay him to clear the land. Lyons, however, prevented Morgan from cultivating as much land as the contract called for. A white man testified in support of Morgan's contention, stating that twenty or twenty-five acres of the land had not been plowed for years if at all. Morgan had worked twenty-five to thirty acres, which would have cost at least two dollars an acre to clear. Lyons's lawyer contended that since there was nothing about payment written into the contract, it was presumed that Morgan had waived any claim for it. The black man knew that he was entitled to compensation and asserted his right by retaining a lawyer and suing Lyons. The judgment went in favor of the freedman and required Lyons to pay $57 in specie and $3 for the sheriff's cost.[10]

Black women were also careful to protect their interests in the crops they worked. Sally Ross of Robertson County brought J. W. Marise into court for nonpayment of wages. She and her two children had entered into a contract with Marise in 1867, but after eight months both parties became dissatisfied—although Marise apparently was not displeased with Ross's work. The Ross family had received about $20 in advances and was still due approximately $46. Ross was paid the $46, and the contract was then terminated.[11] This case indicates that Ross understood the obligations in a contractual relationship and was shrewd enough to realize that unless she received formal release from her agreement with Marise, she could very well have lost everything.

Blacks did not hesitate to seek justice from members of their own community in the bureau's courts. In Bryan, Louisa Moody, who was pregnant, brought charges of assault and battery against a freedman, John Stewart, for kicking her. Although Stewart pleaded not guilty, it was obvious that she had been assaulted. The actions of Stewart were inexcusable, the bureau agent recorded, and "might have been attended with serious result." Stewart was found guilty and sentenced to five days in the guard-house. Angeline Black, a Columbus freedwoman, accused George Powell, a freedman, of taking her horse and selling it. Powell was forced to return the horse.[12]

The disputes between black people that came before the bureau involved all aspects of their lives and indicated that they possessed a universal concept of justice that subordinated individual or family prerogatives to a higher law. Agnes Ewell, a Marshall freedwoman, for example, brought Hayden Ware into court in a dispute over the purchase of some land. In the fall of 1876 she bought a plot of six acres from Ware, and he agreed to take a mule as payment. The freedwoman gave him the mule, but Ware did not produce the deed. Ware admitted that he had made the agreement with the woman and stated that he would give her title to the land as soon as he received the deed from a Mr. Duncan, who had deeded the land to him, or he would pay for the animal. Ewell, however, had made improvements, and wanted to keep the land rather than accept payment for the mule. Finally, she agreed to await the return of Duncan so that arrangements could be made for transfer of the title.[13]

Although the largest number of cases blacks brought before bureau judges dealt with labor contracts, the freedpeople engaged the courts whenever questions arose concerning family and domestic relations and obligations. Perhaps the most important types of these cases entailed recovering orphaned or apprenticed children, whether the family's own or those of deceased or unlocated relatives. Blacks vigorously pursued such matters as soon as they learned that they were free, and continued to do so throughout the early years of Reconstruction. Their continual attempts to reunite their families demonstrate that strong family ties and a sense of family responsibility existed among the freedpeople in Texas—and probably throughout the South—although they had not been allowed to marry legally when they were in slavery.

George Klutz, a black man in the Houston area, induced a bureau agent to send two soldiers with him to San Felipe, in Austin County, to arrest a white man who had carried off Klutz's daughter Susan. Klutz was probably instrumental in having the soldiers arrest yet another white man who had taken two black girls.[14]

In Belton, freedman Ned Duncan petitioned for the return of his two sisters, who had been forcibly detained for their labor by a man named White, their former owner. White believed that because the girls' mother was dead he had a right to their services. Duncan, their nearest of kin, felt otherwise, and proved that he was able to support the two girls. He requested that they be allowed to return home with him. In keeping them, White claimed to be fulfilling the dying wish of the mother, but he could not prove it, and Duncan was awarded the children. The agent who heard the case wrote that because Duncan bore a "good name for honesty and industry," he was to be appointed "guardian pro tem." [15]

Peter Cole and his wife Milly, both black, had custody of Sophy Morgan's daughter Jane, who was about six years old. After they moved from Austin to San Antonio, the Coles died of cholera, and Jane was living with freedwoman Patsy Townes when Sophy Morgan learned of it. Greatly distressed and anxious to have her daughter returned, Sophy Morgan engaged the bureau to recover her, making arrangements to pay for the girl's travel. Before going to the bureau, she twice tried to contact Jane through other blacks going to San Antonio, but they failed to find her. Jane was returned home a month after her mother had become aware of the death of the Coles. [16]

Blacks had very little power in Texas civil courts, and when black children were apprenticed without their parents' knowledge or consent, the freedpeople's only legal recourse was through the bureau courts. When an apprenticeship was adjudicated, the facts were usually published in the newspaper. If no objections were received, the county court would then proceed with the apprenticeship. Because many blacks could not read, they were often not aware of what had taken place. However, they were able to press the bureau courts into reversing or renegotiating many of these apprenticeships.

Charlotte Duckett, a black woman of Boston, Texas, attempted to recover a black girl, Mary Newley, from a white woman, Levinia Lucas; the relationship between Newley and Duckett is not clear. According to the bureau's decision, Newley was to remain with Lucas, who had to post a bond of $200 in addition to the $300 she had originally put up. In the apprenticeship document, Lucas also agreed to treat Newley well and to give her $100 when she came of age. In this case the bureau agent became convinced that Duckett would not be able to care properly for Newley because she lacked money and that it would be in the best interest of the young girl to remain with her white guardian. [17] Duckett's concern, however, enabled Newley to receive a much-improved apprenticeship agreement.

A Boston, Texas, black boy, Guy Johnson, had been bound out by his father to a white man, P. T. Johnson, who may have been their former owner. Apparently the father was not able to take care of the son adequately, and so sought an apprenticeship, which would assure that the boy receive not only an education but also a stipulated sum of money when the contract was terminated. However, about January 1, 1867, Guy ran away from his employer and returned home. P. T. Johnson thereupon filed suit to recover his apprentice, but he was required to put up an additional bond to assure that he would faithfully fulfill the apprenticeship agreement and to promise that when Guy Johnson came of age, he would receive $250.[18]

One of the most significant court cases dealing with the status of black children in Texas in 1868 involved two black families. The case gives a good insight into the concern of blacks to have a healthy moral environment for their children. Overall, the black community protected its members and attempted to control the type of care that black children received, whether from blacks or whites. In this case, Samuel Spencer and his mother-in-law brought suit against Primer Dikes, who had been married to Spencer's sister, Sarah, now deceased. Spencer was contesting the status of three children that his sister had had by a former marriage. Spencer charged that Dikes was treating them cruelly and alleged that he was living with the girl, Anna, in an unlawful manner. Dikes pleaded not guilty to all the charges.[19]

The army of witnesses was impressive. Leading members of the black and white communities testified. Alfred Kent, the white postmaster of Gonzales, where the case was heard, asserted that he thought the children should be given to Spencer's mother-in-law. John V. Law, a prominent white merchant who had been dealing with Dikes since 1865, not only did not believe the allegations but had always found the man to be honest and industrious. Nor had he ever heard any derogatory remarks about Dikes.[20] The children's grandmother, Minty Price, could not prove anything material against Dikes, although she testified that she had seen him playing cards while his wife Sarah was sick in bed. She had also seen him drunk, but not often, and had heard only rumors of his cruel treatment of the children. Minty Price failed to establish the suspected incestuous relationship between Dikes and his stepdaughter Anna Price. Mrs. Price admitted that she wanted the children herself and thought she could take care of them with the assistance of her son. The children were examined after the room had been cleared of the involved parties.[21]

Anna Price emphatically denied the charges brought against her stepfather; she said Dikes had whipped the children only when they deserved it. She firmly defended her stepfather, stating that the three children were treated well. Anna's preference was to live with Dikes, but she told the court she would not object to living with her grandmother if that were the final decision. Peter, who was eleven years of age, confirmed most of Anna's testimony, and nine-year-old Jackson "did not seem to care."[22]

J. T. Price, the former owner of Samuel, Sarah, and Minty, thought the children should be turned over to their grandmother; he was confident she could take proper care of them. Six blacks and one white testified for the complainants, and six blacks and two whites testified for the defense.[23] Whatever the final judgment, the ruling would be important for the black community's solidarity and for how it viewed the care of black children.

It had been observed that Dikes was a fine-looking man, of respectable address and open countenance. He made a favorable impression on the court, but these had been the observations of a white man. In court the children were clean, neatly dressed, and healthy-looking. After counsel for both sides had made their final arguments, the agent interjected and told both the blacks and the lawyers that his office could not be considered a court of law. He stated that he was not governed by state law but by his own common sense and impartiality. He said further that the lawyers' services in bureau courts were not essential, but were an unnecessary burden and expense for the freedpeople. Nevertheless, the presence of the lawyers indicated the black people felt it was an important case. Those present were informed by the agent that he would attempt to work out an amicable settlement, but if his decision did not meet with their approval, they were at liberty to appeal to a higher authority.

After a thorough examination of the case, the agent determined that the charge of cruel treatment was exaggerated and the charge of incest unfounded. Even though the allegations were proved false, the court decided that the grandmother, as the nearest blood relative, would be awarded the children, and she was to receive them January 1, 1869. They were allowed to remain with their stepfather until then so that they might help with the harvest. In the meantime, a guardian selected by a probate judge was appointed for the children.[24]

This case demonstrates that at least one black community in Texas was very concerned about the wholesomeness of the homes that its children would be raised in and suggests that to black society in Texas it was important that family stability be maintained. Community pressures were used to uphold these standards, and charges of immorality were to be dealt with immediately by lawful means. Blacks were saying that they could and would take care of their own. In the Spencer-Dikes case, the problem was not merely that three children were being cared for by a stepfather alone, but also that rumors had been circulated about Dikes that were detrimental to all blacks. To stop these rumors and allegations, Minty Price and her son were willing to use all legal means at their disposal, including the testimony of white witnesses. Dikes pursued a similar course in his own defense and in trying to retain his stepchildren.

Where children were involved, the personal agonies of the freedpeople were intense. Maria Scaggs protested to the bureau court in January 1867 that Campbell Frigg, who had been her husband during slavery, had received an order allowing him to take away the two children she had borne him. She claimed that she had always taken care of the children and that they were removed without her consent. Frigg had obtained the children by concealing from the court the fact that Scaggs was alive and still caring for them. Frigg's interest in his offspring was quite mercenary—after he received them, he immediately hired them out so that he could collect their wages. Maria Scaggs and Campbell Frigg were not able to reach an amicable settlement, so the court imposed its own decision. Since the children in question were a boy and a girl, Scaggs agreed that Frigg should be allowed to keep the boy and she the girl.[25]

If the problem of returning children to their families or relatives posed many difficulties for the black community, so also did marriage relationships. Viable unions had evolved during the uncertain time of slavery, and the black communities in Texas were unsure whether the state would enact marriage laws to legitimize them. In response to this concern, the bureau issued marriage regulations meant to govern the freedpeople's relations and force the Texas legislature into action. All black males under eighteen and females under fifteen years of age were required to obtain the consent of their parents or guardians in order to marry. If neither parents nor guardians were available, then the bureau agent might approve the marriage. A license had to be obtained from the county clerk, and the ceremony performed by a regularly ordained minister or a justice of a state court. No divorces were allowed without due process of law. More importantly, a bureau law of March 3, 1865, recognized that freedpeople cohabiting or associating as man and wife, according to common-law statutes, were regarded as man and wife.[26]

Like any other people, many Texas freedpeople encountered domestic difficulties that they brought to the courts. One case concerned David and Louise Fly, a black couple of Gonzales. David Fly initiated the complaint, charging that his wife constantly abused him, beat him, and would not allow him to sleep with her or have any "matrimonial connections." Louise Fly asserted that her husband was a good-for-nothing "negroe" [*sic*], that she had never loved him, and that she would not permit him to sleep with her because she preferred white men. The court attempted to bring the partners to a mutual understanding. David agreed to buy Louise a bedstead, and she promised not to abuse him any more. Whatever further compromises the couple arrived at on their own, they were able to solve their domestic conflicts: two years later they were still together and had two children. At that point David was a laborer and Louise was keeping house.[27]

Thomas Jones of Columbus informed the court that his wife had left him and was living with another man. She was ordered to return, since she had been regularly married. In Marlin, Thomas Anderson, presumably a white, was fined $450 by the bureau for living with a black woman named Mary. Apparently the community was disturbed about the arrangement and asked that the court terminate the illicit affair. Dinah Behan, a black woman in Marlin, was fined ten dollars for living in open adultery with George H. Myers, a black man.[28] It did not matter whether black men or women were involved; the important point was that legal relationships be established in the black community. The need to stabilize their cultural autonomy precluded transgressions of sexual mores.

Some black women showed considerable skill in fending for themselves, as well as knowledge of what the promise of marriage meant legally, even if it came from a white man. Emma Hartsfield was living in Austin with a white man named Lacy McKenzie. She told the court that McKenzie had induced her to live with him by promising to give her a house and a lot in the city. After living with him for more than a year, Emma Hartsfield became pregnant, and McKenzie insisted that she have an abortion.

When she refused, McKenzie became angry and threatened to sell the house and lot, throw her out, and leave. She informed the Austin bureau court of the threat, and the agent was able to have a lawyer attach the land "to try and frighten him into a settlement." McKenzie was forced to deed to her lot no. 8 in Austin, which came with two houses. In return she "signed an agreement releasing him from all claims."[29]

Despite the evidence that black communities in Texas had preserved the cultural values necessary for organizing and maintaining a stable social order, their reliance upon the bureau courts often left them defenseless against the hostility of the larger social order in which they were to function as equals. In a frontier society, blacks lived in trepidation of vigilante groups. Although they continually complained of personal attacks, there was little blacks or bureau agents could to do alleviate the situation. For example, in Hallettsville, Tom Foley, a freedman, brought suit against

Stewart Campbell, a white, for assault and battery. Witnesses stated that they had seen Campbell strike and cuff Foley just as he had done during slavery. At one point Campbell wanted Foley to ride a wild horse, but Foley expressed fear of being thrown. Campbell told Foley, "G——d d——mn you, I will see if you don't," and then proceeded to knock the black man down and kick him. When Foley got up, Campbell pulled a knife and screamed, "G——d d——mn you, I will cut your life out." Foley then ran. Campbell was fined $50. The same day he was also fined $125 for whipping a black woman with a rope.[30]

In attempting to protect their civil rights, blacks confronted two major difficulties in civil courts: their reluctance to fine whites or to impose bonds that would compel them to keep the peace. The freedpeople regularly brought cases of assault and battery to bureau courts because the civil authorities would not cooperate when these cases were brought to them; grand juries, themselves intimidated, were often unwilling to indict whites. Blacks continued to risk their lives in the process, although not all cases reached a final decision, because the freedmen sometimes failed to appear. For the most part it was not hard to determine why, but this was an issue that neither the black community nor the bureau courts were ever able to solve.

Taking weapons from blacks so that the danger of retaliation would be minimized was another stratagem used by the whites. Again, neither the black community nor bureau or civil courts were able to protect blacks' constitutional right to purchase and keep weapons on their persons or in their households.[31]

In Texas and throughout the South the actions of the courts were quite within the constitutional standards of nineteenth-century America; that is, to provide blacks with a means to protect themselves and uphold equality before the law. Beyond this they were not empowered to go. The most recent judgment has been that "Bureau justice was more civilian than military, more state and local than national." Republicans in Congress assumed that "as a consequence of the war, intrastate equality of legal treatment should exist in their constitutionally governed federal system, as intrinsic parts of each state's constitution, laws, and customs." This meant that the bureau courts were a natural consequence of the Civil War, as were the Thirteenth, Fourteenth, and Fifteenth Amendments and the Reconstruction Acts. Congress and legalists were endeavoring to assure a state-based federalism involving a minimum of federal intervention. The most they would extend to blacks was formal equality with whites before the law; it was up to the former slaves to carry on from that point. This solution was not satisfactory, but the institutional and constitutional restraints against the lawmakers made it impossible for them to proceed further.[37] It was a conservative solution to a complex problem, and it was the freedpeople who suffered most from the lack of federal intervention and protection.

In summary, blacks' response to Texas bureau courts suggests that blacks had access to judicial remedies; they pressed their legal rights aggressively and with an awareness of what the law should do for them. The freedpeople brought cases to these government courts for numerous and varied reasons, establishing that their concepts of business, labor, justice, domestic relations and obligations, and contractual responsibilities were part of a complete ethos in the black community. They realized they were part of the law and could not live outside it, nor did they desire to. Blacks simply wanted the legal system to remedy the injustices done them and to provide protection for their newly won rights and freedom. For a people who had been denied so many rights under slavery, they learned with just a little experience that the bureau courts were generally more receptive to their grievances than the civilian courts.

The way the freedpeople regarded the law contains momentous implications for the study of slave culture. Many slaves had been astute enough observers during the antebellum years to realize that the law conveyed rights to all citizens. For the most part, blacks became acculturated to the legal values of the United States, accepting them readily when fair and impartial justice was dispensed, and fighting through the courts when justice was denied. Without a complex slave culture and ethos, it is unlikely that they would have responded to freedom as they did, using the bureau courts to protect themselves against white society and to maintain stability and harmony in the black community.

The bureau courts, then, were only an institutional vehicle through which blacks expressed their views of justice and their perception of the law. The state judicial system often denied freedpeople similar opportunities. It is not surprising that blacks used the bureau courts as much as they did because they knew that their individual and community survival depended upon how promptly they reacted to their new legal status and how well they protected their culture. That they were able to preserve an autonomous spirit throughout the time of slavery and were ready to express it when freedom finally arrived is seen no more clearly than in their use of the courts and the law in Texas from 1865 to 1868.

66   *Freedom*

NOTES

1. Charles S. Sydnor, "The Southerner and the Laws," *Journal of Southern History* 6 (1940): 3–23. For the slave's dual legal status as a person and as property, see Helen Tunnicliff Catterall, ed., *Judicial Cases concerning American Slavery and the Negro,* 5 vols. (Washington, D.C.: Carnegie Institution of Washington, 1926–1937); David Brion Davis, *The Problem of Slavery in Western Culture* (Ithaca, N.Y.: Cornell Univ. Press, 1966); Robert William Fogel and Stanley L. Engerman, *Time on the Cross: The Economics of American Negro Slavery* (Boston: Little, Brown, 1974); Winthrop D. Jordan, *White over Black: American Attitudes toward the Negro, 1550–1812* (Chapel Hill: Univ. of North Carolina Press, 1968); Maude White Katz, "The Negro Woman and the Law," *Freedomways* 2 (1962): 278–286; Wilbert E. Moore, "Slave Law and the Social Structure," *Journal of Negro History* 26 (1941): 171–202; Kenneth M. Stampp, *The Peculiar Institution: Slavery in the Ante-Bellum South* (New York: Knopf, 1956), 192–236; Peter H. Wood, *Black Majority: Negroes in Colonial South Carolina from 1670 through the Stono Rebellion* (New York: Knopf, 1974); and C. Vann Woodward, *The Strange Career of Jim Crow,* 3rd ed. (New York: Oxford Univ. Press, 1974).

2. W. E. B. Du Bois, "Reconstruction and Its Benefits," *American Historical Review* 15 (1910): 784. See also Martin Abbott, "Voices of Freedom: The Response of Southern Freedmen to Liberty," *Phylon* 34 (1973): 399–405. For Texas slaves' experience with the law, see A. E. Keir Nash, "The Texas Supreme Court and Trial Rights of Blacks, 1845–1860," *Journal of American History* 68 (1971): 622–642, and Nash, "Fairness and Formalism in the Trials of Blacks in the State Supreme Courts of the Old South," *Virginia Law Review* 56 (1970): 64–100.

3. 13 *Statutes at Large* 507–508; Du Bois, "Reconstruction and Its Benefits," 783. See also Du Bois's long chapter on the bureau in *The Souls of Black Folk* (Chicago: McClurg, 1903) and his *Black Reconstruction in America: An Essay toward a History of the Part Which Black Folk Played in the Attempt to Reconstruct Democracy in America, 1860–1880* (New York: Harcourt, Brace, 1935).

4. General Orders, no. 3, HQ Dist., Galveston, Tex., June 19, 1865, in *The War of the Rebellion: A Compilation of the Official Records of the Union and Confederate Armies,* 128 vols. (Washington, D.C.: Government Printing Office, 1880–1901), ser. 1, vol. 48, pt. 2, 929; *Flake's Daily Bulletin* (Galveston), June 29, 1865, 1–2; Charles W. Ramsdell, *Reconstruction in Texas* (New York: Columbia Univ. Press, 1910), 48–49; Robert L. Kerby, *Kirby Smith's Confederacy: The Trans-Mississippi South, 1863–1865* (New York: Columbia Univ. Press, 1972).

5. Circular no. 1, Oct. 12, 1865, Texas, vol. 9, 301, asst. commissioner's records for the state of Texas, Records of the Bureau of Refugees, Freedmen, and Abandoned Lands, Record Group 105, National Archives Building. Unless otherwise indicated, all records and cases cited below are in this record group.

6. *Napoleon Easely v. T. P. Washington,* Oct. 6, 1866, vol. 51, 49.

7. *Richard Cole v. Clarissa Edmunds, Linn Shaffer, John Jordan, and Caroline Green,* Aug. 24, 1866, vol. 123, 7–8.

8. *Lewis Jones (minor) v. R. B. Heath,* June 8, 1867, vol. 138, 58–59; *William Hill v. H. W. Fisher,* Nov. 3, 1868, vol. 113, 21.

9. *Samuel Morgan, v. Patrick Lyons,* June 1, 1868, vol. 154, 91–92.

10. Ibid.

11. *Sally Ross v. J. W. Marise,* Sept. 13, 1867, vol. 156, 27.

12. *Louisa Moody v. John Stewart,* Aug. 10, 1866, vol. 58, 6–7; *Angeline Black v. George Powell,* Nov. 3, 1868, vol. 80, 29.

13. *Agnes Ewell v. Hayden Ware,* Nov. 5, 1868, vol. 136, 54.

14. J. C. DeGress to Lt. Quigley, provost marshall, Hempstead, [Tex.], Oct. 23, 1865, vol. 100, 5; William H. Sinclair, asst. adj. gen., to Ira C. Pedigo, agent, Woodville, [Tex.], Apr. 17, 1866, vol. 4, 188. See also Barry A. Crouch, "The Freedmen's Bureau and the 30th Sub-District in Texas: Smith County and Its Environs during Reconstruction," *Chronicles of Smith County, Texas* 11 (1972): 25.

15. Complaint of Ned Duncan, July 16, 1867, vol. 55, 2–3.

16. Complaint of Sophy Morgan, Oct. 29, 1866, vol. 51, 56; Byron Porter, agent, Houston, to W. C. Hemphill, agent, San Antonio, Oct. 20, 1866, vol. 48, 106–107; Porter to Hemphill, Dec. 12, 1866, vol. 48, 119–120.

17. *Charlotte Duckett v. Levinia E. Lucas,* July 17, 1867, vol. 70, 1–2. Black women apprenticed children to people they trusted, both black and white. Sinclair to Philip Howard, agent, Meridian, [Tex.], Apr. 17, 1866, vol. 4, 189.

18. *P. T. Johnson v. Guy Johnson,* July 17, 1867, vol. 70, 3.

19. *Samuel Spencer and T. M. Harwood v. Primer Dikes,* Oct. 3, 5, 1868, vol. 98, 1–3.

20. Ibid.

21. Ibid., 3–6.

22. Ibid., 6.

23. Ibid., 1–7.

24. Ibid., 5–7; O. T. Steinberg, agent, Gonzales, [Tex.], to M. H. Beaty, probate judge, Gonzales County, Oct. 6, 1868, vol. 98, 7.

25. *Maria Scaggs v. Campbell Frigg,* Apr. 4, 1867, vol. 62, 10–11.

26. Circular no. 9, Mar. 23, 1866, vol. 9, 313; Chauncey C. Morse, acting asst. adj. gen., to F. D. Ingle, agent, Leona, [Tex.], Feb. 22, 1866, vol. 4, 146.

27. *David Fly v. Louise Fly,* Oct. 20, 1868, vol. 98, 10; Manuscript Census Returns, Ninth Census (1870), Gonzales, Tex., vol. 8, 406, Records of the Bureau of the Census, Record Group 29, National Archives Building.

28. *Thomas Jones v. Maria Jones,* Jan. 25, 1868, vol. 80, 8; Complaints and Fines Received, Marlin, [Tex.], Aug. 2, Nov. 18, 1867, vol. 132, 6–7, 12–13.

29. J. P. Richardson, journal, July 6, 1867, vol. 52, 5.

30. *Tom Foley v. Stewart Campbell,* Oct. 25, 1866, vol. 115, 1–2, 4; *Sophie Campbell v. Stewart Campbell,* n.d., vol. 115, 3–4, 6. See also *Abraham Gilmore v. Isaac*

Burleson, Dec. 1, 1868, vol. 62, 70–71; *Mary Morgan v. Silas Morgan,* Aug. 4, 1868, vol. 113, 13; *Martha Downs v. Scott,* May 2, 1868, vol. 170, 2–3; *Edwin Warner v. Plant Williams,* n.d., vol. 123, 31–32.

31. Any of the forty-three volumes of complaints in the Texas bureau records may be consulted for confirmation of these views. The amount of violence committed against blacks was at times overwhelming. See also Barry A. Crouch and L. J. Schultz, "Crisis in Color: Racial Separation in Texas during Reconstruction," *Civil War History* 15 (1970): 37–49.

32. H. M. Hyman, *A More Perfect Union: The Impact of the Civil War and Reconstruction on the Constitution* (New York: Knopf, 1973), 458, 460; Hyman, "Reconstruction and Political-Constitutional Institutions: The Popular Expression," in *New Frontiers of the American Reconstruction,* ed. H. M. Hyman (Urbana: Univ. of Illinois Press, 1966), 1–32; and in the same volume, Alfred H. Kelly, "Comment on Harold M. Hyman's Paper," 40–58. I have been influenced in my legal thinking and interpretations by the following works: Charles Fairman, *Reconstruction and Reunion, 1864–1888,* vols. 6 and 7 of *The Oliver Wendell Holmes Devise History of the Supreme Court of the United States* (New York: Macmillan, 1971), esp. vol. 6, pt. 1; Wallace D. Farnham, "'The Weakened Spring of Government': A Study in Nineteenth-Century American History," *American Historical Review* 68, no. 3 (Apr. 1963): 662–680; James Willard Hurst, *Law and the Conditions of Freedom in the Nineteenth-Century United States* (Madison: Univ. of Wisconsin Press, 1956); Charles E. Larsen, "Nationalism and States' Rights in Commentaries on the Constitution after the Civil War," *American Journal of Legal History* 3 (1959): 360–369; Phillip S. Paludan, "John Norton Pomeroy: States' Rights Nationalist," *American Journal of Legal History* 12 (1968): 275–292; Paludan, "The American Civil War Considered as a Crisis in Law and Order," *American Historical Review* 77, no. 4 (Oct. 1972): 1013–1034.

Four

SEEKING EQUALITY

Houston Black Women during Reconstruction

Contradictory perceptions surround the status and role of black women both in and out of bondage. "On the one hand," Suzanne Lebsock writes, "we have been told that black women, in slavery and afterward, were formidable people, 'matriarchs,' in fact." Nevertheless, "all along, black women were dreadfully exploited." Rarely, she concludes, "has so much power been attributed to so vulnerable a group." A similar paradox embracing black women can be found in the works of America's most famous African American historian. In his early writings, W. E. B. Du Bois described southern black women as tragic figures. In his later books, however, Du Bois noted that although black women suffered countless injustices during slavery and Reconstruction, their sacrifices produced "freedom and uplift" for themselves and their race.[1]

Within the past two decades feminist historians have rewritten women's history from the point of view of the women themselves. Still, only a handful of studies concentrate on the history of black women.[2] This essay will present a case study of black women in Houston during the Reconstruction era. Its larger purpose is to inspire other local studies about black women so that we may fully document their history. Only after we have studied the role of black women through the use of primary-source materials will we be able to resolve some of the paradoxes encountered by historians Lebsock and Du Bois.

The story of Houston's black women during the postwar years is based primarily upon information available in the records of the Bureau of Refugees, Freedmen, and Abandoned Lands (Freedmen's Bureau). The manuscripts vary in quantity for the former Confederate states, Texas having a midsize collection of bureau papers.[3] Before examining them, it is appropriate briefly to explain the bureau's role.

The concept of a major social-welfare agency resulted from the Emancipation Proclamation, and in early 1865 Congress established what eventually became the Freedmen's Bureau. The underlying premise of the bureau was that it would not serve southern blacks as a guardian but would attempt to ensure that they received a fair chance in their struggle for equality. Although the role of the bureau was originally viewed as a limited one, once Reconstruction commenced blacks quickly realized that they would not receive fair trials or justice in the South, and so the bureau established special tribunals to deal with black complaints. "Dissatisfied though blacks so frequently were at the bureau's feebleness and ambivalence," Michael Perman concluded, they nevertheless "knew that without it they would have been far worse off."[4]

Bureau archives constitute a major source of information about what black women in Texas, and especially Houston, were doing in the immediate aftermath of war. Furthermore, these records catalogue some of the serious problems that women encountered in the first years of freedom.

PROTECTING THE FAMILY

It is impossible to know precisely how many blacks were in Houston when the Civil War ended in April 1865, because slaveholders from other states transported blacks to Texas during the war for "safekeeping." By 1870, however, the city counted almost 9,400 residents—approximately 5,700 white and 3,700 black. Houston blacks made up 39 percent of the population.[5] Although the exact number of black women in Houston is not known, it is evident that they were active participants in postwar city life.

With the long and bloody conflict decided and slavery ended, blacks began to search for family members, move back to the vicinity of their old plantations, or locate the nearest bureau office. "While it is true that much of the traveling about that the Freedmen's Bureau paid for was inspired by the wish to try freedom out," historian Willie Lee Rose contends that "a great deal more of it is explained by the laudable urge to find out what had happened to relatives long gone to another part of the world." For the former slave, the "only way was to go and see, since the magic of writing was denied to him."[6]

The bureau generally investigated the "physical and pecuniary" condition of the individuals who applied for financial support to travel in order to determine whether they were "worthy objects of charity to the government." Thus, guided by local teachers, Rachel, an eighty-three-year-old Houstonian, turned to the bureau for assistance. The teachers located and contacted Rachel's only daughter in Charleston, South Carolina, and both mother and daughter attempted to raise money so Rachel could journey to the distant state to "spend her remaining days." Rachel's health was tolerably good, and one of the teachers wrote that if she could "only get started right, she would be okay."[7] In a similar instance, the St. Louis relatives of Hannah Talbot and her children, all of whom lived in Lynchburg, requested that the Texas bureau provide Hannah and her children with the necessary aid to enable them to move to St. Louis.[8]

Another serious problem for freed blacks was that former masters sometimes tried to deny ex-slaves normal family rights. Some whites in postwar Texas "endeavored to prevent wives and children from joining their natural protectors, their husbands and fathers," a bureau agent noticed. Blacks appeared before the Houston bureau charging that former slaveholders were unlawfully detaining their wives and children. Thus Abraham received bureau assistance in retrieving his wife, Hannah, and their six children from a nearby Brazos River plantation. The bureau also gave blacks release orders to deliver to the white individuals holding their families, as they did to James, a freedman who sought his wife and three children. In "nearly every case" whites released ex-slaves upon receiving such orders from the bureau.[9]

Locating and gathering children back into the family became a compelling, exhausting task for many blacks after the war. From late 1865 until the demise of the bureau in 1868, black women and men appeared before the bureau courts and claimed detention of their children by whites. When Mary Busby stated that her twelve-year-old daughter, Louisa, was being kept from her "by some party," this vagueness about the "detainer or detainees" provided the bureau an opportunity to formulate a policy that favored female black parents. "The Mother has the first claim to her child," the bureau stated, adding pointedly that "interference with this right will not be tolerated." Arrest and punishment were the mandated consequences for those who did. The intent of the policy was clear, and black women quickly used its provisions to their—and their children's—advantage.[10]

Black women sometimes used an intermediary when seeking reunification with their children. Lavinia Page enlisted a helper to wrest her daughters Lucy and Winnie from a white doctor in Danville. In another instance, John Lewes, a black Houston resident, also traveled to Danville to reclaim Mary, the daughter of a female acquaintance of his. Single black women who required help in reclaiming their children commonly relied upon other members of the community, often men, to provide it.[11]

The detention of children immediately after the cessation of hostilities but before the enactment of apprenticeship laws may have been a more serious problem for the southern black community than previously has been realized. This situation occurred before the Texas legislature met and had the opportunity to establish apprenticing statutes, which attempted economically to bind black children to whites against the wishes of the black community. It appears that whites detained young black girls more often than boys because it was easier to keep them in a state of semiservitude.[12] The institution of slavery cast many lingering shadows, and the forcible detention of children was one of them.

The Freedman's Bureau attempted to aid black women in their quest for their children, even if this developed into a lengthy or complicated process. Black women challenged even those of their own race who they felt unjustly retained children. Barbara Alfred complained that Jerry Gross, also black, was preventing her child from joining her. She won the case—and her daughter. In another incident, the bureau ordered Louisa, a Sandy Point resident, to turn over Rachel to her mother, Eliza. In a third instance, a Houston black woman claimed that a Galvestonian named Caroline stole her child. The bureau stepped in and ordered the child returned to the Bayou City and her mother immediately. Although a bureau agent and an army officer were themselves accused of kidnapping a black girl in 1866—the *Houston Telegraph* printed lurid headlines suggesting sexual improprieties—local black women continued to seek out the bureau, which became a central judicial agency for the Houston black community.[13]

Black women in Houston often protected children for whom they felt responsible, even if they were not strictly kin. Clara Parker, for example, charged that her "adopted child" was being kept by another black woman, whom the bureau ordered to relinquish custody. In another case, Cynthia Ann Hickman found it necessary, for reasons not recorded, to arrange temporary care for her daughter Martha Allen, aged nine, with Alexander Pierce, a black man. However, she stipulated that while the child was in his care, nobody was to interfere with her unless first getting Hickman's permission or contacting the bureau office. Black women monitored such arrangements closely. Even young women quickly learned the desirability of knowing the law and using it to their advantage. Rosa Johnson, a young black Houstonian, petitioned the authorities in order to have Dony Hamblin, who lived near the "old Government stables," appointed her guardian. All of her relatives were dead, and she wanted Hamblin to be "considered as if she were her mother."[14]

The bureau in Houston began to bind out black children starting as early as 1866. Its agents obtained the required pledges from the white custodians, who, in turn, agreed to a "faithful performance" of signed agreements. Sometimes agreements between the bureau and white people were struck over the apparent objection of black parents. In early 1866, for example, the father of two young black girls, Frances and Lucy, sought the bureau's aid in reclaiming them from a white man. Initially he was successful, for the bureau gave him a written order to the holder, commanding their release. However, the very next day the bureau authorized the white man to keep the children in return for providing their care, culture, and education.[15] In another case, the Houston bureau administrators decided that a thirteen-year-old black girl, Harriet Carson, whose mother was deceased, should continue to live with Virginia Harris, a white resident of adjacent Harrisburg, as a house servant. Her stepfather, Edward Burlington, claiming to be "her next friend or nearest of kin," tried unsuccessfully to gain custody of her. He stated that his stepdaughter had been Harris's slave and had been bound out to her without anyone's knowledge or consent. Nevertheless, young Harriet was obliged to serve as a domestic "in consideration of advantages guaranteed" until she was eighteen, after which she was free to leave. Harris, her white custodian, agreed to furnish her schooling and life necessities; other whites whom the bureau allowed to retain black children often did likewise. Burlington, her stepfather, like other blacks in similar situations, was specifically warned by the bureau not to interfere in any manner with the girl, or to attempt to prejudice her against Harris.[16] Even when the parent was a mother, the bureau might rule that the child remain apprenticed to a white family.

But some black women forced a different resolution. When Ailsie Merrit supplied "satisfactory evidence of her respectability and [proof] that she is able to take care of her child," the bureau ordered a white woman to surrender the child to her mother forthwith.[17] The apprenticing law in Texas allowed the courts to bind out children if their parents were unable or unwilling to support them. It made no reference to race or color, but it was clear to most observers that it was aimed squarely at blacks. The bureau proctored such cases while the law was in effect, from 1866 to its repeal in 1871.[18]

The residents of Houston were concerned about who would care for black orphans in the Bayou City after the war. There were a few instances of both blacks and whites claiming freedchildren, though this happened rarely, and it was up to the bureau to determine with whom they should be placed. In a typical case, the bureau authorized a white woman, O. A. Runnels, to retain two black girls. The bureau required Runnels to "instruct them in rudiments of English" and to supervise their "mental, moral, and physical culture." The same type of agreement applied to blacks when they applied for custody of orphaned children. Thus was Washington Brown, a Houston hack driver who lived on Congress Street, awarded custody of Annette. Although agreements such as these were often supposed to be temporary arrangements, they tended to become permanent.[19]

By 1867 local governments were taking charge of orphans, although they still relied upon the bureau for advice. In Houston that year the Harris County government had control of three orphans. There were also several cases of indigent orphans, too young to take care of themselves, whose relatives, according to the bureau, were too poor to support them. The civil authorities had no legal guidelines for providing care to such children who were under the age for apprenticing. Consequently they were normally assimilated into the black community ad hoc. One agent suggested the establishment of a home for destitute orphans, to be supervised by a bureau employee, but his suggestion was not acted upon.[20] Subsequently an Orphan Society was established to raise funds for the care of these children. In a particularly distressing incident, Octavia Williams, an officer of the society, embezzled fifteen dollars from the proceeds of a fair held to benefit the needy youngsters, and then fled to Galveston. The Orphan Society brought charges against Williams, but the stolen money was evidently never recovered.[21]

BLACK WOMEN, BLACK MEN

While struggling to provide for their children and relatives, black women also began to assert their marital rights and privileges. When necessary, they used the bureau and local courts to pursue their objectives. They charged husbands with nonsupport, infidelity, and related offenses. For instance, when Milly Barnes asserted that Alfred Harroll had committed adultery, a Houston bureau agent negotiated a compromise, and matters were "amicably adjusted," the couple returning home together. Another black Houstonian, Maria Flowers, had a more serious problem. Flowers contended that she had borne Wash Sessuns two children, after which he threatened to leave his family and marry someone else. In mid-1866 Louisa Whiting's complaint echoed that of Flowers. After living with George Washington Holmes for two years, he had deserted Whiting and the children around Christmas 1865, marrying another woman. Whiting believed he should be required to assist in supporting the children, especially since he was a housepainter with a steady income. The bureau sometimes came to the conclusion that it was best for couples to separate. Although it could not issue divorce decrees, it could and did issue orders for people to live apart. Such cases were common in Houston.[22]

It was not only black men who left the family. In one case, the bureau ordered a black woman named Anna Allen to return home to her husband and remain there. Allen's husband pledged to support her, and after studying the situation, a bureau agent concluded that he could "see no reason why you should live apart." Regardless of which partner lodged a complaint, the bureau served as a sort of marriage-counseling agency, hoping to compromise differences between spouses. When persuasion failed, as it sometimes did, bureau agents in Houston simply ordered couples to live together. However, when it became clear to them that a relationship could not be repaired, agents acquiesced and permitted couples to separate. Generally it was women who sought assistance, against husbands who drove them away, ran off with younger women, or just left. When black men entered complaints, it was almost always because their wives were involved with other men.[23]

Whites and blacks in Houston had different perceptions of the behavior of black families. One Houston bureau agent, W. B. Pease, wrote that matrimonial problems among freedpeople had increased in early 1867. Pease claimed that blacks neither comprehended the "solemnity and binding force of the marriage ceremony" nor understood the duties they owed each other in marriage. He thought that the slave custom of "promiscuous intercourse" prevailed among many blacks and reported that infidelity was a common complaint. However, several black couples stated that whites had arbitrarily put slaves together as couples, so they were applying to the bureau for divorce in the mistaken belief that it could grant one.[24] Bureau agents were often in a position to see social practices from different points of view, even if they did not credit them equally.

Houston black women were not reticent about demanding child support from the fathers of their children. Emeline Anderson requested support for her child from George Gentry, whom she identified as the father. Gentry, adjudged the father, was ordered to support his offspring. Julianna Stevens fought a similar battle with Durke Woodall. Initially Woodall had refused Stevens's request for maintenance, but the court decided he should pay five dollars a month. In another instance, Rachel Neal not only testified in court but also brought her child along as evidence.

When couples separated and children were involved, authorities instructed both parents about their obligations to their offspring. The bureau thus reminded Martha and Jacob that if they separated, they were nevertheless "charged morally and legally to assist each other in supporting your children." Part of the bureau's concern was that these children never become part of the public dole, but bureau officials also generally evidenced a strong belief in family life, and thought that youngsters should be raised by their own parents whenever possible.[25]

Pregnant women were among those who appealed to the bureau. Mary Rogers was expecting when her employer threatened to turn her out of the house where she lived. However, she was able to avoid this "until sufficiently recovered from childbirth to work and earn a support." Women who were not pregnant but had been left indigent as a result of pregnancy also asserted their rights. When Malinda Wheeler's husband, Ned, left her impoverished without cause, he was ordered to pay her ten dollars a month support. Some women became so adamant about protecting themselves and what little they had that former husbands found themselves pleading with the bureau to intervene with their former wives so they could retrieve their "personal effects."[26]

After the Civil War there were black women throughout Texas who became indigent and sought assistance from the Freedmen's Bureau. Although this problem was not widespread, it was still too large for the bureau to handle. Between December 1865 and July 1866, the bureau issued only 165 rations to black women in the entire Lone Star State. During June, July, and August 1868, shortly before the bureau concluded its operations, only six women and ten girls received rations from the agency. A ration, which was supposed to care for an entire family, consisted of ten ounces of pork or bacon, sixteen ounces of flour or cornmeal, ten pounds of peas, eight pounds of sugar, two quarts of vinegar, eight eleven-ounce candles, and two pounds of soap, salt, and pepper. In addition, women and children received a supplement of ten ounces of coffee. This ration was inadequate for the needs of a family, but it did help somewhat.[27]

Houston black women numbered among those who found themselves destitute and sought assistance from authorities. Often they turned to the bureau for information and guidance. An unnamed freedwoman approached the Houston bureau for help in taking care of Rachel Hester, who was ill. An agent referred her to a judge, with the recommendation that Hester be sent to the poorhouse, since she had no visible means of support. Tina Washington was another person who lacked the means to support herself; a bureau agent routed her to the county chief justice. Lucinda Graves sought bureau aid because poor health had rendered her

unable to provide for her four children. Joe Moore appealed to the bureau
for help in a sad situation. He related that the child of Nellie Keene had
just died and that she did not have the money to bury it. Keene, through
Moore, sought whatever aid the bureau might see fit to extend.[28] However, such abject need was rare. Blacks across the state, and in Houston,
generally took care of their own. Although the bureau was certainly par-
simonious in distributing rations, it did offer some needed aid to black
women and children.

WOMEN AND WORK

Harris County freedwomen in Houston labored at a va-
riety of tasks when slavery ceased. Some worked for wages and shares as
agricultural laborers on the plantations surrounding the city. Enterprising
black women also found employment in other areas, particularly domestic
service to whites. Both types of work closely resembled the labor they had
performed as slaves. But now the relationship between blacks and whites
had dramatically changed, and black workingwomen in Harris County
took their freedom to work with them. Their change in attitude and behavior did not please white employers, who loudly and often criticized
their lack of servile deference. Black women also complained about whites,
especially when white women charged them with dishonesty. They also
haled other blacks before the bureau for nonpayment of wages and unfair
treatment. Through these cases it is possible to catch a glimpse of how
black women in Houston fought to establish their economic rights.

As employees, black women consistently were treated unfairly. Throughout the Reconstruction era, women who labored in the fields, or who
labored at all, were paid less than men, black or white. For agricultural
labor, first-class workers (always men) received ten dollars in specie per
month; second- and third-class workers, including women, were paid pro-
portionally less. Women who worked on farms, for example, received only
one-half to two-thirds the pay of men when cash was still used as payment
for plantation work. This gender division in the wage system did not
change significantly during the postwar years. When women contracted,
even if married, their agreement with employers was considered binding.
Authorities did not permit husbands to interfere, although spouses were
allowed to make any arrangement concerning working with their wives to
which the employer might consent.[29]

Black women from the surrounding plantation area used the Houston bureau headquarters to bring complaints about threatened or actual physical abuse associated with their employment. They also desired settlement for services rendered, and complained bitterly to the bureau when they were denied their wages. One aggressive woman named Margaret even brought charges against the vice-consul of Russia for defrauding her out of her wages. The bureau warned him that "as a worthy representative of your august Master," he should not "violate with impunity the laws" of the United States.[30]

Black women did not always direct their demands for fair compensation at whites. Kizzy sued Catherine, another black woman, for wages for labor performed in January 1866. Although most individuals compromised their differences between themselves, other conflicts were resolved because women used the bureau to gain additional leverage. The Freedmen's Bureau courts gave these black women a legal tool they had not previously possessed, and the women used it often.[31]

Women who worked the plantations surrounding Houston registered claims to wages or shares for themselves as well as their children when they felt a settlement was unfair. In 1867 a number of white farmers decided to act together in dismissing black women with whom they had contracted for the year. The bureau saw to it that these women remained employed. However, authorities also held black women to their obligations, since contractual agreements bound employees as well as employers. Thus in 1866 C. B. Sojourner was allowed to retain the services of a freedwoman (the "wife of Leroy") until she performed enough work to reimburse him for the cost of transporting her to the job site. She had been destitute with a sick child when Sojourner hired her, and he had employed her at her own request.[32]

At other times, blacks sued other blacks for debts. Mary Vick, a Houston freedwoman, was sued by freedman George Cooper for payment of seven dollars due him for building a small house. Cooper's complaint was sustained, and he collected.[33] A black woman named Minerva also collected. She had worked for W. G. Nolan for four months at ten dollars a month—good wages for her, since this was the standard rate for men. She testified that Nolan had acknowledged his indebtedness and promised to pay her but had not. Minerva claimed she had received only a pair of shoes, worth about two dollars and fifty cents, and that Nolan now was trying to stall by saying somebody else was responsible for half of the money due. Minerva was described as being very destitute and deserving of the money.[34]

Black women were no less aggressive in protecting their working children's economic rights than in protecting their own. While Polly was unsuccessful in trying to collect wages for her children in 1866, because they were judged too young, Rachelle West had more luck a year later in claiming twenty-five dollars for work her children had performed.[35] Black women did not refrain from suing other blacks where payment for their children's work was concerned. Julia Heard hauled Ben Lyons before a bureau court, demanding four dollars in salary, which she received, for the whitewashing her son had done for Lyons. Mary Sellers sought the bureau's help in obtaining child-care pay from Newman Jackson, a black man, who had left two of his children in Sellers's house. He had agreed to pay her six dollars a month and owed her for three months. The bureau ordered Jackson, who worked on a nearby plantation, to pay up.[36]

Houston black women, just emerging from slavery, had very little property, but they did vigilantly guard what they had. Land naturally was of primary importance to them. Tenna's claim for one acre of land was validated, although it is not known how she acquired the real estate. America Lord proved her title to a house erected on the property of Mary E. Shea. When John Kennedy purchased the land, he attempted to remove Lord. However, the bureau prevented this action until Kennedy could prove his right to evict Shea.[37]

Black women in the Bayou City had to be wary about their economic status and their ability to support themselves, lest they become vagrants or paupers. In 1866 Houston authorities charged some indigent freedwomen with vagrancy and compelled them to work on the city's streets. The bureau investigated this and discovered that the police had arrested the black women and a white man for disorderly conduct. Unable to pay the fine for the charge, all were sent to work it off on the street. The bureau agent would have complained had city officials made any distinction in the punishment of blacks and whites, but they had not.[38] However, a bureau agent did intervene to request permission from a city judge for a surgeon to visit Harriet Anthony in the city prison. The surgeon said she had aborted because of hard labor on the street, and the agent also asked that she be released from confinement at once.[39]

Economic catastrophe also forced some black women to enter the world's oldest profession. For those who were young and attractive enough, working as a prostitute was an alternative to vagrancy and poverty. Although the number of black prostitutes in Houston following the war is not known, several young women were brought into court for maintaining a "disreputable house" near the T. & A. Depot.[40]

VIOLENCE: AN ENDURING PROBLEM

For both blacks and whites, the adjustment to freedom was a gradual and often painful process in which blacks were often the victims of force. Many such incidents involved the brutalization of black women. White planter David Hill assaulted Agnes Alexandra, a black woman who worked for him, despite the presence of two witnesses, both of whom later testified against him. Such treatment was sufficient cause for employment contracts to be annulled and blacks freed to seek work elsewhere. That is what happened when Mony, a household worker, was struck many times and generally poorly treated by the white woman who employed her. Although the actions of the white woman were defended as "simply the outbursts of a violent temper provoked by great obstinacy and ill-behavior of the servant," the bureau canceled the work contract between the two, allowing Mony to search for better employment. Sometimes violence was more calculated—a way to try to cheat black workers out of their yearly earnings by running them off the plantation. Premeditated violence against black workers normally occurred toward the end of the contract year, when black workers were due to be paid.[41]

Many former slaveholders abused black women after the war. Selina Parker's suit in early 1866 illustrates how reluctantly some whites relinquished authority and power over their former slaves. Parker was Michael Linney's former slave. Once free, she chose to live with one of Linney's daughters in Liberty, Texas, and in September 1865 she decided to take her daughter and move to Houston. When Linney learned she had decided to make this move, he appeared at her home, physically abused her, stole what money she had (to make any move difficult), and abducted her daughter. After scattering Parker's clothing, he rode off, forcing her little girl to walk in front of his horse. Authorities did not always punish whites for such behavior, but Linney was found guilty of assault, robbery, and kidnapping. He was fined two hundred dollars in gold and was ordered to pay Parker thirty dollars for damages and restitution. Cases similar to this were not uncommon.[42]

While the black community in Houston apparently did not suffer the savage brutalities occurring in rural areas of the Lone Star State, racial violence did take place in the Bayou City. Milly Graham and Emily Matthews complained that the white women who employed them had treated them badly and had physically driven them from their work site. Investigators found Adeline Williams's white employer so abusive that they fined her fifty dollars. In a similar case, the bureau assessed another white employer ten dollars, notwithstanding that the black woman who brought charges against him was "very abusive and used the foulest language." In another incident, a husband-and-wife team, Adeline and Levi Tanks, charged a white physician for chasing them with an open knife. Through out Texas, white-against-black violence continued after slavery had been abolished.[43]

Black women sought to protect their children from violence, and they brought complaints against those who abused their offspring. Julia Brown charged that a white woman who employed her son had beaten him with a cowhide whip, and the bureau ordered the woman to pay the youngster five dollars. However, the bureau did not always rule in favor of black complainants. For instance, Dinah Wren charged a Dr. Hartridge with unjust treatment of her daughter, Rebecca. Investigation, though, revealed that Rebecca was legally apprenticed to Hartridge, as the law required, and that he had agreed, as was normally the case, to furnish her with an education. Investigators found no evidence of abuse on his part and dismissed the charges against him. Rebecca remained under his care. Her mother could have been using the suit as an attempt, for whatever reason, to nullify the apprenticeship contract with Dr. Hartridge. In any event, Wren and other black women consistently attempted to ensure that their children were treated fairly, and the law as well as the bureau helped them do this during Reconstruction.[44]

Violence was a frequent side effect of marital complications for black women in Houston. Dollina Williams, although apparently never legally married to Andrew Johnson Williams, lived with him about three months in late 1865. She complained that during this time Williams drank heavily and beat her. Investigation sustained her charges, and Williams spent ten days at hard labor in a military prison. Emma Matthews made the same complaint against her spouse, who also served ten hard days. The bureau made certain that both men completed their sentences.[45]

Cases of wife abuse often involved other marital complications. Zenobia Johnson, for example, charged that her husband, Wash, not only had mistreated her, but had abandoned her to live with another woman. Moreover, Zenobia complained that she had "contracted a disease from him." Given these circumstances, she had no desire to be reconciled with him, and the bureau allowed her to move and live anywhere she wanted. The bureau's verdict specifically warned Johnson to stay away from Zenobia, lest he be severely punished. However, bureau investigations did not always sustain the accusations made by women. Lucy Ann King, for example, claimed that her husband, Wesley King, abused her, owed her money, and had abandoned her. But the bureau discovered evidence proving that she was not Wesley's wife and that she in fact had an unsavory reputation as a "desperate character, having attempted to poison her master and mistress, also having been put in jail for bad conduct."[46]

Black women also charged black men with other forms of violence against them and their children. They claimed that black men assaulted and battered them and threatened their lives. They also brought charges of rape and attempted rape against black men for attacks on them as well as their daughters. Alice James, for example, alleged that Peter Smith had tried to ravage her daughter. Melissa Hill brought the same charge against Albert Williams in 1867, and the bureau referred the complaint to the Houston city recorder. Hill was unable to prove her accusation to the satisfaction of the officials, who therefore dismissed the charge against Williams. In other similar complaints, men had to post rather large bonds—up to five hundred dollars—to assure their appearance before the bureau or civil court. Although rape was not a common crime in the postwar Houston black community, it did happen occasionally. There were also instances of women fighting violence with violence. The records reveal cases of women being charged with drawing knives, disorderly conduct, fighting, and using "bad language."[47]

CONCLUSION

Black women in Houston made strides in consolidating whatever social and economic rights they could establish through a combination of their own efforts, the law, the Freedmen's Bureau courts, and community resources. They focused first upon the reunification of families and kin, especially the locating of children. Encountering white opposition, and occasionally conflicts within their own community, they used the bureau and whatever other support they could muster to bring children into families. This included the few indigent or orphaned black children in the Bayou City. They also did their best to see that black children were adequately supported, by pressing claims for child support. Although not completely successful, black women tried to limit the social and economic violence done to themselves and to their children in postwar Houston. The early years of Reconstruction were characterized by turbulence and disorder for urban black women who lived and worked in and around Houston. They struggled to carve out a niche for themselves and to consolidate the gains they had been reluctantly granted by Congress, despite a begrudging, often outwardly hostile, white South. Within their own community, the adjustment to freedom brought forth turmoil and clashes between blacks themselves. To ascertain what rights and protection they had, black women in Houston used the bureau and, occasionally, civil officials to determine where they stood legally. They were quick to employ the few legal redresses to which they were entitled, and attempted to begin defining a dignified existence for themselves. By the end of the Reconstruction era, a stable black community had begun to form in Houston. Much of the credit for this properly belongs to women who asserted and tested their newly won legal rights.

Some recent arguments contend that blacks gained little or nothing from emancipation or from national efforts to reconstruct the South. But surely, as Willie Lee Rose has observed, the "difference between slavery and freedom is about the greatest difference in status we can imagine, no matter how kindly a view some historians might want to take of slavery, no matter how limited and curtailed freedom may have turned out to be."[48] By frequently using the Freedmen's Bureau courts in postwar Houston to prevent curtailment of their freedom, black women in the Bayou City established a legacy for the future and forged a base for continued progress.

NOTES

1. Suzanne Lebsock, *The Free Women of Petersburg: Status and Culture in a Southern Town, 1784–1860* (New York: Norton, 1984), 88; W. E. B. Du Bois, *The Souls of Black Folk: Essays and Sketches* (Chicago: McClurg, 1903), 68–69, and *Darkwater: Voices from within the Veil* (New York: Harcourt, Brace and Howe, 1920), 164–165, 169–170, 178. See also his "Reconstruction and Its Benefits," *American Historical Review* 15 (July 1910): 781–799, and his *Black Reconstruction in America: An Essay toward a History of the Part Which Black Folk Played in the Attempt to Reconstruct Democracy in America, 1860–1880* (New York: Harcourt, Brace, 1935). An overview is in Darlene Clark Hine, "Lifting the Veil, Shattering the Silence: Black Women's History in Slavery and Freedom," in *The State of Afro-American History: Past, Present, and Future,* ed. Darlene Clark Hine (Baton Rouge: Louisiana State Univ. Press, 1986), 223–249.

2. The most important histories of black women are Jacqueline Jones, *Labor of Love, Labor of Sorrow: Black Women, Work, and the Family from Slavery to the Present* (New York: Basic Books, 1985); Deborah Gray White, *Ar'n't I a Woman? Female Slaves in the Plantation South* (New York: Norton, 1985); Gerda Lerner, ed., *Black Women in White America: A Documentary History* (New York: Pantheon, 1972). There are several other books on black women, but they are polemical, poorly

researched, or written for a popular audience, making them of little value. Although not concentrating on women, an extremely valuable work for this period is Herbert G. Gutman, *The Black Family in Slavery and Freedom, 1750–1925* (New York: Pantheon, 1976).

3. Barry A. Crouch, "Hidden Sources of Black History: The Texas Freedmen's Bureau Records as a Case Study," *Southwestern Historical Quarterly* 83 (Jan. 1980): 46–58; Crouch, "Freedmen's Bureau Records: Texas, a Case Study," in *Afro-American History: Sources for Research,* ed. Robert L. Clarke (Washington, D.C.: Howard Univ. Press, 1981), 74–94. A local study is Crouch, "The Freedmen's Bureau and the 30th Sub-District in Texas: Smith County and Its Environs during Reconstruction," *Chronicles of Smith County, Texas* 11 (Spring 1972): 15–30. See also Ross N. Dudney, Jr., "Texas Reconstruction: The Role of the Bureau of Refugees, Freedmen and Abandoned Lands, 1865–1870, Smith County (Tyler), Texas" (master's thesis, Texas A&I University, 1986). It is characteristic of the Texas bureau records that blacks are sometimes referred to only by a first name, as had been the practice during slavery.

4. Michael Perman, *Emancipation and Reconstruction, 1862–1879* (Arlington Heights, Ill.: Harlan Davidson, 1987), 24. It is also important to see John A. Carpenter, *Sword and Olive Branch: Oliver Otis Howard* (Pittsburgh: Univ. of Pittsburgh Press, 1964); George R. Bentley, *A History of the Freedmen's Bureau* (Philadelphia: Univ. of Pennsylvania Press, 1955), esp. 152–168, 249–253; William S. McFeely, *Yankee Stepfather: General O. O. Howard and the Freedmen* (New Haven, Conn.: Yale Univ. Press, 1968); Herman Belz, *Emancipation and Equal Rights: Politics and Constitutionalism in the Civil War Era* (New York: Norton, 1978), and Sara Rapport, "The Freedmen's Bureau as a Legal Agent for Black Men and Women in Georgia: 1865–1868," *Georgia Historical Quarterly* 73 (Spring, 1989): 26–53.

5. Cary D. Wintz, "Blacks," *The Ethnic Groups of Houston,* Fred R. Von der Mehden, ed. (Houston: Rice Univ. Studies, 1984), 15–20, 22; David G. McComb, *Houston: A History,* rev. ed. (Austin: Univ. of Texas Press, 1981), 57, 60; Kenneth W. Wheeler, *To Wear a City's Crown: The Beginnings of Urban Growth in Texas, 1836–1865* (Cambridge, Mass.: Harvard Univ. Press, 1968), 150–166. See also Susan Jackson, "Slavery in Houston: The 1850s," *Houston Review* 2 (Summer 1980): 66–82; Paul D. Lack, "Urban Slavery in the Southwest," *Red River Valley Historical Review* 6 (Spring 1981): 8–27. For a comparison, see Alwyn Barr, "Occupational and Geographic Mobility in San Antonio, 1870–1900," *Social Science Quarterly* 51 (Sept. 1970): 396–403.

6. Willie Lee Rose, *Slavery and Freedom* (New York: Oxford Univ. Press, 1982), 101.

7. Julia B. Nelson, interview with Louis W. Stevenson, Oct. 30, 1869, Box 42, Records of the Bureau of Refugees, Freedmen, and Abandoned Lands, Texas, Record Group 105, National Archives, Washington, D.C. See also Barry A. Crouch and Larry Madaras, "Reconstructing Black Families: Perspectives from the Texas Freedmen's Bureau Records," *Prologue: Journal of the National Archives* 18 (Summer

1986): 109–122, reprinted in *Our Family, Our Town: Essays on Family and Local History Sources in the National Archives,* comp. Timothy Walch (Washington, D.C.: National Archives and Records Administration, 1987), 156–167; Robert H. Abzug, "The Black Family during Reconstruction," in *Key Issues in the Afro-American Experience,* 2 vols., ed. Nathan I. Huggins, Martin Kilson, and Daniel M. Fox, 2:26–41 (New York: Harcourt Brace Jovanovich, 1971). A marvelous survey of blacks regarding their family and social activity is Leon F. Litwack, *Been in the Storm So Long: The Aftermath of Slavery* (New York: Knopf, 1979). Unless otherwise indicated, all references are to the Texas bureau records in RG 105.

8. J. C. de Gress (agent, Houston) to James R. Lynch (commander, Houston), Oct. 24, 1865, vol. 100, 7; Charles C. Hardenbrook (agent, Houston) to S. H. Lathrop (commander, Houston), Sept. 18, 1866, vol. 100, 263; J. D. O'Connell (agent, Houston) to J. M. Davis, Aug. 30, 1867, vol. 102, 173–174; L. H. Warren (agent, Houston) to Edward Miller (agent, Millican), June 22, 1867, vol. 102, 46.

9. Byron Porter (agent, Houston) to C. C. Morse, Jan. 5, 1866, vol. 100, 127–128; George Gladwin (agent, Houston) to Mr. Calhoun, Dec. 30, 1865, vol. 100, 108; Gladwin to C. Culsheans (Fort Bend County), Jan. 15, 1866, vol. 100, 162; Porter to Mr. Hills, Jan. 15, 1866, vol. 100, 166.

10. George Gladwin to John H. Murphy, Dec. 29, 1865, vol. 100, 104; Gladwin to Henry Sampson, Jan. 2, 1866 (three letters), vol. 100, 118–119; de Gress to "Whom It May Concern," Dec. 1, 1866, vol. 100, 364–365; Byron Porter to William Austin (Crockett), Jan. 27, 1866, vol. 100, 182; Porter to M. Joseph Jerkes (Navasota), Feb. 12, 1866, vol. 100, 192. The legal aspects of black rights at the time are explored in Donald G. Nieman, *To Set the Law in Motion: The Freedmen's Bureau and the Legal Rights of Blacks, 1865–1868* (Millwood, N.Y.: KTO Press, 1979).

11. Byron Porter to Dr. Whitehead (Danville), Mar. 12, 1866, vol. 100, 202; de Gress to William Austin (near Danville), Nov. 6, 1866, vol. 100, 315.

12. Chauncey C. Morse to provost marshall (Houston), Oct. 1, 1865, vol. 4, 10; Order by Byron Porter, Jan. 3, 1866, vol. 100, 123; Porter to Hugh Kelly (Clear Creek), Jan. 6, 1866, vol. 100, 137.

13. Porter to Dr. Tait (Tyler), July 5, 1866, vol. 100, 238–239; *Barbara Alfred v. Jerry Gross,* Sept. 5, 1868, vol. 108, 184–185; George Gladwin to Louisa (freedwoman), Jan. 11, 1866, vol. 100, 153–154; *Doney Hamilton v. Caroline Flash,* Aug. 25, 1868, vol. 108, 176–177. The relationship between the army and the Bureau is told in William L. Richter, *The Army in Texas during Reconstruction, 1865–1870* (College Station, Tex.: Texas A&M Univ. Press, 1987), 32–46. For the alleged involvement of a bureau agent in a kidnapping, see Byron Porter to C. C. Gillespie (editor, *Houston Telegraph*), Sept. 5, 1866, vol. 100, 261, and Richter, *Army in Texas,* 151.

14. *Clara Parker v. Louisa Hutt,* Aug. 19, 1868, vol. 108, 170–171; de Gress to Cynthia Ann Hickman, Oct. 15, 1866, vol. 100, 275; *Case of Rosa Johnson,* Feb. 12, 1868, vol. 108, 104–105.

15. Byron Porter to Mr. Fulton, Jan. 4, 1866, vol. 100, 125, and Jan. 5, 1866, vol. 100, 135; de Gress to Fulton, Oct. 29, 1866, vol. 100, 297.

16. W. B. Pease to "To Whom It May Concern," Feb. 28, 1868, vol. 103, 69. The Texas bureau believed, in principle, that black parental rights were supreme. This seems not to have been the case in North Carolina, where Rebecca Scott has drawn an overly harsh portrait of bureau agents in "The Battle over the Child: Child Apprenticeship and the Freedmen's Bureau in North Carolina," *Prologue: Journal of the National Archives* 10 (Summer 1978): 10–23.

17. W. B. Pease to Sarah White (freedwoman), Feb. 1, 1868, vol. 103, 54–55; Byron Porter to Martha Rodgers (white custodian), Jan. 1, 1866, vol. 100, 111–112.

18. Byron Porter to T. C. Powell (Waverly), Jan. 18, 1866, vol. 100, 171; George Gladwin to A. F. Oliver (Austin County), Dec. 23, 1865, vol. 110, 102; Theodore Brantner Wilson, *The Black Codes of the South* (Tuscaloosa: Univ. of Alabama Press, 1965), 110; *General Laws of the State of Texas Passed by the Eleventh Legislature* (Austin, 1866), 61–63; John Pressley Carrier, "A Political History of Texas during the Reconstruction, 1865–1874" (PhD diss., Vanderbilt Univ., 1971), 75. For civilian action, see "Book of Indentures to Bonds of Apprenticing, 1867–1870" (University Archives, James G. Gee Library, East Texas State University [Commerce]), and Carrier, "The Era of Reconstruction, 1865–1875," in *Tyler and Smith County, Texas: An Historical Survey,* ed. Robert W. Glover, 65–66 (Marceline, Mo.: Walsworth Publishing Co., 1976).

19. Byron Porter to O. A. Runnels, July 18, 1866, vol. 100, 244–245; Porter to Washington Brown (freedman), May 1, 1866, vol. 100, 216. For additional examples, see Porter to Sarah W. Gover (Polk County), Jan. 19, 1866, vol. 100, 172; Porter to Carrie Toland, Jan. 20, 1866, vol. 100, 173; Porter to J. E. Foster, Jan. 27, 1866, vol. 100, 181.

20. W. B. Pease to J. P. Kirkman (acting asst. adj. gen.), Mar. 6, 1867, Operations Reports, P-149, Box 13.

21. *Orphan Society v. Octavia Williams,* June 10, 1867, vol. 108, 4–5. See also Kathleen C. Berkeley, "'Colored Ladies Also Contributed': Black Women's Activities from Benevolence to Social Welfare, 1866–1896," in *The Web of Southern Social Relations: Women, Family, and Education,* ed. Walter J. Fraser, Jr., R. Frank Saunders, Jr., and John L. Wakelyn, 181–203 (Athens: Univ. of Georgia Press, 1985). A general survey of the Texas effort is Ira Christopher Colby, "The Freedmen's Bureau in Texas and Its Impact on the Emerging Social Welfare System and Black-White Social Relations, 1865–1885" (PhD diss., Univ. of Pennsylvania, 1984).

22. *Milly Barnes v. Alfred Harroll,* June 24, 1867, vol. 108, 16–17; *Lucinda Reed v. Charles Reed,* Aug. 22, 1868, vol. 108, 174–175; *Maria Flowers v. Wash Sessuns,* Feb. 3, 1866, vol. 109, 38–39; Byron Porter to William H. Sinclair, July 11, 1866, vol. 100, 241–242; L. H. Warren to Maj. De Bathligethy, July 10, 1867, vol. 102, 78; *Priscilla Bennett v. Peter Bennett,* June 25, 1868, vol. 108, 134–135. For back-

ground, see Christie Farham, "Sapphire? The Issue of Dominance in the Slave Family, 1830–1865," in *"To Toil the Livelong Day": America's Women at Work, 1780–1980,* ed. Carol Groneman and Mary Beth Norton, 68–83 (Ithaca, N.Y.: Cornell Univ. Press, 1987).

23. De Gress to Rhode Ann Licks, Oct. 8, 1866, vol. 100, 270; de Gress to Anna Allen, Oct. 22, 1866, vol. 100, 286; *Moses Jackson v. Carlinda Jackson,* July 6, 1867, vol. 108, 24–25; *Charles Smith v. Lizzie Smith,* Aug. 24, 1868, vol. 108, 176–177; *Smith Welton v. His Wife,* May 25, 1866, vol. 109, n.p.; *Amy Robinson v. Richard Robinson,* May 2, 1866, vol. 109, n.p.; O. E. Pratt to agent, Houston, Oct. 1, 1866, vol. 46, 3; Byron Porter to John (freedman), Jan. 12, 1866, vol. 100, 156. In one strange case, a woman complained that her husband had married another woman, but the complaint was dismissed without reason; see *Millie Lisles v. James Lisles,* Aug. 25, 1868, vol. 108, 176–177.

24. W. B. Pease to J. P. Kirkman (acting asst. adj. gen.), Mar. 6, 1867, Operations Reports, P-149, Box 13; McFeely, *Yankee Stepfather,* 131. For information on forced marriages among Texas slaves, see Edwin H. Fay to "My Own Darling Wife," Jan. 24, 1863, in *"This Infernal War": The Confederate Letters of Sgt. Edwin H. Fay,* ed. Bell Irvin Wiley, 216–217 (Austin: Univ. of Texas Press, 1958).

25. *Emeline Anderson v. George Gentry,* Apr. 28, 1868, vol. 108, 114–115; *Juliann Stevens v. Durke Woodall,* Sept. 15, 1868, vol. 108, 194–195; *Rachel Neal v. Adam Neal,* Feb. 9, 1866, vol. 109, 38–39; Byron Porter to Jacob (freedman), Jan. 10, 1866, vol. 100, 146–147.

26. *Mary Rogers v. Colonel Anderson,* June 12, 1867, vol. 108, 6–7; W. B. Pease to Judge Noble, Feb. 1, 1868, vol. 103, 55; *Malinda Wheelers v. Ned Wheelers,* Nov. 9, 1867, vol. 108, 54–55; L. H. Warren to Carlinda Jackson, July 5, 1867, vol. 102, 70; de Gress to "To All Whom It May Concern," Dec. 11, 1866, vol. 100, 384.

27. "Rations Issued to Women by the Bureau since December 1, 1865," vol. 4, 271–272; Byron Porter to C. C. Morse, Jan. 5, 1866, vol. 100, 128–129; Porter to J. E. George (Danville), Aug. 22, 1866, vol. 100, 256; L. H. Warren to H. R. Bell (judge, Montgomery County), Aug. 2, 1867, vol. 102, 128; Joseph B. Kiddoo (assistant commissioner, Texas) to J. D. O'Connell, June 18, 1867, vol. 5, 82; Warren to O'Connell, Aug. 10, 1867, vol. 102, 142.

28. William M. Van Horne (agent, Houston) to Judge John Brashear (chief justice, Houston), Sept. 3, 1867, vol. 102, 181; Dec. 2, 1867, vol. 103, 20; J. D. O'Connell to Dr. Moodie, Aug. 19, 1867, vol. 102, 165; Nov. 22, 1867, vol. 102, 210–211; Joseph J. Reynolds (assistant commissioner, Texas) to Oliver Otis Howard (commissioner), Oct. 20, 1868, vol. 5, 438.

29. Byron Porter to John M. Sapp (Montgomery), Jan. 31, 1866, vol. 100, 184; Porter to Orra M. Carter (Plantersville), Mar. 28, 1866, vol. 100, 209; Order by Porter, Jan. 24, 1866, vol. 100, 176; Jan. 26, 1866, vol. 100, 180. For an analysis of the relationship between black and white workers elsewhere in the South at this time, see Julie Saville, "A Measure of Freedom: From Slave to Wage Laborer in South Carolina, 1860–1868" (PhD diss., Yale Univ., 1986); Jonathan W. McLeod,

"Black and White Workers: Atlanta during Reconstruction" (PhD diss., Univ. of California at Los Angeles, 1987); Richard Paul Fuke, "Planters, Apprenticeship, and Forced Labor: The Black Family under Pressure in Post-Emancipation Maryland," *Agricultural History* 62 (Fall 1988): 57–74; and Peter J. Rachleff, *Black Labor in Richmond, 1865–1890* (Urbana: Univ. of Illinois Press, 1989).

30. A. A. Emerson (agent, Houston) to Mr. Wolf (vice-consul of Russia), Oct. 1, 1866, vol. 4, 350.

31. George Gladwin to Thomas Taylor (Washington County), Jan. 3, 1866, vol. 100, 122, plus a series of similar letters immediately following; Gladwin to Catherine, Jan 6, 1866, vol. 100, 138; Byron Porter to R. D. Inge (agent, Leona), May 4, 1866, vol. 100, 218; Charles C. Hardenbrook to H. W. Allen (agent, Hempstead), May 30, 1866, vol. 100, 226–227.

32. Byron Porter to C. B. Sojourner, Jan. 15, 1866, vol. 100, 166–167. See also *Kizzy King and Miranda King v. Josiah King,* Feb. 14, 1866, vol. 109, 40–41; *Parcilla Enridge v. Mr. Pugh,* Jan. 6, 1868, vol. 108, 88–89; L. H. Warren to Dave Roberts, July 5, 1867, vol. 102, 67–68.

33. *George Cooper v. Mary Vick,* July 5, 1867, vol. 108, 22–23.

34. W. B. Pease to Abner Doubleday (agent, Galveston), Feb. 7, 1867, P-8, Box 42; L. H. Warren to John Brashear (chief justice, Harris County), June 24, 1867, vol. 102, 48.

35. *Case of Polly,* May 2, 1866, vol. 109, 48–49; William Van Horne to Mr. Hennessey, Dec. 16, 1867, vol. 103, 35; *Moses Anthony v. Mr. Alexander,* June 20, 1867, vol. 108, 12–13; L. H. Warren to Mr. Alexander, June 20, 1867, vol. 102, 41; Byron Porter to Mr. Taylor (Grimes County), Jan. 9, 1866, vol. 100, 145; J. D. O'Connell to Edward Miller (agent, Millican), Aug. 13, 1867, vol. 102, 157–158.

36. *Julia Heard v. Ben Lyons,* June 13, 1867, vol. 108, 8–9; William Van Horne to J. S. Randall (agent, Sterling), Sept. 2, 1867, vol. 102, 178–179.

37. W. B. Pease to John Kennedy, Jan. 21, 1868, vol. 103, 50; *Tenna v. Mr. Raphael,* July 17, 1867, vol. 108, 28–29; J. D. O'Connell to E. M. Wheelock (agent, Galveston), Aug. 13, 1867, vol. 102, 156–157; Byron Porter to Dan Linton (Montgomery), Jan. 11, 1866, vol. 100, 153; William Van Horne to J. J. McKeever, Dec. 24, 1867, vol. 103, 37–38; *Joe Davis v. Patience Wynn,* June 12, 1867, vol. 108, 6–7. For writings on the rights of white women, see Suzanne Lebsock, "Radical Reconstruction and the Property Rights of Southern Women," *Journal of Southern History* 43 (May, 1977): 195–216.

38. A. A. Emerson to de Gress, Oct. 26, 1866, vol. 4, 363; de Gress to H. A. Ellis (acting asst. adj. gen.), Oct. 26, 1866, vol. 100, 296. It is worth noting, however, that no white women were ever put to work on the city's streets.

39. *Julia Wilkes v. City of Houston,* June 11, 1867, vol. 108, 4–5; de Gress to Judge Hadley, Oct. 24, 1866, vol. 100, 289.

40. L. H. Warren to Judge Fuller, June 24, 1867, vol. 102, 51; Warren to George Lancaster (agent, Hempstead), June 8, 1867, vol. 102, 13.

41. Byron Porter to Charles F. Allen (agent, Hempstead), May 22, 1866, vol. 100, 223; *Mony v. Mary Mortimer,* Aug. 24, 1867, vol. 89, 3–4. For white violence on Texas black women, see Barry A. Crouch, "A Spirit of Lawlessness: White Violence, Texas Blacks, 1865–1868," *Journal of Social History* 18 (Winter 1984): 217–232.

42. *Selina Parker v. Michael Linney,* Jan. 22, 26, 1866, vol. 109, 28–29, 34–35.

43. *Milly Graham v. Louisa Thompson,* May 2, 1866, vol. 109, 48–49; *Emily Matthews v. H. F. Matthews,* June 7, 1867, vol. 108, 2–3; Charles C. Hardenbrook to Marple, July 27, 1866, vol. 100, 250; *U.S. v. Tobin,* Dec. 19, 1865, vol. 109, 12–13; *Levi and Adeline Tanks v. Dr. Blake,* June 18, 1867, vol. 108, 12–13; L. H. Warren to Judge Fuller, June 22, 1867, vol. 102, 44; *Margaret Downs v. Milton McGowan,* May 2, 1866, vol. 109, 46–47.

44. *Julia Brown v. Jamison,* May 4, 1866, vol. 109, 54–55; *Dinah Wren v. Dr. Hartridge,* June 18, 1867, Vol. 108, 10–11.

45. *Dollina Williams v. Andrew Johnson Williams,* Feb. 12, 1866, vol. 109, 38–39; *Emma Matthews v. Frank Matthews,* Feb. 15, 1866, vol. 109, 40–41; Byron Porter to Officer in Charge of Military Prison, Feb. 23, 1866, vol. 100, 194; W. B. Pease to Judge Fuller, June 18, 1867, vol. 102, 37; July 27, 1867, vol. 102, 120–121. See also Elizabeth Pleck, *Domestic Tyranny: The Making of Social Policy against Family Violence from Colonial Times to the Present* (New York: Oxford Univ. Press, 1987).

46. De Gress to "To All Whom It May Concern," Dec. 3, 1866, vol. 100, 367; *Lucy Ann King v. Wesley King,* Jan. 2, 1866, vol. 109, 18–19.

47. Houston Agent to Autry Wright, Aug. 9, 1867, vol. 102, 142–144; *Lucinda Reed v. Osburn Smith,* Sept. 14, 1867, vol. 108, 192–193; L. H. Warren to Mayor DeDigethaby, June 13, 1867, vol. 102, 24; Warren to Judge Fuller, June 26, 1867, vol. 102, 57–58; *Melissa Hill v. Albert Williams,* June 13, 1867, vol. 108, 6–7; *U.S. v. M. McGuire,* Dec. 30, 1865, vol. 109, 16–17; *U.S. v. Holda Cotton,* Dec. 28, 1865, vol. 100, 104; Dec. 28, 1865, vol. 109, 16–17; *Kissya Lee v. November Ashville,* Nov. 12, 1867, vol. 108, 58–59; *Virginia Haardley v. Louisa Fernandos,* Dec. 14, 1867, vol. 108, 72–73. See also Jacquelyn Dowd Hall, " 'The Mind That Burns in Each Body': Women, Rape, and Racial Violence," in *Powers of Desire: The Politics of Sexuality,* ed. Ann Snitow, Christine Stansell, and Sharon Thompson, 328–349 (New York: Monthly Review Press, 1983).

48. Rose, *Slavery and Freedom,* 93; Eric Foner, *Nothing but Freedom: Emancipation and Its Legacy* (Baton Rouge: Louisiana State Univ. Press, 1983); Barry A. Crouch, "Black Dreams and White Justice," *Prologue: Journal of the National Archives* 6 (Winter 1974): 255–265. Bess Beatty portrays how black women were viewed in black newspapers during this time in "Black Perspectives of American Women: The View from Black Newspapers, 1865–1900," *Maryland Historian* 9 (Fall 1978): 39–50.

POSTSCRIPT TO PART II

Barry Crouch was one of the pioneer social historians who used primary sources to study how ordinary people lived. His main focus was on the African American community in Reconstruction Texas. He mined Record Group 105 of the Texas Freedmen's Bureau's reports and letters to the local agents and gave a view of Reconstruction from the point of view of the newly freed slaves. Professional historians refer to this approach as history from the bottom up.

The three essays in this selection were influenced by the iconoclastic and sprawling view Herbert Gutman presents in *The Black Family in Slavery and Freedom, 1750–1925* (Pantheon, 1976), which argues that the slave family was more stable—and that former slaves were less promiscuous—than previously thought. Crouch himself lent his notes on the Texas Freedmen's Bureau to Gutman for his chapters on Reconstruction.

Each of the essays illustrates how the newly freed African Americans attempted to reconstitute their families and negotiate fair labor contracts for themselves and humane apprenticeship agreements for their children. Much more research needs to be done in these areas. Did Gutman, for example, exaggerate the stability of the slave family to play down the idea of a matriarchy? How well did the former slaves negotiate labor contracts? How forceful and successful were black women in achieving a stable community?

A good starting point for the reader is the essays by James Smallwood cited in Crouch's footnotes. His book *Time of Hope, Time of Despair: Black Texans during Reconstruction* (Kennikat Press, 1981) remains the best overview on the subject. Unfortunately, it is out of print, though it deserves a second edition. Both Smallwood and Randolph B. Campbell in *Grass-Roots Reconstruction in Texas, 1865–1880* (Louisiana State Univ. Press, 1997) deny that a black matriarchal family developed in the years following slavery. For a comparison with African American women's responses to

Reconstruction in other states, see Leslie A. Schwalm, *A Hard Fight for We: Women's Transition from Slavery to Freedom in South Carolina* (Univ. of Illinois Press, 1997); and Mary J. Farmer, "'Because They Are Women': Gender and the Virginia Freedmen's Bureau's 'War on Dependency,'" in *The Freedmen's Bureau and Reconstruction: Reconsiderations* (Fordham Univ. Press, 1999), edited by Paul A. Cimbala and Randall M. Miller. An important overview can be found in *Women's Radical Reconstruction: The Freedmen's Aid Movement* by Carol Faulkner (Univ. of Pennsylvania Press, 2004), which analyzes the role of black and white abolitionist-feminists and their conflicts with male counterparts. For the struggle of blacks to achieve economic independence, see Nancy Cohen-Lack, "A Struggle for Sovereignty: National Consolidation, Emancipation, and Free Labor in Texas, 1865," *Journal of Southern History* (1992).

PART III *Reaction*

Five

A SPIRIT OF LAWLESSNESS
White Violence, Texas Blacks, 1865–1868

S outhern history, though rich and compelling, is stained by the theme of violence. Both before the Civil War and long after, violence was an accepted facet of southern society. Reconstruction, however, may have been that region's most violent era. Blacks and whites struggled to redefine their roles within an atmosphere of bitterness, frustration, and resentment. Racial tensions, always an important characteristic of southern life, reached new extremes that appalled even contemporaries. From Paris, Texas, a year after emancipation, Mrs. L. E. Potts, a native Tennesseean, implored President Andrew Johnson to do something about the plight of the "*poor* negro" and "their persecution." Just a few months out of slavery, she wrote, "their masters are so angry to loose [*sic*] them that they are trying to persecute them back into slavery." Killing black people was not considered a crime, she continued, and "they are often run down by blood hounds, and shot because they do not do precisely as the white man says." Black Texans needed federal protection, for the area "savors of rebellion." When blacks did work, Potts concluded, they "scarcely get any pay, and what are they to do [?]." [1]

Violence was a major component of postwar race relations. Revisionist historians of Reconstruction emphasize in particular the political implications of widespread violence by southern whites against blacks after the Civil War. Leon Litwack has been especially forceful in accentuating the role of Reconstruction violence and dramatically portraying some of its effects and results. The number of blacks, "beaten, flogged, mutilated, and murdered in the first years of emancipation," he maintains, "will never be known." Litwack contends that accurate body counts or statistical breakdowns fail to reveal the "barbaric savagery and depravity—the severed ears and entrails, the mutilated sex organs, the burnings at the stake, the forced drownings, the open display of skulls and severed limbs as trophies." No amount of industry or deference, he concludes, protected a freedperson suspected of harboring "dangerous tendencies" or seeming to be a "'smart-assed nigger' who needed chastisement."[2]

Litwack's graphic description of white violence against blacks is useful in calling attention to this issue, but it has not led to an examination of individual acts of violence. Most writings focus either on political violence, the rise and depredations of the Ku Klux Klan, or the major riots and racial confrontations between blacks and whites.[3] Still to be published is a detailed account of violence following emancipation, when, in the words of Willie Lee Rose, "coming to terms with freedom would be the first challenge" for whites.[4] No one has attempted to assess the different aspects of white violence in the immediate postwar era, to analyze the whites who perpetrated it, to ascertain its rationale, or to determine in what social and geographical context the violence occurred. Nor have statistical compilations been undertaken comparing white and black violence, the numbers killed, and the percentage of a specific black population murdered.

Fortunately, some of these issues can be explored in the case of Texas. Two extant sets of evidence related to the Lone Star State permit a detailed look at white violence against blacks from mid-1865 until mid-1868. The first is the conclusions reached by a special committee on lawlessness and violence established by the 1868 Texas constitutional convention. The second is the violence register compiled by the Texas Freedmen's Bureau.

These records reflect certain limitations and biases and must be used with caution. Republican sentiment inspired both documents, and recorders probably stressed rather than minimized white violence against blacks. In addition, the state committee only recorded homicide totals, thus hindering the detection of any statistical errors. Often the bureau sources provide only minimal background material. Frequently, the age and sex of the black victims are missing and have to be inferred. The information about whites and their backgrounds is sketchy at best. Although the type of assault committed is included, recurrently the motivation for the crime is ignored. Furthermore, local bureau agents depended upon various sources for their data, since they did not witness all the violence themselves. Officials throughout the districts submitted reports collected in various fashions. Surely, some were based on hearsay and distortions, thus skewing the figures.[5]

Another critical difficulty with violence records is that many events were never recorded, so the figures in both documents must be weighed against possible omissions. General Joseph J. Reynolds stated in 1868: "The official reports of lawlessness and crime (for Texas), so far from being exaggerated, do not tell the whole truth."[6] In spite of these problems, these documents represent a rich source of information for the Presidential Reconstruction years. To ignore their content is to limit our knowledge about white violence and black suffering in a postwar southern state.

The special committee's report is less comprehensive than the bureau's record. Dealing only with homicides, the data was gathered from state department records (from about forty counties) in which indictments had been found, Freedmen's Bureau materials for approximately sixty counties, and sworn statements of witnesses throughout the state. The committee recognized this was a "very imperfect view of the actual violence and disorder in the State."[7]

According to the committee, the homicide figures reveal a "frightful story of blood." During the three-year period from June 1865 to June 1868, Texans killed 939 people (see Table 5.1). Of this total, 373 were blacks murdered by whites, but only 10 were whites killed by blacks. Additionally, the committee reported 8 blacks killed by unknown assailants. The committee also indicated another 40 homicides in which the victim's race was not specified. It concluded that the "great disparity between the numbers of the two races killed, the one by the other, shows conclusively that 'the war of races' is all on the part of the whites against the blacks."[8]

The Texas Freedmen's Bureau compiled the second, and more important, violence record. This report consists of three massive volumes entitled *Criminal Offences Committed in the State of Texas* and focuses on the same years as the special committee's findings. These immensely detailed records provide information regarding the town and county where acts of violence were committed, the particulars of crimes, the names and races of the people involved, the circumstances surrounding outrages, the mechanisms by which crimes were reported, and any action the bureau or the civil authorities took.[9]

The statistical breakdown of the 2,225 offenses catalogued by the Texas bureau (see Table 5.2) not only corroborates the special committee's report on lawlessness and violence, but also reveals much more.[10] The bureau attempted to describe all physical acts of violence, not simply homicides. Even though there are some minor discrepancies between the state committee's death statistics and those of the bureau, what should command attention is the high death rate caused by white males killing primarily black males.[11]

More to the point is the meaning of the number of blacks killed from June 1865 to June 1868 in relation to the black population of Texas. Excluding the 8 blacks killed by assailants whose race was not known, 124.33 blacks were killed each year, on average, by whites. According to the 1870

TABLE 5.1. TEXAS HOMICIDES, JUNE 1865–JUNE 1868

| Year | Number of victims | | | Total |
	Black	White	Unknown	
1865	38	39		77
1866	72	70		142
1867	165	166		331
1868	133	171		304
Year unknown	21	24		45
Total blacks and whites	429	470		899
Total homicides	899		40	939

| Race of assailant | Number of victims | | | Total |
	Black	White	Unknown	
White	373	460★		833
Black	48	10		58
Unknown	8	—		8
Total blacks and whites	429	470		899
Total homicides	899		40★★	939

Average number of Texans killed each year: 313

★The *Report* (cited below as a source) mistakenly uses the number 464. The Reconstruction Convention *Journal* originally listed it as 460.

★★The sources do not give a racial breakdown of those killed by "parties whose race is unknown."

Source: Journal of the Reconstruction Convention, Which Met at Austin, Texas, June 1, A.D., 1868 (Austin, 1870) (June 30, 1868), 194; *Report of Special Committee on Lawlessness and Violence in Texas* (Austin, 1868), 4.

census, 253,475 blacks lived in the Lone Star State. Thus, the estimated annual death rate for blacks from white-inflicted outrages was 49.05 per 100,000. But this violence was not distributed equally: both the sex and the age of a potential victim affected the likelihood of a black Texan being murdered by a white one, and adult black males were by far the most likely to be killed. Although the bureau neither recorded the ages of those killed nor identified all according to sex, the statistics on black women slain (discussed later) indicate that 97 percent of the identified dead blacks

TABLE 5.2. WHITE AND BLACK VIOLENCE IN TEXAS, 1865–1868

Crime	Number of victims			
	W/B*	B/W	W/W	B/B
Killing	499	15	241	48
Assault and battery/ aggravated assault and battery	487	9	38	90
Whipping	126	—	—	—
Shooting	81	5	17	3
Assault—intent to kill	61	2	47	17
Assault	50	3	13	5
Threatening to kill	45	—	11	4
Robbery	29	1	6	2
Shooting at	28	1	5	5
Threatening to shoot	15	—	1	1
Stabbing	14	—	1	—
Driving from crop	11	—	—	—
Other	78	6	46	14
Total	1,524	42	426	189
Total acts of violence: 2,239**				

*Race of assailant/race of victim (B: black, W: white)

**Indians, Mexican Americans, or unknowns were involved in 58 cases.

Texas population (1870): 818,579; Whites: 564,700; Blacks: 253,475; Indians: 379; Chinese and Japanese: 25.

Source: Criminal Offences Committed in State of Texas, assistant commissioner, Austin, vols. 11–13, Records of the Bureau of Freedmen, Refugees, and Abandoned Lands, Texas, Record Group 105 (National Archives); *The Vital Statistics of the United States, Ninth Census* (1870), 3 vols. (Washington, D.C., 1872), 2:560, 2:608, 2:658. All tabulations by the author.

were males. Thus of the 124 blacks killed each year by whites, an estimated 120 were male and 4 were female. Of the 253,475 blacks recorded by the 1870 census, 126,278 were males. If, as estimated above, 120 of these males were killed by whites each year, the violence-specific death rate for black males rises to 95.03 per 100,000. The census records 44,804 black men in the 18–45 age range; internal evidence derived from Texas bureau manuscripts suggests that most of the black men killed were in this age range. Assuming that "most" means as much as 90 percent, the annual death rate for black men age 18–45 killed by whites was 241.05. This figure equals an annual death rate of 0.24 percent, so over the course of the three-year period, 0.72 percent—a figure approaching 1 percent—of black men age 18–45 were killed by whites.[12]

Of all the southern states at the close of the war, Texas had three distinctive factors that may have affected its violence record: the state's relative immunity from the devastation of the war, its location on the frontier, and its low population density. Texas is so large that its eastern half is the size of Mississippi and Alabama combined, yet in 1870 only 818,579 citizens resided in the state. Thus, the army had a difficult job trying to enforce order and protect the ex-slaves, and the bureau never had more than 100 agents. Moreover, most of the army's troops were stationed on the vast frontier, not in the heavily populated areas, where they could have protected the freedpeople. That Texas was never invaded successfully, and therefore did not accept defeat easily, also helped produce conditions for individual and group attacks by whites against blacks.[13]

The Lone Star State's vast size permitted individuals or groups to elude the law and justice, even when local officials did not connive to aid them in escaping punishment. By 1868 there were 5,000 pending homicide indictments in Texas. Yet from the end of the war until the fall of 1868, there was only one legal execution in the state, ironically of a Houston freedman. In the same year, General Reynolds, commander of the Fifth Military District, reported that "civil law east of the Trinity River is almost a dead letter" and that the "murder of negroes is so common as to render it impossible to keep an accurate account of them."[14] Geography, the frontier, a lax system of law enforcement, and inadequate support from the army or the bureau all conspired to make rural blacks general targets for white violence.

Did whites commit the violence individually or in groups (a group being defined as two or more people)? Litwack argues that "much of the violence inflicted on the freedmen had been well organized, with bands of white men meting out extra-legal 'justice' and anticipating the Klan-type groups that would operate so effectively during Radical Reconstruction." The evidence from Texas does not bear out Litwack's argument. Of the 1,524 total attacks or threats on blacks from 1865 to 1868, 1,037 (or 68 percent) were perpetrated by individuals. Blacks were terrorized by groups in 301 cases, mostly by desperadoes, in some cases by bandits, or in a few instances by the Ku Klux Klan, which made its first appearance in early 1868. In 186 actions, the party or parties were unknown. In many of these unsolved outrages, the black person was found dead, and no identification of the attacker could be made. Black families were enumerated in only 35 altercations.[15]

White violence against Texas blacks took many forms and resulted from a variety of causes, which are difficult to pinpoint. It was, for example, sometimes related to political or labor activities, sometimes to social relations and mores. It was directed at women and children and at institutions such as schools and churches. The well-documented viciousness and seemingly random nature of many instances of violence may indicate that it was related to the peculiar psychological condition of a people frustrated and enraged by defeat in a long and painful civil war.

Two questions might be raised about this spate of white-on-black violence. First, were certain types of violence more frequently committed by groups of whites or by individuals? Second, were some classes of whites more prone to use group or mob violence than others? Some kinds of violent attacks, of course, were committed by both individuals and groups, but patterns may be established for specific motivations. The question of which classes were likely to commit violence is much more difficult to answer, and a complete accounting will need further supporting studies.[16]

In past writings about Reconstruction, historians have too often narrowly focused on politically motivated violence against blacks. This was certainly a central part of the violence equation, but there were, to be sure, many other reasons for outrages ending in injury or death for blacks. At work or play, while drinking, in institutional settings, or when refusing to sanction old social mores, blacks were subject to numerous outrages. Although black Texans are seen largely as victims in this essay (a concept not without evident pitfalls), the major conclusion to be drawn is that whites used violence in different guises to control blacks politically, economically, and socially. Texas whites resented black political equality, a free-labor ideology, and more equitable social relations. Blacks most assuredly responded to white violence and committed individual acts against whites. But the figures in Tables 5.1 and 5.2 substantiate the judgment that black violence against whites was minimal compared to what whites were doing to them. Obviously not all whites were participants in the outrages—some even abhorred the incidents—but the high number of incidents suggests there was little concerted action to stop them.[17]

The following examples of violence are representative of the categories of violence discussed in the remainder of the essay. There are enough cases to draw tentative conclusions about postwar Texas violence, although it is impossible to construct a chart for corroborative purposes because of the lack of continued specific information on the background and motivation of white perpetrators. Nonetheless, categories, though not precise statistics, do emerge from the data.

Once blacks organized, met politically, and were enfranchised, they became sources of potential and real conflict in the political arena. The rise in the death rate of Texas blacks, and the careful recording of it, coincides precisely with the congressional Republicans' struggle to control the Reconstruction process and with the emergence of local blacks as voters, community leaders, registrars, and Union Leaguers. From 1866 to 1867, when freedmen won the right to vote, the total number of blacks slain by whites doubled. But worse lay ahead. According to the state committee, 69 percent of the blacks murdered by whites died during 1867 and 1868. Republicans, both black and white, states Otto Olsen, "provoked a hatred from their opponents so intense that it soon turned Reconstruction into an age of violence and terror." White Texans, as one historian has noted, perceived political rights for blacks as a temporary aberration that "could be taken back by the state after it was readmitted to the Union." Thus, violence, terror, and intimidation became acceptable means for the destruction of black political equality.[18]

The case of George E. Brooks, a politically active minister from Millican, Texas, is instructive. His decomposing body was found after a clash between Millican's blacks and whites in mid-1868. The incident originated when a black man was murdered near the sheriff's residence: the culprit was not arrested for two days, and was then released on his own recognizance. When blacks protested this lenient treatment, the Ku Klux Klan entered the affray, inciting a racial imbroglio, which resulted in the killing of prominent members of Millican's black community. In the Millican affair, it seems likely that whites, with substantial economic and political interests in the community, were concerned about blacks banding together, asserting their rights, and demanding justice. The killing of Brooks, who was a prominent local politician, registrar, and Union League member, was a "deliberate murder" and one of a "most outrageous character."[19]

Even if black Texans simply wished to learn more about their rights, they risked danger. While on his way to hear the bureau's assistant commissioner speak, James Cole of Walker County was besieged by a mob of "white rowdies," assaulted, and pistol-whipped. The same thing happened in Harrison County, only the whites involved in that incident were described as "civil officers" and the "disloyal."[20] Where politics motivated violence, whites used both individual and group tactics, depending upon whether blacks had protested the denial of their rights, served a political function, or attended meetings. The evidence suggests that all classes of whites participated in the attacks, especially where blacks emerged as a vocal segment of the body politic.

Violence associated with labor-related behavior was prevalent in the postwar years. Activities such as contracting, working, moving for better jobs, securing rations, arranging credit bills, seeking wages, dividing shares, or being driven off the land without compensation led to violence. Because of the refusal of blacks to work in gangs, and the dominance of sharecropping, much of the violence was committed against individuals. Whites perpetrating the attacks were property holders, the bureau records suggest, probably former planters who were concerned about maintaining a reliable, dependent, and available labor pool. For example, Wyatt Hooks, a Bowie County freedman, lost his life when he decided to leave his former owner and seek employment in Arkansas. He was murdered in cold blood by the man he had served under as a slave. A Dr. Phillips chained, whipped, and threatened the life of his former slave when the latter refused to stay and work for him. The black man appeared at the Houston bureau office still wearing the chain.[21]

Violence also occurred when blacks sought to assert their freedom. Three years after the official decree abolishing slavery in the Lone Star State, some black Texans were still enslaved. Violent efforts to perpetuate slavery involved planters refusing to accept the idea of black freedom. Protesting his continued enslavement, Albert, a Washington County slave/freedman, challenged his master/employer, Irving Randall, in the fall of 1866. Randall informed Albert he was still a slave, whereupon the black man questioned Randall's veracity. Albert's "boldness" caused him to be shot in one arm, necessitating amputation. About the same time, another black man was killed for attempting to leave a plantation after being officially freed. A former owner whipped and kicked a Dallas County black woman who tried to assert her freedom in early 1868.[22]

Disciplining blacks to the "new" labor relations was another component of white violence. When Texas blacks decided to control their own labor and make the best arrangements for working, their actions provoked physical assaults, injuries, and even death. Again, this type of violence was largely individual. In rare instances, gangs of white men (perhaps hired by the planters) whipped blacks who refused to sign new contracts; this happened in Davis County. Those who controlled the land after the war liberally used the lash to suppress any notions of independence that blacks may have entertained. But blacks were not only whipped for seeking a new work environment: some were killed, as were a mother and her baby in 1868 in Rusk County when she left her employer. Others were murdered when they refused to return to their "masters."[23]

That Texas blacks now enjoyed total freedom of movement aroused indignation in those concerned about a stable labor force. Blacks were not permitted to look for better jobs or more advantageous share arrangements, and leaving the farm without permission was certainly a transgression of the old pass system. A few owners went to great lengths to find and punish blacks who departed without consent. In Fort Bend and Walker counties whites used dogs to chase two black men (one was shot at twice) because they had failed to check with the farm owner before leaving. A Fort Bend County freedman named Shade was confined two days in the "calaboose" for attempting to move. Families had to be careful about allowing their offspring freedom of movement. Stephen Bryant and his wife, Liberty County freedpeople, were handcuffed, whipped, and beaten because two of their sons left the farm without asking the owner's permission.[24]

White violence against black Texans, however, involved more than just the contracting process or moving away from the confines of the plantation. It lurked over the freedpeople's everyday working life. Texas blacks were beaten and wounded for being too sick to work, for taking too long to eat breakfast, for being late to work, for hoeing too slowly (100 lashes), for incompetence, for laziness, for carelessness, or for paying too much attention to an ailing relative. One freedman appeared at the Freedmen's Bureau office in Seguin covered with large scabs and scars. He informed the agent that because he was too sick to pick cotton, he had been whipped with a strap that had a two-inch iron buckle. Miles, a Fort Bend County freedman, told a similar story: his employer had beaten him over the head and back with a heavy walking stick. Much of this ill treatment was parcelled out by owners themselves or their hired foremen and managers.[25]

Labor-related violence often surfaced at the end of the contracting year or after the harvesting of crops, when it was time to collect wages or, more commonly, divide shares. The complaint books of the Texas Freedmen's Bureau contain a large number of cases indicating the role of planters in violence against blacks. Laborers deluged the bureau with grievances asserting they received too little or no compensation whatsoever from their employers. According to Texas freedpeople, they were shot, struck with pistols, cut with hatchets or knives, whipped, beaten with clubs and chains, assaulted with monkey wrenches, stabbed, or threatened with shotguns and pistols. If a freedperson actually was able to get his or her employer before a bureau court for nonpayment, retaliation was too often the result. Oliver, a Montgomery County freedman, was killed for bringing his employer before the bureau, and an Anderson County black man, Henry Jones, was waylaid and murdered by his boss because Jones had sued him for seven dollars.[26]

Whether blacks sued their employers, demanded a fair settlement, looked for a more advantageous position, or challenged whites about specific contract provisions, their conceptions of freedom and fairness clashed with landowning whites' old perceptions of how blacks should behave. The planters struggled to survive against the frustrations of nature, low cotton prices, and a labor force that now desired an opportunity to make decisions for itself. Adjusting to these staggering economic changes brought forth white violence to keep blacks "disciplined" to the prewar ways and to guarantee that a pliant and steady work force would always be available. Much of the conflict in labor and labor-related activities was due to two completely different viewpoints of what freedom meant to employers and employees, and blacks generally were the losers. A Texas planter neatly summarized the contest, contending "the struggle seems to be who will get the negro *at any price*."[27]

Still, antiblack violence was not prompted solely by economics and labor relations. In social relations, whether implementing or maintaining acceptable social mores or monitoring the social activities of blacks, white Texans followed antebellum patterns. Black Texans could not make insulting noises, speak disrespectfully or out of turn, talk back, dispute the word of whites, or disobey a command. Further, they had to stand at attention when whites passed, step aside when white women were on the sidewalk, address whites properly, and remove their hats in their presence. "Improper actions" by blacks resulted in swift retaliation. Although outrages of this sort were not common, the ones that did occur demonstrated to black Texans that social intercourse was still governed by harsh rules.[28]

The social code, a combination of whites' racial and class attitudes, was interrelated with social mores and activities and guarded exactingly by all classes of whites. The sources suggest that planters did not become involved as much in this type of violence as they did when labor and economics was concerned, but this may be because of the scarcity of incidents compared to those from the labor arena. Urban and small-town whites apparently used this type of violence to prevent erosion of the social order. A case in point is that of a young white woman allegedly insulted by a Montgomery County freedman when they passed on the street. The woman's father and brothers attacked the black man, who was rescued by the sheriff, only to be brought before a justice of the peace on trumped-up charges. Though acquitted, the freedman was later taken into the woods by his previous attackers, stripped of his clothing, laid face down, and severely whipped. In two other instances, black men were murdered because they reportedly insulted white women. A Prairie Lea black man was publicly whipped for addressing a white man he had known all his life as "Tom" instead of "Master Tom." Another black man was stabbed in the arm while standing in church, the white assailant exclaiming, "God damn your black soul. I will learn you to stand in the way of white ladies." [29]

Texas whites who attempted to guard and maintain old social mores generally did so individually, though there were exceptions. Whites who attacked blacks at dances, parties, or social functions did so in groups, apparently angered that blacks had found ways to enjoy themselves. Such a "gang," as the bureau referred to it, entered a Palestine saloon where local blacks were dancing and threw several of them through the upper-story windows. A similar occurrence in Panola County in 1868 ended with three black men dead and four wounded. The white ringleader was the county sheriff. Freedmen were also murdered at celebrations. [30]

Texas whites did not respect sex when committing outrages. Whites victimized black women in 183 incidents (see Table 5.3), according to a tabulation of bureau records. Too often in discussions of the antiblack violence that followed the Civil War, males are the major focus. The rather significant number of offenses perpetrated against black women strongly indicates that there was a deep rage underlying many of the attacks and that much of the violence was purposeless, almost elemental and irrational. Some black women were attacked but not killed, receiving especially gruesome treatment. A Limestone County freedwoman, Jo Brooks, had her ears cut off and her arms burned to a crisp, for no stated provocation. Others, even if not so horribly violated, were nonetheless brutalized. When women were attacked for reasons unrelated to labor, the crimes were perpetrated by individuals who, the sources suggest, had little economic standing in communities and came from a desperate, socially irresponsible class. [31]

Nor were children immune from white violence. Like adults, they suffered from whipping, flogging, beating, assaults, castration, and murder. Much violence against children seems to have been random, motivated by nothing more than whites' deep rage. Children were whipped and kicked, stabbed to death, shot at, and had turpentine placed on their "fundaments." In the fall of 1866, a Bosque County black boy was whipped to death, and a seven-year-old girl, Dolla Jackson, suffered an attempted rape and was robbed of twenty-five cents. The bureau viewed the white assailants in

TABLE 5.3. VIOLENCE BY WHITES AGAINST BLACK TEXAS WOMEN, 1865–1868

Crime	Incidents
Assault and battery	76
Aggravated assault and battery	48
Murder	15
Whipping	12
Assault and rape	9
Shooting and assaulting	9
Threatening to kill	6
Shooting at	3
Holding in slavery	2
Robbery	1
Cutting off ears	1
Abduction	1
Total	183

Source: Criminal Offences Committed in State of Texas, assistant commissioner, Austin, vols. 11–13, Records of the Bureau of Freedmen, Refugees, and Abandoned Lands, Texas, Record Group 105 (National Archives). All tabulations by the author.

these cases as characters of a desperate and mean sort, with no established economic or community standing. This may lead to the surmise that all whites who brutalized black children were from the lower economic stratum and were thus presumably more frustrated than wealthier persons, but this conclusion is not entirely valid. For example, three prominent citizens of McLennan and Bosque counties, two of whom were doctors, committed what a bureau agent called one of the "most atrocious deeds in the annals of barbarity," castrating a freedboy. Perhaps in the same social group was the planter who shot a freedchild because the mother left his employ. However, child assault instigated by influential whites remained rare. Most of the recorded outrages were as brutal, but there is nothing to indicate that the perpetrators were of the same class as the doctors or planter cited above.[32]

Two treasured institutions of the black community, schools and churches, also were the objects of white violence. In Anderson County, where the population was almost equally divided between black and white, a white mob stoned the black church, twice broke the windows, and threatened the minister. In Washington County, congregation members were beaten. A white mob attacked a Harris County Baptist church in September 1868.

The whites assaulted the former minister, an "old man," his son, and his daughter-in-law, brutally kicking, mauling, and mangling them, nearly killing the elderly preacher and his daughter-in-law. Teachers and schools suffered the same fate. The former were driven from counties or killed. The latter were trashed and burned. Northern white soldiers, apparently not immune to racial hatred, fired on a black school on their way to the frontier, leading to a "regular skirmish" between the two races and leaving four wounded, two on each side. Whites also entered schools with drawn pistols, disrupting classes.[33]

Although individual acts of violence accounted for over two-thirds of the total, white desperadoes committed the most destructive forms of group violence against blacks. In the immediate postwar years, these bandits robbed, plundered, harassed, and murdered blacks who lived in northeastern Texas and along the Arkansas border. Marauding bands, composed of ex-Confederate soldiers and other economically dispossessed men, hated both blacks and Yankees. Blaming the war and Northern invaders for their bleak circumstances, they attacked with an intensity bordering on the fanatical. Four groups in particular, led by Cullen Baker, Benjamin F. Griffith, Ben Bickerstaff, and Buck Taylor, were responsible for the majority of attacks. Bickerstaff was once arrested, but a judge refused to try him because he had been a good Confederate soldier; a bureau agent later killed him. Many of these desperadoes, as one contemporary observed, would kill a freedman for seventy-five cents and boast of the deed as a "laudable one to high minded chivalry." One governmental official referred to Baker as a "highwayman and murderer." In a perceptive report, he accounted for Baker's appeal, writing that

> such a character is as essential to the ends and aims of the
> citizens of this part of the country as hounds are to a hunter.
> Through such instrumentalities the chivalry govern the lower
> grades of society even more effectually than they could by
> legal enactments by narrating their deeds of valor to the ig-
> norant freedmen who recount them by their evening firesides
> with horror and consternation.[34]

Texas whites often killed blacks for no obvious reason other than racial hatred or the satisfaction of sadistic fantasies. Some reportedly shot freedmen to "see a d———d nigger kick" or because they just wanted to shoot a "damned nigger." Others shot them, apparently, to test their skills as marksmen. The very presence of free blacks led to murders. In Grayson County, for instance, where blacks composed only 18 percent of the population and therefore were not a political threat, three whites murdered three freedmen because, they said, they felt a need to "thin the niggers out and drive them to their holes."[35]

Antiblack violence in Texas from 1865 to 1868 was significant because of its high yearly death toll and because of the percentage of the population affected. The death rate for black Texans during this era was more than twenty times the rate for all races in nineteenth-century Philadelphia, and three and a half times the rates for Dallas, Houston, and New York City in recent times.

The size of the state and the isolation of many sections of it largely account for white attacks against blacks having been committed mainly by individuals and only occasionally by groups. Certain patterns emerge, however, in relation to the motivations behind the various categories of white violence.

Labor violence was largely perpetrated by individual planters; the constant references in the sources suggest that former "owners" and "masters" expected to subordinate blacks and prevent them from achieving economic independence. There were some attacks on working blacks that can be classified as random, but most were purposeful. Whipping was still widely practiced as a means of discipline and punishment, but whites also found other ingenious ways of using violence to keep blacks working and tied to the land.

Antiblack violence against persons who violated prewar social relations or mores is more difficult to classify. When attacks focused on schools and churches, lower-class white crowds or mobs were the villains. Often these gangs would wreak havoc on black social gatherings such as dances and parties.

Whites who attacked blacks because of political motivations came from varied backgrounds. Much of the political violence was perpetrated by individuals or small groups that harassed, intimidated, and sometimes murdered black Texans who participated in some fashion in politics or simply desired to live a free life. Small groups described as bullies and rowdies also attacked blacks, such as registrars, directly involved in politics.

The group confrontation that occurred at Millican (and led to the death of minister George E. Brooks) involved a cross-section of both the white and black communities. Certain crimes, however, were more likely to be associated with whites of higher socioeconomic status. Prominent members of the white community apparently took part of the Millican affray, and were perhaps involved when blacks were attacked for holding some official position.[36]

A suggestion by a bureau agent that the upper classes used desperadoes—and by implication, the lower classes—to control blacks is significant. By allowing those who committed attacks on blacks to go free or to pay a ridiculously small fine, local officials did nothing to discourage these crimes. This made other whites aware that violence against blacks would not be punished. The idea of one white class supporting violence by another worked both ways. For example, a "mob of citizens" attempted to break into the jail and free the three men who castrated the freedboy mentioned above. Moreover, there was even talk of assassinating the agent and others who maintained the criminals in custody. The threat of violence was an effective psychological weapon, and as the bureau agent implied, it could be used by an upper class to control a lower one and to keep yet another class, of a different color, in constant fear.

During the early years of Texas Reconstruction, conditions were "anomalous, singular, and unsatisfactory," according to General Philip H. Sheridan (famous for reportedly saying that if he owned both Texas and hell, he would rent out Texas and live in hell). Texas was all this and more, particularly for blacks who tried to take advantage of their supposed freedom. Clearly more studies of violence in other southern states are necessary before we can conclude, as does James M. Smallwood, that an "examination of sources" suggests "there was little difference in the degree of harassment suffered by Texas blacks and those of other states." If the remainder of the old Confederacy had a scale of violence similar to that which occurred in Texas, then the southern black populace faced an even more desperate situation than had been earlier assumed.[37] All this serves as a reminder that Reconstruction was fraught with wrenching experiences. Texas blacks needed extraordinary resilience to prevent their potential social, economic, and political gains from turning into terrible losses.

NOTES

This project was originally conceived in a National Endowment for the Humanities Summer Seminar under the direction of Professor Stanley L. Engerman. I would like to thank him for his generous contribution to the essay. Friends and colleagues who have provided inestimable help include Anne M. Butler, Arnoldo

De León, Larry Madaras, and John V. Van Cleve. Jim Samuels was a wonderful booster.

1. Mrs. L. E. Potts to Mr. President (June 1866), Phillip H. Sheridan Papers, Container 4 (Manuscript Division, Library of Congress); H. G. Wright to Geo. Lee, July 21, 1866, Sheridan Papers, Container 4; John A. Carpenter, "Atrocities in the Reconstruction Period," *Journal of Negro History* 47 (1962): 234–247; and James L. Roark, *Masters without Slaves: Southern Planters in the Civil War and Reconstruction* (New York: Norton, 1977), 111–209.

2. Leon F. Litwack, *Been in the Storm So Long: The Aftermath of Slavery* (New York: Knopf, 1979), 276–277; Robert Cruden, *The Negro in Reconstruction* (Englewood Cliffs, N.J.: Prentice-Hall, 1969); Eugene D. Genovese, "Re-examining Reconstruction," *New York Times Book Review,* May 4, 1980, 40. The role of Reconstruction violence is debated in William C. Harris, *The Day of the Carpetbagger: Republican Reconstruction in Mississippi* (Baton Rouge: Louisiana State Univ. Press, 1979); in the review of that book by Richard N. Current, *American Historical Review* 85 (1980): 465; in the exchange of letters in the same issue, 1048–1049; and in Eric Foner, "Reconstruction Revisited," *Reviews in American History* 10 (1982): 82–100.

3. For accounts of violence connecting politics, race, and the Klan, see George Calvin Rable, "But There Was No Peace: Violence and Reconstruction Politics" (PhD diss. [2 vols.], Louisiana State Univ., 1978) and *But There Was No Peace: The Role of Violence in the Politics of Reconstruction* (Athens: Univ. of Georgia Press, 1984); Melinda Meek Hennessey, "To Live and Die in Dixie: Reconstruction Race Riots in the South" (PhD diss., Kent State Univ., 1978); Barry A. Crouch, "Postbellum Violence, 1871," in *Congress Investigates: A Documented History, 1794–1974,* 5 vols., ed. Arthur M. Schlesinger, Jr., and Roger Burns, 3 : 1689–1846 (New York: Chelsea House, 1975); Allen W. Trelease, *White Terror: The Ku Klux Klan Conspiracy and Southern Reconstruction* (Baton Rouge: Louisiana State Univ. Press, 1979); James M. McPherson, *Ordeal By Fire: The Civil War and Reconstruction* (New York: Knopf, 1982), 491–619; William H. Fisher, *The Invisible Empire: A Bibliography of the Ku Klux Klan* (Metuchen, N.J.: Scarecrow Press, 1980).

4. Willie Lee Rose, *Slavery and Freedom,* ed. William W. Freehling (New York: Oxford Univ. Press, 1982), 78; David Grimsted, "Making Violence Relevant," *Reviews in American History* 4 (1976): 334; Richard Maxwell Brown, *Strain of Violence: Historical Studies of American Violence and Vigilantism* (New York: Oxford Univ. Press, 1975).

5. William S. McFeely in *Grant: A Biography* (New York: Norton, 1981), writes that by 1867 bureau commissioner Oliver Otis Howard "had thousands of *carefully documented* reports from his agents of murders and mutilations of freedmen all across the South," 260 (emphasis added). W. Eugene Hollon states that the statistics submitted by the lawlessness and violence committee "were generally accepted as valid by both radical and conservative members" of the convention (*Frontier*

Justice: Another Look [New York: Oxford Univ. Press, 1974], 221–222). Two Texas newspapers did criticize the committee, but not for the figures it presented: the *Brownsville Ranchero,* July 17, 1868, 4, and the *Galveston Daily News,* 1–2. For minor questions and an analysis that fails to understand the implications of the numbers killed, see Betty Jeffus Sandlin, "The Texas Reconstruction Constitutional Convention of 1868–1869" (PhD diss., Texas Tech Univ., 1970), 65–95; Merline Pitre, "A Note on the Historiography of Blacks in the Reconstruction of Texas," *Journal of Negro History* 66 (Winter 1981–1982): 342–343.

6. U.S. Department of War, *Report of the Secretary of War, November 20, 1869,* 41st Cong., 2nd sess., House Executive Document 1, Part II (Serial 1412), 705 (Washington, D.C., 1869).

7. *Journal of the Reconstruction Convention, Which Met at Austin, Texas, June 1, A.D. 1868* (Austin, 1870), 193 (June 30, 1868). A copy is in the Thomas W. Streeter Texas Collection (Beinecke Rare Book and Manuscript Library, Yale University). It is also reprinted in Senate Miscellaneous Documents, 40th Cong., 2nd sess., No. 109 (Serial 1319), 3–8. See also Hollon, *Frontier Violence,* 48–52, 221–222.

8. *Journal of the Reconstruction Convention,* 194–195. In a supplementary report (July 21, 1868, 501), the committee raised the total killed of both races to 1,035 but did not attempt to separate the new numbers according to murders by race. One Texas historian claims that "probably the number of murders was far greater." The lawlessness and violence committee's "damning statistics leave no doubt. Texas was the scene of a race war in which Negroes and their protectors suffered great loss of life" (Edgar P. Sneed, "A Historiography of Reconstruction in Texas: Some Myths and Problems," *Southwestern Historical Quarterly* 72 [1969]: 445). Comparisons with other Southern states are difficult because of the paucity of figures, but see Edward Magdol, *A Right to the Land: Essays on the Freedmen's Community* (Westport, Conn.: Greenwood, 1977), 270–271; and Jesse Parker Bogue, Jr., "Violence and Oppression in North Carolina During Reconstruction, 1865–1873" (PhD diss., Univ. of Maryland, 1973). The Texas statistics refute the conclusion of Joe Gray Taylor of Louisiana, who states that "most violence inflicted upon black people in Louisiana, and *elsewhere for that matter,* was inflicted by black people." No "statistical comparison is possible," he continues, "but this student is convinced that for every black man killed by a white man, for political or other reasons, two were killed by other black men" (*Louisiana Reconstructed, 1863–1877* [Baton Rouge: Louisiana State Univ. Press, 1974), 421 [emphasis added]). This essay supports Trelease's assertion in *White Terror* that "black men were more often the victims than the perpetrators of interracial violence" (19).

9. *Criminal Offences Committed in State of Texas,* assistant commissioner, Austin, vols. 11–13, Records of the Bureau of Freedmen, Refugees, and Abandoned Lands, Texas, Record Group (RG) 105, National Archives. A brief description is in Crouch, "Hidden Sources of Black History: The Texas Freedmen's Bureau Re-

cords as a Case Study," *Southwestern Historical Quarterly* 83 (1980): 224–225. Also see Brown, "The Archives of Violence," *American Archivist* 41 (1978): 431–443.

10. Although the bureau numbered 2,316 offenses, the compiler of the cases skipped from number 909 to 1,000, thus making the official count 2,225. This minor flaw does not affect the argument. The establishment of the various categories and all the counting was done by Crouch. The Texas Freedmen's Bureau only catalogued the violence; it did not break down the list into usable statistics.

11. Table 5.2 lists only those categories of violence for which ten or more violent acts were committed. Since whites often left the physical property of blacks unharmed, it may be assumed they were intent upon brutalizing the freedpeople. For examples of black property destroyed (there were only twelve incidents), see *Criminal Offences Committed in State of Texas,* case nos. 28, 230–231, 526, 531, and 2,258. Hereafter the report will be cited as *Criminal Offences,* and the case number of the outrage will follow.

12. *The Statistics of the Population of the United States, Ninth Census* (Washington, D.C.: Government Printing Office, 1872), pp. x–xii, 606–607. On black women, see Table 5.3.

The calculations for the death rates are as follows:

Average number of blacks killed per year (June 1865–June 1868) by whites: 373/3 = 124.33.

Number of blacks in Texas: 253,475 (1870 census).

Estimated annual death rate (per 100,000) for blacks killed by whites: (124.33) (100,000)/253,475 = 49.05.

Of the blacks killed, 97 percent were male, so of the 124 blacks killed by whites each year on average, 120 were males [(0.97)(124)] and 4 were females.

The 253,475 blacks in the 1870 census included 126,278 males and 127,197 females.

The annual death rate for black males (per 100,000) killed by whites: (120)(100,000)/126,278 = 95.03.

It is impossible to know how many of the 120 black males killed each year by whites were from the 18–45 age group, but evidence suggests that "most" of them were.

If "most" means as much as 90 percent, then of the 120 black males killed each year by whites, as many as 108 [(0.90)(120)] were from this age range.

According to the 1870 census, there were 44,804 black males age 18–45 in Texas.

The annual death rate (per 100,000) for black males age 18–45 killed by whites: (108)(100,000)/44,804 = 241.05.

The percentage of black males age 18–45 killed by whites each year was 0.24 percent (108/44,804).

The bureau personnel seem to have been quite careful in specifically identifying women, children, and older black people; for children, see *Criminal Offences,* nos. 179, 413, 526, 584, 1,021, 1,141, and 1,185; for older blacks, see nos. 159, 283, 1,130, 1,334, 1,441, and 2,076.

13. Ludwell H. Johnson, *Red River Campaign: Politics and Cotton in the Civil War* (Baltimore: Johns Hopkins Univ. Press, 1958); Randolph B. Campbell and Richard G. Lowe, *Wealth and Power in Antebellum Texas* (College Station, Tex.: Texas A&M Univ. Press, 1977), 17; *The Vital Statistics of the United States, Ninth Census,* 3 vols. (Washington, D.C.: Government Printing Office, 1872), 2:560; Michael Perman, *Reunion without Compromise: The South and Reconstruction, 1865–1868* (Cambridge: Cambridge Univ. Press, 1973); Alfred B. Sears, "Slavery and Retribution," *Southwestern Social Quarterly* 41 (1960): 9. Mustering out orders for the army precluded "any massive occupation of the state" (Robert W. Shook, "The Federal Military in Texas, 1865–1870," *Texas Military History* 6 [1967]: 8).

14. *Report of the Secretary of War, 1869,* 705; Shook, "Federal Military in Texas," 41; *Report of the Special Committee on Lawlessness and Violence,* 9; Jesse Dorsett, "Blacks in Reconstruction Texas, 1865–1877" (PhD diss., Texas Christian Univ., 1981), 168–175. For the army specifically, see Shook, "Federal Occupation and Administration of Texas, 1865–1870" (PhD diss., North Texas State Univ., 1970); William Lee Richter, "The Army in Texas during Reconstruction, 1865–1970" (PhD diss., Louisiana State Univ., 1970).

15. Litwack, *Been in the Storm So Long,* 278–279; G. David Garson and Gail O'Brien, "Collective Violence in the Reconstruction South," in *Violence in America: Historical and Comparative Perspectives* (rev. ed.), ed. Hugh Davis Graham and Ted Robert Gurr, 243–260 (Beverly Hills, Calif.: Sage, 1979). There was Klan violence in Texas, but it was minimal in this early period; see *Criminal Offences,* nos. 509–510, 1,081, 1,682, 1,688, 1,867, 1,918, 1,963, 2,027, 2,121–2,122, 2,158–2,160, and 2,124–2,126; and Trelease, *White Terror,* 137–148.

16. Bureau records give only minimal data about whites. However, some general profiles can be constructed based upon the nature of the crime, the type of violence, the reasons for the attack, the circumstances of the incident, and the comments of the bureau. These factors, somewhat sporadically provided, nonetheless enhance general impressions about white participants.

17. I am preparing an essay on black violence against whites for this same period. The limited black response to the violence of white Texans (see Tables 5.1 and 5.2) was due to a lack of numbers, fear of more retribution, a lack of weapons, the absence of cities (perhaps), a frontier geography, and fewer towns in which to congregate on weekends. Blacks were not nearly as well armed as whites in Reconstruction Texas, although the lawlessness and violence committee suggested otherwise. Whites took every opportunity to disarm blacks; see *Report of the Special Committee,* 4–5; and *Criminal Offences,* nos. 273, 399, 740, 1,103, 1,284, 1,492, 1,737, 1,994, 1,995, 1,996, and 2,086. The question of protecting blacks from white violence did arise in the state legislature; see Carl H. Moneyhon, "George T. Ruby and the Politics of Expediency in Texas," in *Southern Black Leaders of the Reconstruction Era,* ed. Howard N. Rabinowitz (Urbana: Univ.

of Illinois Press, 1982), 363–392. According to General Sheridan and General Reynolds, white Texans were more concerned about Indians killing whites on the frontier than about whites murdering blacks in the interior. The movement of troops from the frontier to the interior, Reynolds reported, would weaken the former posts, "but the bold, wholesale murdering in the interior of the State seems at present a more urgent demand for the troops than Indian depredations" (*Report of the Secretary of War, 1869,* 706). Sheridan wrote: "It is strange that over a white man killed by Indians on an extensive frontier, the greatest excitement will take place; but over the killing of many freedmen in the settlements, nothing is done" (Sheridan to J. A. Rawlins, November 6, 1866, Sheridan Papers, Container 71). In the papers of James W. Throckmorton (governor, 1866–1867) at the Texas State Library, there is not one complaint about whites killing blacks, but a stream of letters about the Indians.

18. The percentages are based upon the figures in Table 5.1. Otto H. Olsen, ed., *Reconstruction and Redemption in the South* (Baton Rouge: Louisiana State Univ. Press, 1980), 9; Billy D. Ledbetter, "White Texans' Attitudes toward the Political Equality of Negroes, 1865–1970," *Phylon* 60 (1979): 253. See also Harrell Budd, "The Negro in Politics in Texas, 1867–1898" (master's thesis, Univ. of Texas, 1925); John Pressley Carrier, "A Political History of Texas during Reconstruction, 1865–1874" (PhD diss., Vanderbilt Univ., 1971); Carl Moneyhon, *Republicanism in Reconstruction Texas* (Austin: Univ. of Texas Press, 1980); James D. Smallwood, *Time of Hope, Time of Despair: Black Texans during Reconstruction* (Port Washington, N.Y.: Kennikat Press, 1981), 128–158; Ann Patton Malone, "Matt Gaines: Reconstruction Politician," in *Black Leaders: Texans for Their Times,* ed. Alwyn Barr and Robert A. Calvert (Austin: Univ. of Texas Press, 1981), 49–81.

19. "Criminal Offences," nos. 1954–1961; Nathan H. Randlett to Vernou, July 23, 1868, assistant commissioner, Letters Received, R-178, Box 9, Texas, RG 105; Crouch, "Self-Determination and Local Black Leaders in Texas," *Phylon* 39 (1978): 349–352; Hennessey, "To Live and Die in Dixie," 77–78. It is interesting to note that of all the materials consulted about Millican, which included about ten newspapers, the bureau was the only source correctly reporting the affair and the numbers killed or injured.

20. *Criminal Offences,* no. 1,865

21. Ibid., nos. 373, 377, 381–382, 355, 473, 324. Also see nos. 128, 202, 203, 293, 356, 386, 404, 512, 649, 658, 744, 906, 1,191, 1,314, 1,407, 1,427, 1,775, 1,843, 1,906, 1,981–1,982, and 2,032; Foner, "Reconstruction and the Crisis of Free Labor," in *Politics and Ideology in the Age of the Civil War* (New York: Oxford Univ. Press, 1980), 120; and *Nothing but Freedom: Emancipation and Its Legacy* (Baton Rouge: Louisiana State Univ. Press, 1983); Stanley L. Engerman, "Economic Adjustments to Emancipation in the United States and British West Indies," *Journal of Interdisciplinary History* 13 (1982): 192.

22. *Criminal Offences,* nos. 127, 128, 386, 557, 558, 904, 905, 906, 1,017, 1,190, 1,023, 1,281.

23. Ibid., nos. 316 and 324.

24. Ibid., nos. 205, 209, 200–201, 208, and 2,195.

25. Ibid., nos. 217, 320, 141, 321, 222, 229, 318–319, 474, 476, 77, 658, and 1,891; and nos. 219, 1,074, and 1,161.

26. Ibid., nos. 213, 243, 378, 484, 779, 446, 1,304–1,305, 1314, 1,885, 1,775, 2,275, 2,043, 193, 230, 244, 387, 410, 484, 525, 820, 1,146, 1,163, 1,553, 1,986, 2,042, 2,087, 228, 1,147, 1,828, 2,278, and 597. The reports also came from other states. Sara Baker of Panola, Texas, complained to the Shreveport, Louisiana, agent that she had never received any wages and that her employer had shot at her son and driven both off the farm ("Record of Complaints," Shreveport, vol. 44, 14 [June 25, 1866], Louisiana, RG 105).

27. Foner, "Reconstruction and Free Labor," 118. (The Texas planter is quoted on the same page, emphasis added.) These observations are based upon the material in notes 21 through 25. See also Roger L. Ransom and Richard Sutch, *One Kind of Freedom: The Economic Consequences of Emancipation* (Cambridge: Cambridge Univ. Press, 1977); Carl N. Degler, "Rethinking Post-Civil War History," *Virginia Quarterly Review* 57 (1981): 250–267; Smallwood, "Perpetuation of Caste: Black Agricultural Workers in Reconstruction Texas," *Mid-America* 61 (1979): 5–23.

28. *Criminal Offences,* nos. 199 and 241; C. Vann Woodward, "Not So Freed Men," *New York Review of Books,* Aug. 13, 1979, 8; Bertram Wilbur Doyle, *The Etiquette of Race Relations in the South: A Study in Social Control* (Chicago: Univ. of Chicago Press, 1937), 109–135; Bertram Wyatt-Brown, *Southern Honor: Ethics and Behavior in the Old South* (New York: Oxford Univ. Press, 1982), suggests how deeply embedded these beliefs were.

29. *Criminal Offences,* nos. 220, 233, 114, 102, 902, 199, 245, 1,672, 2,044, 2,045, 396, 1,189, 245, 1,614, 816, 1,721, and 1,672.

30. Ibid., nos. 441, 36, 412, 521, 582, 873, 1,657–1,662, 784, 282, 1,227, and 2,232.

31. Ibid., nos. 838, 1,133, 308. Other examples are nos. 140, 204, 274, 430, 485, 486, 517, 537, 584, 1,706, 1,151, 1,588, 1,653, 1,660, 1,664, 1,761, and 2,076. Some of these same mutilations were practiced during slavery.

32. Ibid., nos. 66, 1,185, 1,022, 1,020, 1,548, 2,077, 112, 178, 198, 324, 413, 526, 584, 1,017, 1,021, 1,101, 1,141, 1,185, 1,251, 1,281, 1,589, 1,731–1,733, and 1,940; A. F. Morse (agent, Waco) to J. B. Kiddoo (assistant commissioner, Texas), January 20, 1867, vol. 167, 5, 7, 9; also the correspondence about the castration case in vol. 165, 29, 31, 37, 39, 43.

33. *Criminal Offences,* nos. 157, 158, 210, 873, 2,168, 2,169, 2,170, 220, 241, 427–428, 445, 591, 592, 1,036, 1,433, 542, 702, 2,072, 1,552, 1,694, 1,736, 1,827, and 2,258. See also Smallwood, "The Black Community in Reconstruction Texas: Readjustments in Religion and Evolution of the Negro Church," *East Texas Historical Journal* 16 (1978): 16–28; "Black Education in Reconstruction Texas: The Contributions of the Freedmen's Bureau and Benevolent Societies," *East Texas*

Historical Journal 19, (1981): 17–40; "Early 'Freedom Schools': Black Self-Help and Education in Reconstruction—Texas, a Case Study," *Negro History Bulletin* 41 (1978): 790–793; Alton Hornsby, Jr., "The Freedmen's Bureau Schools in Texas, 1865–1970," *Southwestern Historical Quarterly* 76 (1973): 397–417.

34. *Criminal Offences,* nos. 199, 123, 265, 267, 536, 539, 556, 567, 596, 1,281, 1,894–1,901, 1,902, 2,004, 1,837–1,840, 1,201–1,204, 2,073–2,075, 2,082–2,085, 2,119, 2,124, 2,240–2,244, and 2,257; V. V. Smith (agent, Lewisville, Ark.) to Jonathan E. Bennett, November 30, 1867, Narrative Reports, assistant commissioner, LR-1593, Box 11, Arkansas, RG 105. See also C. C. Rister, "Outlaws and Vigilantes of the Southern Plains, 1865–1885," *Mississippi Valley Historical Review* 19 (1933): 538–545, 552–554; Boyd W. Johnson, "Cullen Montgomery Baker, The Arkansas-Texas Desperado," *Arkansas Historical Quarterly* 25 (1966): 229–239.

35. *Criminal Offences,* nos. 179, 1,104, 750, 265, 265, 266, 267, 692, 539, 264, 727, 281, 1,454, 736, 1,890, 1,334, 1,441, and 454; also nos. 139, 1,021, 1,296, and 1,297. See also George Calvin Rable, "Bourbonism, Reconstruction, and the Persistence of Southern Distinctiveness," *Civil War History* 29 (1983): 135–153.

36. Hennessey, "To Live and Die in Dixie," 77.

37. Sheridan to Rawlins, November 6, 1866, Sheridan Papers, Container 71; James E. Sefton, *The United States Army and Reconstruction, 1865–1877* (Baton Rouge: Louisiana State Univ. Press, 1967), 92; Smallwood, *Time of Hope,* 160. There is some information on state violence in Olsen, *Reconstruction and Redemption,* but not enough for comparisons, and most of it involves the period after 1872. Trelease's *White Terror* is a veritable state-by-state catalogue of southern lawlessness. Sefton claims that Louisiana was "unquestionably the most turbulent state in the whole South" from 1872 to 1877 (239). The number one ranking might be given Texas during 1865 to 1868.

Six   # CRISIS IN COLOR

Racial Separation in Texas during Reconstruction

BARRY A. CROUCH AND L. J. SCHULTZ

A s Winthrop D. Jordan has shown in his recent work, the white man's attitude toward the black did not originate in this country in 1619. The seeds of racial bias were planted even earlier, when Englishman first encountered African. These early English concepts flourished in America, bolstering and shoring up the "peculiar institution," and finally becoming identified as an inseparable part of it.[1] With this in mind, it hardly seems feasible that the Thirteenth Amendment would foster economic, social, or psychological conditions that would guarantee, or even encourage, mixing of the white and black races in the South. A purely legal prelude to civil and social equality simply would not erase the phenomenon of "white over black." The war was an intermission during, not an alteration of, a situation that had existed since the sixteenth century. The forces for racial polarization are not easily categorized under subheadings of politics, social customs, and the psychological effect of the Civil War.

The problem of determining the beginnings of racial separation is a continuing source of controversy among historians. Unquestionably, urban slavery, in both the North and South, gave rise to segregation, but the postwar period is open to interpretation. The major point of departure has been C. Vann Woodward's *The Strange Career of Jim Crow,* which places the establishment of segregation in the 1890s.[2] Others, ignoring Woodward's caution, have followed him almost blindly.[3] In the last decade, studies by Leon F. Litwack, V. Jacque Voegeli, Richard C. Wade, Joel Williamson, and most recently Roger A. Fischer, have questioned Woodward's essentially legal argument.[4] Racial barriers undoubtedly existed in Texas before and during the Civil War, but they emerged most clearly, not only psychologically but also legally, immediately afterward.

In 1865, there was no need for southern apologists versed in the defense of slavery. "Slavery" no longer existed, but the historical, biblical, scientific, economic, and sociological antebellum polemics were revived. Although the arguments had once served their purpose, the case had to be won anew. The institution had been stripped of its legal support, and the mind of the South bore an acute awareness that the old arguments were undergoing a severe test. Southerners, however, were perfectly confident that their inept black dependents would never rise to the occasion of accepting the responsibility of becoming a "freed man." To southerners, Texans not excepted, the freedman was simply a poor "nigger," out of place politically, socially, and economically. In November 1865, when many of the Negroes in Texas did not even know they were free, George W. Paschal expressed the new facts of life in a letter to the *Southern Intelligencer:*

> We have lost negro slavery; let us hope that, by prudence, we will have gained the liberty of conscience and the freedom of thought and speech for the white man, which have not been tolerated for a long time. . . .
>
> In saying that the negro is free, and that he must be allowed all the rights of a freedman, let none understand me as meaning, that he is thereby entitled to social equality and political equality at the polls. . . .
>
> All men who have ever observed the working of society know that even social equality depends upon so many natural and artificial laws that it can not be said to absolutely exist in any community. Everyone must take his social position according to the circumstances of his case. These depend less upon political laws than upon the developments of mind, moral deportment, avocation and taste.[5]

Paschal then pointed out that suffrage was not an inherent part of liberty.

The black man in his new role was to be pitied—and indeed he was. From the halls of Congress to the editorial pages of southern newspapers echoed the statement that he had been better off in his prewar servitude. The charge rang true, and it served as a prologue to the redefinition of the Negro's role in postwar southern society.

The Black Codes were the supposed underwriters of the new freedom. One historian contends that the South looked at the postwar codes "as vital protection for their women and children, the only practical method of inducing the freed Negro to support himself, and a generous softening of prewar legal controls of the free Negro."[6] A brief glance at any of the Black Codes, including the milder ones of Texas, demonstrates, however, that they went much further than reorienting the black man to his new role in southern society. In this context, one can hardly doubt the integrity of northern congressmen who at this time saw the codes as an extralegal attempt to again enslave the Negro.[7]

The 1866 bills dealing with civil rights and the Freedmen's Bureau were essentially a reaction to the codes. During the House debate over the first version of the latter bill, Ignatius Donnelly of Minnesota offered an amendment to provide "a common-school education to all refugees and freedmen who shall apply therefor." It was his belief that an education offered to the Negro would "fit him to protect himself in that not distant day when the [Freedmen's] bureau must necessarily be withdrawn." Donnelly further asserted:

> The enemies of the black man, those who opposed his liberation, now point to him and say, "See the condition to which you have reduced him. He is worse off than before. His race is perishing from the face of the earth under the innumerable miseries which liberty has inflicted upon it."[8]

The accusation was valid in some respects, but at least the freedman was free. Three months later, Colonel Caleb B. Forshey of Texas, in testimony before a congressional committee, stated: "I believe that so far from the black man's degradation by slavery, he was exalted by it, and that to the best condition he has ever enjoyed, and to the best of which, as a race, he is capable."[9]

On July 16, Congress passed a revised Freedmen's Bureau bill, which included an educational provision similar to Donnelly's, over Johnson's veto. Now Texas gentlemen were faced with the disconcerting possibility that their sons and daughters would have to share the same schoolrooms with former slaves. Their apprehension gave rise to the practice of racial separation in education, which would end only in 1954, with the *Brown vs. Board of Education* decision.

At this time there existed a strong fear that the new authorities in education would vindictively push integration of public schools upon an unwilling populace. In 1866, the *Brownsville Ranchero* came out for free schools for blacks, conducted at night. The schools were to be located in "proper localities." Thus, not only segregated classes, but also the removal of Negro schools from the proximity of whites was urged.[10]

In Austin and Galveston, the Methodist Church took up the education of Negroes and provided locations for the new schools. The black arm of the Methodist Church also advocated the establishment of day schools and the ordination of colored ministers to fill the new need for clergy- men for black congregations. In August 1866, the *Galveston Weekly News* praised the Negro Methodist Church in that city for recognizing the idea of separatism in religion. The article expressed satisfaction that the African Methodist had no desire whatsoever to unite with the white Southern Methodist Church.[11]

Although most Texans favored the denominational education of the freedmen, many still feared that the Radical government in Austin might not meet the situation in the same manner. In 1871, Colonel Jacob C. De- Gress, the military superintendent of public instruction, stated that he was placing the matter of mixed schools entirely in the hands of local school boards. The *Brenham Banner* breathed a sigh of relief in an article headlined "THE PUBLIC AND FREE SCHOOLS NOT TO BE MIXED." L. P. Rucker, president of the school directors for Washington County, passed his verdict by declaring:

> Information has been given already, both publically and in private conversations with prominent men in every town and neighborhood of the county that the Board of School Directors for this county has passed a unanimous resolution declaring that for the peace and success of the whole, separate schools should be established for the white and the colored pupils.[12]

Less than two weeks later the *Banner* reported that there were thirteen colored schools and twenty-seven white schools in operation. Evidently the president of the school board was defining a system that was already in operation.

It became common in the 1870s for newspapers to report the number of "free white" and "free colored" schools. In general, the attitude toward these educational ventures regarding the freedmen was not unkind. The pride in his educational progress was very similar to the paternal pride taken in these same black dependents prior to the war. Alternatives to free schools were always open, but the cost of tuition was prohibitive for poor whites as well as blacks. Even the threat or rumor of tuition was at times successful in stopping Negro attendance at schools intended for them.[13]

The Texas State Educational Convention met on January 1, 1873. In- cluded in the school system plan to be presented to the state legislature was the structure that lasted until 1954: "The boards of directors shall be fully empowered to make any separation of the pupils in their districts into separate schools, that the peace, harmony and success of the schools and the good of the whole may require." [14] Another resolution extended the racial separation to institutions of higher learning. It proposed: "That an institution for the higher instructions of the colored population and especially for the education of colored teachers, should be established by the Legislature." [15] Finally, practice had become statute.

In the cities, the black population usually had its own locale. In Austin, it was known as "Pleasant Hill." Located in the area east of Waller Creek, it contained between forty and fifty small houses "occasionally varied by a substantial stone residence." In general, Austin citizens were content with the progress being made in the little settlement, removed as it was from the rest of the city. By February 1872, the influx of residents into Pleasant Hill had given it the appearance of a military encampment, and many of the black inhabitants passed the winter in tents. They had their own community life, held their own camp meetings, and for the most part conducted their lives quite apart from the mainstream of life in Austin. [16]

Not all of the activities in Pleasant Hill met with the approval of the white residents of Austin, however. Complaints were frequently seen in the *Austin Democratic Statesman,* wherein a citizen was alarmed at the noise or disturbances that seemed to be daily routine in the black settlement. If any Negro resident of Pleasant Hill had business to conduct in the city proper, he had to be quick, alone, and discreet. Gatherings of "colored folk" were frowned upon, and their appearance in the city sometimes prompted enforcement of the vagrancy laws. Evidence exists that Pleasant Hill was not alone in Texas as an early ghetto prototype. Houston also had its "Freedmen's Town," and a local column in one Galveston paper refers to "negro dens," where Negro women congregated when they left their place of employment. [17]

C. Vann Woodward contends that "as a rule . . . Negroes were not aggressive in pressing their rights, even after they were assured . . . by law." He further states that there were very few attempts at entry into public lodging facilities due to the possible unpleasantness of a rebuff. [18] The fact remains, however, that in Texas the avenue of entry was not open even for trial acceptance. In 1875, the *Panola Watchman* recorded that the Civil Rights Bill "has played the devil with hotel men throughout the country."

> The Texas Senate has passed a bill taking the licenses off all hotels which make them private houses, and as they are thus

made private houses, the General Government will lose a
large revenue from this source, and proprietors of hotels can
admit whom they please as inmates.

If all the States will emulate the example set by Texas in
this matter, the civil rights bill will be a dead letter so far as
forcing the negro into bed with the white man when he is
traveling is concerned.[19]

Civil rights thus meant a black bedfellow, and the legislature had reacted
accordingly. The only acceptable black citizens were "respected by their
white neighbors—respected, because the negroes know their place, and
keep it."

Another tactic for keeping the Negro in his place was the vagrancy law.
Although the vagrancy laws under the Black Codes had been dissolved,
there was elation when General Oliver O. Howard, commissioner of the
Freedmen's Bureau, declared that vagrancy laws could be applied to the
Negro, provided they were not discriminatory. The Texas vagrancy law
stipulated that the first offense should be accompanied by work on public
projects for a period not to exceed one week, subsequent offenses being
punishable by terms not longer than three weeks. The order for arrest
might be issued "on the affidavit of three credible householders" of the
county. The law defined a vagrant as "an idle person without visible means
of support, and making no exertion to obtain a support by an honest employment." According to this definition, most freedmen could legally be
called vagrants. A vagrant might have the right to trial by jury, but little
evidence exists that the Negro had such recourse even in major criminal
cases.[20] As a matter of record, the more serious the crime, the higher the
possibility that the Negro might face trial by riotous tribunal.

The threat of the vagrancy laws was not lost upon black citizens. Vio-
lations and punishments occurred often and were fairly well publicized.
Constant requests from white citizens for stricter enforcement of the law
were seen in the local columns of the newspapers. On very few occasions were the vagrants classified as Negroes. One Austin citizen, however,
leaves no doubts as to the target of his complaint.

Has the city an ordinance against vagrancy? If not, one should
be passed and rigidly enforced. There are numbers of idle,
ragged, shiftless negroes who congregate on the street cor-
ners, loaf around all day, and prowl and steal at night, who, if

driven out of the city and forced into the country as tillers of the soil, would add to the wealth and productiveness of the country.[21]

There is no reason to believe the complaints went unheeded. In one instance a Negro man in Brenham was sentenced by a district court to two years in prison for stealing a bottle of whiskey. In another case, a black man in Austin had been thrown in jail because he had a headache and had stopped to rest. The case was complicated by the fact that the Negro said he was carrying fifty dollars at the time of the arrest and the officer said it was only fifteen.[22]

Further evidence of hostility between the races is found in a newspaper article entitled "Web Flanagan with His Arm Around a Big Black Nigger." It reported:

> The individual whose name heads this article is before the people of this district, as the nigger nominee for the senate. As a man, we have no unfriendly feelings toward him, but as a "little puny, political" squirt, made by the accidental force of circumstances, he justly deserves the contempt of the honest, intelligent and laboring people of the 5th District. . . . The Convention . . . composed partly of State Police and murderers, nominated Mr. Flanagan. . . .
>
> One Peter Choice said that he was glad he lived and that his old master was dead, and that he thanked God the day had come when he could walk over his grave. . . .
>
> Others were in the Convention who had committed crime and outrages upon the people of our Country, and to cap the whole thing, Cam Fitzhue, who some years ago castrated himself, and who it is said, threw his seed to the chickens in the yard, and who Maj. Flanagan said in a political speech he thanked God he could not perpetrate his species.[23]

Again, fraternization and political equality were construed to mean social equality, thus the charge that "R. Hillebrand has been putting himself on an equality with negroes by openly and publically drinking lager beer with them in Louis Schieek's saloon." It was quoted sequentially in no less than three newspapers in two states. Hillebrand, the state senator from Bastrop and Fayette counties, had even stated that he would have no objections should his daughter receive the attentions of, or even marry, one of the darker race.[24]

Indeed, Texas was not ready to accept the redefinition of the black man in southern society. To do so would be to dispense with those principles so long ago accepted as the foundations of slavery. The war had removed legal protection from these principles, but it had not removed the dogmatic acceptance of them. "Civil rights" was just another phrase for "black bedfellow," and Texans were in no mood for such sacrilege. In November 1865, the *Southern Intelligencer* carried an article warning that if the black infringement on white rights should result in a race war then

> the final result could not be doubted by any person capable
> of tracing causes to their legitimate consequences . . . the
> negroes would be subdued, the superior race would again
> assert its supremacy, and the people who had so multiplied in
> bondage, would, under their new condition of freedom, be
> forced to follow the retreating footsteps of the buffalo and the
> Indian.[25]

Underlying all antagonism and hostility between the races was the new political arena of the Reconstruction era. The political old guard of Texas was now aware that the black man was more than a threat to be physically controlled and racially separated. Now he was also in a position to exercise his franchise and win control over his white political foe. Political warfare had not yet singled him out for political emasculation, even if such a thing could have been carried out under Radical rule. Since he could not legally be disfranchised, nor subjugated to the legal monster of Jim Crow, he was made the target of racist attacks. Politics became overt displays of racism. Since the arguments could not be legislated, the appeal had to be made to emotion and to the principles that had shored up the old institution by proving satisfactorily to southerners that the inferior race was meant only to serve the superior one. Biblical and psychological arguments were again polished and put to new use. If the Democratic South were to unite, it would have to fly the white banner. Newspaper reports of Republican and Negro political meetings and rallies were composed of strings of racial cliches. In commenting on a Negro convention in Panola County, the *Watchman* stated with biblical allusion that "some dusky son of Ham moved Mr. Burbon Anderson, Democratic candidate for the Legislature, be elected chairman of the meeting."[26] Then, changing to a theme which had been an Anglo prejudice for three centuries, the report continues that the "ugliest and most apeish looking negro in the audience . . . was elected chairman."[27]

Whenever racial antagonism threatened to fade from public expression, a local, state, or national election breathed new life into it. The hostile attitude toward the "inferior race" and its Republican mentors was never left to run its own course. The psychological counterparts of this bitter feeling were many. The myths of the black man's sexual prowess and his longing for the white woman, products of the sixteenth century, once again carried racial hate into a new environment.

In *White over Black,* Jordan describes the pre-sixteenth-century use of color as seen in the *Oxford English Dictionary.* The connotations of white were, in part, virginity, innocence, purity, and perfect human beauty and health; qualities characterized by the color black included "deeply stained with dirt; soiled, dirty, foul . . . iniquitous, atrocious, horrible, wicked." Jordan writes that "no other colors so clearly implied opposition . . . no others were so frequently used to denote polarization." "White and black," Jordan says, "connoted purity and filthiness, virginity and sin, virtue and baseness, beauty and ugliness, beneficence and evil, God and the devil."[28]

In Reconstruction Texas, the psychological implications of the color white were revived. In the *Southern Intelligencer* appeared the headline "Symbolic Meaning of Color." Without citing a source, the article listed the significance of the colors white, yellow, blue, green, red, violet, and black, and then white with black:

> White was the emblem of light, religious purity, innocence, faith, joy and life. In the judge, it indicates integrity; in the sick man, humanity; in the woman chastity. . . .
>
> Black expressed the earth, darkness, mourning, wickedness, negation, death, and was appropriate to the Prince of Darkness. In some old illuminating manuscripts, Jesus in the temptation, wore a black robe. White and Black together signify purity of life, and mourning or humiliation.[29]

The black man found himself superimposed against a tableau of the southern belle and all the ideals of southern chivalry. It was ungentlemanly to follow any other course but that of white solidarity.

Articles that revived the fear of miscegenation were also circulated. One report even tried to prove that the percentage of white men sleeping with black women was greater in the North than in the South; the proof offered was the greater population of mulattoes and Negroes in the North.[30]

To accept the fact that segregation did not exist during this time in southern history would be to agree with *Plessy vs. Ferguson.* Between 1865 and 1876 in Texas, equality was doubtful, but separatism was definitely a fact of life. Public entertainment, public lodgings, and even most public streets were off-limits, or at least fraught with danger, for the black population. When public entertainment was held, blacks and whites attended separate functions; marriage announcements were reported as "white" or "colored"; and when a citizen advertised for domestic help, he usually specified black or white. Trial by jury was almost nonexistent for black citizens, and a dual standard of justice was present in almost all cases, especially in those involving vagrancy.[31]

Adding to the social stress of racial separation was the constant threat of violence against Negroes. In at least one case, racial polarization prompted the murder of a freedman, by his fellow blacks, for proclaiming himself a member of the Democratic Party. The effectiveness of white violence in preventing blacks from taking full advantage of their new citizenship should not be underrated. Recountings of whites murdering Negroes for overstepping their place were well publicized, and jailbreaks or escapes by whites who were apprehended in such cases were not infrequent.[32]

Probably the most brutal case of violence committed by whites came in the "Houston Massacre" on February 8, 1875. An armed band invaded Freedmen's Town during church services; twenty-five blacks were surrounded and slaughtered. "Stripping them of their coverings amid horrible jokes, and unfeeling laughter," a newspaper reported, "they disemboweled and quartered the poor victims, hanging them by the legs like hogs." A disgusted newspaper correspondent vented his indignation at the gruesome spectacle. He was appalled that the incident

> excited no comment from any of the ministers, no notice was taken of it in any of the congregations, save by a few men who, with glad and eager looks, left their pews, and a few women who, with smiles gave each other knowing nods.
>
> . . .
>
> [The Negroes were] slain in the broad open daylight of the Sabbath morning, within the incorporate limits of the city of 20,000 inhabitants, and not an official raised his hand to prevent it, or to arrest the perpetrators of the deed; not a citizen who raised his voice in protest.[33]

Underscoring the validity of the report is the fact that it appeared in a staunch Democratic paper. And whether the comment was true or not, one can be sure that the reporter's last words inspired a good amount of fear in the heart of the freedman: "This tale of murder is about as true as you hear of being committed on negroes in the South."[34]

One year earlier, almost to the day, the epitome of racial separation in Texas had been noted by the *Panola Watchman* in a statement by C. W. Butler. His arguments are infused with the accepted shibboleths of the day.

The Negro Question

Perhaps no question has so fully engrossed the mind of the American people for the past fourteen years. . . . But one thing we feel certain, and that is, that we would be far better off without them. This was almost the universal mind of the southern people at the close of the war.

In the section of his letter entitled "How to Get Rid of Them," Butler suggests: "Do not employ them, rent, lease or sell to them. This is a cheap and an easy way, with but little danger of having yankee bayonets bristling around us." In the final portion of his letter, "What Benefit Will It Be to Us?" Butler gives four main reasons, and in his polemic lies the embodiment of the separation of the races during this period.

1st. The further we are removed from the negro, the better. Who would want a negro for a bed-fellow, a roommate, a son-in-law or daughter-in-law? . . . God save me from such a situation.

The wider the space between us and the negro, the better for both. If the same room is too near, why not the same neighborhood, county, State, or United States? I greatly prefer that the ocean should divide us.

2nd. When the negroes get out of the way, the noble-hearted white man will take his place, and be our friend brother. . . . If it was certainly known that our county had not, nor would not have a negro in it, I imagine there would be a rush from our native, negro-ridden [*sic*] States . . . to be our neighbors.

3rd. Society would be better. Who would not live in a purely white settlement than a black one for good society, yea, or even a mixed one? Undoubtedly the purer the better.

4th. Our stock and property of every kind would be more secure. . . . Therefore, it would be worth more , and with the approving smile of kind heaven resting upon us, we would be far richer in purse and soul. Happy and contented, we would thank a kind heavenly Father, and move forward to join the white-robed in the celestial land.[35]

The politics of the day were those of white supremacy, and they were inextricable from the social feelings of the time. Political, civil, and social equality were seen as one, and the resultant racial hostility bred withdrawal by both factions. The generally accepted thesis that mixing of the races was common practice during Reconstruction, at least in Texas, is not borne out in fact. In summary, then, it might be said that racial separation in Texas did not wait until the decade of *Plessy vs. Ferguson* to solidify. Rather, it was a basic fact of life during the years 1865 to 1877.

NOTES

1. Winthrop D. Jordan, *White over Black: American Attitudes toward the Negro, 1550–1812* (Chapel Hill: Univ. of North Carolina Press, 1968), and Jordan, *The Negro versus Equality, 1762–1826* (Chicago: Rand McNally, 1969). See too, Joel Williamson's review of *White over Black* in *American Scholar* 38 (Spring 1969): 339–341. One might also profit from Thomas F. Gossett, *Race: The History of an Idea in America* (Dallas: Southern Methodist Univ. Press, 1963); William Stanton, *The Leopard's Spots: Scientific Attitudes toward Race in America, 1815–1859* (Chicago: Univ. of Chicago Press, 1960); John C. Greene, "The American Debate on the Negro's Place in Nature, 1780–1815," *Journal of the History of Ideas* 15 (June 1954): 384–396.

2. Although Woodward does discuss social and psychological attitudes, his thesis is primarily economic; see *The Strange Career of Jim Crow*, 2nd rev. ed. (New York: Oxford Univ. Press, 1966); *Origins of the New South, 1877–1913* (Baton Rouge: Louisiana State Univ. Press, 1951), 205–212; and *Reunion and Reaction: The Compromise of 1877 and the End of Reconstruction* (Boston: Little, Brown, 1966), in which he acknowledges his debt to Charles A. Beard.

3. John S. Ezell *The South since 1865* (New York, 1963); Charles Crowe, ed., *The Age of Civil War and Reconstruction, 1830–1900: A Book of Interpretative Essays* (Homewood, Ill., 1966), 549; Barton J. Bernstein, "*Plessy v. Ferguson:* Conservative Sociological Jurisprudence," *Journal of Negro History* 48 (July 1903): 190–205.

4. Leon F. Litwack, *North of Slavery: The Negro in the Free States, 1790–1860* (Chicago, 1961); V. Jacque Voegeli, *Free but Not Equal: The Midwest and the Negro during the Civil War* (Chicago and London, 1967); Voegeli, "The Northwest and the Race Issue, 1861–1862," *Mississippi Valley Historical Review* 50 (Sept. 1963): 235–251; Richard C. Wade, *Slavery in the Cities: The South, 1820–1860* (New York, 1964); Joel Williamson, *After Slavery: The Negro in South Carolina During Reconstruction, 1861–1877* (Chapel Hill: Univ. of North Carolina Press, 1965); Williamson, *The Origins of Segregation* (Boston, 1968); Roger A. Fischer, "Racial Segregation in Ante-Bellum New Orleans," *American Historical Review* 74 (Feb. 1969): 926–937; Fischer, "A Pioneer Protest: The New Orleans Street-Car Controversy of 1867," *Journal of Negro History* 53 (July 1968): 219–233. See also Vernon L. Wharton, *The Negro in Mississippi, 1865–1890* (Chapel Hill: Univ. of North Carolina Press, 1947); Charles E. Wynes, *Race Relations in Virginia, 1870–1902* (Charlottesville: Univ. of Virginia Press, 1961). James M. McPherson expresses a different idea in his review of Williamson's *After Slavery* in *Journal of Negro History* 50 (July 1965): 210–212.

5. *Austin Southern Intelligencer,* Aug. 11 and Nov. 16, 1865. Returning from Washington, Judge Paschal also stated that part of the terms for the readmission of Texas was to "recognize the rights of the negro as a freeman, not implying thereby the social equality of the negro with the white, or his equality at the polls" (*New Orleans Daily Picayune,* Dec. 8, 1865); William S. McFeely, *Yankee Stepfather: General O. O. Howard and the Freedmen* (New Haven: Yale Univ. Press, 1968), 68, 160; Fawn M. Brodie, *Thaddeus Stevens: Scourge of the South* (New York, 1959), 235.

6. Theodore B. Wilson, *The Black Codes of the South* (University, Ala., 1965), p. 139.

7. McFeely writes that "In February 1866 Texas could draft a 'more liberal' black code than those enacted in some other cotton states, because the Bureau in Texas had already established strict vagrancy rules" (*Yankee Stepfather,* 153). Charles Ramsdell, *Reconstruction in Texas* (New York: Columbia Univ. Press, 1910), 100–101; W. C. Nunn, *Texas under the Carpetbaggers* (Austin, 1962), 7–8; Kenneth M. Stampp, *The Era of Reconstruction, 1865–1877* (New York, 1965), 78–79; Rembert W. Patrick, *The Reconstruction of the Nation* (New York, 1967), 45; cf. Edgar P. Sneed, "A Historiography of Reconstruction in Texas: Some Myths and Problems," *Southwestern Historical Quarterly* 72 (Apr. 1969): 438. For the integrity of northern congressmen, consult Hans L. Trefousse, *The Radical Republicans: Lincoln's Vanguard for Racial Justice* (New York, 1969), 321–322, 324; LaWanda and John H. Cox, "Negro Suffrage and Republican Politics: The Problem of Motivation in Reconstruction Historiography," *Journal of Southern History* 33 (Aug. 1967): 303–330.

8. Marion M. Miller, ed., *Great Debates in American History* (New York, 1913) 7:185; Martin Ridge, *Ignatius Donnelly: The Portrait of a Politician* (Chicago and London, 1962), 102; Eric L. McKitrick, *Andrew Johnson and Reconstruction* (Chicago, 1960), 274–325.

9. *Galveston Weekly News,* May 9, 1866. H. C. Smith, a Negro, probably best expressed the idea of freedom: "In speaking for myself I speak for every colored man I know, and I say that freedom, in poverty and in trials and tribulations, even amidst the most cruel prejudices, is sweeter than the best fed or the best clothed slavery in the world" (*San Antonio Express,* Sept. 23, 1867).

10. *Brownsville Ranchero,* as cited in the *Galveston Weekly News,* Dec. 7, 1866. And see the *Austin Tri-Weekly State Gazette,* June 24, 1868. The aims of the *Gazette* were to make "uncompromising warfare upon Radicalism in every shape and under every disguise, opposing negro suffrage, negro juries and negro office-holding to the last" (Apr. 29, 1868); *Harrison Flag,* June 21, 1866; *Flake's Bulletin* (Galveston), Feb. 16, 1868.

11. *New Orleans Crescent* as cited in the *Galveston Weekly News,* Apr. 25 and Aug. 1, 1866; *Marshall Texas Republican,* Oct. 20 and Nov. 24, 1865; *Austin Southern Intelligencer,* Mar. 14, 1867; *Austin Democratic Statesman,* July 29 and Sept. 19, 1871; *Corpus Christi Nueces Valley,* Aug. 31, 1872.

12. *Brenham Banner,* Sept. 1 and 12, 1871. Colored school attendance was given as male, 240, female, 265.

13. *Corpus Christi Nueces Valley,* Mar. 9 and July 20, 1872. The number of white students was given as 200, colored, 75; *Galveston Weekly News* as quoted in the *Brenham Banner,* Oct. 12, 1866; and *Banner,* Feb. 1871 to Jan. 1875. Rates for the select schools ran from about $2.50 to $5.00 a month. The *Austin Democratic Statesman,* Sept. 3, 1871, and Sept. 12, 1871, recorded the opening of a new colored school for boys, but very few pupils came, probably resulting "from the report having in some way become circulated that those who sent their children would have to pay tuition." A new school for black girls was also held in the colored Methodist church (*Austin Southern Intelligencer,* Jan. 24 and Feb. 14, 1867). The *New York Times* reported there were 16,000 Negroes attending schools in Texas (Apr. 1, 1866).

14. *Austin Democratic Statesman,* Jan. 1, 1873. An education separation bill had passed the state senate in 1871 (*Flake's Bulletin* [Galveston], Apr. 1, 1871); and see the *Austin Tri-Weekly State Gazette,* June 24, 1868.

15. *Austin Democratic Statesman,* Jan. 1, 1873.

16. Ibid., Aug. 29 and 31, 1871; Feb. 8 and July 2, 1872.

17. Ibid., Feb. 13, Aug. 29, and Sept. 10, 1872; *Panola Watchman,* Feb. 24, 1875; *Galveston Weekly News,* Sept. 26, 1866. See the *Austin Tri-Weekly State Gazette,* Oct. 25, 1867, for comment on the *Forum Africanum,* where the Negroes congregated.

18. Woodward, *Strange Career of Jim Crow,* 28.

19. *Panola Watchman,* Mar. 10 and Aug. 4, 1875.

20. *Austin Southern Intelligencer,* Nov. 9, 1865; *Panola Watchman,* Sept. 2, 1874. Whites broke into a jail in Center City and hanged two Negroes. After the outrage had been committed, a public meeting was held to denounce it. See also

John A. Carpenter, *Sword and Olive Branch: Oliver Otis Howard* (Pittsburgh, 1964), 135; James E. Sefton, *The United States Army and Reconstruction, 1865–1877* (Baton Rouge: Louisiana State Univ. Press, 1967), 147–148.

21. *Austin Democratic Statesman*, Feb. 15, 1872; *Brenham Banner*, Feb. 1871 to Jan. 1875, especially Nov. 30, 1871, and Mar. 1, 1873; *Galveston Weekly News*, Sept. 1, 1873.

22. *Brenham Banner*, June 7, 1873; *Austin Democratic Statesman*, Oct. 21, 1871.

23. *Henderson Times* as quoted in the *Panola Watchman*, Nov. 12, 1873.

24. *LaGrange New Era*, citing the *New Orleans Weekly Picayune*, and finally quoted in the *Austin Democratic Statesman*, Aug. 10, 1871.

25. *Austin Southern Intelligencer*, quoting the *New York Times*, Nov. 30, 1865.

26. *Panola Watchman*, Nov. 5, 1873. In the article, another note of antagonism appeared when the paper reported the "nigger . . . Stephen Brown . . . made a disconnected, nonsensical talk of some half to three quarters of an hour in length, the substance of which was that the white folks were not capable of making laws for the poor nigger, and thought that the Legislature ought to be composed equally of whites and blacks." For Negroes in Texas conventions see Stampp, *Era of Reconstruction*, 169; Patrick, *Reconstruction of the Nation*, 112; Forrest G. Wood, *Black Scare: The Racist Response to Emancipation and Reconstruction* (Berkeley and Los Angeles: Univ. of California Press, 1968), 119. A report of Negroes meeting and planning to take over Alabama, Mississippi, Louisiana, and Texas can be found in William C. Harris, *Presidential Reconstruction in Mississippi* (Baton Rouge: Louisiana State Univ. Press, 1967), 90.

27. *Panola Watchman*, Nov. 5, 1873. On the theory of Ham and the association of the ape with the Negro, see Jordan, *White over Black*, 17–20, 28–32.

28. Jordan, *White over Black*, 7. See also John Hope Franklin, ed., *Color and Race* (Boston: Houghton Mifflin, 1968).

29. *Austin Southern Intelligencer*, Oct. 26, 1865.

30. *Galveston Weekly News*, July 4, 1866. The article was entitled "The Mingling of the Races North and South." Also, see the *Houston Times* as quoted in the *Brenham Banner*, Dec. 14, 1871, and the *Banner*, Apr. 30, 1875, which reported that Matt Gaines, a prominent Negro legislator, was taken into custody by the sheriff of Fayette County for stating that the colored population might marry whomever they pleased; Wood, *Black Scare*, 152.

31. *Galveston Weekly News*, June 13 and Sept. 12, 1866; *Panola Watchman*, July 1873 and Mar. 31, 1875; *Austin Democratic Statesman*, Nov. 16, 1871. In at least one election, the certificates issued to Negroes had "written on the back in red the words, 'colored voter'" (*Austin Southern Intelligencer*, June 8, 1867).

32. The amount of violence in Texas during this period is truly staggering. One finds atrocity stories in almost any newspaper. For representative examples, see the *Panola Watchman*, Nov. 19, 1873, and Sept. 9, 1874; *Galveston Weekly News*, Oct. 5, 1866, and Feb. 1, 1867; McFeely, *Yankee Stepfather*, 69, 207; Sefton, *Army and Reconstruction*, 54, 92, 95, 191, 193; Carpenter, *Sword and Olive Branch*, 128,

130; Brodie, *Thaddeus Stevens,* 328; Otis A. Singletary, *Negro Militia and Reconstruction* (Austin: Univ. of Texas Press, 1957), 9, 18; W. R. Brock, *An American Crisis. Congress and Reconstruction, 1865–1867* (New York: St. Martin's, 1963), 184; Claude Elliott, "The Freedmen's Bureau in Texas," *Southwestern Historical Quarterly* 56 (July 1952), 1–24; Ann P. Baenziger, "The Texas State Police during Reconstruction: A Reexamination," *Southwestern Historical Quarterly* 72 (Apr. 1969), 470–491; Robert W. Shook, "The Federal Military in Texas, 1865–1870," *Texas Military History* 6 (Spring 1967), 3–53; and compare E. Merton Coulter, *The South during Reconstruction, 1865–1877* (Baton Rouge: Louisiana State Univ. Press, 1947), 117–118.

33. *Panola Watchman,* Feb. 24, 1875. The headline read "Terrible Massacre at Houston, Texas—Twenty-five Blacks Weltering in Blood!!"

34. Ibid. For accounts of the massacres at Millican and Hempstead, see *New Orleans Daily Picayune,* June 18, 1868; *Austin Tri-Weekly State Gazette,* July 22, 1868; *San Antonio Express,* July 19 and 24, 1868; *Flake's Bulletin* (Galveston), Jan. 18, 1868.

35. *Panola Watchman,* Feb. 11, 1874. Although he does not deal with the Reconstruction period, Lawrence D. Rice in "The Negro in Texas, 1874–1900" (PhD diss., Texas Technological College, 1967), in part supports the findings in this article. Rice states that "despite the absence of Jim Crow laws until the 1890s there arose during Reconstruction a definite pattern of segregation in the social contacts of the races, a pattern which was to increase in rigidity in succeeding years" (411). See also Robert Cruden, *The Negro in Reconstruction* (Englewood Cliffs, N.J.: Prentice-Hall, 1969).

Seven

"ALL THE VILE PASSIONS"

The Texas Black Code of 1866

Surveying the state literature on the Civil War and Re-construction, Randolph B. Campbell observed that Texas's versions of the infamous black codes of 1865–1866 have been defended as models of discretion compared to those adopted in other states, but the very existence of such legislation indicates that Texans did not mean to accord blacks equality before the law.[1] Although increasing attention has been paid to Texas history during the post–Civil War years, little has focused upon the passage of the black codes, what they portended for the Reconstruction status of the Lone Star State, and whether these enactments really embodied a spirit of judiciousness toward the recently emancipated slaves.

Scholars of Texas history have alluded to and briefly mentioned the substance of the 1866 black code, but they have not analyzed it in detail or included in their discussions the various other statutes that reinforced the code and additionally limited black rights and equality. Until the 1980s, with few exceptions, writers on the Texas experience believed the Texas laws to be rather mild and more favorably disposed toward blacks than those of any other southern state. Recently, Texas historians have revised previous interpretations of the code, but their discussions have tended to be brief and to follow past ideas with a slightly different twist, blaming the army and the Freedmen's Bureau.

Because the 1866 Texas black code has been viewed as an anomaly, it is necessary to set the laws in context and analyze them. First, by briefly scrutinizing past perspectives on the code, we can ascertain how Texas Re-construction historiography has perceived them. Second, through a short discussion of the political and economic situation at the time the Texas legislature passed these statutes, the reasons for their passage become clear. Finally, a dissection of the laws themselves and of how they attempted to regulate and coerce black Texans demonstrates that the state's politicians intended to circumscribe severely the freedmen's constitutional rights and maintain a stable laboring force.

The southern black codes were a series of laws directly or indirectly applied to the former slaves and passed by the states of the defeated Confederacy. Enacted between the close of the Civil War in 1865 and the imposition of Congressional Reconstruction in early 1867, the statutes dealt with labor and contracts, apprenticeship, vagrancy, enticement, domestic relations, property holding, court testimony, litigation procedures, criminal penalties, convict leasing, and numerous other aspects of the freedpeople's lives. Designed to restrain and control the free blacks, they penalized, fined, and imprisoned them for the slightest transgression.[2]

Nineteenth-century Texas writers, some of whom had been participants in the events they wrote about, found the black codes necessary. Charles Stewart, a former Texas congressman, claimed that the 1866 convention and subsequent legislature followed presidential and congressional requirements, which included providing for the "future education of the negroes; for the equal preservation of their lives, liberty and property, and for the bestowal of other rights and privileges upon them." Oran M. Roberts believed that emancipation "made it incumbent upon the Legislature to endeavor to regulate the conduct and control of a large body of persons, who had heretofore been provided for, taken care of, and governed for the most part by the owners."[3]

A majority of Texas historians have viewed the black codes in a similar vein. Charles W. Ramsdell saw the laws as "harsh and stringent," but thought them "necessary both for the good conduct and for the protection of the negroes for whom alone [they were] intended." Seth Shepard McKay considered them merely "toned down" versions of antebellum legislation. T. R. Fehrenbach declared the code essential, since blacks "delighted in taking no orders, a perfectly human reaction after years of forced labor." Ernest Wallace wrote that the legislature saw the codes as "imperative" and that they did not "offend the radicals." John C. McGraw found the codes "absolutely necessary" because of the "total irresponsibility and depravity" of blacks in 1866.[4]

Joe B. Frantz, in his brief bicentennial history of the state, stated that the 1866 Constitution as "a whole treated blacks more generously than the fundamental law of any other state of the recent Confederacy," but the labor code was a "subterfuge for keeping the black in some sort of peonage." Like Frantz, Nora E. Owens insists that the 1866 Texas constitution "gave more specific guarantees to blacks than did any other state,"

although the code, while less severe and "much less rigid" than those imposed by other former Confederate states, was nevertheless discriminatory.
Finding the laws generally lenient, with the exception of the contract provision, John P. Carrier states that they avoided "most of the more obvious
abuses" of earlier legislation.[5]

Winnell Albrecht, in the most comprehensive treatment of the code,
asserted that the freedmen received "more rights and privileges and their
welfare was more fully protected in Texas than in any other Southern
state." Despite the "vindictiveness against the North and the prevailing
prejudice against the colored race, so evident in the Senate and House
Journals and in most of the state's newspapers, the legislators were discreet
in their final decisions, giving to the state a Black Code which they felt was
both fair and workable." Examining the legislative process reveals that the
lawmakers curbed a "large number of unacceptable actions on the part of
the laborer," representing "another victory for the moderate view."[6]

From a broader historiographical perspective, Theodore Brantner Wilson, in 1965, expressed the prevailing view of the 1866 constitutional convention and the Eleventh Legislature when he described the members
as "paragons of discretion." He concluded that the constitution "spelled
out more specific guarantees" for blacks "than did any" of the previous
southern conventions. Protecting them "in all their rights of person and
property," it allowed their testimony "in all cases in which Negroes were
interested parties" and gave them "equal access to the courts." Criminal
prosecutions against former slaves would be conducted in the same manner as those against whites, and similar penalties would apply equally to
both races.[7]

William L. Richter wrote that the "Black Codes have been attacked
by recent historians, but they were an honest attempt by the legislature,
blinded as it was by racial prejudice, to make what it thought was a workable system of free labor." He posited that because the Texas government
did not reorganize until 1866, "she benefitted from Northern criticism
leveled at Black codes passed by other Southern states." Planters observed
that "no civil law dealt with the blacks as freedmen"; the Freedmen's Bureau was too temporary, irregular, and, he should have added, sympathetic
to depend upon, and employers thought "some form of compulsory black
labor was necessary." These attitudes found legal recognition in the code.[8]

In Richter's eyes, the Eleventh Legislature simply codified "army orders" and bureau promulgations. Thus, both agencies "helped entrench
the lien and sharecropping system in agriculture" and promoted vagrancy
laws in order to force blacks to work. Absolving the legislature of any

underhanded intentions, Richter actually blamed the stringent statutes on the intrusion of outside forces that promoted the concept of national sovereignty. The legislators desired to clarify blacks' role in society so they could attract white immigrants. They were searching, in Richter's phrase, for a "practical alternative" to black labor.[9]

Subsequently, Richter found the laws to be more "complex" than their denouncers would have us believe. Richter implies that by repealing all prewar legislation involving slaves and free blacks and making the code nondiscriminatory, the legislature acted magnanimously and simply followed bureau guidelines with a little "more vigor." He did admit that the punishment provision of the contract law "smacked of slavery under another guise." The "horror the new laws aroused in Union ranks was probably more the product of who wrote them than what they said," Richter concluded, "although some farsighted loyalists realized that a black population controlled by peonage could not deliver a reliable bloc vote in the future."[10]

In 1969, Edgar P. Sneed contended that myth had pervaded and prejudiced the writing of Texas Reconstruction history. The "euphemistic explanation" often given for why the Eleventh Legislature found it necessary to pass the black codes involved the preservation argument. White Texans may have regarded these laws as necessary to establish stability and protection from the freedmen. But as a "historical judgment of the true nature of the black codes and of Texan motives," Sneed asserted, this interpretation is "subject to grave doubt." White conduct toward blacks in 1866 "simply will not substantiate the professed motives for enacting the codes. Against whom did Negroes require protection?" he asked.[11]

Few Texas Reconstruction writers have dissented from the older viewpoints or grappled with Sneed's question. Historians who have discussed these laws, observed James M. Smallwood, have "praised the Texas legislature's codes as more liberal than those of other Southern states." But the assemblymen "publicly admitted that they intended the proscriptions to apply exclusively to blacks." The nondiscriminatory aspect veiled their obnoxiousness. Walter T. Chapin agreed. The code intended to "insure" that blacks "would remain a cheap, docile, and disciplined source of labor," he wrote. The laws were "exacting," and whites could provide "additional coercions" to a "politically powerless, physically defenseless people."[12]

Revisionists have begun in a small way to respond to past interpretations and Sneed's query. Alwyn Barr wrote that even though the code was "based in part on labor, vagrancy, and apprenticeship laws used also in the North," the laws "left employers so much discretion and control that conditions under them in some ways would approximate slavery." Campbell, in *A Southern Community in Crisis,* stated that the "Negro worker was placed in a position as near to slavery as a free man might be." Indeed, the Texas code was "in the class with the infamous Black Codes created earlier in other southern states which added to the determination of Radical Republicans in Congress to block Presidential Reconstruction." [13]

Smallwood has taken the most extensive revisionist look at the code. Presaging Richter's argument, he found that the legislators, "influenced by white public opinion" and "guided by army and bureau precedents," considerably modified (Richter's "vigor") the bureau's labor policy "because most local agents tended to be fair with blacks." They also desired the agency's removal. Comparable to the Alabama and Louisiana codes, the statutes "certainly proved to be oppressive and in violation of the Civil Rights Act of 1866." The legislature "intended the proscriptions to apply exclusively to blacks." Other extensions to the basic apprenticeship, contract, and vagrancy provisions reinforced the blacks' inferior status. [14]

In summary, earlier writers believed the code to be necessary to regulate, monitor, and control black labor. A newer generation of historians found the various laws to be moderate, discretionary, and, even if unwise politically, certainly offering a "practical alternative" to the response of other southern states to black freedom. In addition, some found the army and the bureau responsible for providing a basis for the code through their pronouncements and policies. These historians thus absolve the legislature of much of its political ineptitude in enacting a black code that was especially harsh, restrictive, and stringent, whether considered on its own merits or compared to previous laws.

To stimulate a resurgence of southern loyalty, President Andrew Johnson desired to bring the defeated states back into the Union as quickly as possible. Therefore, he never enunciated precise and clear terms upon which the South would be readmitted. A discussion of some possibilities, which included the removal of the Freedmen's Bureau and the cessation of martial law—if southerners protected and provided good treatment to the freedmen and demonstrated that they were, in fact, law-abiding—became part of a wide-ranging debate. Misreading Johnson's intentions, Texas conservatives believed they could blithely ignore his recommendations and what other southern states had done in 1865 and early 1866, and deal with the freedmen in their own way. [15]

Because of the ambiguity in the requirements for readmission to the Union, the South defined the former slaves as inferior individuals with few basic rights. Actually, the enactment of the black codes occurred in two stages. The first series of laws relating to the freedpeople appeared before the passage of the Civil Rights Act of 1866 and came out of South Carolina, Mississippi, Alabama, Louisiana, and Florida. The actions of these legislatures, according to Daniel J. Flanigan, "gave ample evidence as to Southerners' intentions concerning blacks if left unmolested by national authority." Only the pressure of northern public opinion, the army, and the Freedmen's Bureau prevented them from passing even more draconian measures.[16]

Although still a states' righter at heart, John H. Reagan, the former Confederate postmaster general, in his famous Fort Warren letter and in his open missive to the people of Texas, understood more definitively than local Texas politicians what the North required. To be readmitted, the state had to recognize the authority of the United States government and the abolition of slavery. But even this might fail to attain the desired results "unless provision shall be made, by the new State government, for conferring the elective franchise on the former slaves," albeit with an intellectual, moral, and property qualification. Texas might also have to accept the admissibility of blacks' testimony on the same condition as whites'.[17]

Provisional governor Andrew J. Hamilton supported Reagan's viewpoint and urged the constitutional-convention delegates to fully protect and provide for freedmen's civil rights. To do otherwise "would procrastinate our return to our original position in the Union." From published circulars and newspaper articles, Hamilton had "reason to apprehend" that his views would not be acceptable to the convention majority. He warned "of the evil results which may be expected to follow any system of legislation in the Southern States, intended to operate only upon the freedmen, and to keep them in a condition of necessary dependence upon their former masters, at the same time that their nominal freedom is acknowledged."[18]

Meeting in February 1866, the Texas Constitutional Convention did not deal extensively with the rights and privileges of the emancipated slaves. The increasing split between the president and Congress left the future course of Reconstruction in limbo. The delegates undoubtedly also clearly believed that these matters should come under the purview of the legislature, so they considered the freedmen only cursorily. Refusing to ratify the Thirteenth Amendment, since African slavery had been "terminated" by "force of arms" and "its re-establishment being prohibited," they declared that bond or involuntary servitude could not exist except as punishment for a crime of which the party had been duly convicted.[19]

The constitution guaranteed that blacks would be "protected in their rights of person and property by appropriate legislation." Granted the right to enter into contracts, sue, and be sued, they could buy, sell, and convey property. Criminal prosecutions brought against them would be similar to those brought against whites, with blacks subject to "like" penalties. Blacks could testify in any civil or criminal case involving an injury or crime against *their* persons or property under rules of evidence applicable to whites. They could testify "in all other cases" under proscribed regulations "as to facts hereafter occurring." The constitution left for the legislature to specify what rules would surround black testimony.[20]

If Gov. James W. Throckmorton did not encourage the legislature to restrict black freedom and civil rights, he nonetheless supported what it planned to do. He wrote to his friend Benjamin Epperson in late 1865: "I am sure we will not be allowed even to contend for gradual emancipation [long after black freedom had become an established fact] [b]ut I do believe we will be enabled to adopt a coercive system of labor." He refused to entertain the thought of providing black Texans with any other rights, such as testifying, because this would lead the "hellhounds of radicalism" to demand for blacks the right to sit on juries, enfranchisement, and "finally to perfect social and political equality."[21]

In addressing the legislature, Throckmorton stressed frontier defense and called for the removal of the Freedmen's Bureau and the occupation forces. He encouraged minimal legal protection for the freedpeople to achieve this end. Well-satisfied Texans would "do justice to the freedmen," but Throckmorton felt that "there has been a laxity in enforceing [sic] the laws; not particularly as to this class of people, but generally, that requires the serious consideration of the law-abiding power of the government." Texans should bear with the freedmen's "foibles and make charitable allowance for the want of industry and steadiness of purpose manifested by the great mass of them," for they were "not answerable for our late civil war and national calamities."[22]

Throckmorton was neither as politically astute as past and present historians have made him out to be nor as dedicated to protecting Unionists and blacks as some writers have suggested. A basically mean-spirited man who laid the blame for Texas's troubles on the Republicans, he made little attempt to influence the legislature. By complaining that he had no control over their deliberations and capitulating to their actions in regard to black Texans, Throckmorton did not understand the depth of Northern emotion, and this failure paved the way for his removal a year later. His unwillingness to compromise and his deeply ingrained bias against blacks ensured that the legislature would enact a black code as severe as those passed by other states in 1865.[23]

The Eleventh Legislature had been in session for over a month when it commenced deliberations about the freedpeople. Within two weeks it had established a black code comparable in every way to previous Southern legislation. On October 27, 1866, it approved a lien law and an apprenticing statute. On November 1, it enacted an enticing law relating to laborers and apprentices, and five days later it moved to a gun-restriction law and an all-encompassing labor code, which irrevocably tied blacks to the land. On November 8, vagrancy legislation further limited black rights. Passed separately, these laws collectively became the Texas black code. They never mentioned race, but the freedmen were their sole focus.[24]

Similar to state statutes in Alabama, Mississippi, the Carolinas, and Tennessee, the Texas laws defined black rights, as had the 1866 constitution. Determining that persons with one-eighth or more "African blood" (i.e., with at least one black great-grandparent) were Negroes, the law granted them the ability to enter into and "enforce contracts, to sue and be sued, to inherit, purchase, lease, hold, sell, and convey real, personal and mixed estate." They could also make "wills and testaments." Empowered to "enjoy the rights of personal security, liberty, and private property," they were now subject to all "remedies and proceedings for the protection and enforcement of the same." No discrimination would exist "in the administration" of the state criminal laws.[25]

The legislature prohibited blacks from marrying whites or testifying against them, serving on juries, holding office, voting, homesteading on the public domain, and serving in the militia, and confined public education to white children. It provisionally authorized the Board of Managers to purchase twenty-six acres of land for a "Lunatic Asylum" for the benefit of "Insane Negroes," if it was deemed "expedient" to do so. They set aside ten thousand dollars to buy the property and make improvements. A nascent Jim Crow law required each passenger train to attach one car "for the special accommodation of Freedmen."[26] But the heart of the 1866 black code consisted of the labor, vagrancy, and apprenticing statutes.

The contract (labor) law declared that any person desiring to work for longer than one month had to sign a written agreement in the presence of a justice of the peace, county judge or clerk, notary public, or "two disinterested witnesses," to be read aloud to the laborer. It had to be signed in triplicate and would be in effect for the specified time. A copy would be filed and signed by the county court clerk in the county where the employer resided, with an endorsement verifying the date. For a fee of twenty-five cents, the particulars would be entered alphabetically in a book, showing names, date of filing, and duration. Disputes would be "decided before a court of competent jurisdiction" with the power to enforce its decisions.[27]

Every laborer had "full and perfect liberty to choose" an employer within a specified deadline (which basically nullified any attempt at negotiation by the worker), but once the employee made his decision, he would not be allowed to leave until the contract had been fulfilled. In an effort to force black women and children back into the field, the law also stipulated that agreements could be made only "with the heads of families," embracing the labor of all the members and "binding on all minors." It could be terminated only by the employer's consent or by harsh treatment or breach of contract on his part. If a laborer quit "without cause or permission," he forfeited all wages.[28]

The longest section (9) of the contract law dealt with the governance of laborers. The worker had to "obey all proper orders" of the employer or agent and "take proper care" of all stock animals and agricultural implements. The employer had the right to "make a reasonable deduction" from the laborer's wages for injuries to animals or breakage of tools, or "for bad or negligent work." Disobedience was defined as "failing to obey reasonable orders, neglect of duty, leaving home without permission, impudence, swearing or indecent language to, or in the presence of" the employer, his family, or agent, or "quarrelling and fighting" with another laborer. A fine of one dollar would be imposed for every such action.[29]

For lost time without the employer's permission (unless due to sickness), the laborer paid a fine of twenty-five cents an hour. For absence without leave, the employer could fine the worker two dollars a day, "fines to be denounced at the time of the delinquency." Although not required to labor on the Sabbath, employees had to take "necessary care of stock" and other property on the plantation or do the required cooking and household chores "unless by special contract for work of necessity." Further limitations on the freedpeople's independence provided that workers could neither have livestock without the employer's consent nor receive visitors during working hours.[30]

The laborer could be dismissed for "gross misconduct," which the legislature defined as "disobedience, habitual laziness, frequent acts of violation of their contracts, or the laws of the State." The employer settled all difficulties arising with the employee and imposed all fines, although the lawmakers did grant the freedmen the right of appeal to the nearest justice of the peace and two freeholders (citizens), one to be chosen by the employer and one by the worker. The decision of this three-person tribunal was final. Even if the laborer had a legitimate complaint, the judicial remedy did not provide significant protection, since most civil officials sided with the former owners or came from the same class.[31]

The contract law also included domestic laborers and household employees. The servant would be on call "all hours of the day or night, and on all days of the week" and would "promptly answer" all requests and "obey and execute all lawful orders and commands of the family" unless otherwise stipulated. Failure to fulfill the family's orders, except for sickness, would be termed disobedience. Required to be "especially civil and polite to their employer, his family and guests," servants should "receive gentle and kind treatment." Employers could make no call for services after ten o'clock at night or on Sunday, nor make any other demands "which exigencies of the household or family do not make necessary or unavoidable."[32]

The Eleventh Legislature enacted a lien law that was similar to the contract laws and agricultural relations of other southern states. Whenever the employer provided farm animals, advances for necessary provisions, farm implements, or cash to purchase these items in order to make a crop, the employee had to sign a written obligation that he or she had obtained this assistance in "good faith" and that without it he or she would not be able to proceed. The advance, or the "amount thereof," would be a lien upon the crop and the stock furnished or bought with the cash given. This lien would have preference over all others "except that for the rent of the land" on which the crop was raised. Liens would be recorded in the county court offices.[33]

The legislature also enacted an apprentice law. All minors under fourteen years of age could be bound by their father, mother, or guardian until the age of twenty-one unless they married. If fourteen or older, the minor could agree to the apprenticeship if not opposed by their mother or father. If the minor's age could not be ascertained (and most black children had no evidence of their birth date), then the judge affixed it. This latitude in determining a youth's age led to abuses. Applications had to have ten days' public notice, and no minor would be indentured except at the regular term of the court. The law gave judges "exclusive jurisdiction" and required them to approve all indentures, which the county clerk recorded.[34]

The county judge had to require a bond, of which he established the sum, from the master or mistress making the indenture. One or more "good and sufficient sureties" guaranteed that the apprentice would be furnished sufficient food and clothing, treated humanely, taught a "specified trade or occupation," and given medical attention. The sureties would oversee the "general and faithful compliance with the terms stipulated in the indentures." If the master or mistress failed to comply with the terms of the contract, a suit could be instituted by the father, mother, or guardian, or the county judge, for damages sustained. Any damages recovered would be applied to the benefit of the apprentice under guidelines prescribed by the county judge.[35]

The power to "inflict such moderate corporeal chastisement as may be necessary and proper" could be used to control the apprentices. If they ran away or left without permission, they could be recaptured, brought before a justice of the peace, and remanded into the service of the master or mistress. An apprentice who refused to return would be jailed or allowed to give bond for an appearance at the county court's next term. An apprentice who left without "good and sufficient cause" would receive punishment as provided for by the vagrancy laws until he or she agreed to return to his or her master or mistress. If the judge determined the apprentice had reason to violate the indenture, he could annul the agreement.[36]

Additionally, the legislature passed a separate punishment law to prevent individuals from persuading, tampering with, enticing away, harboring, secreting, or feeding a laborer or apprentice. Upon conviction, the violator, in addition to being held liable for damages, would be punished by a fine of not more than five hundred or less than ten dollars, imprisonment in the county jail for six months, or both. It was a misdemeanor for any individual to employ a contracted laborer or apprentice and thereby deprive the contractor of the worker's services. A person convicted of doing so would receive a fine of not less than ten nor more than five hundred dollars "for each and every offence," or imprisonment not exceeding thirty days in the county jail, or both, and liability for damages could be imposed.[37]

The legislature enacted a vagrancy statute as another method of controlling the black population. By defining a vagrant as "an idle person, living without any means of support, and making no exertions to obtain a livelihood, by any honest employment," the law encompassed a large variety and class of persons. Vagrants included fortunetellers who were not licensed to exhibit "tricks or cheats in public"; prostitutes; professional gamblers or those who kept houses for them; beggars of alms not afflicted with a disablement, physical malady, or misfortune; habitual drunkards;

and "persons who stroll idly about the streets of town[s] or cities, having no local habitation, and no honest business or employment."[38]

If those charged with vagrancy did not pay their fines "within a reasonable time," then they could be forced to labor for the town or county as provided by the police court or municipal authorities.

At stated periods, such authorities would "make regulations prescribing the kind of work at which vagrants are to be employed." This generally meant laboring on public works or roads. The guilty vagrant who refused to work for the town or county and failed to pay the fine and costs would be lodged in jail in "close confinement, on bread and water, until he or she may consent to work." To ensure that local jurisdictions would receive some benefit from vagrants, days spent in incarceration would not be computed "in estimating the time for satisfying the fine and costs."[39]

To prevent the freedmen from carrying pistols, the legislature made it unlawful for anyone to carry guns on the "enclosed premises or plantation" of any citizen without the owner's or proprietor's consent. This prohibition did not apply to persons in the "lawful discharge" of a civil or military duty, or to planters and their managers, thereby placing the freedpeople at a further disadvantage when trying to protect themselves. For violating the statute, the fine was not less than one nor more than ten dollars, or imprisonment in the county jail for not less than one day nor more than ten, or both, at the discretion of the court or jury deciding the issue.[40]

Although the penal laws were not, strictly speaking, part of the black codes, the legislature revised them with an eye toward ensnaring blacks. For theft of property valued under twenty dollars, a conviction brought imprisonment in the county jail for a term not exceeding one year and a fine not exceeding one hundred dollars, or imprisonment without a fine. For stealing a cow, sheep, goat, or hog valued at twenty dollars or more, a person was to be incarcerated in the state penitentiary for not less than two or more than five years. If the value of the livestock was less than twenty dollars, the sentence was imprisonment in the county jail for a term not exceeding two years and a fine not over one hundred dollars, or incarceration without a fine.[41]

Livestock became the central focus of a long amendment to the penal code. An individual who took, drove, used, or removed any stock belonging to another from its "accustomed range," or without the owner's consent, with intent to defraud, would be charged with theft. If convicted, a defendant would receive a maximum two-year penitentiary term, or be assessed a fine not to exceed one thousand dollars, or both, at the discretion of the court and jury. The same act, if not deemed theft, was a mis-demeanor punishable by a fine not to exceed twice the value of the stock. The only necessity was to prove the act of killing, destruction, driving, using, or removing range stock, and the accused had to "show any fact under which he can justify or mitigate the offense." [42]

A law clearly aimed at black Texans, although, like the others, appar-ently nondiscriminatory, required severe punishment for conviction of rape. "Whoever shall be guilty of rape," the legislature declared, "shall be punished by death, or by confinement in the Penitentiary for life, or for any term of years not less than five, in the discretion of the jury." Even writers such as Albrecht and Wilson, who find the general code dis-cretionary and acceptable, believed this legislation unjust. Albrecht stated that it "exhibited a clear anti-Negro bias" because rape was one of the "criminal activities in which," many believed, blacks "were most likely to engage." Wilson admitted that the "wide latitude in punishment" under the rape law "is suspicious." [43]

Anticipating an increase in the number of inmates in local jails, the legislature permitted officials to employ those convicted of petty offences on public utility works. The police court could lawfully employ upon the public buildings, works, or roads of the county anyone convicted of a mis-demeanor or lesser crime and sentenced to a term in the county jail, for the whole term of the imprisonment or any part thereof. Officials could also employ or lease for hire convicts for any mechanical or other employment. Inmates could also be made to labor to pay off fines, at the rate of one dollar a day. When the fine and costs were worked off, the inmate would be discharged, but could be employed from when he was first imprisoned until the trial. [44]

Finally, although few historians of Texas Reconstruction have com-mented on the ramifications of the practice, the Eleventh Legislature pro-vided for the beginning of convict leasing, no doubt realizing that blacks would be sentenced to the penitentiary in droves. The legislators enacted a comprehensive law that concentrated on employing convicts to build rail-roads, dredge rivers, irrigate, mine, and labor in foundries. They divided the inmates into two classes; the first, comprised of those convicted of murder, arson, rape, horse stealing, burglary, perjury, and robbery, would labor inside the penitentiary. Those convicted of all other crimes would be employed outside the penitentiary on "works of public utility" directed by a Board of Public Labor. [45]

A comparison of the Texas black codes with those enacted by other southern states in 1865 and 1866 reveals no substantive differences. As Albrecht stated, a "compilation of a code for freedmen entailed more borrowing than innovation." Whether dealing with labor, vagrancy, or apprenticeship, the requirements and restrictions placed upon persons by Texas laws were similar to those in Georgia, Louisiana, Maryland, North Carolina, and Virginia. The early black codes of South Carolina, Mississippi, Alabama, and Florida may have been more detailed and have been applied only to freedpeople, whereas the Texas legislature, responding to a changed political situation, modified the statutes to make no distinction according to race, but in this it only seemed more enlightened.[46]

Although the legislature disguised its true purpose through nondiscriminatory laws, the restrictions it placed upon the freedpeople paralleled those in other southern states; it is simply untrue that the Texas laws were less severe. Except that they do not apply solely to the freedpeople, the Texas black codes are interchangeable with those enacted by any other southern state. To label the legislators who saw a necessity for this repressive legislation as "paragons of discretion" is to distort the truth, even considering the atmosphere in which they lived. Everyone understood what was being attempted with the codes.

The Eleventh Legislature did not require previous Northern laws or regulations from the army or the Freedmen's Bureau to serve as models for its black code; the antebellum years had shown how to control a minority population. Moreover, by slightly changing the laws that had applied to free blacks before the war and by avoiding any reference to race, the legislature could perpetuate white domination. The legislators believed that they would be allowed to shape general laws toward specifically repressive ends. By attempting the ruse of enacting nondiscriminatory laws, the legislature led Texas toward the reimposition of military Reconstruction.

If the labor policies of the army and the Freedmen's Bureau were so coercive and inimical to black interests, then why did the planters reject them as untenable? Because they allowed blacks the opportunity to make their own decisions. As Herman Belz has written, these institutions "were committed to the independence of the freedmen in a way that former masters and most white southerners were not." To say that the 1866 Texas black codes merely copied into state law statutes from the North and modified what the army and bureau required is to miss the essential point. One also has to consider the intent of the framers. The South was looking backward and "seemed to be saying that for blacks Reconstruction would begin and end with the codes."[47]

The 1866 legislature enacted the black codes for several reasons. First, it wanted to regulate stringently the freedmen's labor. Second, it hoped that the laws would render the Freedmen's Bureau unnecessary. Third, it initiated, perhaps intentionally, the incipient stages of segregation and Jim Crowism. Fourth, it believed that through this series of laws the Fourteenth Amendment might become a dead issue. Fifth, by implying that these ordinances applied to all citizens, the legislators attempted to forestall any criticism that they would be used only against the freedmen.

Finally, they would satisfy the economic elite of the state by placing blacks in a category of semislavery.

Although historians have argued that the 1866 Texas Constitution and black code appeared to be generous and indeed to guarantee the freedpeople numerous rights that they had not formerly enjoyed, this misrepresents the intent and underlying purpose of the statutes. To contend that the legislature was magnanimous because it conferred certain limited rights upon black Texans is nonsense. The established social, economic, and legal restrictions prevented black Texans from participating as equals in a system weighted enormously against them. Refusing to accept national sovereignty and a new emphasis on integrating blacks into the constitutional system, Texas legislators circumscribed black equality at every turn.[48]

To argue, as do Richter and, occasionally, Barr and Smallwood, that the 1866 black code was the desire and responsibility, no matter how tenuous, of the army and the Freedmen's Bureau absolves the white citizens and the legislature of most of the harshness and animosity they exhibited toward blacks. The intention of the directives from the army and bureau was entirely different from the motivation behind the code. To deny similarities in some of the Texas laws and governmental announcements would be preposterous, but the code went far beyond anything the bureau attempted and relegated blacks to the bottom of the economic and social ladder.

Even if we grant that the legislature passed a nondiscriminatory code in the hopes it would stalemate the bureau, force its removal, and bring about quicker recognition from the president, it does not mean that the overriding influence came from two national agencies. For attempting to bring some order out of the postwar chaos, the army and the bureau are once again being castigated as the villains of Reconstruction. This interpretation, though Richter has updated it with massive research, echoes the historiography of the Ramsdell school rather than viewing the code for what it actually was. Freedom under the bureau was very different from freedom under the legislature.

In minor ways the labor policies of the bureau did resemble those set up by the black code. For example, the agents stressed the fact that blacks could not both live in idleness and honor their contracts. But these officials, "highly suspicious of Southerners' motives," saw the code "as a means of coercing freedmen into unfair contracts with planters." The code also made vagrancy and contract violation "punishable by long terms of forced, uncompensated labor," which merely reinforced the bureau's mistrust of the legislature's intent. Criminal laws covertly allowed courts to punish blacks with harsher penalties; the code included an apprenticeship statute that controlled black children. In short, the statutes denied the freedmen the personal rights that whites expected and possessed.[49]

What we must realize about the black code is that the Texas legislators did not require the army and the bureau as tutors. Former slaveholders and Confederate patriots understood antebellum history. After all, free blacks had received these minimum guarantees before the war, but they still had not been equal. Those who enacted the code had a year and a half to observe and contemplate national events. They ignored them. A conservative (Reagan) and a moderate (Hamilton) attempted to inform them of the wisest course. In the meantime, Throckmorton demonstrated no leadership qualities and the legislature blithely legislated.

To be sure, the North had nasty laws concerning vagrants and laborers. Historians now make much of this comparison. But it does not mean intentions were similar. The Texas black code went far beyond any of the Northern laws and approached the earlier strictures of the most virulent of southern statutes, with the aim of making blacks forever legally subservient, as had been attempted in South Carolina and Mississippi. The trap, for most, is the way the Eleventh Legislature approached its impending legislation. All precedents suggested that success lay with a tough but non-discriminatory code. It responded in excess, angering Congress and leading to the reimposition of military rule.

A conservative Republican, the Virginia-born John L. Haynes, wrote to E. M. Pease that the legislature had "completed its series of bills to reenslave the negroes." The legislators included a labor bill requiring all to contract by January 10 or be declared vagrant, and an apprentice law "to gobble up the young negroes under 21 and give them a suitable (i.e., white) guardian, with the power of a little moral suasion of the birch." The legislators also required all workers to give up their arms, forbade them to "enter upon any premises without consent," and outlawed tampering with any laborer. This is the program, he concluded. "Is it not more infamous than that of any other State?" Haynes asked. He thought so, and so did many others.[50]

NOTES

1. Randolph B. Campbell, "Statehood, Civil War, and Reconstruction, 1846–76," in *Texas through Time: Evolving Interpretations,* ed. Walter L. Buenger and Robert A. Calvert (College Station: Texas A&M Univ. Press, 1991), 194 (quotation). For additional insights see Ralph A. Wooster, "The Civil War and Reconstruction in Texas," in *A Guide to the History of Texas,* ed. Light Townsend Cummins and Alvin R. Bailey, Jr., 37–50 (New York: Greenwood Press, 1988); Barry A. Crouch, "'Unmanacling' Texas Reconstruction: A Twenty-Year Perspective," *Southwestern Historical Quarterly* 93 (Jan. 1990): 275–302.

2. Older views are expressed in John M. Mecklin, "The Black Codes," in *South Atlantic Quarterly* 16 (July 1917): 248–259; George A. Wood, "The Black Code of Alabama," *South Atlantic Quarterly* 13 (Oct. 1914): 350–360; J. G. de Roulhac Hamilton, "Southern Legislation in Respect to Freedmen, 1865–1866," in *Studies in Southern History and Politics* (New York: Columbia Univ. Press, 1914), 137–158.

3. Charles Stewart, "Reconstruction in Texas," in *Why the Solid South? or, Reconstruction and Its Results,* ed. Hilary A. Herbert (Baltimore: Woodward, 1890), 353 (1st quotation); O. M. Roberts, *Our Federal Relations from a Southern View of Them* (Austin, Tex.: Eugene Von Boeckmann, Printer, 1892), 79 (2nd quotation). Hubert Howe Bancroft barely mentioned the codes in his *North Mexican States and Texas,* 2 vols. (San Francisco: The History Co., 1886, 1889), 2:485–486. Stewart's memory was faulty, as the legislators did not provide for black education. Had the government required that blacks be enfranchised, he insisted, it would have been implemented. Texans would have submitted to these conditions due to the "arbitrament of the sword" and as a duty imposed upon "brave men" ("Reconstruction in Texas," 353). See James Marten, "'What is to Become of the Negro?' White Reaction to Emancipation in Texas," *Mid-America: An Historical Review* 73 (Apr.–July 1991): 115–133.

4. Charles William Ramsdell, *Reconstruction in Texas* (New York: Columbia Univ. Press, 1910), 122, 125 (1st quotation), 126 (2nd quotation); Ramsdell, "Presidential Reconstruction in Texas," *Quarterly of the Texas State Historical Association* 12 (Jan. 1909): 217–218; Seth Shepard McKay, *Making the Texas Constitution of 1876* (Philadelphia: Univ. of Pennsylvania Press, 1924), 13 (3rd quotation); T. R. Fehrenbach, *Lone Star: A History of Texas and the Texans* (New York: Macmillan, 1968), 402 (4th quotation). Fehrenbach adds that the "stabilization [black codes] of 1866 could have saved many planters, but it was overturned" (419). Ernest Wal-

lace, *Texas in Turmoil, 1849–1875* (Austin: Steck-Vaughn, 1965), 185 (5th and 6th quotations), 186.

Actually, the code did offend the Republicans, but they could do little to prevent its implementation. John Conger McGraw, "The Texas Constitution of 1866" (PhD diss., Texas Technological College, 1959), 227 (7th and 8th quotations), 228, 233. McGraw misses the fact that "petty officials" under all these laws had enormous power and that the freedpeople, because of their social and economic position, could do little to challenge the system. The underlying purpose of the vagrancy statute was to keep blacks out of urban areas and on the plantation (228).

5. Joe B. Frantz, *Texas: A Bicentennial History* (New York: Norton, 1976), 116 (1st and 2nd quotations); Nora Estelle Owens, "Presidential Reconstruction in Texas: A Case Study" (PhD diss., Auburn Univ., 1983), 165 (3rd and 4th quotations); John Pressley Carrier, "Constitutional Change in Texas during the Reconstruction, 1865–1876" (MA thesis, North Texas State Univ., 1967), 62 (5th quotation). Carter, "A Political History of Texas During the Reconstruction, 1865–1874" (PhD diss., Vanderbilt Univ., 1971), 125–140, elaborates on his earlier ideas. Most southern states gave blacks basic rights. In this sense, Texas was no different, and therefore, no more generous.

6. Winnell Albrecht, "The Black Codes of Texas" (MA thesis, Southwest Texas State Univ., 1969), 95 (3rd quotation), 96 (4th quotation), 101 (1st quotation), 102 (2nd quotation). Albrecht concludes that "regardless of the vindictiveness shown in many of the committee reports and despite the motivation which might have been involved, the Eleventh Legislature gave to Texas freedmen more rights than did any other Southern state" (85). Her statements seem largely irrelevant and are untrue. Although she did compare the Texas codes with those of the other southern states, Albrecht seems to have completely ignored the similarities and their significance in placing heavy burdens upon black freedom. Indeed, the code was "workable," but fair is another matter entirely.

7. Theodore Brantner Wilson, *The Black Codes of the South* (Tuscaloosa: Univ. of Alabama Press, 1965), 108 (1st quotation), 108–109 (2nd quotation), 109 (3rd quotation), 111, 118, 142. The 1866 Civil Rights Act required that similar criminal penalties apply to blacks and whites. A new monograph on the southern black codes of 1865–1866 is sorely needed.

8. William L. Richter, *The Army in Texas during Reconstruction, 1865–1870* (College Station: Texas A&M Univ. Press, 1987), 59 (2nd–4th quotations), 61 (1st quotation). A convenient summary is William L. Richter, "The Army and the Negro during Texas Reconstruction, 1865–1870," *East Texas Historical Journal* 10 (Spring 1972): 7–19.

9. Richter, *Army in Texas,* 59 (1st and 2nd quotations), 60. For a different outlook, see J. Thomas May, "Continuity and Change in the Labor Program of the Union Army and the Freedmen's Bureau," *Civil War History* 17 (Sept. 1971): 245–254; Harold D. Woodman, "Post–Civil War Southern Agriculture and the

Law," *Agricultural History* 53 (Jan. 1979), declared that the "yearlong written contract for wage labor, instituted by the army in occupied areas during the war and continued with the support of the Freedmen's Bureau after the war, gave southern labor relations a peculiarity from the start" (321). Also see Nancy Cohen-Lack, "A Struggle for Sovereignty: National Consolidation, Emancipation, and Free Labor in Texas, 1865," *Journal of Southern History* 58 (Feb. 1992): 57–98

10. William L. Richter, *Overreached on All Sides: The Freedmen's Bureau Administrators in Texas, 1865–1868* (College Station: Texas A&M Univ. Press, 1991), 94 (1st quotation), 95, 97 (3rd quotation), 290 (2nd and 4th quotations). An equally unsubstantiated argument on the same subject can be found in Amy Dru Stanley, "Beggars Can't Be Choosers: Compulsion and Contract in Postbellum America," *Journal of American History* 78 (Mar. 1992): 1283–1286.

11. Edgar P. Sneed, "A Historiography of Reconstruction in Texas: Some Myths and Problems," *Southwestern Historical Quarterly* 72 (Apr. 1969): 438 (quotations). See also Stephen Stagner, "Epics, Science, and the Lost Frontier: Texas Historical Writing, 1836–1936," *Western Historical Quarterly* 12 (Apr. 1981): 165–181. The myth of democratic institutions is expressed in Merline Pitre, "A Note on the Historiography of Blacks in the Reconstruction of Texas," *Journal of Negro History* 66 (Winter 1981–1982): 341.

12. James M. Smallwood, *Time of Hope, Time of Despair: Black Texans during Reconstruction* (Port Washington, N.Y.: Kennikat Press, 1981), 54 (1st and 2nd quotations); Walter T. Chapin, "Presidential Reconstruction in Texas, 1865–1867" (MA thesis, North Texas State Univ., 1979), 127–128, 129 (3rd quotation), 129–130 (4th–7th quotations). Even Jesse Dorsett, who tends to accept the older views of Texas Reconstruction, found the legislation "unjust." Most opposed "granting the negro any political rights whatever, insisting that he should be made to work by uniform laws." The few who "urged a more liberal stand were driven into silence" ("Blacks in Reconstruction Texas, 1865–1877" [PhD diss., Texas Christian Univ., 1981], 13).

13. Alwyn Barr, *Black Texans: A History of Negroes in Texas, 1528–1971* (Austin: Jenkins; Pemberton Press, 1973), 56–57 (1st quotation); Randolph B. Campbell, *A Southern Community in Crisis: Harrison County, Texas, 1850–1880* (Austin: Texas State Historical Association, 1983), 265 (2nd quotation), 266 (3rd quotation). Campbell further states that "this labor contract reveals the intention of most white Texans during Presidential Reconstruction to keep Negro workers as close to slaves as possible" (266).

14. Smallwood, *Time of Hope,* 54 (quotations), 55. He does emphasize, however, that there was a significant difference between bureau-sanctioned contracts and those to be initiated under the legislature's confining code. If followed, he argues, they would have removed the bureau's influence and given the "landlords predominate power in law" (56). Even for all its alleged vaunted influence, the bureau could never remove the relatively constant economic suppression (57). The *New York Tribune* quoted the *New Orleans Tribune,* Dec. 12, 1866, which referred

to the lawmakers as the "most ignorant set of men that ever assembled in this state" and who represented "all the vile passions engendered by a civil war" (quoted in Smallwood, *Time of Hope,* 175).

15. LeRoy P. Graf, Ralph W. Haskins, and Paul H. Bergeron, eds., *The Papers of Andrew Johnson,* vol. 9, *September 1865 –January 1866* (Knoxville: Univ. of Tennessee Press, 1967); Hans L. Trefousse, *Andrew Johnson: A Biography* (New York: Norton, 1989), 215–271; Eric Foner, *Reconstruction: America's Unfinished Revolution, 1863–1877* (New York: Harper and Row, 1988); Michael Perman, *Reunion without Compromise: The South and Reconstruction, 1865–1868* (Cambridge: Cambridge Univ. Press, 1973), 68–109; Eric L. McKitrick, *Andrew Johnson and Reconstruction* (Chicago: Univ. of Chicago Press, 1960), 153–213; Dan T. Carter, *When the War Was Over: The Failure of Self-Reconstruction in the South, 1865–1867* (Baton Rouge: Louisiana State Univ. Press, 1985). A study of just how Johnson viewed Texas and the conditions therein would be invaluable. For a partial explanation see Owens, "Presidential Reconstruction in Texas."

16. Daniel J. Flanigan, "The Criminal Law of Slavery and Freedom, 1800 – 1868" (PhD diss., Rice Univ., 1973), 271 (quotation). Additional background and political maneuvering can be found in Foner, *Reconstruction: Unfinished Revolution;* Leon F. Litwack, *Been in the Storm So Long: The Aftermath of Slavery* (New York: Knopf, 1979).

17. John H. Reagan, *Memoirs: With Special Reference to Secession and the Civil War,* ed. Walter Flavius McCaleb (New York: Neale, 1906), 288 (quotation), 290 – 291; Ben H. Procter, *Not without Honor: The Life of John H. Reagan* (Austin: Univ. of Texas Press, 1962), 178–182; Forrest G. Wood, *Black Scare: The Racist Response to Emancipation and Reconstruction* (Berkeley and Los Angeles: Univ. of California Press, 1968), 83–85.

18. John L. Waller, *Colossal Hamilton of Texas: A Biography of Andrew Jackson Hamilton, Militant Unionist and Reconstruction Governor* (El Paso: Texas Western Press, 1968), 88–89; Wilson, *Black Codes,* 94 (1st and 2nd quotations), 108 (3rd quotation).

19. *The Constitution of the State of Texas, 1866* (Austin: Joseph Walker, State Printer, 1866), Article VIII, 27. The only detailed work on the Constitution, which must be used with caution, is McGraw, "Texas Constitution of 1866." In actuality, the 1866 document was but a slight revision of the 1845 Constitution.

20. Ibid.

21. Eric Foner, *Nothing but Freedom: Emancipation and Its Legacy* (Baton Rouge: Louisiana State Univ. Press, 1983), 49 (1st quotation); Claude Elliott, *Leathercoat: The Life History of a Texas Patriot* (San Antonio: Standard Printing, 1938), 122–178; Ruby Crawford Holbert, "The Public Career of James Webb Throckmorton, 1851–1867" (MA thesis, Univ. of Texas at Austin, 1932), 60 (2nd and 3rd quotations).

22. Holbert, "James Webb Throckmorton," 84 (3rd and 4th quotations); Elliott, *Leathercoat,* 147–178; Wilson, *Black Codes,* 88 (1st and 2nd quotations).

23. The most recent exposition is William L. Richter, "General Phil Sheridan, the Historians, and Reconstruction," *Civil War History* 33 (June 1987): 131–154. In *Overreached on All Sides,* Richter continues to praise Throckmorton for his astuteness, but even a cursory reading of his post–Civil War speeches and some of his correspondence suggests how deeply he detested blacks and other minority groups. The only biography, Elliott's *Leathercoat,* appeared in 1938, and a new one is much needed.

24. Good summaries but weak interpretation of the legislature's action can be found in Albrecht, "Black Codes of Texas," 68–102; McGraw, "Texas Constitution of 1866," 197–236; Thomas Wesley Kremm, "Race Relations in Texas 1865 to 1870" (MA thesis, Univ. of Houston, 1970), 35–40; Carrier, "Political History of Texas during the Reconstruction," 125–140; Owens, "Presidential Reconstruction in Texas," 156–191.

25. H. P. N. Gammel, comp., *The Laws of Texas, 1822–1897 . . .,* 10 vols. (Austin: Gammel Book Co., 1898), 5:988 (1st quotation), 5:1049 (2nd–6th quotations). For a comparison with the other states mentioned, see U.S. Department of War, *Letter of the Secretary of War communicating . . . a synopsis of laws respecting persons of color in the late slave States* (Jan. 3, 1867), 39th Cong., 2nd sess., Senate Executive Document 6, Serial 1276 (Washington, D.C., 1867).

26. *Laws of Texas,* vol. 5, 977, 1015 (4th quotation), 1049–1050, 1088–1092, 1121–1122, 1125 (1st–3rd quotations), 1154–1156.

27. Ibid., 994 (1st quotation), 995 (2nd quotation), 997; *Synopsis of laws respecting persons of color,* 222–224. For Richter's analysis of the labor law, which differs from most others, see *Overreached on All Sides,* 96–98. Wilson writes that "a majority" of the legislators "were sorely tempted to pass a severe Black Code" but "they yielded to discretion." The labor law was a "considerably softened version of the original bill" as the senate at one point adopted a provision that "'all common laborers' *must* make annual contracts early each January." This and "other injudicious provisions were eliminated." He does admit, however, that the "contract law was the most inequitable in the Black Code of Texas" (*Black Codes,* 109).

28. *Laws of Texas,* 5:994–995 (1st quotation), 5:995 (2nd–4th quotations); *Synopsis of laws respecting persons of color,* 222.

29. *Laws of Texas,* 5:995–996 (quotations); *Synopsis of laws respecting persons of color,* 223.

30. *Laws of Texas,* 5:996 (quotations); *Synopsis of laws respecting persons of color,* 223. The legislature amended the act preventing work on Sunday, stating that "any person or persons who shall labor, or who shall hire, compel, or permit, his or her employees, children, or apprentices, to labor on the Sabbath" (*Laws of Texas,* 5:1139–1140) would be guilty of a misdemeanor and upon conviction be fined not less than ten or more than fifty dollars, provided, of course, that "household duties, works of necessity, and charity" were not prohibited by the law (5:1140). The assemblymen then listed a host of jobs and occupations exempted from the rule, which essentially negated the effect of the law. In addition, and this could

very well have applied to freedmen, they prevented hunting game either with a gun or dog. Conviction carried a fine of not less than five or more than twenty-five dollars. If the stock of any person was injured or killed, the fine would be double the above amount and the violator would pay all damages. Those who traded or bartered on the Sabbath were guilty of a misdemeanor and fined not less than ten nor more than fifty dollars (5:1141).

31. *Laws of Texas,* vol. 5, 996–997 (quotations), 999; *Synopsis of laws respecting persons of color,* 222–224. At the expiration of the contract, or if a laborer or apprentice were released, they could request a "written certificate of discharge." If the employer or master or mistress refused, they could be charged with a misdemeanor and upon conviction fined a sum not exceeding one hundred dollars. The law also required that at each term of their court, the district judges would give the "act specially in charge to the grand jury" (*Laws of Texas,* 5:999). Legislators gave minimal consideration to protecting laborers or apprentices. They desired a stable labor force, children to be bound so they would not be a drain upon a county's monetary resources, cheap labor for whites, and laws that regulated blacks' movements.

32. *Laws of Texas,* 5:997 (quotations); *Synopsis of laws respecting persons of color,* 224. For Richter's analysis of the contract law, which differs from most others, see *Overreached on All Sides,* 96–98.

33. *Synopsis of laws respecting persons of color,* 221 (quotations), 223. What many have not realized is that the legislature made it easy and convenient to impoverish blacks for any type of use or abuse of a farm animal. Thus, the law declared that for the theft of agricultural products, farm animals, or any other property, or its "wilful destruction" or injury, the worker had to pay double the value of the object, one-half to go to the employer, one-half to a general fund (*Laws of Texas,* 5:996).

34. *Laws of Texas,* 5:979 (quotation), 5:981; *Synopsis of laws respecting persons of color,* 224–226.

35. *Laws of Texas,* 5:979, 5:980 (quotations), 5:981; *Synopsis of laws respecting persons of color,* 225–226. The legislature surely realized that the freedpeople would not have money to initiate suits for blacks' failure to abide by apprenticeship agreements. The apprenticeship could be terminated, the individual released, and the bond cancelled if the master or mistress brought their ward before a county judge and proved "on good and sufficient cause" that the apprentice would not be "injured thereby" (*Laws of Texas,* 5:980). The apprentice could not reside outside the county in which the agreement had been made without a written order from the county judge. When a judge granted permission for leave, then the judge of the county where the apprentice resided assumed jurisdiction over him or her. Any apprentice moved without permission and retained for more than thirty days "shall not be held liable for a further compliance with his indentures" (5:981). They could, however, choose to remain in the indenture.

36. *Laws of Texas,* 5:980; *Synopsis of laws respecting persons of color,* 225. Apprentices would not have had the necessary cash to post bail.

37. *Laws of Texas,* 5:998 (quotation); *Synopsis of laws respecting persons of color,* 221–222. Once again Richter attributes this portion of the code to the bureau, specifically to Joseph B. Kiddoo, the second assistant commissioner, in his Circular Order No. 14 (*Overreached on All Sides,* 96). Judicial authorities retained considerable power under the black codes. In fact, they became the single most important body directing and controlling the requirements of the laws and supervised apprentices. Judges had the power to "hear and determine and grant all orders and decrees" at any time (*Laws of Texas,* 5:981). To prevent individuals, family members, or relatives from enticing away, concealing, or harboring a "deserting" apprentice, the law levied a five-dollar-a-day fine, and the offending party would be liable for damages sustained by the master or mistress "on account of such willful" conduct (5:981). This made it especially difficult for black relatives to dissolve an indenture or ascertain if its provisions were being upheld (*Synopsis of laws respecting persons of color,* 226–227). In *Overreached on All Sides,* Richter stated that the apprenticing law was a "measure long awaited by citizens and the bureau alike" (95). The bureau had refused permission to state authorities to bind out children before the law's passage (96).

38. *Laws of Texas,* 5:979, 5:1020–1021 (1st quotation), 5:1021 (2nd–3rd quotations); *Synopsis of laws respecting persons of color,* 226. The statute mandated that sheriffs, justices of the peace, and county civil officers report to the judges of the county court "all indigent or vagrant minors" and also those minors whose parent or parents did not have the means, or who refused, to support their youngsters. The county judge initiated the process to apprentice these youngsters to some "suitable or competent person" under court directed terms, "having particular care to the interest of said minor." The legislature did not intend to provide extensive protection for the rights of children or vagrants who would be apprenticed. Although nondiscriminatory on the surface, it was essentially aimed at black children, who would provide whites with a cheap source of labor. (All quotations above are from *Synopsis of laws respecting persons of color,* 224.)

39. *Laws of Texas,* 5:979, 5:1021 (1st quotation), 5:1022 (2nd–4th quotations); *Synopsis of laws respecting persons of color,* 226–227. Youthful and juvenile vagrants would be sent before the police court to be bound out under the apprenticing act. The fines and penalties prescribed in the vagrancy statute "shall conform to the provisions of the Criminal Code in relation to the same offences" (*Laws of Texas,* 5:1022). County courts, justices of the peace, mayors, and recorders of incorporated towns and cities had the power to order the arrest of vagrants "of their own motion" or on written complaint by some "credible person" (5:1021). After a magistrate issued a warrant, a peace officer would arrest and bring the offender before the court. If a law official were unavailable, it could be directed to any "private person" (5:1021). Upon appearance of the alleged vagrant, the court had to determine if the evidence substantiated the charge. The accused could demand a trial by jury. A fine of not more than ten dollars could be levied on someone convicted of the charge, but the defendant could not be released until the fine

and court costs were paid. Richter views the vagrancy law as part of the bureau's "legislative desire" (*Overreached on All Sides*, 95).

40. *Laws of Texas*, 5:1008 (quotations); *Synopsis of laws respecting persons of color*, 222. Richter suggests that the rule prohibiting blacks from carrying firearms "could be seen as a measure to disarm black laborers but, as it was not racially specific, it loosely followed bureau directives on such matters" (*Overreached on All Sides*, 95). He falls into the old trap of arguing that because the laws were nondiscriminatory, they therefore had to be more enlightened than statutes enacted by southern states before the Texas legislation. The bureau did attempt to disarm citizens within the limits of a town, but the effort was more directly aimed at whites.

41. *Laws of Texas*, 5:1118–1119. These provisions did not "apply to cases of theft, where a different punishment, for any specific offence is expressly provided by law" (5:1118). Another revision of the penal code provided double punishment for any adult convicted of aiding or instigating the committing of a crime by an underage apprentice (5:1106).

42. Ibid., 5:1105 (1st quotation), 5:1106 (2nd quotation). If a person marked or branded with an unrecorded identification any stock not already so identified, a misdemeanor resulted. For those convicted of this offense, a fine would be imposed equal to double the value of the stock. Similarly, altering or changing a mark or brand, whether upon a person's own stock or upon stock that was under his control, without recording it was also a misdemeanor and carried the same fine. If a person killed an unmarked or unbranded "sheep, hog, goat, cow, calf, ox or beef steer," this constituted a misdemeanor, and conviction led to a fine of not less than twenty-five dollars nor more than one hundred dollars or a sentence of "hard labor on public works" of the county or state for not less than three or more than six months. The law did not include "counterbranding."

In addition, if a person should take up, use, or milk any cow not his own and without the owner's consent, a fine not exceeding ten dollars for every offence would result.

43. *Laws of Texas*, 5:1079 (1st quotation); Albrecht, "Black Codes of Texas," 100 (2nd quotation); Wilson, *Black Codes*, 111 (3rd quotation).

44. *Laws of Texas*, 5:1037–1038. All money realized under this act would he paid into the county treasury and appropriated for the county's benefit as directed by the police court. If acquitted, the defendant would receive not less than twenty-five cents nor more than one dollar a day, "provided, that before trial and conviction no person shall be held to labor by order of said Court, without his consent" (5:1038).

45. Ibid., 5:1110, 5:1111 (quotation), 5:1112–1113. To benefit works "of obvious and manifest public utility," convicts would work in gangs of not less than twenty (5:1111). The state treasurer, a member of the Board of Public Labor, would negotiate contracts with individuals, companies, or corporations for file leasing of the inmates, and the board would superintend the convicts in all their activities. For all convicts leased out, the state would provide their clothes, sub-

sistence, and medical attention. If they attempted to escape, refused to work, or demonstrated refractory conduct, they would be sent back to the penitentiary at "hard labor" (5:1113). When a convict completed his term, and if he had been leased, he would receive one-third of the net proceeds of his work. Moreover, inmates were not allowed to converse with each other.

By the time that the legislature enacted this law, the number of blacks in the penitentiary had dramatically increased. This continued to be the case over the next few years. See Donald R. Walker, *Penology for Profit: A History of the Texas Prison System, 1867–1912* (College Station: Texas A&M Univ. Press, 1988); Herman Lee Crow, "A Political History of the Texas Penal System, 1829–1951" (PhD diss., Univ. of Texas at Austin, 1964), 70–83, 85–86; Barry A. Crouch, "The Fetters of Justice: Texas Black Convicts and the Reconstruction Penitentiary" (unpublished paper). Within a year after emancipation, blacks composed over 40 percent of the prison population.

46. Albrecht, "Black Codes of Texas," 3 (quotation); Joe M. Richardson, "Florida Black Codes," *Florida Historical Quarterly* 47 (Apr. 1969): 365–379; Donald G. Nieman, "The Freedmen's Bureau and the Mississippi Black Code," *Journal of Mississippi History* 40 (May 1978): 91–118; Nieman, *To Set the Law in Motion: The Freedmen's Bureau and the Legal Rights of Blacks, 1865–1868* (Millwood, N.Y.: KTO Press, 1979), 72–102.

47. Wilson, *Black Codes,* 108 (1st quotation); Herman Belz, *Emancipation and Equal Rights: Politics and Constitutionalism in the Civil War Era* (New York: Norton, 1978), 72 (2nd quotation); Gerald David Jaynes, *Branches without Roots: Genesis of the Black Working Class in the American South, 1862–1882* (New York: Oxford Univ. Press, 1986), 17 (3rd quotation).

48. Wilson, *Black Codes,* 108–109; Albrecht, "Black Codes of Texas."

49. Nieman, *Set the Law in Motion,* 72 (1st quotation), 73 (2nd and 3rd quotations).

50. J. L. Haynes to E. M. Pease, Oct. 4, 1866 (quotations), Pease-Graham-Niles Papers (Austin History Center, Austin Public Library); James Marten, "John L. Haynes: A Southern Dissenter in Texas," *Southern Studies,* new series, 1 (Fall 1990): 270. On Haynes, see Carl H. Moneyhon, *Republicanism in Reconstruction Texas* (Austin: Univ. of Texas Press, 1980).

Eight   THE FETTERS OF JUSTICE

Black Texans and the Penitentiary
during Reconstruction

At the 1897 National Prison Association convention, Thomas J. Goree, superintendent of the Texas penitentiary from 1877 to 1891, regaled the audience with an apocryphal tale about emancipation, blacks, and their propensity for theft. At war's end, Goree's mother informed her slaves they were free and that all laws now applied to them. A plantation blacksmith asked Mrs. Goree if this included "stealing." Yes, she replied, since this violated the criminal code. The former slave artisan claimed he should have been trained as a brick mason instead of as a blacksmith because if blacks were sent to prison for theft, the state would have to build a wall extending five miles out on the prairie to hold all those convicted.[1] His statement proved to be prophetic.

A study of black prisoners confined in the Texas state penitentiary during the years immediately following the Civil War catalogues the patterns of crime, rates of violence, and reasons for imprisonment for the former slaves. In the early years of Reconstruction, the Lone Star State experienced mayhem of epidemic proportions. Yet blacks, who were most often the victims of violence, rarely responded in a like manner. As compared to whites, black individuals did not commit much violence, nor were black communities plagued by it. Nevertheless, one year after the end of the war, blacks composed almost one-half of the total prison population in the state penitentiary at Huntsville.

A watershed in southern prison development, the Civil War "changed the status of half of the population—the slaves—who were most liable to penal action, and it thus created a wholly new situation for the penal system to deal with." Blacks were "jammed into overcrowded and dilapidated penal facilities constructed in antebellum days primarily 'for whites only.'" According to C. Vann Woodward in *Origins of the New South*, "among the institutions of the Old Order that strained to meet the needs of the New, none proved more hopelessly inadequate than the old penitentia-

ries." Called upon to assume the "plantation's penal functions," prisons
had neither the proper facilities nor the personnel to function effectively.[2]

Works that focus upon the Reconstruction-era Texas penitentiary, like
those about other southern prisons, largely ignore or only pay lip service
to the dramatic increase in the number of black inmates during the early
years of Reconstruction, when the Conservatives were in power. Most
of the published and unpublished historical scholarship on the Texas state
prison (again, similar to works on other southern prisons) deals with a later
period (when convict leasing was the vogue), the administrative history
of the prison, or its political relationship with the state government, often
giving only a cursory glance at the prisoners. What occurred before the
advent of convict leasing is every bit as significant.[3]

By 1849 the impulse to build penitentiaries had reached its southern-
and westernmost point. Texas erected a prison at Huntsville, the second
largest in the South. Modeled after Mississippi's penal institution, it resembled a textile factory, which it was, and later returned considerable profits.
In its first decade of operation, the Texas penitentiary was comparable to
those of other southern states. In 1850, ten inmates resided in the prison,
and by 1851 the roll had swelled to thirty-eight. The first woman entered
in 1854. Convicted of infanticide, she served a one-year confinement.
Although the records are somewhat vague for 1849–1860, five slaves seem
to have served time in Huntsville during that period.[4]

The prison population fluctuated during the war. Texas established
military prisons, specifically at Camp Groce, but also used Huntsville to
house thirty-three prisoners of war. Moreover, to assist its Union-occupied
neighbors—Louisiana, Arkansas, and Missouri—the Texas government
volunteered to incarcerate any person from these three states sentenced to
"hard labor." As the war turned against the South, no institution was safe
from plundering—including the prison, which produced wagon sheets,
flour sacking, and other cloth products for the Confederate Army. Perhaps
looking for clothing or other items, a Confederate colonel and his men
robbed the penitentiary. To their surprise, the raiders discovered blacks in
the prison.[5]

Ironically, on January 1, 1863, six black crewmen off the U.S. steamer
Harriet Lane were captured in Galveston harbor and transported to the penitentiary, despite their assertions of being free. Three weeks later, twenty-
nine more blacks—twenty-two slaves and seven free blacks—were taken
from the ship *Morning Light* at Sabine Pass and put in the custody of the
Harris County sheriff. Uncertain of what to do with them because the
"free Negro" and "runaway" laws of Texas did not take into account this

particular state of affairs, law-enforcement officials asked the legislature to alter the statutes so "as to meet the exigency of the times." No one knew "how soon" a "brigade of Negroes of like character" would need to be confined at Huntsville.[6]

At the close of the Civil War, the United States was still basically a rural society. On the horizon lay a social revolution of considerable proportions, since the former slaves would have to be integrated into the body politic. What this meant for the whole nexus of the law, police officials, and penal institutions would have far-reaching consequences, even until the present day. In the antebellum period, the South had found no need to erect large penitentiaries, although it has historically always been the country's most violent region. Slavery served as an institution for controlling blacks, and white recalcitrants were often dealt with by local authorities.[7] When the guns fell silent, blacks found themselves in a new relationship with the law.

On August 10, 1865, George Martinas, a Guadalupe County freedman not two months out of slavery, was arraigned before the county court for "wilfully and feloniously" stealing a horse owned by B. R. Schafer, a white man. Martinas pleaded not guilty. An all-white male jury disagreed with his plea and sentenced him to ten years in the state penitentiary at Huntsville. Although the value of the horse is unspecified and how Martinas appropriated the animal is unclear, we know that he entered prison on December 6, 1865. Martinas became one of a host of freedpeople imprisoned in state penitentiaries across the South in the aftermath of the war. The crimes often involved animals or the theft of farm products.[8]

The status of the prison at the war's termination remained confused. In 1866 the Eleventh Legislature postponed action on a lease plan until Governor James W. Throckmorton could sort out the situation. The legislators did, however, establish the Board of Public Labor, which had the power to "hire out" convicts to mines, foundries, and public-utility projects such as railroads, inland and intercoastal waterways, and irrigation works. In a precursor to convict leasing, the board leased 148 prisoners to the Airline and Brazos railroads. Financially unstable, these corporations abused the prisoners and failed to pay the state for their labor. Meanwhile, the prison remained in dire monetary need and was overcrowded. Its inmate color line had also changed.[9]

The superintendent of the Texas state penitentiary in the immediate postwar years was James Gillespie. Appointed by Governor Throckmorton, Gillespie had previous experience as a prison administrator, having served as the director of Huntsville from 1850 to 1858. A Virginian by birth, he had fought in the war for Texas independence, the war against

Mexico, and the Civil War. Sympathetic to Presidential Reconstruction and Throckmorton's political ideas, Gillespie found the penitentiary situation chaotic and the institution deeply entangled in the conflict between the occupation army and the elected state government. Later, when Throckmorton was removed from the governorship, Gillespie resigned as superintendent.[10]

From June 19, 1865 ("Juneteenth," the official emancipation day for black Texans), until December 31, 1865, Huntsville received 31 freedpeople. By mid-1866, the inmates numbered 261: 95 whites, 41 Mexicans, 4 Native Americans, 117 black men, and 4 black women. Blacks, who made up 31 percent of the Texas population, constituted 46 percent of the total prisoners, and together with Mexicans and Indians composed 64 percent of all those imprisoned in the state penitentiary. By the end of 1866, Gillespie reported that Huntsville had 298 prisoners: 98 white men, 35 Mexicans, 155 black men, and 10 black women. Black Texans fueled the increase. Gillespie stated that "we are having almost daily acquisitions, most of all of whom are negroes."[11]

With the Conservatives firmly entrenched in power, their newspaper supporters exulted in the diminution of "worthless" blacks in Texas society. The *Texas Republican* declared that the "penitentiary is already full to overflowing and in less than two years all of the idle, vicious negroes in the State will find their way there."[12] Local courts responded enthusiastically to these calls to incarcerate "disruptive blacks," or those who did not conform to how the majority perceived the new social order. Blacks as slaves had primarily been disciplined by their owners, but after emancipation, black criminality moved from the private to the public sector. The state legislature responded with laws that courts readily used to entrap blacks.

Although the 1866 revision of the penal laws by Conservatives did not create a special category for freedpeople—the statutes were supposedly nondiscriminatory—they did have a considerable impact upon the Texas black community. For stealing a cow, sheep, goat, or hog worth twenty dollars or more (and in cases involving blacks, animals were almost always valued at twenty dollars or higher), a person was to be imprisoned in the penitentiary for not less than two or more than five years. If the property stolen was valued at less than twenty dollars, the individual would be incarcerated in the county jail for a term not exceeding two years and fined not over one hundred dollars, or confined without a fine.[13]

These new laws and other statutes ensured that black Texans arrived in significant numbers at Huntsville. At least one resident of the town took notice of the racial shift in the penitentiary's inmate population. The observer, James C. Devine, was the Freedmen's Bureau agent whose head-quarters graced the prison town. A former captain in the Twenty-eighth Pennsylvania Infantry, Devine was mustered out in Brenham, Texas. (Yes, he was a carpetbagger.) He received an appointment to the bureau's Bren-ham office shortly after the tragic fire in that town in 1866. Later assigned to Huntsville, Devine served there seven months. He became a Freedmen's Bureau traveling agent in May 1867. During the yellow-fever epidemic that year, Devine contracted the disease and died at the age of twenty-seven.[14]

Six months before Devine's death, however, he alerted bureau head-quarters to the steadily increasing number of former slaves arriving at the prison. Although little is known about his beliefs or attitudes, it is certain Devine was an astute observer. He estimated that between 140 and 150 freedpeople inhabited the institution at the time, and he had begun to in-quire why so many blacks were being imprisoned. From "good authority," the Huntsville agent learned that most of the blacks had been committed for two years or "upwards for the most trivial offences," such as stealing a few ears of corn, or had had cases brought against them for petty larceny, which involved anywhere from a few cents up to twenty dollars.[15]

Having found evidence of prisoners being improperly confined at Huntsville, Devine believed that the "object" of the penitentiary had been "perverted." Incarcerations were not "for a less period" than two years. He queried headquarters, "Is it not the intention to punish and confine in County jails persons convicted of minor" crimes? Devine cited the case of a freedman who had perpetrated a petty illegal act and who, instead of be-ing sent to the county jail for a few weeks or months, was now sentenced to the state prison "for a term not less than two and frequently as many as three, four and five years." Devine requested authority to approach the penitentiary's superintendent in order to "obtain a report of all freed-people confined" in the institution, including information on background particulars and the crimes they had committed.[16]

In early 1867 Devine again apprised the bureau's central office of the "daily additions being made of Freedpeople [to the penitentiary] from all parts of the State." His interpretation of why blacks were being incarcer-ated differed from the "idle, vicious Negroes" syndrome proffered by the *Texas Republican,* and he indicted the Conservatives. "It can only be hoped that a change of the form of State Government will end in the liberation of many confined therein," he wrote. Devine claimed the blacks' only "fault consisted in having incurred the anger of former masters and [they] are now the victims of their persecution, or being found guilty by a bitterly prejudiced jury of theft" or "petty larceny, and sentenced from two to ten years imprisonment."[17]

The bureau's new assistant commissioner, Charles Griffin, became increasingly concerned about Devine's observations and decided to survey the condition of the Texas penitentiary. In February 1867, William H. Sinclair, a bureau inspector, traveled to Huntsville to undertake this task. Born in Ohio and reared in Michigan, Sinclair joined a Michigan regiment when war came, served in the First Michigan Light Battery, and then transferred to the adjutant general's office. On the staff of Bvt. Maj. Gen. David S. Stanley of the Army of the Cumberland, he fought in several campaigns. Entering Texas with the occupation army, Sinclair was a "natural staff officer with a gift for the complex regulations and paperwork requirements of the army."[18]

Sinclair's talents soon attracted the attention of the Freedmen's Bureau. Serving in various capacities (Sinclair was incredibly versatile), he became so valuable to the agency that he advised J. B. Kiddoo, the state's second bureau commissioner, and made four long tours throughout Texas at Kiddoo's request. Sinclair traveled over much of the eastern half of the Lone Star State and became familiar with white attitudes toward blacks. Although he "suffered" himself, according to William L. Richter, "from a condescending view of black people," Sinclair was concerned with the unequal treatment of blacks and the prevalence of white injustice. He had earlier complained to Governor James W. Throckmorton about the treatment of two black prisoners in the Marlin (Falls County) jail.[19]

With the assistance of Devine and the permission of prison superintendent Gillespie, Sinclair first examined the records of the prison. From these he "could obtain nothing more definite than the general charge which is generally theft." A unique and fascinating piece of work, Sinclair's effort seems to be the only serious and intensive investigation that attempted to ascertain from blacks themselves the conditions and reasons surrounding their crimes. To determine the "specific act[s]" for which the freedpeople had been imprisoned, the inspector believed he had no "other recourse than to go among them and take their statements."[20] Sinclair may have been condescending, but he was certainly thorough in his examination of the inmates.

In February 1867, when Sinclair made his investigation, he found a total of 411 inmates; of this number, 225 (or 55 percent) were black, and 14 of those were women. Although Sinclair found no white females incarcerated, he remarked that two prisoners listed as freedwomen and who admitted they had been slaves before the war were "almost as white as any caucassian [*sic*]." Sinclair spoke to many other black prisoners, and several strange stories emerged.[21] There is no suggestion by Sinclair or anyone else that the inspector was ever hampered by state authorities in his canvassing of the black inmates. It was a rather remarkable accomplishment, but typical of Sinclair's thoroughness.

Sinclair "did not believe all the statements" submitted to him were "correct and truthful"; he was a too savvy veteran of the war to be that naive. He also understood the "inclination of convicts to plead their innocence and assert the injustice of their imprisonment." Despite this, Sinclair thought the "majority" of the prisoners' statements were reliable. Any "person listening to their simple frank statements and looking into the black and honest faces," he wrote, "could not believe otherwise." The severity of the sentences appalled Sinclair, and he highlighted for Assistant Commissioner Griffin the "crimes committed or alleged and to the punishment inflicted."[22]

Sinclair emphasized that many of the crimes for which blacks were now "undergoing punishment" had been, in the antebellum era, taken care of through the "lash." (He was not advocating a return to this system of discipline.) The average sentence was a "little over three years," and by the time Sinclair began his interviews, many of the freedpeople had been incarcerated for over a year. But their time at Huntsville did not always represent how long they had served, for "each of them before conviction was confined in a county jail for longer or shorter periods" of time, which in a significant number of cases extended to six months. (This preliminary imprisonment did not count toward prison time.) Sinclair's conclusion was simple and direct: "Their fate is indeed hard and unjust."[23]

Even though Sinclair despaired about the state of the criminal-justice system in Texas, he did find that prison hygiene and penitentiary conditions in general were about as good as could be expected. He candidly admitted that the "convicts are well fed[,] well clothed and kindly treated by the prison keepers." There is no reason to believe that the bureau inspector exaggerated, but the status and physical state of the inmates deteriorated in the next three years as the state moved toward the implementation of convict leasing. Superintendent N. A. H. Dudley reported in 1870 that "a great many of the convicts were in such a bad state of health that they were unfit for the performance of any labor."[24]

Although Sinclair saw none of the physical harshness of prison life, he did support his observations with a lengthy analysis of 223 freedmen and women, which listed their names, their home counties, their crimes, their sentences, and most important, statements from the prisoners themselves.

It is significant to note that Sinclair found that 89 percent (198 of 223) of the crimes committed by black prisoners had been committed against property, most of them agriculturally related. In light of one historian's claim about the violent nature of Louisiana freedpeople, the incredibly few incidents of Texas blacks being imprisoned for injuring or killing another person, of either race, is important. Only twenty-five cases (11 percent) involved violent crime.[25]

Whites, too, were mostly imprisoned for theft, but their imprisonment rate for violent crime was higher than that of blacks. Sinclair gave no indication of the reasons for white incarceration, and prison records provide no statistical evidence of the racial classification of inmates until a report submitted in 1876, nine years after Sinclair's investigation. This later account is the only available statistical source that identifies the race of the prisoners and the reasons for confinement. From August 31, 1875, to September 1, 1876, 635 prisoners were received at Huntsville, 229 of them white. Of these felons, 177 (77 percent) had been committed for various kinds of theft, and 40 (18 percent) for perpetrating violence on another person.[26]

Freedpeople who committed more-serious crimes may have been victims of vigilante "justice," and thus would never have made it to prison, but the evidence does not suggest such a pattern. To be sure, postwar Texas was an incredibly violent place, and blacks were often killed for trivial reasons, but the violence records of the Freedmen's Bureau, the army, and the 1868 state constitutional convention do not indicate any widespread killing of blacks who may have committed rape or murder. Many blacks were eliminated for political and economic reasons, but there is simply no documentation, except for some wildly impressionistic interpretations offered by newspapers and later historians, that blacks went on murdering and maiming sprees once they became free.[27]

It is within the realm of possibility that most of the outrages committed by black Texans fell within the category of black-on-black violence, which the white authorities did not bother to investigate or punish. Judges and other law-enforcement officials may have simply ignored the abuse that occurred in the Texas black community and focused upon those freedpeople who physically attacked whites. Apathy toward black offenders who assailed members of their own race, as well as the summary punishment visited upon those who attacked whites, might account for the small percentage of Texas blacks imprisoned for such crimes. Although these conjectures are within the realm of possibility, the records for postwar Texas indicate relatively little upheaval within the black community.[28]

And if blacks who resorted to violent action against a white person were lynched before a trial or imprisonment could take place, there is little evidence of that in Reconstruction-era Texas. In Kentucky, lynching became common immediately after the war, but white Texans preferred other methods of dealing with alleged offenders. The bureau's violence compendium, the most thorough available, lists only seven hangings for the years 1865 to 1868. Many lynchings may have gone unreported, but studies do not suggest this. It is possible that more whites were dispatched by this method than blacks. Blacks received extralegal justice at the hands of whites, but the rope was not the preferred weapon.[29]

The violence trends in Texas do resemble those that prevailed in Louisiana. In both states, blacks and Republicans were "blamed for provoking whites to violence" and for committing most of it. The statistics for Louisiana and Texas, however, belie those accusations. As Gilles Vandal has demonstrated, rural Louisiana blacks (those outside New Orleans), who composed 60 percent of the state's population (twice the percentage in Texas), accounted for only 25 percent of all homicides between 1865 and 1884. During Reconstruction, blacks in Louisiana perpetrated less than 20 percent of the murders but were victims in 80 percent of Louisiana killings, figures comparable to those in Texas. Vandal discovered that blacks "regularly committed" robberies after the war, but they "rarely" slew anybody.[30]

Vandal did not indicate how many blacks the state of Louisiana imprisoned during Reconstruction, but the patterns of crime among blacks there were quite similar to those in the Lone Star State. (Louisiana penitentiary records would suggest this same trend.) Violence and imprisonment are intimately connected, but projecting recent conditions onto the black communities of the past is unwarranted. To be sure, Vandal compiled statistics on black violence, and Sinclair attempted to determine why blacks had been incarcerated. What they discovered was that blacks in both states were the primary victims of white violence, committed only a small portion of violent crimes themselves, but ran afoul of the law because of nonviolent theft.

After the war, horses, ponies, and mules were valuable commodities in the South. In a region devastated by war, the theft of these animals brought harsh retribution from the courts, and blacks especially were severely punished for stealing these beasts. Generally, the circumstances surrounding the thievery did not concern the legal establishment: instead, courts were interested in whether the animals were alive or dead and how the accused thieves intended to use them. The lengths of the sentences clearly reflect how important white and black society believed animals to be in an agricultural economy. None of the terms in the thirty cases of horse, pony, and mule theft for which Sinclair's interviewees were convicted were for less than five years, and almost one-half (twelve) were for longer periods.[31]

Some freedpeople were victims of their own poor judgment and perhaps should have thought longer about the consequences of what they were doing. However we may evaluate the reasons for black theft of farm animals, some did have plausible stories for their actions. A few asserted they were owed money for services rendered, and when they failed to receive monetary satisfaction, they made the drastic and unwise decision to take an animal as compensation. When they were caught, they received sentences of five to seven years. For example, Richard Johnson, a Johnson County freedman, took a horse valued at twenty dollars "in lieu of $30.00 owed him by his employer." This was a major mistake on Johnson's part: the court sent him to Huntsville for seven years.[32]

Luke Bird, a Polk County freedman, admitted that he took the horse he had been convicted of stealing, but claimed that he did so only after his employer, who had allegedly killed two white men, shot at Bird twice. Although Bird may have been removing himself from a volatile situation the fastest way he knew how, he chose a method of transportation that belonged to a white man. It cost Bird seven years of his life. A Bastrop County freedman named Daniel Reno told Sinclair that he bought a pony for thirty dollars from his employer and promised to work off the purchase price. Reno did so, but later the employer desired the horse back and agreed to pay Reno the same price. Unable to obtain the money from his employer, Reno took back the horse; he received seven years.[33]

Two more horse-theft cases are worth noting. Levi Barns of Victoria County and Henry Clompton of Harris County apparently ran afoul of a "master" and a "mistress." The Victoria County freedman said that his employer "loaned" him a horse, but when he "refused to live with her another year" (the assumption is that he referred to labor contracting), she prosecuted him for theft. Clompton stated to Sinclair that his "master" went to Mississippi and left a horse in "his charge." While on his visit, the white man died. Clompton, or Sinclair, left many questions about the incident unanswered. The Harris County freedman declared that because he could not prove he was simply caring for the animal, "he was accused and convicted of theft."[34]

Swine ranked in popularity after horses, ponies, and mules on the animal-theft scale. In thirteen hog-stealing cases, involving twelve men and one woman, the quantity did not matter: all received two-year sentences.

Four cases involved men who either took or killed hogs "in lieu of rations" or "could not" or "did not" get enough to eat. One man admitted butchering three pigs because his diet consisted only of beef. Prince of Wales, a Cherokee County freedman, blamed his son-in-law for the theft, but confessed that he had accompanied him. For Thomas Ravis, a Rusk County freedman, revenge played a role. After Ravis and his employer had butchered some hogs, the employer gave him two pigs, which he took home. Later, Ravis was arrested, charged with theft, and sent to prison.[35]

One case involving the theft of seven pigs' feet also demonstrated how a former master or employer could dispose of a nonproductive worker. Sinclair described John Montgomery of Dallas County as a "lame old man[,] crippled in both feet and goes on crutches." Montgomery informed Sinclair that he received permission from the "mans cook" to take the pork, since he had been in the "habit of getting it when he wanted it, and had general permission to do so from him." The "owner," as Sinclair characterized the white man, coerced the cook into swearing that "she did not give" Montgomery "permission" to take the pigs' feet. The court gave him two years. Sinclair concluded that it was an "extremely hard case."[36]

Killing or stealing steers, calves, oxen, sheep, or chickens—or absconding with meat, bacon, pigs' feet, or wool—drew the same two-year confinement for Texas blacks. There were seventeen cases of this nature, all involving men, and the reasons they related to Sinclair for their acts paralleled those of many others in Huntsville. A few blacks, tired of laboring for almost nothing or seeing the ration provision of their contracts violated, took meat, animals, or fowl in lieu of rations or because they had not received any of their stipulated allotment and were hungry. Some of them openly admitted their culpability, with no attendant attempt at justification.[37]

Some fascinating twists occurred in cases of cotton, wheat, and flour theft. All involved men. The sentences ranged from two to five years, but only two individuals received confinements longer than the standard two-year incarceration. A few of the men had taken grain or cotton because they had not received any remuneration from their employers. Two Smith County freedmen, Hank Watts and Charles Richardson, had been convicted of stealing cotton, but Richardson was sentenced to four years and Watts to five. In their defense, they stated they had been hired to haul the cotton for a white man. Unknown to them, it had been stolen. In short, Watts and Richardson were serving time for a white man's crime.[38]

Corn will serve as a good example of why so many blacks were charged with theft. There were seventeen cases of stealing corn, with an almost uniform two-year sentence imposed in each. (Two exceptions, noted below, did not drastically change the pattern.) It made little or no difference how much blacks took: whether they stole eight or twenty-four ears, one-half to two bushels, or a load of corn worth twelve dollars, they faced twenty-four months in the state penitentiary. The two variations to the sentencing pattern involved Taylor Perkins, a Harrison County freedman who received three years for "stealing" twenty-one bushels, and Charles Bowen, a freedman from Walker County whose crime included taking six and a half bushels; he faced five years.[39]

Perhaps the strangest case Sinclair encountered, although surely not the most tragic, was that of George Barnett, a freedman from Anderson County. Barnett's story borders on the incredible, but because of the circumstances nevertheless could be true. Barnett related that he was cleaning out his employer's smokehouse and found one and a half pounds of wool along with some other trash. The freedman, being thrifty and diligent, cleaned the wool and made a pair of socks out of the residue. Barnett was prosecuted by his employer for stealing the wool, convicted, and sentenced to two years in the state penitentiary. Unfortunately, there is nothing to suggest precisely why Barnett's employer took this misguided action.[40]

Sinclair, bureau agents in the field, and concerned whites often commented upon how malice, revenge, and hatred motivated some people to connive at sending blacks on an extended tour of the state penitentiary. The revenge came in many forms. For those who had betrayed the "cause," the consequences were intended to be severe, as in the case of George Powell. At the end of the war, Powell, a Harris County freedman, directed a U.S. Army officer to seventeen hundred bales of cotton hidden by the Confederates. Powell was not arrested until one year after the alleged theft occurred; the obviously trumped-up charge was not even listed in the books of the prison.[41]

Other than the brief details Sinclair provided, there is almost no information on black female prisoners in Texas. The fourteen females at Huntsville came from thirteen counties spread across all parts of the state; they accounted for 6 percent of all black inmates and about 3 percent of all prisoners at the penitentiary, percentages that remained constant throughout the rest of the century. All but one of the freedwomen were convicted of theft; twelve were serving two-year sentences, one a three-year, and one a five-year. Carrie Petty, a Smith County freedwoman, received the longest sentence: she was serving five years for stealing three dresses. When

Sinclair recorded his interview with Petty, he wrote, "Has Babe—Accuser took her dresses and then Carrie took accusers."[42]

Like Petty, Jane Grisham, a Brazos County black woman, also had a "small child babe," according to Sinclair. Grisham had been convicted of stealing ten dollars and sentenced to two years. Upshur County resident Rose Moore had, along with her husband, been sent to Huntsville for two years for stealing a hog. Moore informed Sinclair that her husband had taken the pig—she "knew nothing of it." When Moore discovered the pork, "she made a party." Other freedwomen were charged with taking nightgowns, dresses, petticoats, shirts, stockings, rings, or cash. Elvira Mays of Harrison County was the only woman who served time for a crime other than theft or burglary. Convicted of giving her husband "a pick axe to get out of jail," she joined him at Huntsville for two years.[43]

Mary Burns, a Gonzales County black woman, had been convicted on the evidence of her daughter. She twice denied to Sinclair that she had taken a box containing thirty dollars belonging to her employer, and claimed the confession had been forced. Burns said that she and her daughter had been "hung up by [the] neck" twice to extract an admission of guilt. (There is no evidence the daughter served time.) This may have been the same Mary Burns about whom D. C. Dickson, the prison financial agent who employed Burns during her prison stay, was speaking when he said he had never known a "more exemplary negro." She carried the keys to the house and had "ample" opportunity to "indulge a propensity for stealing if she had any." Dickson requested that the governor pardon Burns.[44]

The bureau's continued involvement with ferreting out injustices against the freedpeople, along with Sinclair's investigation and recommendations for reducing the number of blacks in the penitentiary, further strained relations between the bureau and the civil authorities, especially the conservative regime of Governor Throckmorton. The bureau inspector surmised that the Texas situation was quite similar to what had occurred in Alabama, where blacks had also been sentenced to the penitentiary in droves. From his extensive discussions with black prisoners and the circumstances surrounding their convictions, Sinclair suggested that the state of Texas pardon many of them, just as the Alabama governor had done for inmates there.[45]

The bureau's suggestion to grant amnesty to black prisoners resulted in an intense controversy with Governor Throckmorton. T. R. Fehrenbach, in a popular Texas history written in the 1960s, argued that a "Bureau official [Sinclair], passing through [Huntsville], had interviewed this group and decided their offenses were all trivial. He did not investigate." The assistant commissioner, Charles Griffin, requested that Throckmorton evaluate these cases and release all the black prisoners. Fehrenbach says the governor "gave this unprecedented request the reply it deserved." Griffin, "deeply offended," never "forgave the 'Reb General.'"[46] This misinterpretation of the bureau's desires has often been perpetuated.

What the bureau suggested was that Throckmorton investigate the more egregious cases, and if the circumstances warranted, grant pardons. Bureau officials did not expect the governor to free every black prisoner. They based their request upon the events in Alabama, in which that state's prison had become "filled with freedpeople under almost the same circumstances" as in Texas. When Wager Swayne, assistant commissioner of the Freedmen's Bureau in Alabama, called the governor's attention to the conditions "under which they were arrested and convicted," the state's chief executive issued many pardons. The Texas bureau believed that "executive clemency" should be used to liberate those who had been victimized by an unjust system.[47]

In March 1867, Governor Throckmorton responded to the bureau's concern about the large number of blacks in Huntsville. Throckmorton reminded the bureau authorities that the "class of freedmen now confined in the Penitentiary, as a general rule," was the "most vicious and dishonest of the entire freed population of the State and instead of astonishment being expressed at the number" incarcerated, Throckmorton thought it spoke well for the freedpeople themselves and "is a contradiction of the charge of white oppression, that the number should be no greater than it is." (At the time, blacks represented 55 percent of the prison population.) Throckmorton felt it "remarkable indeed that a greater number of crimes were not committed, and a much greater number of convictions had."[48]

The governor, who hated the bureau, continued his diatribe for eight pages. Throckmorton contended that the conviction of only 225 persons of color for the crimes referred to showed that there could not have been much, or any, "oppression or injustice done this class of people." He found Sinclair's efforts to "certainly" be "a novel proceeding," but did not believe it "justifiable that an application of this character should be based *upon the statements of the convicts.*" Quite frankly, Throckmorton asserted that black testimony could not be trusted and that the facts had to "come from the officers of the courts where the parties were tried or from citizens of respectability who are acquainted with the previous character of the convicts."[49]

According to historian William Richter, the "whole question soon became moot" because bureau records show that "61 percent of the blacks held at Huntsville and interviewed by Sinclair had completed their terms or been pardoned" by Throckmorton before he was ousted in 1867.[50] If this assertion is true—and the evidence is vague, uncertain, and doubtful—then those blacks who were pardoned were simply being replaced by another group. In short, it is highly unlikely that such a large percentage of black prisoners were released. Regardless, Griffin, who remembered the governor's rebuke, had the final say. He influenced Philip H. Sheridan, head of the fifth military district, to remove Throckmorton as an "impediment" to reconstructing Texas.[51]

A revision of Texas penitentiary history (and possibly those of other southern states) in the postwar period is now necessary. First, contrary to past assertions, Texas blacks were convicted of petty crimes at an alarming rate. Second, the laws were changed to entrap blacks for theft and to ensure they served a minimum of two years. Third, although we know little about the background of the convicts, they were not the most "vicious" and "dishonest" of the freedpeople, as described by James W. Throckmorton. Fourth, the Freedmen's Bureau never suggested that the governor pardon all blacks in the state penitentiary. This myth has been perpetuated to discredit the bureau and prove Throckmorton's essential correctness.

The fact that the majority of blacks went to prison for crimes against property and not against other people, either white or black, suggests that, contrary to what Throckmorton emphasized, the legal system was functioning precisely the way the Conservatives desired. Another Texas Reconstruction penitentiary superintendent, N. A. H. Dudley, declared that the "negro or Union man stood but a poor chance for acquittal when tried before a jury composed necessarily of those who held their political sentiments as sufficient to merit their fullest condemnation."[52] In effect, penal slavery became one method by which the disgruntled losers in the war punished their former chattels. Huntsville became its embodiment.

At the beginning of Reconstruction in Texas, violence escalated against blacks, who faced a bigoted judicial system that felt compelled to rid the community of black thieves and use the penitentiary as a clearinghouse. Slavery had imposed rules and obligations upon whites, and their behavior toward bondspeople was expected to conform to these cultural restrictions. After emancipation, the old order collapsed, paternalism disappeared, and

Texas whites used not only weapons but also the "majesty of the law" to punish the freedpeople. Blacks were sentenced to the penitentiary for theft, not for violence, and eighteen months after the war they made up more than half of the inmate population.

NOTES

1. Thomas J. Goree, "Some Features of Prison Control in the South," *Proceedings of the Annual Congress of the National Prison Association of the United States held at Austin [Texas], December 2–6, 1897* (1898), 131–132. On Goree, see Thomas Cutter, ed., *Longstreet's Aide: The Civil War Letters of Major Thomas J. Goree* (Charlottesville: Univ. of Virginia Press, 1995). An early survey of Reconstruction crime is Edith Abbott, "The Civil War and the Crime Wave of 1865–70," *Social Service Review* 1 (June 1927): 212–234.

2. Mark T. Carleton, *Politics and Punishment: The History of the Louisiana State Penal System* (Baton Rouge: Louisiana State Univ. Press, 1971), 13; C. Vann Woodward, *Origins of the New South, 1877–1913* (Baton Rouge: Louisiana State Univ. Press, 1951), 212. Also important is Blake McKelvey, "Penal Slavery and Southern Reconstruction," *Journal of Negro History* 20 (Apr. 1935): 153–179.

3. James Robertson Nowlin, "A Political History of the Texas Prison System, 1849–1957" (master's thesis, Trinity Univ., 1962); Herman Lee Crow, "A Political History of the Texas Penal System, 1829–1951" (PhD diss., Univ. of Texas at Austin, 1964); Thomas E. Sullenberger, "An Interpretive History of the Texas Convict Lease System, 1871–1914" (master's thesis, Sam Houston State Univ., 1974); Thomas Michael Parrish, "'This Species of Slave Labor': The Convict Lease System in Texas, 1871–1914" (master's thesis, Baylor Univ., 1976); Donald R. Walker, *Penology for Profit: A History of the Texas Prison System, 1867–1912* (College Station: Texas A&M Univ. Press, 1988).

4. "Texas Penitentiary," *Journal of Prison Discipline and Philanthropy* 15 (Jan. 1860): 7–17; C. W. Raines, comp., *Year Book for Texas, 1901* (Austin: Gammel Book Co., 1902), 318–319; Crow, "Texas Penal System," 84–86: Bowen C. Tatum, "The Penitentiary Movement in Texas, 1847–1849" (master's thesis, Sam Houston State Univ., 1970), 16–21; Hilda Jane Zimmerman, "Penal Systems and Penal Reforms in the South Since the Civil War" (PhD diss., Univ. of North Carolina, 1947), 22; Edward L. Ayers, *Vengeance and Justice: Crime and Punishment in the Nineteenth-Century South* (New York: Oxford Univ. Press, 1984), 68; James A. Wilson, "Frontier in the Shadows: Prisons in the Far Southwest, 1850–1917," *Arizona and the West* 22 (Winter 1980): 323; Blake McKelvey, "Penology in the Westward Movement," *Pacific Historical Review* 2 (Dec. 1933): 418–438; Walker, *Penology for Profit,* 13–17. The early history of the Texas prison is similar to that of Alabama; see Mary Ann Neeley, "Painful Circumstances: Glimpses of the Alabama

Penitentiary, 1846–1852," *Alabama Review* 44 (Jan. 1991): 3–16. Alabama did not incarcerate slaves. In 1846 two white women inhabited Wetumpka (the Alabama penitentiary), one for manslaughter and one for incest.

5. Thomas W. Markham (penitentiary physician) to Col. John C. Easton, Apr. 24, 1863, and S. B. Hendricks (superintendent) to Governor Pendleton Murrah, Dec. 6 and 28, 1863, Penitentiary Papers, Texas State Library, Austin (hereinafter cited as Penitentiary Papers); Charles C. Nott, *Sketches in Prison Camps: A Continuation of Sketches of the War* (New York: Randolph, 1865), 133–135; Leon Mitchell, Jr., "Camp Grove: Confederate Military Prison," *Southwestern Historical Quarterly* 67 (July 1963): 15–21; F. Lee Lawrence and Robert W. Glover, *Camp Ford, C.S.A.: The Story of Union Prisoners in Texas* (Austin: Texas Civil War Centennial Advisory Committee, 1964); William Best Hesseltine, *Civil War Prisons: A Study in War Psychology* (Columbus: Ohio State Univ. Press, 1930).

6. James A. Baker (for Henry E. Perkins) to Board of Directors of the State Penitentiary, Feb. 13, 1863, and B. P. Lanham (sheriff, Harris County), Statement of Account, Jan. 28, 1863, Penitentiary Papers; Leon Mitchell, Jr., "Prisoners of War in the Confederate Trans-Mississippi" (master's thesis, Univ. of Texas at Austin, 1961), 139–142.

7. Perceptive studies are Philip J. Schwarz, *Twice Condemned: Slaves and the Criminal Laws of Virginia, 1705–1865* (Baton Rouge: Louisiana State Univ. Press, 1988); Daniel J. Flanigan, "The Criminal Law of Slavery and Freedom, 1800–1868" (PhD diss., Rice Univ., 1973); and David J. Bodenhamer, "The Efficiency of Criminal Justice in the Antebellum South," *Criminal Justice History* 3 (1982): 81–95.

8. *State of Texas v. George (a freedman)*, No. 527, Indictment and Judgment, Oct. 4, 1867, Governor's Papers [E. M. Pease], and "A List of Freedmen and Women Confined in the Texas Penitentiary," Nov. 6, 1866, Penitentiary Papers.

9. "Minutes of the Board of Public Labor," 3–18, Penitentiary Papers; H. P. N. Gammel, comp., *The Laws of Texas, 1822–1897,* 10 vols. (Austin: Gammel Book Co., 1898), 5:1110–1113; Walker, *Penology For Profit,* 19–22; Zimmerman, "Penal Systems and Penal Reforms," 67–69; Sullenberger, "Texas Convict Lease System," 19–21; Parrish, "'This Species of Slave Labor,'" 37–39; Nowlin, "Texas Prison System," 1–22. For an example of the type of abuse that occurred under convict leasing, see William Warren Rogers and Robert David Ward, *Convicts, Coal, and the Banner Mine Tragedy* (Tuscaloosa: Univ. of Alabama Press, 1987).

10. Claude Elliott, *Leathercoat: The Life History of a Texas Patriot* (San Antonio: Standard Printing Co., 1938), 173–174; Ruby Crawford Holbert, "The Public Career of James Webb Throckmorton, 1851–1867" (master's thesis, Univ. of Texas at Austin, 1932), 106–117. According to Sullenberger, "Governor Throckmorton's questionable management of penitentiary affairs further exacerbated a situation which was already approaching disaster" ("Texas Convict Lease System," 21). Walker agrees, stating that the Throckmorton administration "botched things" where the prison was concerned (*Penology for Profit,* 23).

11. "Freedmen and Women in the Texas Penitentiary," Penitentiary Papers; *Texas Almanac for 1867* (Galveston: Richardson and Co., 1867), 202.

12. *Texas Republican,* Aug. 25, 1866.

13. For an analysis of these statutes, see Barry A. Crouch, "'All the Vile Passions': The Texas Black Code of 1866," *Southwestern Historical Quarterly* 97 (June 1993): 29. Walker argues that this penal codification "brought a reduction in sentence for those convicted of stealing cattle, sheep, goats, or hogs" (*Penology for Profit,* 115–116). Because the value of the animal had to be twenty dollars or more before someone accused of stealing it would be confined in the penitentiary, Walker believes this revision of the 1857 law was not "an attempt to ensnare blacks and feed them into the state prison system." (Of course, the 1857 law did not apply to slaves.) But the later law also declared that anyone who took, drove, used, or removed any stock belonging to another from its "accustomed range," or without the owner's consent, with intent to defraud would be charged with theft. If convicted, the accused could receive a maximum two-year prison term, or a fine not exceeding one thousand dollars, or both. Contrary to Walker's argument, these statutes were used almost exclusively against the freedpeople. Although the 1866 enactments cannot be described as "pig laws" (laws designed to ensnare blacks because of their so-called propensity to steal pork), they were certainly akin to them. Walker also confuses the immediate postwar laws with those later passed under the redeemers.

14. *General Orders, Special Orders, Circulars, and Rosters, 1865–1869,* assistant commissioner, Texas, Records of the Bureau of Refugees, Freedmen, and Abandoned Lands, Texas, Record Group 105, National Archives, Washington, D.C., vol. 9, (hereinafter, references to the Texas bureau records will be cited as RG 105); Harry E. Estill, "The Old Town of Huntsville," *Quarterly of the Texas State Historical Association* 3 (Apr. 1900): 271; William L. Richter, *Overreached on All Sides: The Freedmen's Bureau Administrators in Texas, 1865–1868* (College Station: Texas A&M Univ. Press, 1991), 177–178. See also Richter, "The Brenham Fire of 1866: A Texas Reconstruction Atrocity," *Louisiana Studies* 14 (Fall 1975): 287–314.

15. James C. Devine to Henry A. Ellis, Oct. 4, 1866, vol. 110, 3, RG 105.

16. Ibid.

17. Devine to Sinclair (agent, Galveston), Jan. 12, 1867, D-151, Operations Report, RG 105.

18. William H. Sinclair (inspector) to J. T. Kirkman (acting assistant adjutant general), Feb. 26, 1867, box 21 (hereinafter cited as Sinclair Report), RG 105; William L. Richter, "Who Was the Real Head of the Texas Freedmen's Bureau? The Role of Brevet Colonel William H. Sinclair as Acting Assistant Inspector General," *Military History of the Southwest* 20 (Fall 1990): 124. On Griffin, see Richter, "Tyrant and Reformer: General Griffin Reconstructs Texas, 1865–66," *Prologue: Journal of the National Archives* 10 (Winter 1978): 225–241; and Crouch, *Freedmen's Bureau* (1992), 27–32.

19. Sinclair to Throckmorton, Jan. 17, 1867, Letters Sent, vol. 5, 415, RG 105; Richter, "Head of the Texas Freedmen's Bureau?" 136, 155.

20. Sinclair Report, RG 105.

21. Ibid. A brief exposition of this document is in Crouch, "Freedmen's Bureau Records: Texas, a Case Study," *Afro-American History: Sources for Research,* ed. Robert L. Clarke (Washington, D.C.: Howard Univ. Press, 1981), 79–84; and Richter, "Head of the Texas Freedmen's Bureau?" 136–138. For a comparison, see E. C. Wines and Theodore W. Dwight, *Report on the Prisons and Reformatories of the United States and Canada: Made to the Legislature of New York, January, 1867* (Albany: Van Benthuysen and Sons, 1867).

22. Sinclair Report, RG 105.

23. Ibid.

24. Ibid.; *Report of the Condition of the State Penitentiary, Huntsville, February 10, 1870* (1870), 10. For comparable conditions, see Paul G. Hubbard, "Life in the Arizona Territorial Prison, 1876–1910," *Arizona and the West* 1 (Winter 1959): 317–330.

25. Sinclair Report, RG 105; Joe Gray Taylor, *Louisiana Reconstructed, 1863–1877* (Baton Rouge: Louisiana State Univ. Press, 1974), 421. A similar perception of black violence is found in Joel Williamson, *The Crucible of Race: Black-White Relations in the American South since Emancipation* (New York: Oxford Univ. Press, 1984), 58. Cf. Eric Foner, *Reconstruction: America's Unfinished Revolution, 1863–1877* (New York: Harper and Row, 1988), 121; and Leon Litwack, *Been in the Storm So Long: The Aftermath of Slavery* (New York: Knopf, 1979), 276–282.

26. *Report of the Inspector of the Texas State Penitentiary, Located at Huntsville, Texas, to the Governor of Texas, Submitted October 16, 1876* [H. K. White, inspector] (1876), 6–24, 33. Of the twelve white convicts who did not fall into the theft or violence category, ten had no offense listed, one had been imprisoned for bigamy, and one for false swearing. By September 1, 1876, the prison population was almost 65 percent black (1,028 out of 1,590), around 28 percent white (439), and a little more than 7 percent Mexican (121); in addition, there were 2 Native Americans.

27. *Criminal Offences Committed in State of Texas,* 3 vols., RG 105; *Abstracts of Crimes Committed in Counties of Texas, January 1869–March 1870,* 3 vols., Office of Civil Affairs, Records of United States Army Continental Commands, 1821–1920, Record Group 393, National Archives; *Journal of the Reconstruction Convention, Which Met at Austin, Texas, June 1, A.D. 1868* (Austin: Tracy, Siemering, 1870), 193–195, 501. Texas violence for the first three years after the war is explored in Barry A. Crouch, "A Spirit of Lawlessness: White Violence, Texas Blacks, 1865–1868," *Journal of Social History* 18 (Winter 1984): 217–232; and Gregg Cantrell, "Racial Violence and Reconstruction Politics in Texas, 1867–1868," *Southwestern Historical Quarterly* 93 (Jan. 1990): 333–355. In general, see George C. Rable, *But There Was No Peace: The Role of Violence in the Politics of Reconstruction* (Athens: Univ. of Georgia Press, 1984). One observer quipped that murder was an "inalienable" state right in Texas.

28. See the sources cited in note 27 above.

29. *Criminal Offences Committed in State of Texas,* RG 105. On Kentucky, see George C. Wright, *Racial Violence in Kentucky, 1865–1940: Lynchings, Mob Rule, and "Legal Lynchings"* (Baton Rouge: Louisiana State Univ. Press, 1990), 41–46. On lynching in general, see James Elbert Cutler, *Lynch-Law: An Investigation Into the History of Lynching in the United States* (New York: Longmans, Green, 1905); National Association for the Advancement of Colored People, *Thirty Years of Lynching in the United States, 1889–1918* (New York: Arno Press, 1919); Richard Maxwell Brown, *Strain of Violence: Historical Studies of American Violence and Vigilantism* (New York: Oxford Univ. Press, 1975), 214–216; and Edward L. Ayers, *The Promise of the New South: Life After Reconstruction* (New York: Oxford Univ. Press, 1992), 156–159, 495–497. The best study is probably W. Fitzhugh Brundage, *Lynching in the New South: Georgia and Virginia, 1880–1930* (Urbana: Univ. of Illinois Press, 1993).

30. Gilles Vandal, "Black Violence in Post–Civil War Louisiana," *Journal of Interdisciplinary History* 25 (Summer 1994): 47, 53, 63. For further confirmation, see Vandal, "'Bloody Caddo': White Violence against Blacks in a Louisiana Parish, 1865–1876," *Journal of Social History* 25 (Winter 1991): 373–388. A solid comparison of crime and justice in the North and South from the colonial era to the late nineteenth century is provided by three works of Michael Stephen Hindus: "The Contours of Crime and Justice in Massachusetts and South Carolina, 1767–1878," *American Journal of Legal History* 21 (1977): 212–237; "Black Justice under White Law: Criminal Prosecutions of Blacks in Antebellum South Carolina," *Journal of American History* 63 (Dec. 1976): 575–599; and *Prison and Plantation: Crime, Justice, and Authority in Massachusetts and South Carolina, 1767–1878* (Chapel Hill: Univ. of North Carolina Press, 1980).

31. Sinclair Report, RG 105. For the importance of animals to the southern economy, see Roger L. Ransom and Richard Sutch, *One Kind of Freedom: The Economic Consequences of Emancipation* (New York: Cambridge Univ. Press, 1977).

32. Sinclair Report, RG 105.

33. Ibid.

34. Ibid.

35. Ibid.

36. Ibid.

37. Ibid.

38. Ibid.

39. Ibid. It severely stretches the imagination to believe that Perkins would steal an entire load of corn, since that much grain would be difficult to dispose of quickly.

40. Ibid.

41. Ibid.

42. Ibid.; J. U. Wright (district court clerk, Smith County) to Thad McRae

(private secretary to E. M. Pease), Dec. 20, 1867, Penitentiary Papers; Jane Howe Gregory, "Persistence and Irony in the Incarceration of Women in the Texas Penitentiary, 1907–1910" (master's thesis, Rice Univ., 1994), 9. The literature on nineteenth-century female prisoners is growing. See works by Nicole Hahn Rafter: "Female State Prisoners in Tennessee: 1831–1979," *Tennessee Historical Quarterly* 39 (Winter 1980): 485–497; "Prisons for Women, 1790–1980," *Crime and Justice* 5 (1983): 129–181; "Gender, Prisons, and Prison History," *Social Science History* 9 (Summer 1985): 233–247; *Partial Justice: Women in State Prisons, 1800–1935* (Boston: Univ. Press of New England, 1985), 131–156; see also Estelle B. Freedman, *Their Sisters' Keepers: Women's Prison Reform in America, 1830–1930* (Ann Arbor: Univ. of Michigan Press, 1981), 7–45; Anne M. Butler, "Still in Chains: Black Women in Western Prisons, 1865–1910," *Western Historical Quarterly* 20 (Feb. 1989): 18–35; and Gary R. Kremer, "Strangers to Domestic Virtues: Nineteenth-Century Women in the Missouri Prison," *Missouri Historical Review* 84 (Apr. 1990): 293–310.

43. Sinclair Report, RG 105.

44. Ibid.; D. C. Dickson (prison financial agent) to Governor E. M. Pease, Nov. 20, 1867, Penitentiary Papers.

45. Sinclair Report, RG 105.

46. T. R. Fehrenbach, *Lone Star: A History of Texas and the Texans* (New York: Macmillan, 1968), 403; Rupert Norval Richardson, Ernest Wallace, and Adrian N. Anderson, *Texas: The Lone Star State,* 3d ed. (Englewood Cliffs, N.J.: Prentice-Hall, 1970), 210–211, 221; 4th ed. (1981), 250–251; and 5th ed. (1988), 233–234; Lawrence D. Rice, *The Negro in Texas, 1874–1900* (Baton Rouge: Louisiana State Univ. Press, 1971), 153–156, 165; William L. Richter, "General Phil Sheridan, the Historians, and Reconstruction," *Civil War History* 33 (June 1987): 131–154.

47. Sinclair Report, RG 105. On Swayne, see Kenneth B. White, "Wager Swayne: Racist or Realist?" *Alabama Review* 31 (Apr. 1978): 92–109.

48. James Oakes to J. T. Kirkman (acting assistant adjutant general), Mar. 15, 1867, vol. 48, 156–157, RG 105; J. W. Throckmorton to Oakes (commander, Austin), Mar. 18, 1867, J. W. Throckmorton Papers, Center for American History, University of Texas Archives, Austin (hereinafter cited as Throckmorton Papers). There is also a copy of the letter in vol. 46, n.p., RG 105.

49. Throckmorton to Oakes, Mar. 18, 1867, Throckmorton Papers; Oakes to Kirkman, Mar. 25, 1867, vol. 48, 161, RG 105.

50. Richter, "Real Head of the Texas Freedmen's Bureau?" 138. There is simply no indication of where the figure "61 percent" came from or how it was derived. For an opposing view, see Butler, "Still in Chains," 26–27, n. 20; and the Penitentiary Papers, which suggest that maybe 40 percent or less of the freedpeople were pardoned.

51. Throckmorton, "To The People of Texas," Aug. 10, 1867, Throckmorton Papers.

52. *Condition of the State Penitentiary, Huntsville,* 10. It would not be until the latter part of the nineteenth century that the progressives influenced a southern penal-reform movement. See Hilda Jane Zimmerman, "The Penal Reform Movement in the South during the Progressive Era, 1880–1917," *Journal of Southern History* 17 (Nov. 1951): 462–492; and Paul M. Lucko, "The 'Next Big Job': Women Prison Reformers in Texas, 1918–1930," in *Women and Texas History: Selected Essays,* ed. Fane Downs and Nancy Baker Jones, 72–87 (Austin: Texas State Historical Association, 1993).

POSTSCRIPT TO PART III

The essay by Crouch and Schultz was a response to
C. Vann Woodward's revisionist view in *The Strange Career of Jim Crow*
(Oxford 1955), which argued that legal segregation occurred in the 1890s,
much later than historians had previously assumed. Rejecting Woodward's
interpretation, Crouch and Schultz, in one of the earliest state studies,
demonstrate that segregation in Texas began immediately after the Civil
War ended. This essay was Crouch's first study of Texas Reconstruction
and was based upon a careful reading of contemporary newspapers. See
also James M. Smallwood, "The Woodward Thesis Revisited: Race Relations and the Development of Social Segregation in Reconstruction Texas:
A Brief Essay," *Negro History Bulletin* (1984). For a useful compilation of
the controversy surrounding Woodward's thesis, see *When Did Southern
Segregation Begin?,* readings selected and introduced by John David Smith
(Bedford/St. Martin's, 2002).

Crouch's essay on the Texas Black Code of 1866 reinforces his critique
of the Woodward thesis and argues that whites were determined to keep
blacks in their place and restrict their freedom and mobility. Even though
the Thirteenth Amendment abolished slavery, whites hoped to circumscribe blacks' movements and use them as a compliant labor force.

Two essays in this section indicate Crouch's creative use of government sources and Freedman's Bureau records. In "A Spirit of Lawlessness,"
Crouch uses two Reconstruction-era reports—the first from a special
committee on lawlessness and violence established by the 1868 Texas Constitutional Convention, and the second (a register of criminal offenses)
from the Texas Freedmen's Bureau—to elaborate on the amount of mayhem in Reconstruction Texas, most of it perpetuated by whites against
blacks. This essay was path-breaking, even though his conclusion about
the randomness of the violence was challenged by Gregg Cantrell, who
argued for a direct relationship between political activism and violence

in "Racial Violence and Reconstruction Politics in Texas, 1867–1868," *Southwestern Historical Quarterly* (1990). Clearly a full-fledged monograph on Texas violence is needed, and should be modeled after Gilles Vandal's *Rethinking Southern Violence: Homicides in Post–Civil War Louisiana, 1866–1884* (Ohio State Univ. Press, 2000).

Even more research needs to be done on incarceration in the Reconstruction era. Crouch's "The Fetters of Justice: Black Texans and the Penitentiary during Reconstruction" concludes that blacks were sent to prison mainly for committing crimes against property, such as stealing horses, and not for perpetuating violent crimes against whites or other blacks; his findings need to be substantiated by more research not only on Texas history but also on case studies of other states during this period, similar to those found in *Vengeance and Justice: Crime and Punishment in the Nineteenth-Century South* by Edward L. Ayers (Oxford, 1984). A useful early study is Blake McKelvey, "Penal Slavery and Southern Reconstruction," *Journal of Negro History* (1935). Michael Stephen Hindus provides a comparative perspective in *Prison and Plantation: Crime, Justice, and Authority in Massachusetts and South Carolina, 1767–1878* (Univ. of North Carolina Press, 1980). An important overview is William D. Carrigan, *The Making of a Lynching Culture: Violence and Vigilantism in Central Texas, 1836–1916* (Univ. of Illinois Press, 2004), but see the critical review essay by Bertram Wyatt-Brown in the *H-Net Book Review* (March 2005).

PART IV *Freedmen's Bureau Agents and African American Politicians*

Nine

GUARDIAN OF THE
         FREEDPEOPLE

         Texas Freedmen's Bureau Agents and
         the Black Community

Created by Congress in March 1865, the Bureau of Refugees, Freedmen, and Abandoned Lands, known as the Freedmen's Bureau, supervised the transition of the slaves from bondage to freedom. The bureau was directed by a national commissioner; the office in each former Confederate state was headed by an assistant commissioner, who administered bureau operations; and field personnel (subassistant commissioners) stationed in the major cities and towns across the region conducted daily bureau business. Often ignored in the historical literature, these men who constantly interacted with the black community became the heart of the Reconstruction process. Throughout their tenure, they faced numerous obstacles and stupefying responsibilities.

Texas provides a unique opportunity to observe the actions of the local agents and the many barriers they encountered. The state is geographically huge, and local bureau officers supervised enormous areas, often covering 1,500 square miles. These men had to contend with a great deal of white-on-black violence and numerous outrages perpetrated among whites themselves. Although postrevisionist historians have seen the agency as being too solicitous of planter approval and too conservative where black interests were involved, Texas agents did not necessarily conform to this pattern.

The Freedmen's Bureau has often been explored nationally and at the state level from an administrative perspective. The focus has been upon either Oliver Otis Howard, the national commissioner, or the agency in a particular southern state. More often than not, the organization has been condemned. Originally, historians believed it to be politically involved and too supportive of black equality. In current studies, the bureau is castigated for not doing enough to assist the newly freed slaves and for dashing their efforts at autonomy.[1] Regardless, any executive-level view tells us almost nothing about how personnel in the field worked for the legal and political equality of blacks.

A brief look at the field agents who served in the Texas Freedmen's Bureau is necessary: how they interacted with the black community, the problems and difficulties they confronted, and what steps the bureau took to ensure that agents fulfilled their responsibilities to the freedpeople. Intertwined with an agent's duties were his relations with civil authorities and planters, who constantly attempted to discredit the bureau and its personnel.

These agents, or subassistant commissioners, have also been viewed disdainfully. "When it came to the Bureau agents below the rank of assistant commissioner," stated John A. Carpenter, Oliver Otis Howard "was not so fortunate." He "had little control" over the men picked by the state bureau chief, and Carpenter claims that even those who headed the state agency had little voice in the selection of men who supervised local districts. The state commissioners had to depend upon officers who were detailed from the regular army (generally from the Veteran Reserve Corps) and had been disabled in some fashion during the war.[2] This seems to be an unnecessarily negative view of all bureau agents.

Throughout its existence, the Bureau lacked manpower. A shortage of funds meant it could not pay civilian agents, and the army consistently mustered out individuals. Before his death, Carpenter identified 2,441 bureau agents who had served throughout the organization's existence. At its peak, wrote Eric Foner, the bureau never employed "more than 900 agents in the entire South." For example, Alabama had a maximum of only 20 field agents, and but a dozen served in Mississippi in 1866. Eastern Texas, which is the same size as Alabama and Mississippi together, never had more than 65, and for much of the bureau's tenure the numbers allotted to cover such a vast region remained abysmally low.[3]

Recent scholarship has seriously revised the negative portrait of the Texas agents. Cecil Harper, Jr., finds that a total of 202 men served as subassistant commissioners during the Bureau's Texas tenure. "Those who served as assistant commissioners in Texas made every attempt to secure men of ability and proven loyalty to serve as local agents," writes Harper, "but clearly, they were not always successful." Some agents, Harper notes, were drunks, functionally illiterate, or criminally dishonest, but these cannot be characterized as "typical." In general, the agents' commitment was real, and overall they can be characterized as men of ability, integrity, and honesty, "who did the best they could."[4]

A local agent's duties and responsibilities can only be described as daunting. Activities "included introducing a workable system of free labor in the South, establishing schools for freedmen, providing aid to the destitute, aged, ill, and insane, adjudicating disputes among blacks and between the races, and attempting to secure for blacks and white Unionists equal justice from the state and local governments." Serving as "diplomat, marriage counselor, educator, supervisor of labor contracts, sheriff, judge, and jury," each had to "win the confidence of blacks and whites alike in a situation where race and labor relations had been poisoned by mutual distrust and conflicting interests," wrote Eric Foner.[5]

Bureau agents did not view black Texans with an open mind. Imbued with the racial attitudes of the nineteenth century, they performed in a manner that is nevertheless surprising, even for the time. Though they occasionally perceived the black community as backward, believed their work rhythms did not always coincide with free-labor ideology, and at times saw their morals as suspect, they blamed these "deficiencies" upon slavery. Considering the agents' backgrounds, as well as the social and racial milieu within which they performed, their collective efforts on behalf of the legal rights, education, and social problems of the former slaves were sincerely given. They demonstrated honesty and perseverance in the face of incredible odds.

Writing his monthly report from Sumpter, Texas, in November 1867, Hiram S. Johnson, a citizen agent, declared (often underlining his points) that the "*spirit* of *slavery* and a *love* of the '*Lost Cause*' still animates and *lives* in about *half* our people." They "*hate* the *government, its laws* and its *officials*" and lose "no opportunity to throw *every obstacle* in the way of their *administration*." Only the "*full* and *rigid* enforcement of the *Congressional policy* of *Reconstruction*" would remedy this state of affairs. Whites attempted to "*cheat, swindle* and *oppress*" the freedpeople, "at *all* times and in *every* way." If not for "*fear* of the *Military Authorities*," he concluded, the "*woods* would *stink* with the *carcasses* of *dead freedmen*."[6]

A. H. Cox, the agency official in Liberty, Texas, found time to be the final arbiter in making "all things right." Where a bureau agent "does his duty," Cox informed headquarters, the "freedmen have confidence in him and they will obey all that he may say to them and they think it all wright [*sic*], but where he is constantly doing them wrongs they very correctly consider him the worst enemy they have instead of being their friendly adviser in all instances." Later he observed that he had "heard both white and black complain of Agents being partial to either the one race or the other," which Cox found to be a "natural consequence," since "no man can do justice and please all and when that is done one feels as his duties are done."[7]

From Hempstead, Texas, in 1867, John H. Archer wrote Assistant Commissioner Joseph B. Kiddoo that it must "be clear that the Bureau is positively necessary (and if President [Andrew] Johnson will only take his seat in my office for a week I will undertake to convince him of the fact) and if the Bureau is necessary troops are also necessary, as without troops to sustain him, I cannot conceive it possible" for an agent "to fully carry out his instructions, execute the orders of the Bureau and the Laws of Congress; and if he cannot do that he may just as well be at the 'Hub of the Universe', as at his post."[8] Johnson, Cox, and Archer, at the center of local-level Reconstruction, experienced what all agents faced every day.

Abner Doubleday, of baseball fame, asserted that "every kind of business, wherein freedmen are concerned, is transacted by this office when consistent with the laws and regulations of the Bureau." Another agent simply could not keep abreast of all his responsibilities and complained that he had "more to do than I ought to," since he also served as post adjutant and acting assistant quartermaster. One Houston official summarized the plight of every Texas agent when he wrote that almost every day "my office has been thronged with Freed people and I have had more business to do than I could well attend to." Combined with the excessive size of their subdistricts, agents found the lack of time, space, and military support a constant source of frustration.[9]

One of the first actions an agent took when he arrived at his post was to seek out the local black leader. Often using this person as an intermediary, a bureau official could more effectively serve the black community. In Columbia, for example, when it appeared that there might be difficulties in preserving the peace during the 1867 Christmas season, the subassistant commissioner appointed a freedman, Anderson Hendrick, as chief of a "special police force" to maintain harmonious relations between whites and blacks. To a large extent, he succeeded.[10]

When Texas blacks approached a bureau agent, they quickly determined how sympathetic the officer would be to their individual plight. Blacks made a distinction among the agents and divided them into two categories. James C. Butler, the Huntsville subassistant commissioner, received complaints from freedmen living in Leon, Houston, and Polk counties, areas outside his subdistrict. Although he referred them to the agents in their own counties, blacks claimed that these were "'Southern Bureau's,'" meaning the officer in their section sympathized with the planters. Butler's subdistrict was already so large that he could only refer the cases to head-quarters and to the agents of whom the freedmen had complained.[11]

Charles F. Rand, who characterized Clarksville (the headquarters for his subdistricts) as a "blood thirsty hole," understood that because of the size of the area he supervised, freedpeople would have problems travel-ing to his office. So, Rand went to them. On one tour, he visited all the counties in his subdistricts with the exception of Lamar. It took Rand two weeks to cover the area. In Cotton Gin, David S. Beath indicated the danger involved in freedpeople traveling a long distance to consult a Bu-reau agent: "This district is too large for one agent to attend to," he wrote headquarters, "as some of the freedpeople have to come 50 miles and are liable to be assassinated."[12]

Texas bureau agents reiterated again and again that the freedpeople feared retaliation by whites if they informed the agency of some transgres-sion. Always a reality, it too often came true. Neil Kirk, a Nacogdoches freedman, reported William Furra to the local agent for threatening his life and shooting at him. The local agent fined Furra $20. On Christmas Day 1867, Furra lured Kirk into the woods and shot him off his horse (the bullet grazed Kirk's forehead). Furra then tied Kirk's hands behind him and fired a bullet into each arm and another into his shoulder. In Paris, the agent claimed blacks feared challenging whites in bureau courts, prefer-ring to "suffer wrong and abuse than suffer death for complaining of their wrongs.[13]

Freedmen persevered, however. They approached agents in the middle of the night to explain existing conditions in a specific area. At midnight on June 30, 1867, the Sterling officer, J. L. Randall, was "awakened by two freedmen, who came so noiselessly upon the verandeh" [*sic*] where he slept that Randall "thought they had come for a bad purpose." Randall drew a derringer, but recognized one of the men as the "most influential freedman in the county." The individuals related accounts of being "beat and whipped and shot, and that nobody was punished for it and the blacks would not stand it any longer." The agent warned that they might be killed if they retaliated. The freedmen said they were "prepared for that kind of business."[14]

One of the agent's major functions was to nurture the implementation of a contract labor system based largely upon an amalgamation of European and American economic philosophies. This process intimately involved a subassistant commissioner with black workers, the signing of contracts, the protection of economic rights under the law, fair compensation at the end of the harvest season, and, in general, the treatment of laborers. Agents often clashed with planters, who hoped to maintain complete control over their labor forces. The bureau effectively negated many of the coercive aspects of the 1866 black code, so employers sought other methods to enhance their bargaining position and discredit the agency.

In Brazos County, Edward Miller observed that "there seems to be a reluctance on the part of the freedmen, to have their contracts approved, by anybody" but a bureau agent, and some even refused "to go before a Magistrate." Blacks declared that "contracts have been read to them different from what their purport is now," and the agent apprehended a "great deal of trouble from that source." Because of fraud and false statements, Texas blacks often expressed the fact that the "white man can read and write" and would promise them a great deal, but put "what he pleases in the contract." They felt that having an agent read the provisions would reduce their chance of being swindled.[15]

Agents attempted to annul dishonest contracts, but whites challenged their authority. In Huntsville, M. M. Elmore accused freedman Fred Smiley of violating his contract, which had been drawn up in accordance with the 1866 labor law, part of the Texas black code. The civil court ordered Smiley to return to Elmore's employ under the original agreement, or he could work "in the street, thus reducing him to the state of a peon." The agent had previously disapproved of the document and informed Smiley he could "go where he pleased." Unfortunately, the court's decision aroused "very injurious feelings in the minds of the freedmen," the agent wrote, and made them "suspicious of the Bureau, thinking that it has no authority."[16]

End-of-harvest settlements demanded an agent's "presence on nearly every plantation." Said one subassistant commissioner, few freedmen would have received "their equitable portion" unless "given to him by" an agent. One bureau man had almost one hundred plantations in his territory and admitted he would not be "able to do justice to all freedpeople" unless he could hire special agents. The Livingston bureau official believed he was "getting them down badly" when he visited plantations and divided the crops. He had taken his stand "in justice to all," he wrote, "and if they do not kill me or the Government cut my head off by relieving me," he would teach employers to pay the freedmen "what they justly owe him, and stop their abuses of them."[17]

The largest number of an agent's cases involved disputes over accounts and fines between employers and employees. E. M. Whittmore handled such disagreements by reading to the freedmen the items of each account and "disallowed any articles they denied having received." Planters also made efforts to have the freedmen pay transportation costs if they had been hired from another area. Even into 1868, planters argued for the right to deduct from the wages of black laborers for loss of time, disobedience, impertinence, and neglect. If permitted, such practices would place laborers entirely in their employer's power and leave them in a "state of beggary and dependence" at the end of the year, observed one distressed bureau agent.[18]

Blacks desired equal justice under the law, and this became a primary bureau goal. Blacks often received the same judicial treatment as whites did in bureau courts. Agents accepted black testimony and affidavits long before local, county, and state officials ever considered such a course of action. Agents also promoted the idea that the freedpeople should be allowed to serve on juries and participate in the legal process. They constantly attended courts in action to determine if the freedpeople received fair treatment. Hiram Clark, headquartered in Clinton, attended district courts in Victoria and DeWitt counties to observe how the civil authorities dealt with freedmen involved in civil and criminal trials.[19]

In addition to their many other duties, agents also served as justices of the peace, or as one official stated: "I dispose of business after the fashion of the Old English Magistrates." Informing headquarters of how he conducted his court, the Sherman agent described it thus: "I summon the parties to appear at my office on a certain day bringing witnesses on each side, I hear the evidence and thus give my judgment according to what I conceive to be right, which has given, so far, I believe entire satisfaction to both races." And the caseload was heavy. One agent reported that in January 1868 he heard seventy-two cases of debt between blacks and whites and eighty-four cases among blacks involving debts and quarrels.[20]

Securing justice for blacks proved to be an exasperating task. The incompetence, uncooperativeness, and fearfulness of civil officials hampered an agent's efforts to promote legal equality. In Huntsville, an agent referred to a justice of the peace as "not only a rebel" but as a "bigoted superannuated old fool and not in any way competent to perform his duties." One bureau official observed that "if the civil authorities could be but induced to act firmly and justly and in unison with" the government, "then perhaps it might be possible to get along without troops." The local leaders feared to do their "duty as the mass of whites" were opposed to extending the "protection of the law" to blacks.[21]

Civil authorities administered the law with indifference and apathy. Their inactivity, wrote the Wharton subassistant commissioner, became a "shield not to the innocent but the guilty and is oftener used as a means of persecution and to control the freedmen than protect him in his interests and to do him justice." Blacks could not rely upon these antediluvian individuals for either justice or protection. Nesbit B. Jenkins somewhat exaggeratedly believed that the "presence of only one U.S. Soldier here would be a greater guarantee and security to the freedman than all the civil courts and authorities." One agent stated to headquarters: "you can perceive what justice these civil courts render to the negro."[22]

The Sumpter agent, Charles Schmidt, wrote that his experience had taught him that the nearer a subassistant commissioner could "approximate his position to that of a Civil Magistrate the better, and the same protection extended to him by the Military should be extended to *all*." He observed that the greatest trouble that civil officers labored under was that they were "*afraid* to act." Schmidt believed that though often intimidated, "they should be assured of protection and then compelled to act." Few complaints arose when they did perform their duties; the "complaint is they fail to act." Their failure was due to their timidity, and they attempted to "throw it upon" the agent, "thinking him better protected than they are."[23]

Agents often commented that the "civil law is a farce." Freedmen "dare not report an outrage—a justice dare not issue a warrant, or a sheriff serve it if the freedman be the accuser." Force seemed to be the only way to assure black equality. There is, and "always has been, and probably will be, difficulty in controlling these people by civil law," contended one bureau official, since "they have never been educated to respect it." He believed that soldiers would "produce more peace and quiet than all the civil codes of law in Christendom." As for the freedpeople, they stood "no chance" in civil law unless the bureau closely monitored its enforcement. The "revolver," not legality, one agent lamented, "rule[d] the day."[24]

Along with lax law enforcement, agents encountered devious planters, who were "anxious to have an Agent address their freedpeople." They would cheerfully send a horse or buggy to convey him to the plantation in the hope it might influence the agent. Planters also took every opportunity to destroy any relationship an agent established with the black community. With "avidity and eagerness," the planters told "their employees that the [bureau] "is defunct never to be resurrected, endeavoring to impair the confidence of the freedpeople in the Agents." With a "peculiar blindness," they sought to "show the freedman that the 'Bureau' is deposed, its powers vanished, [and] their unswerving friendship for them . . . [a] strange inconsistency!" said one.[25]

Although some planters openly acknowledged the "necessity of Bureau agents," they had a visible disposition to weaken black confidence in agents in order to more easily "play upon their ignorance." Many planters attempted to take advantage of the freedmen "without making themselves amenable to the law." Some risked the consequences anyway, but the "fact that the Bureau has an eye upon them," believed one official, "will have a salutary influence." Planters did have a "wholesome realization of the fact (however unpleasant it may be) that the freedmen have rights as well as themselves and that the Government stands ready to enforce these rights." By keeping the freedpeople in "moral and intellectual darkness," the planters maintained control.[26]

Rumors and bribes became two staples of planter efforts to discredit an agent in the eyes of the black community. After returning from leave, a man informed the Cotton Gin bureau official, Charles E. Culver (who remained anonymous), that the agent had absconded with $15,000 belonging to the freedman. That lie and "thousands of equally voracious rumors were spread all over the county," wrote Culver. "It was all done to discourage the freedmen," he explained. In fact, Culver thought that General Philip Sheridan must have been through Freestone County when he "made that memorable remark concerning Texas."[27] (Sheridan is rumored to have said that if he owned both Hell and Texas, he would rent out Texas and live in Hell.) Indeed, agents who were controlled by planters found their way into the Texas bureau ranks, but they were not a majority.

J. L. Randall of Sterling spoke of planters who attempted to bribe and threaten agents. "If anything serious occurs parties will attempt to bribe" the subassistant commissioner wrote, "and at the same time insinuate that if he acts in the case, he will be strung up to a post oak, or shot like a dog while riding through the country attending to his legitimate business." Rather than use bribes and threats, some malcontents impersonated agents to bilk freedmen out their money and discredit the bureau. In Sumpter, H. S. Johnson fined Dick Gibson twenty-five dollars, imprisoned him for five days, and forced him to make restitution of the money he had extorted from local blacks by impersonating an agent."[28]

The Texas Freedmen's Bureau administrators used a variety of ways to learn whether agents adequately served the freedpeople. In every monthly report, headquarters had agents respond to this request: "Report such Bureau Agents and Civil Officers as have neglected their duties, or been guilty of abuse of freed people, with statement of circumstances, etc." Field officers reported their comrades for failing to perform their duties. From Huntsville, an official declared that "from the condition of affairs" at

Crockett (Houston County), he judged "that either the agent or the civil officers neglect their duties." Headquarters also acted upon complaints from freedmen and removed unsympathetic agents.[29]

Two very able and conscientious inspectors, William H. Sinclair and George T. Ruby, one white, one black, traveled throughout eastern Texas interviewing agents as well as speaking with members of local freedmen's communities. Their recommendations about which subassistant commissioners to retain and which ones to terminate were generally accepted at headquarters. Through this method, the Texas bureau managed to eliminate rather quickly those officials who did not support black equality and rights.[30]

In July 1867, Ruby became a Texas Freedmen's Bureau official. He investigated conditions in Brazos, Robertson, and Falls counties. At Millican, a critical railhead, he found the bureau agent, Edward Miller, sick with "bilious fever." Miller complained to Ruby of the "multiplicity of his duties" and wished to be transferred to a position that had "less labor and care." Miller impressed Ruby (he saw him transact business) "as an earnest officer who would do all he could but who rather lacks the 'savoir faire' in execution." The freedmen, Ruby observed, "have more or less complaints against him and allege, the more thoughtful ones," that murder was so "rampant" that Miller "dared not act as he should."[31]

Ruby believed the subdistrict that Miller supervised was "an exceedingly rough one" and almost as bad as those he discovered in adjacent areas. The traveling agent suggested that the "people need a little rough handling." Incapacitated as Miller was for such activity, Ruby suggested that the area needed "an energetic faithful officer who can and will materially aid in the work of 'Reconstruction.'" Nevertheless, Ruby did not remain inactive himself while visiting Brazos County. Although he refused to mention the name, Ruby organized a chapter of the Union League with the assistance of two registrars. One of the men who had been appointed to enroll black voters, a man named Kelsey, told Ruby few union men lived in the county.[32]

In Robertson County, Ruby encountered a "terrible state of affairs." Even whites avoided the bureau. The agent, J. L. Randall, Ruby believed to be "on the right side and determined to do his duty," but the rebels avowed their intention of "shooting the 'Bureau.'" Randall had been sick with the "bilious fever" and "though he sent repeatedly for the doctors *not one would come near him.*" The only Union man in the county was a bookkeeper for a business firm. Ruby breathed a sigh of relief when he left Brazos and Robertson counties. He felt more comfortable and safe in Falls County, where "everything is quiet and orderly" and the bureau "possesses a judicious firm officer who endeavors to do his duty despite reports to the contrary."[33]

While investigating R. B. Sturgis, who supervised Falls and Bell counties, Ruby heard from leading Union men that on "several occasions" Sturgis had been guilty of refusing to listen to freedmen's complaints about ill-treatment from planters through the use of "blows and sticks." Ruby concluded that the freedman did seem to be "unfairly treated." This mistreatment would only increase, since registration for the fall elections had commenced. Ruby asked the complainants if their county was quiet and did the agent "really do all he can?" They asserted that under Sturgis the subdistrict had been "quiet and orderly when disorder and murder have stalked rampant all about him."[34]

Bell County, Ruby wrote headquarters, was noted for its lack of murders and "grave outrages" during the war. Following the war, circumstances changed. The freedmen were now abused and the union cause suffered. Why not confront Sturgis, Ruby queried the Unionists, and inform him that "he is unwittingly perhaps frightening the freedmen from any action in the work of Reconstruction?" Although they had already approached Sturgis, the group agreed to try again. Ruby also informed Sturgis how matters stood, and the agent expressed a "warm desire to act in harmony with the party." Ruby discovered the agent to be a "very affable courteous gentleman," whom he hoped would work out his differences with the black and white union men.[35]

Without cavalry to assist him in support of his duties, an agent faced tremendous opposition. Agents often related to headquarters that being unsupported in the field made their attempts to aid the freedmen exceedingly difficult. The Bastrop bureau man wrote that the primary obstacle in performing his responsibilities was "having no power either to enforce" his decisions or to "protect freedpeople in their rights." He could not arrest offenders "who murder or outrage the blacks" and could not protect himself "from insult and violence while in the discharge" of his duties. Many of the freedpeople lived far from the agent's office, and he had no "means" to ensure a safe visit to his official headquarters.[36]

The freedmen as well as the agents realized that the bureau's effectiveness was severely limited without recourse to troops. And they had to be cavalry. "Infantry are but little adapted to police purposes," wrote the agent headquartered in Sumpter. "Three good horsemen can do more service and police the county better than twenty footmen." The continued presence of soldiers did have a salutary effect on the local inhabitants and their treatment of the freedpeople. The "sight of a Blue Coat is sufficient, in many instances, to suppress a disposition to commit crime," an agent informed headquarters, and their "presence is a guarantee that I . . . will maintain public peace and good order."[37]

A subassistant commissioner who had no troops stationed at his post pointedly observed that

> it will be almost impossible for me to perform my duty ef-
> ficiently without troops for there are an infernal set of rebel
> executive officers in the County and they glory in thwarting
> and defeating the very object I am here for. The freedpeople
> will not be protected without troops, and the only protection
> I can afford them is to report any outrage to headquarters.

It would be impossible for the bureau to be of much service without "some force to act in conjunction with it, either military or a well regulated civil force." In fact, "without the protection of the U.S. Government [blacks] would be in a worse condition than a dog without a master."[38]

Freedmen in Texas experienced rampant violence. An agent remarked that whether the state was "reconstructed or not, if the troops" were re-moved, he believed the "freedpeople will be practically re-enslaved." Sub-assistant commissioners complained that without soldiers they could not protect the freedmen, force civil authorities to give blacks legal equality, or ensure fairness in the settlement of wages or the division of shares. A Livingston bureau agent succinctly summarized what southern occupation meant: "if the military power of the government fails at this juncture to carry out its desires the freedom of the Negro will prove to be the worst calamity that has ever befallen him or his race."[39]

The lack of power to compel civil authorities to provide a semblance of fair legal treatment for the freedpeople continued to plague the efforts of bureau officers until the agency was terminated. One agent asserted that he needed military support to "bring dishonest men and rascals to justice." When these "tricky and designing men" were in "their element," they would "evade" the agent if possible when they discovered him to be the "least crippled or without authority." Another subassistant commis-sioner received no cooperation from area residents, and they continually attempted to deceive and intimidate him. The citizens legally opposed the agent and published lies in rebel newspapers to discredit him among the freedmen.[40]

Eric Foner wrote that "perhaps the greatest failing of the Freedmen's

Bureau was that it never quite comprehended the depths of racial antagonism and class conflict in the postwar South."[41] A majority of Texas bureau agents remained sensitive to the plight of blacks. Their letters and reports include observations about the attitudes and responses of various classes of whites to emancipation and Reconstruction. Bureau agents understood the racial hatred that accompanied the changed status of blacks. They often commented on class divisions and on how whites of varying economic background treated the freedpeople in everyday relations. Unquestionably, a great deal of underlying enmity existed.

In Victoria, the agent observed that the disposition of lower-class whites toward blacks "is not friendly"—"at least not in town; they seem to be jealous of the freedpeople, especially those that make a good living, and are able to dress their families decent, and educate their children, and express their ill feeling, by arguing to make them ridiculous." Educated whites treated the freedmen with "indifference," and only a few took "an interest in their welfare." Overt hostility was the hallmark of "some half-grown rowdies, who formerly belonged to the rebel Army." Blacks, however, "seldom take notice of them, and unless they are assaulted, no difficulties occur, between freedmen and whites."[42]

One agent opined that he had "neither language [n]or words to express the hatred and malice towards the freedpeople." In Wharton, the agent found white resentment "latent and strong" and requiring "but the slightest spark to kindle it into a blaze of animosity and wish for their extermination." Among whites, class lines blurred when justice for blacks became the issue. One judge, the Waco subassistant commissioner reported, refused to try a gang of outlaws because they had been "good" Confederate soldiers and "they had only robbed 'Damned Niggers.'" Besides, blacks could not testify against a "white gentleman." In South Texas, blacks stood "in an equality with the poorer class of Mexicans."[43]

Willie Lee Rose wrote that "surely the difference between slavery and freedom is about the greatest difference in status we can imagine, no matter how kindly a view some historians might want to take of slavery, no matter how limited and curtailed freedom may have turned out to be."[44] In Texas, the Freedmen's Bureau enhanced the opportunities for blacks to experience the full realities of freedom, no matter how harsh the lessons might have been. Within the boundaries established by Congress, working in a hostile environment, and receiving little financial assistance, the Texas bureau was neither as dismal as past historians have pictured it nor as successful as it might have been. It did make a difference for the freedpeople.

Bureau agents became the embodiment of all war-related frustrations for white society. They often served in isolated places, amid a hostile populace, and with no troops for protection. Depending upon the agents' demeanor and their relations with blacks and whites, they often became targets of abuse, ostracism, and violence. Thus, their personal safety could never be guaranteed and was often precarious. "The agents which the Bureau could command," W. E. B. Du Bois wrote, "varied all the way from unselfish philanthropists to narrow-minded busybodies and thieves," but more often than not the "average was far better than the worst."[45]

In general, bureau historiography has condemned the organization for betraying the aspirations of southern freedpeople. The field personnel, the agents, have also been subjected to many negative interpretations, though these have been unsubstantiated. And whether in Texas or in other southern states, the bureau has been judged by a standard that would be impossible for most current or past organizations to attain. For all the limitations that surrounded it, and the extent of these cannot be exaggerated, the Texas Freedmen's Bureau, on the whole, performed rather well. Indeed, black Texans would have been much worse off without its presence.

However one views the attempts of the Freedmen's Bureau to initiate the former slaves into the mysteries of freedom, its agents, at least in the Lone Star State, certainly acquitted themselves rather well. Life in the South during the turbulent early years of Reconstruction, when all classes of people had to make adjustments, cannot have been easy. Old institutions had been destroyed, and new ones were being designed to bring equality and citizenship to blacks, as well as a different form of race and labor relations. The bureau found itself at the center of post–Civil War life when it attempted to implement these changes, mandated by Reconstruction. Local agents set this transition in motion through their very presence.

Hostile whites, turbulent race relations, a lack of military support to enforce their decisions, truculent local officials, and scheming planters all meant that a Texas bureau agent had to be cautious. More important, although often commented upon, is how they interacted with the black communities they served. In contending with the pressures from local citizens, headquarters, the legal system, and their own biases, the agents came across attitudes and feelings, from both whites and blacks, spanning the emotional spectrum. An agent faced a formidable task, one that required a multitude of skills.

Du Bois concluded that the bureau's "successes were the result of hard work, supplemented by the aid of philanthropists and the eager striving of black men." Its failures resulted from "bad local agents, inherent difficulties of the work, and national neglect." Although many factors limited the bureau's success, it was "committed to the independence of the freedmen in a way that former masters and most white southerners were not," writes Herman Belz.[46] This rings true of the Texas Freedmen's Bureau. From our perspective, it may not be the freedom and independence we would have envisioned for black Texans, but the Texas Freedmen's Bureau did what was humanly possible, and the agents did the best they could for their day.

NOTES

1. There is no current essay specifically on Freedmen's Bureau historiography. See, in particular, LaWanda Cox, "From Emancipation to Segregation: National Policy and Southern Blacks," in *Interpreting Southern History: Historiographical Essays in Honor of Sanford W. Higginbotham,* ed. John B. Boles and Evelyn Thomas Bolen, 199–253 (Baton Rouge: Louisiana State Univ. Press, 1987); Richard Lowe, "The Freedmen's Bureau and Local Black Leadership," *Journal of American History,* 80 (Dec. 1993): 989–998.

2. John A. Carpenter, *Sword and Olive Branch: Oliver Otis Howard* (Pittsburgh: Univ. of Pittsburgh Press, 1964), 99.

3. Cox, "Emancipation to Segregation," 228n50; Eric Foner, *Reconstruction: America's Unfinished Revolution, 1863–1877* (New York: Harper and Row, 1988), 143.

4. Cecil Harper, Jr., "Freedmen's Bureau Agents in Texas: A Profile" (paper presented at the meeting of the Texas State Historical Association, Galveston, 1987), 2–13. For two quite different perspectives on the Texas Bureau, see Barry A. Crouch, *The Freedmen's Bureau and Black Texans* (Austin: Univ. of Texas Press, 1992); and William L. Richter, *Overreached on All Sides: The Freedmen's Bureau Administrators in Texas, 1865–1868* (College Station: Texas A&M Univ. Press, 1991).

5. Foner, *Reconstruction,* 142–143. Perhaps the best summary of how historians interpret blacks' feelings about the bureau is contained in Michael C. Perman's observation that "dissatisfied though blacks so frequently were at the bureau's feebleness and ambivalence, they knew that without it they would have been far worse off" (*Emancipation and Reconstruction, 1852–1879* [Arlington Heights, Ill.: Harlan Davidson, 1987], 24. Black response to the bureau, however, cannot be so easily dismissed by suggesting that only southern blacks found it feeble and ambivalent.

6. H. S. Johnson (agent, Sumpter) to J. P. Richardson (acting assistant adjutant general [AAAG]), Nov. 30, 1867, J-42, Operations Reports, Records of the Bureau of Refugees, Freedmen, and Abandoned Lands, Texas, Record Group 105, National Archives (references to the operations reports contained in the re-

cords of the Texas bureau hereafter cited as OR); Richter, *Overreached on All Sides,* 192–194.

7. A. H. Cox (agent, Liberty) to Charles A. Vernou (AAAG), July 31, 1868, C-108, OR; Cox to Vernou, Sept. 30, 1868, C-132, OR.

8. J. H. Archer (agent, Hempstead) to Joseph B. Kiddoo (assistant commissioner [AC], Texas), Jan. 10, 1867, A-81, OR.

9. A. Doubleday (agent, Galveston) to J. T. Kirkman (AAAG), March 1, 1867, D-153, OR; William M. Van Home (agent, Houston) to Richardson, Apr. 1, 1868, V-9, OR; W. B. Pease (agent, Houston) to Kirkman, Jan. 1867, P-147, OR.

10. A. F. N. Rolfe (agent, Columbia) to Richardson, Dec. 31, 1867, R-74, OR.

11. James P. Butler (agent, Huntsville) to Kirkman, Aug. 31, 1867, B14, OR. Headquarters reprimanded or removed agents when they received complaints from blacks that field personnel were ignoring their problems or were too sympathetic to whites.

12. Charles F. Rand (agent, Clarksville) to Roberts, Apr. 30, 1868, AC, LR, R-146, OR, Rand (agent, Marshall) to Kirkman, Apr. 19, 1867, AC, LR, R-109, OR; David S. Beath (agent, Cotton Gin) to Vernou, Sept. 30, 1868, B-247, OR. See also, William L. Richter, "'This Blood-Thirsty Hole': The Freedmen's Bureau Agency at Clarksville, Texas, 1867–1868," *Civil War History* 38 (Mar. 1992): 51–77.

13. J. F. Grimes (agent, Nacogdoches) to Richardson, Feb. 4, 1868, G-39, OR; DeWitt C. Brown (agent, Paris) to Richardson, Apr. 30, 1868, B-139, OR; T. M. K. Smith (agent, Nacogdoches) to Richardson, Dec. 5, 1867, S-94, OR.

14. J. S. Randall (agent, Sterling) to Kirkman, June 29, 1867, R-179, OR.

15. Edward Miller (agent, Millican) to Kirkman, Mar. 2, 1867, M-312, OR; and Mar. 31, 1867, M-313, OR; E. M. Whittmore (agent, Seguin) to Richardson, Feb. 4, 1868, W-30, OR; Nesbit B. Jenkins (agent, Wharton) to Richardson, Feb. 29, 1868, J-50, OR; and Mar. 31, 1868, J-54, OR; William H. Rock (agent, Richmond) to W. H. Sinclair (agent, Galveston), Jan. 12, 1867, R-110, OR; Barry A. Crouch, "'All the Vile Passions': The Texas Black Code of 1866," *Southwestern Historical Quarterly* 97 (July 1993): 13–34.

16. James P. Butler (agent, Huntsville) to Richardson, Feb. 29, 1868, B-93, OR.

17. Edward Miller (agent, Bryan City) to Richardson, Nov. 30,1867, M-85, OR; M. H. Goddin (agent, Livingston) to Garretson, Sept. 30, 1867, G-19, OR.

18. Edward Miller (agent, Millican) to Kirkman, Mar. 2, 1867, M-312, OR; and Mar. 31, 1867, M-313, OR; Whittmore to Richardson, Feb. 4, 1868; Jenkins to Richardson, Feb. 29, 1868, and Mar. 31, 1868; William H. Rock (agent, Richmond) to W. H. Sinclair (agent, Galveston), Jan. 12, 1867, R-110, OR.

19. Hiram Clark (agent, Clinton) to Richardson, Apr. 4, 1868, C-63, OR.

20. H. S. Johnson (agent, Sumpter) to Charles Garretson (AAAG), Sept. 30, 1867, J-13, OR; Anthony Bryant (agent, Sherman) to Kirkman, June 30, 1867, B-17, OR; W. B. Pease (agent, Houston) to Richardson, Jan. 31, 1868, P-38, OR.

21. James C. Butler (agent, Huntsville) to Richardson, Mar. 21, 1868, B-105,

OR; N. B. Jenkins (agent, Wharton) to Richardson, Apr. 30, 1868, J-30, OR; A. G. Malloy (agent, Marshall) to Richardson, Mar. 31, 1868, M-179, OR.

22. N. B. Jenkins (agent, Wharton) to Richardson, Apr. 30, 1868, J-30, OR; James P. Butler (agent, Huntsville) to Richardson, May 2, 1868, B-121, OR.

23. Charles Schmidt (agent, Sumpter) to Vernou, May 31, 1868, S-216, OR.

24. Charles R. Rand (agent, Marshall) to Kirkman, Apr. 19, 1867, AC, LR, R-109, OR; Rand to Richardson, February 1, 1868, R-105, OR; Hiram Clark (agent, Clinton) to Richardson, March 3, 1868, C-49, OR; John Dix (agent, Corpus Christi) to Richardson, Feb. 29, 1868, D-36, OR; Dewitt C. Brown (agent, Paris) to Richardson, Mar. 31, 1868, B-106, OR. See also William L. Richter, "'The Revolver Rules the Day!' Colonel DeWitt C. Brown and the Freedmen's Bureau in Paris, Texas, 1867-1868," *Southwestern Historical Quarterly* 93 (Jan. 1990): 303–332.

25. James C. Devine (agent, Huntsville) to Kirkman, Mar. 1, 1867, D-154, OR; Charles E. Culver (agent, Cotton Gin) to Charles Garretson (AAAG), Nov. 1, 1867, C-19, OR.

26. James C. Devine (agent, Huntsville) to William H. Sinclair (agent, Galveston), Jan. 12, 1867, D-151, OR; J. L. Randall (agent, Sterling) to Kirkman, Apr. 30, 1867, R-120, OR; James Hutchison (agent, Columbia) to Kirkman, Apr. 30, 1867, H-203, OR.

27. Charles E. Culver (agent, Cotton Gin) to Garretson, Nov. 1, 1867, C-19, OR. On Culver, see James Smallwood, "Charles E. Culver, a Reconstruction Agent in Texas: The Work of Local Freedmen's Bureau Agents and the Black Community," *Civil War History* 27 (Dec. 1981): 350–361.

28. J. S. Randall (agent, Sterling) to Kirkman, June 29, 1867, R-179, OR; H. S. Johnson (agent, Sumpter) to Garretson, Sept. 30, 1867, J-13, OR.

29. Edwin Tumock (agent, Centreville) to Richardson, Mar. 1, 1868, T-16, OR; James P. Butler (agent, Huntsville) to Richardson, Jan. 31, 1868, B-80, OR.

30. William L. Richter, "Who Was the Real Head of the Texas Freedmen's Bureau? The Role of Brevet Colonel William H. Sinclair as Acting Assistant Inspector General," *Military History of the Southwest* 20 (Fall 1990): 121–156; Barry A. Crouch, "Politics through Education: George T. Ruby and the Louisiana and Texas Freedmen's Bureau," author's MS. Richter's thesis about Sinclair seems to me somewhat far-fetched.

31. George T. Ruby (Marlin) to Kirkman, July 26, 1867, AC, LR, R-186, OR.

32. Ibid.

33. Ibid. Ruby (Marlin) to Kirkman, July 27, 1867, AC, LR, R-187, OR.

34. Ruby (Marlin) to Kirkman, July 27, 1867, AC, LR, R-187.

35. Ibid. Ruby indicated he wrote on the subject "as the matter may assume proportion."

36. Byron Porter (agent, Bastrop) to Richardson, Apr. 1, 1868, P-51, OR; Anthony Bryant (agent, Sherman) to Kirkman, June 30, 1867, B-17, OR.

37. H. S. Johnson (agent, Sumpter) to Kirkman, Aug. 31, 1867, J-9, OR; and May 1, 1867, J-74, OR.

38. James P. Butler (agent, Huntsville) to Richardson, Feb. 29, 1868, B-93, OR; DeWitt C. Brown (agent, Paris) to Richardson, Apr. 30, 1868, B-139, OR; J. H. Archer (agent, Hempstead) to Joseph B. Kiddoo (AC, Texas), Jan. 10, 1867, A-81, OR.

39. S. H. Starr (agent, Mount Pleasant) to Richardson, Feb. 29, 1868, S-153, OR; M. H. Goddin (agent, Livingston) to Garretson, Sept. 30, 1867, G-19, OR.

40. James P. Butler (agent, Huntsville) to Richardson, Mar. 21, 1868, B-105, OR; M. H. Goddin (agent, Livingston) to Garretson, Sept. 30, 1867, G-19, OR.

41. Foner, *Reconstruction,* 170.

42. Edward Miller (agent, Victoria) to J. B. Kiddoo (AC, Texas), Jan. 11, 1867, M-309, OR.

43. John H. Morrison (agent, Palestine) to C. S. Roberts (AAAG), Apr. 30, 1868, M-189, OR; Nesbit B. Jenkins (agent, Wharton) to Vernou (AAAG), June 30, 1868, J-66, OR; Charles Haughn (agent, Waco) to Vernou, June 30, 1868, H-236, OR; R. S. Mackenzie (agent, Brownsville) to Richardson, Dec. 20, 1867, R-65, OR. On Mackenzie, see Michael D. Pierce, *The Most Promising Young Officer: A Life of Ranald Slidell Mackenzie* (Norman: Univ. of Oklahoma Press, 1993).

44. Willie Lee Rose, "Blacks without Masters: Protagonists and Issue," in *Slavery and Freedom,* ed. William W. Freehling (New York: Oxford Univ. Press, 1982), 93.

45. W. E. B. Du Bois, "The Freedmen's Bureau," *Atlantic Monthly* 87 (March 1901): 360; John and LaWanda Cox, "General O. O. Howard and the 'Misrepresented Bureau,'" *Journal of Southern History* 19 (Nov. 1953): 427–456; J. Thomas May, "The Freedmen's Bureau at the Local Level: A Study of a Louisiana Agent," *Louisiana History* 9 (Winter 1968): 5–19. The experience of Texas agents is recounted in James Smallwood, "The Freedmen's Bureau Reconsidered: Local Agents and the Black Community," *Texana* 11 (1973): 309–320; Smallwood, "Charles E. Culver, a Reconstruction Agent in Texas," 350–361; Richter, "'The Revolver Rules the Day!'" 303–332. For a discussion of the secondary material, see Crouch, *Freedmen's Bureau,* 177–181.

46. Du Bois, "Freedmen's Bureau," 363; Herman Belz, *Emancipation and Equal Rights: Politics and Constitutionalism in the Civil War Era* (New York: Norton, 1978), 72.

Ten

HESITANT RECOGNITION
Texas Black Politicians, 1865–1900

In his novel *Texas* (1985), James A. Michener creates a scenario in which the governor establishes a task force to "snap" the Lone Star State "to attention regarding its history." Instructed to compile a list of seven ethnic groups whose "different cultural inheritances" had contributed significantly to the state's history, it was to investigate the antecedents of each group. Blacks were fifth on the task force's agenda, described as being the "great secret of Texas history," their background "muted" and their "contributions" to the historical development of the state denied.[1] Although writing fiction, Michener clearly recognized the absence of blacks in past writings about Texas history.

Peculiarly, the Lone Star state, although its background and history are unique, has not attracted many individuals who want to explain the complex nature of black history in Texas. Alwyn Barr summarized the status of blacks throughout Texas history when he wrote that the "roles of black people in the development of Texas have been significant since the sixteenth century, with the greatest influence in the nineteenth and twentieth centuries when blacks formed from 10 to 30 percent of the population." There is cause for optimism. Since 1950, Barr continues, "a growing number of black and white historians have begun to present a more complex and sensitive understanding of institutions within the black community, as well as a more objective view of efforts to attain equal treatment." As a result, the "quantity and quality of writing on black Texans during recent years is impressive," but many topics deserve additional attention.[2]

What we now require, Barr contends, are "broad studies of slavery, racial ideas, religious activities and beliefs, fraternal groups, and roles of women." Other important topics for further consideration would be "sports, violence, migration, and urbanization."[3] Some of the gaps are being filled, but the black Texans of the last century still require incisive analysis into their social and political behavior, how they voted, and how the representatives they elected to office performed in their tenure in the state legislature. Here it is useful to provide a brief summary of the published material available on the history of black Texans in the latter third of the nineteenth century.

Even for the years following the Civil War, when blacks first became free and organized politically, books on Texas blacks are scarce. With the exception of Carl M. Moneyhon's book on Reconstruction Republicanism, which includes an extensive discussion of blacks and their interaction with the Republican Party, little significant information has been printed. The University of Texas Press published Moneyhon's study in 1980, but no book focusing on Texas blacks in the years 1865 to 1874, or even later, no matter the theme, has been published under the aegis of an outstanding or well-known press in the past fifteen years. Now almost two decades old, there is only one general history of how black Texans contributed to the state's development.[4] This is not an imposing compendium.

One can persuasively argue that the best overall perspective on Texas during the immediate post–Civil War era is provided by a doctoral dissertation completed in 1971. The intervening years have produced five books that concentrate solely on some phase of the Texas black experience from 1865 to 1900. Although black political participation is discussed in more detail than perhaps any other subject, there is much we do not know about how black legislators worked within the system or how they related to the black and white communities they served. In addition, a general survey delineates their political role in a wider cultural context, but because it is an overview, the contribution of Texas blacks to political development is slighted.[5]

Recent scholars of the black community in the postwar South, and specifically Texas, fall into two camps: (1) the new social historians, who tell the story of Texas blacks from their own perspective with a great deal of sympathy; and (2) the new political historians, who have abandoned the Dunning view of Reconstruction for a more sympathetic treatment of the hostile climate and sensitive issues faced by black politicians and their white allies. Yet the latter historians, who often employ prosopography, or collective biography, are critical of urban middle-class black politicians for having failed to meet the needs of their rural lower-class constituents.[6] Except in their backgrounds, these officeholders seem to have been quite like all other politicians—concerned mainly with safeguarding their own interests and the interests of those they served.

At a minimum, we need biographical sketches of as many nineteenth-century elected Texas black officials as possible. The lesser political officers— district clerks, like Johnson Reed of Galveston, sheriffs, justices of the peace, inspectors of hides and animals, and constables (who accounted for most of the elected black officials from 1870 to 1900)—are barely known; their stories should become part of a composite picture of black leaders who integrated themselves into the Texas political arena. Studies of local Reconstruction leaders and their influence would undoubtedly aid in presenting a composite picture of all nineteenth-century black politicians in Texas.[7]

A true pioneer in this regard is Donald G. Nieman. Combining politics and criminal justice, he argues that blacks influenced the system in a number of ways. Focusing upon Washington County blacks, who composed approximately 52 percent of the county population between 1860 and 1890, he points out not only which political positions blacks could contend for, but also how they were organized in the county, who the candidates were (and some background on them), and which whites they supported in various elections. Nieman has given us a careful and highly revealing look at political and judicial awareness in the Texas county with the largest number of black inhabitants.

Although they "did not win a share of county offices equal to their percentage of the population, and no black man received the party's nomination for the powerful positions of sheriff, district judge, or county judge," Nieman writes, they nevertheless were "not excluded from the spoils." Winning most of the Republican nominations for the state legislature during the 1870s and 1880s, blacks also "secured the party's nomination for such county-wide offices as clerk of court and treasurer." As Republican political organizations evolved over the decades and the party came to rely even more heavily upon black voters, black politicians continued to be elected to local and state offices. Later, they consistently won two of the four available seats on the county commission.[8] What Nieman has done for Washington County will probably be impossible to replicate for every Texas county with a significant postwar black population. What is required, however, before we can do much at this level is an interpretive monograph that synthesizes and analyzes the information about those blacks who served in the state legislature.

The recent appearance of a book focusing upon Texas black politicians during the latter third of the nineteenth century provides an opportunity to explore in depth what we do and do not know about these men. How do these black lawmakers compare in background, experience, and characteristics with their brethren in other states during the Reconstruction years and after? Merline Pitre argues that "we still do not know very much about these [Texas] black legislators who served the state from 1868 to 1898."[9]

Unfortunately, the little information we do possess about these mostly unknown figures is repeated again and again, and little new material has been forthcoming. A few of the more prominent black Texans who were elected to state office, or who were figures in a major political party, have received excellent treatment. Lesser-known persons, however, largely have been passed over. Even some of the most important black politicians have been written about only cursorily, or else would benefit from new explorations into their backgrounds and careers. We also need to know these men's origins—especially slave or free. Once elected, how did they perceive their commitment to their black constituents?

Moreover, although Texas was predominantly rural, there was a major difference between those representing more urbanized areas, such as George T. Ruby of Galveston, and, for example, Benjamin F. Williams (the tallest of all Twelfth Legislature members), who served largely rural and small-town Lavaca and Colorado counties. In 1870, Galveston was a town of about 4,000 (the county comprised 15,289 people: 12,053 whites and 3,236 blacks), and Williams's two counties had a combined population of 17,494 (11,086 whites and 6,408 blacks).[10] It certainly would aid our understanding of black lawmakers if we had some idea of the types of black communities they represented. Again, most were agriculturally based, since blacks performed a majority of the farming labor, but clearly, as the above demonstrates, they were not uniform.

What is now necessary is a composite analysis of the legislators. Pitre, whose book is the first in five decades to deal solely with black politicians, provides a biographical pastiche of most of the legislators who served between 1868 and 1900, but focuses upon five legislators. To each of these five she assigns a subtitle suggesting what motivated their political careers. All bases are covered: we get a militant, a party loyalist, an opportunist, an accommodationist, and a "climber of sorts."[11]

Three of the newer prosopographical frameworks—Thomas Holt's look at South Carolina legislators, and the analyses of Texas assemblymen by Alwyn Barr and Barry A. Crouch—are also helpful for understanding the background and status of black Texas legislators of the last century. What is required, as this essay attempts to develop, is the employment of collective biographical techniques to explore in greater detail Texas's biracial politics, beginning with the end of the Civil War. Although blacks did not vote until Congress assumed control of Reconstruction in 1867, they did begin to organize their communities as soon as freedom became a reality.

It is important to understand the individual and collective behavior of these black legislators. For example, consider the five black politicians Pitre chose for "a preview." Ruby, the previously mentioned black Galvestonian, serves as a brief case study. Although significant, and Pitre's essay on Ruby is an adequate summary, he has been the subject of much attention by historians. Without question the fullest and most interpretative examination of Ruby is in *Southern Black Leaders,* Moneyhon's detailed and critical examination of Texas's most famous Reconstruction black politicians. In addition, there are two other journal articles on Ruby, plus additional material in other essays, which are also quite satisfactory.[12]

Pitre's book reveals what we do and do not know about many of these politicians. For example, she has chapters on Matthew Gaines and Robert L. Smith, two men whose careers spanned the whole era of black political participation (1868–1900) in the state legislature. Although Gaines (at five feet tall, one of the shortest men in the Twelfth Legislature) has remained an often-mentioned but unexplored black enigma, Ann Patton Malone left little unsaid about him in her careful and probing insights into the most radical of Texas blacks.[13] Robert L. Smith, surely one of the most important black politicos of the latter nineteenth-century, has received much less attention. Any future investigator of Smith must use the Booker T. Washington Papers at the Library of Congress, which will surely add a new dimension to Smith's career. His quite extensive correspondence with the "Wizard of Tuskegee" sharply delineates his role in the Texas black community.[14]

Blacks "held the ace card of the Republican party in their hand," states Pitre. Providing basic support for the newly established Texas organization, blacks had not only votes but numerical "power" as well. Pitre believes that in discussions of blacks and the political arena, one should always distinguish between the "sources," "bases," and "exercise" of power. Potential sources of power, according to Pitre's survey of black lawmakers, such as "voting, holding office, favorable population distribution, economics, and wealth," were in themselves "passive and inert." They might be "converted into real power only when appropriate means for operationalizing them are available and utilized." In her estimation, blacks failed to "operationalize."[15]

A specific instance in the life of Norris Wright Cuney exemplifies Pitre's belief of how blacks missed opportunities to utilize their newly won power. In 1877 a wildcat strike occurred among the black railroad workers in Galveston. Wages, the black laborers complained, were so low they could not support their families. According to Pitre, "some white leaders," who are not identified, "urged blacks to press the railroad company for damage[s] and use violence if necessary to get what they wanted." Cuney counseled otherwise, stating that force would not aid their cause and that troops from Houston would simply quell the protest. Allegedly he told blacks to return home and accept whatever wage they could get the following day. "Although enraged," writes Pitre, "blacks dispersed peacefully."

Pitre cites two reasons for Cuney's action. One possibility is that "he was working for white employers who wanted blacks to return to work." The second is that Cuney, "being a climber of sorts," was "trying to establish himself as a leader of these urban blacks." Neither answer seems entirely satisfactory, although Pitre claims that "an analysis of this period reveals" that the "actions of black leaders were impacted upon by whites." Perhaps Cuney was attempting to avoid what would have been a virtual bloodbath for blacks by making efforts to negotiate behind the scenes. A state Democratic administration, hostile to blacks, would not have been reluctant to call in armed troops, since this had occurred in other areas. Cuney clearly understood that he was not negotiating from the strongest of positions, so he had to be most tactful in trying to avoid violence.[16]

Cuney's life needs much further analysis than Pitre could allot it. He was unquestionably a complex and gifted man. Though the most important black Republican in post-Reconstruction Texas, he has not received the historical attention that he warrants. This black Galvestonian (carrying on the tradition of Ruby), who led the Texas Republican Party from 1883 to 1896, and was described by the biographer of Governor James Stephen Hogg as one of the "greatest political leaders in Texas," still needs a solid monograph—even a long essay would be welcome. Unfortunately, there is no large body of Cuney papers: the source material about him is scattered, diverse, and not readily accessible.

Pitre identifies Cuney as a "climber." He was certainly that and more. Ambitious and politically astute, this black Texas powerbroker comes across no more clearly in recent analyses than in previous ones. It should be noted that Cuney was never elected to the state legislature. His position as collector of customs for the Port of Galveston gave him considerable influence in recommending and dispensing offices. Because of his power, the white leaders of the Republican Party respected Cuney and often listened to his advice. Until something better appears, we will have to be satisfied with Virginia Neal Hinze's 1965 master's thesis.[17]

The same difficulties are present with other legislators and politicians, and even less is known about them. Richard Allen is a prime example of an intriguing man who first became prominent during the turbulent years of Reconstruction but whose background is somewhat muddled. His role and status in local, state, and national Republican and convention politics is not altogether certain. Pitre labeled the Houstonian "an opportunist." That he may have been, but surely there was more to his character and philosophy than simply striving to get ahead. Allen might be described more aptly as a "survivor," since he was able to continue his political career longer than any other nineteenth-century black leader.

Allen is a particularly fascinating individual both because of the area from which he was elected and because of his longevity (relatively speaking) in Texas politics. Born a slave in Virginia in the latter 1820s, he became a skilled artisan and learned to read. In the early years of Reconstruction (he was from a predominantly white district in Harris County), he served both on the county voter registration board and as a Union League organizer, and held Republican Party convention offices. As a contractor, he had, "by his industry and enterprise," purchased a "comfortable home" for his family. A member of the Radical wing of the Republicans, Allen supported the interests of black voters and promoted a black labor convention in 1869.

Allen succeeded in having two Houston organizations incorporated, the Gregory Institute for black children and the Drayman's Savings Club. In the legislature, he joined an informal club of Radicals whose purpose was to prevent the governor from vetoing bills that provided government aid to railroads. He ended his political career as an at-large delegate to the Republican National Convention in 1896, the last political participant of the original Reconstruction legislators.[18]

Although information is limited on many of these state politicians, Pitre attempts a composite and comparative analysis of the forty-two (actually there were forty-three) nineteenth-century black Texas legislators and the ten who either served in the constitutional conventions of 1868–1869 and 1875 or were delegates to the national Republican conventions. She concludes that the "majority of these black politicians did not differ markedly from most of those they sought to lead." The "average black lawmaker" was born a slave, dark complected, and the son of an "uprooted slave immigrant." During the Civil War he had probably been a runaway slave rather "than a soldier fighting beside his master." Their educational attainments varied from illiteracy to higher education: one completed college, six either attended or finished a two-year normal school, three made it through the elementary grades, and twenty-seven had a "rudimentary education." Only four were uneducated.

They generally came from the lower middle class, although they were, according to Pitre, "far more fortunate in term[s] of occupation and wealth than the overwhelming majority of freedmen." While she believes there was some distance between the social origins of the leaders and the masses, "it was never as great as that which existed in Louisiana and South Carolina, where the leadership consisted of a disproportionately high number of mulatto and well-educated blacks with considerable property."[19] On this latter point there is some reason to be doubtful of Pitre's conclusion, since a comparison between those blacks who served in the Texas legislature and those who were elected in other states across the South suggests that there were more similarities in their backgrounds than has been otherwise believed.

Earlier works and models can serve as sources of ideas for a study of Texas black politicians, and of material that can be extrapolated to make comparisons with other southern state black legislators. The one that immediately comes to mind is Thomas Holt's superb monograph on South Carolina's black politicos. Using a combination of traditional archival sources and computer-generated voting models, he tells us more than we have ever known about the inter- and intraracial contacts and dealings of South Carolina's first black elected officials. In addition, Holt provides a chart that straightforwardly summarizes the backgrounds of black legislators.[20]

A similar effort needs to be done for Texas. The primary materials Holt used were extensive, and these same kinds of original manuscripts must be consulted in any future investigation of Texas black officeholders and politicians. The amount of research necessary to piece together the lives of black legislators in Texas is exemplified in the work of Moneyhon on Ruby and of Malone on Gaines. One must follow every lead possible when reconstructing the background and contributions of black assemblymen, whether in the Lone Star state or in the remainder of the South. Works on black legislators in Georgia and Louisiana, although not as sophisticated as Holt's, also might be used as guides for future studies of Texas black leaders.[21]

Barr has provided a model for future scholars in his essay "Black Legislators of Reconstruction Texas." Let us briefly examine Barr's refined analysis of the Twelfth Texas Legislature (1870), the fourteen blacks—twelve in the House, two in the Senate—who served in it. (It had been claimed previously there were thirteen blacks in this legislature.) They made up 12 percent of the total members (120), and in their states of origin, average age, occupations, literacy, economic status, leadership ability, and prewar condition, they "reflected a striking diversity." All came from outside

Texas, with one possible exception, Goldsteen Dupree. Only one, Ruby, was a Northerner.

The fourteen state legislators averaged thirty-nine years of age. Their occupations included farming, ministering, working as a mechanic, and other jobs requiring skill. All but three seem to have been literate. They were men on the rise: almost three-quarters held some form of property. None could be considered wealthy, but they did exhibit a certain material success. Because of their social and economic success, they generally had good relations with the white community. Only four were elected from areas with black majorities.[22]

Barr contends that these legislators agreed on three major issues: protection from violence for all people, particularly blacks; education; and frontier defense for those exposed to attacks by the Native Americans. Economic issues also generated some unanimity, especially in attempts to protect the rights of laborers through a general strengthening of legal rights. These included more carefully drawn apprenticeship and contract labor laws, lien reform, and civil-suit protection. On other issues the coalition broke down, each becoming more concerned about local needs than the interests of the state generally. Black legislators supported the governor's vetoing of extraneous railroad legislation, but they never failed to vote yea when the railroad interests were in their own backyard.

A summary of voting records demonstrates that black legislators balanced a concern for state-government expenses against the needs of individual districts. Black Texans did not vote for projects that would excessively drain the state of funds. Fiscally responsible, they often have been portrayed as precisely the opposite. In fact, they performed little differently from their white Republican counterparts when it came to deciding on the major issues of the day. In sum, the background, behavior, and character traits of these black legislators compare favorably with those of their counterparts in other southern states during this period. It will be necessary to compile this type of information for all black Texas legislators before a comprehensive portrait can emerge.[23]

Contrary to Pitre's assertion, the backgrounds, education, and occupations of black Texas Reconstruction-era legislators were similar to those of black lawmakers in Louisiana and South Carolina; there were greater differences in economic status and place of birth. Black South Carolina politicians' origins and orientations were basically "bourgeois." But because of enough "differences in socioeconomic background," these same legislators demonstrated divergent views on some of the important issues of the day.

In Texas, only two black legislators (15 percent) had been free before the Civil War, whereas the figure in South Carolina was 25 percent. Unlike Louisiana and South Carolina, Texas could not rely upon a large class of prewar free blacks to assume leadership roles: the Lone Star State had only 355 free blacks on the eve of the Civil War. When comparing slave background, occupations, and education, the differences among black leaders in Texas, Louisiana, and South Carolina, according to Barr, seem "minimal." But there were differences. Only one black Reconstruction legislator in Texas was a native, but 90 percent had been born in the South, compared to approximately 70 percent in South Carolina and Louisiana. Only 46 percent of the South Carolinians held property, while 71 percent of the black Texans did, as did a majority of the Louisianians. One factor is clear: Texas blacks could not rely upon a large class of prewar free blacks to assume leadership roles as could Louisiana and South Carolina, because the Lone Star state had only 355 free blacks on the eve of the Civil War.[24] Unquestionably, further analysis and comparison of Texas black legislators to those of other Confederate areas is necessary.

In other Deep South states (Alabama, Florida, Georgia, and Mississippi), about two-thirds of the black legislators came from districts with black majorities; in Texas the figure was 29 percent (4 of 14). Those elected from other areas needed the assistance of white Unionists who supported the Republican Party. Even though blacks composed a large majority of the Republican base in Texas, they were not able to assume significant leadership positions. In the Lone Star State the upper echelon of the Republican Party was dominated by whites. Because Texas had a smaller black populace than either South Carolina or Louisiana, there were few predominantly black districts—and, therefore, fewer black legislators. Nevertheless, the profiles of the constituencies, voting records, and biographies of all the legislators from Texas, Louisiana, and South Carolina, asserts Barr, "seem similar in many ways."

Interesting distinctions did occur. Regardless of economic background, Texas black legislators voted for bills to aid laborers, unlike their counterparts in South Carolina. Texas was a new state with a small free-black population before the war, so economic divisions between blacks were not nearly as pronounced as they were in older areas such as South Carolina and Louisiana. As is well known, those two states had large, active, and economically solid free-black enclaves during the antebellum years. "Yet on broader economic issues," Barr observes, black Texans "showing a greater diversity of voting patterns which, as in South Carolina, seemed to be based upon both regional interests and socio-economic factors."

Overall, the Texas Reconstruction black legislators evinced an interest in the legal, political, educational, and economic matters of the black community, which is contradictory to some of the conclusions reached by Pitre. According to Barr, these men had "achieved leadership experience, economic stability, and literacy" before they were elected to the legislature. Although they had almost no political experience, they quickly learned to function within the electoral system. Committed to the Republican Party and their black supporters, these Reconstruction legislators also responded to the diverse economic needs of their districts. Unified on some subjects, they were cognizant of local, party, and state necessities. They responded accordingly.[25]

Past organizational models have not been informative about the personal data of black Texas legislators or convention delegates. From 1978 to 1993, much material has been accumulated about black state legislators and nonelected politicians. No one has seen fit to organize it into an understandable pattern. Moreover, the nuances of what this group of men endured and how they went about their political duties has eluded most historians attempting to weave a coherent interpretation. Previous historians have separated black Texas legislators into unnecessary categories, but a more organized reference now seems necessary: this background information needs to be assimilated into one easily accessible table for future scholars.

The table at the end of this essay combines all the material presented by Pitre and others into a succinct analysis of who these men were. Such a chart is more comprehensive than Barr's, which was confined to one legislature. A collective study of all nineteenth-century black Texas legislators would raise new questions and give us a better answer to the political problems faced by black legislators and other political officials. The precarious nature of blacks' positions in the community regarding their own people had to be balanced against the power and influence of whites. Even blacks from predominantly black districts had to steer a delicate course. Fear of violent retaliation from whites for engaging in politics was an ever-present reality.

Nineteenth-century Texas black politicians need more extensive analysis than they have hitherto received. Pitre's 1985 book is a beginning, but her work is somewhat confusing and a little exasperating. What is now required are more journal pieces on (and for some, book-length assessments of) black leaders who have been ignored or only briefly sketched. Such portraits should relate these black politicians to their local communities in order to set the stage for their sojourn into county and state politics. Barr's recent analysis of black legislators in Reconstruction Texas is a good, but modest, beginning.

Barr's analysis is one model to follow, as are the works of Holt on South Carolina, Vincent on Louisiana, and Drago on Georgia. Additionally, the collective biographical data collected in the appendix to this essay provides a basis for comparing the backgrounds of black Texas lawmakers with those of other southern black legislators. From this groundwork, a composite picture could be painted of the areas from which Texas black state leaders emerged and of the political experience they gained. An even more detailed analysis, one including all other political roles, would present a clearer picture of these men. In short, a prosopographical approach would enlighten all.

Texas state historiography has progressed to the point that blacks can be taken on their own terms, without nineteenth- and early twentieth-century racial stereotypes, or even later ones, being taken as models for viewing their behavior. Black Texas politicians from the last third of the nineteenth century deserve better treatment and more detailed analyses than they have received in past writings. Unquestionably, their accomplishments have to be weighed against their failures, for there were both, but future accounts will need to be finely crafted studies, interweaving political, social, and economic history.

From many past writings we get some isolated sense of what the black political experience was like, but the social and economic milieus of these legislators, individually and collectively, need intensive investigation. More studies concentrating solely upon blacks are necessary and welcome. Before we fully understand postwar black Texans, we need much more information about prewar blacks. This is a very difficult task, since only recently has a study of slavery in Texas been published. But with that history, one essential part of the puzzle has been completed. Until similar works appear in the future, we will have to be content with a poor foundation regarding the nineteenth-century black political experience.

APPENDIX

The following is a summary of the background data available on Texas black politicians, 1868–1900. Most has been compiled from secondary data, but it is the first time, to my knowledge, that it has been presented in such a format. Questionable information is indicated by brackets.

TABLE 10.1. BACKGROUND DATA FOR BLACK TEXAS POLITICIANS, 1868–1900

Name	Offices, dates	County of residence	Prewar status/ color	Year and place of birth	Occupation: prewar/ postwar	Education	Wealth
David Abner [Abnar], Sr.	SR 74 CC 75	Harris	slave/ black	1820 Alabama	farmer/ farmer	literate	$35,000 [?]
Richard Allen	SR 70,73 DD 68,76 ALD 92	Harris	slave/ black	1826 [1830?] Virginia	mechanic, builder, carpenter/ bridge contractor	literate	home
Edward Anderson		Montgomery Harris	slave/ black	[1834]	——/ farmer		
Alexander Asberry	SR 89 DD 88 ALD 92	Robertson	slave/ black	1861 Texas		Hearne Profess. Academy	
H. A. P. Bassett	SR 87	Grimes					

(continued)

TABLE 10.1. *Continued*

Name	Offices, dates	County of residence	Prewar status/ color	Year and place of birth	Occupation: prewar/ postwar	Education	Wealth
Thomas Beck	SR 74,79 81	Madison Grimes		[1839] Mississippi	——/ farmer		
Edward J. Brown	SR 74	Harrison		[1840] Alabama	——/ carpenter		
D. W. Burley	SR 70	Robertson	free/ black	1844 Virginia			
Charles W. Bryant	CC 68	Harris	slave/ black	[1840] Kentucky	——/ minister	literate	
Walter M. Burton	SS 74,76 79,81 AD 72	Fort Bend	slave	[1829] North Carolina	farmer/ farmer	literate	
Silas (Giles) Cotton	SR 70	Robertson	slave	[1814] South Carolina	farmer/ farmer	illiterate	

Name	Office	County	Status	Birth year/place	Occupation	Literacy
Norris Wright Cuney	DD 72, 76, 80 ALD 84, 88, 92	Galveston	slave/mulatto	1846 Texas	——/customs inspector	private
Stephen Curtis	CC 68	Brazos	slave/black	[1806] Virginia	——/carpenter, laborer	illiterate
B. B. ("Bird") Davis	CC 75	Wharton	slave	[1827] [1835] North Carolina	——/farmer	
R. Goldsteen Dupree	SR 70	Montgomery		[1846] Texas		literate
R. J. Evans	SR 79 DD 84	Grimes Robertson	slave	1854 Louisiana	——/teacher	common
Jacob E. Freeman	SR 74, 79	Waller Fort Bend	slave/black	[1841] Alabama	——/mechanic	
Matthew Gaines	SS 70, 73	Washington	slave	[1840] Louisiana	blacksmith shepherd/farmer, minister	literate

(continued)

TABLE 10.1. *Continued*

Name	Offices, dates	County of residence	Prewar status/ color	Year and place of birth	Occupation: prewar/ postwar	Education	Wealth
Harriel G. Geiger	SR 79,81	Robertson		[1839] South Carolina	——/ blacksmith lawyer		
Melvin Goddin	CC 75	Walker					
B. A. Guy	SR 79	Washington	slave	[1842] Virginia	——/ farmer		
Nathan H. Haller	SR 93,95	Brazoria	slave	1845 South Carolina	blacksmith		
Jeremiah Hamilton	SR 70	Washington	slave	[1839] Tennessee	——/ teacher, carpenter	literate	
William H. Holland	SR 76 ALAD 76 ALD 80	Waller	slave/ mulatto	1841 Texas	——/ teacher, principal postal employee	Oberlin	1 lot

Name	Reference	County	Status/Race	Birth	Occupation	Literacy	Value
Wiley W. Johnson	CC 68	Harrison	slave/ black	[?] Arkansas	shoemaker		
Mitchell M. Kendall	CC 68 SR 70	Harrison	slave/ black	[1818] Georgia	blacksmith/ farmer, blacksmith	literate	$2,400
Robert A. Kerr	SR 81 ALAD 68, 92	Bastrop	mulatto	1833 Louisiana	barber, shipping clerk	common	
D. C. ("Doc") Lewis	SR 81	Wharton		[1844]	——/ farmer		
Ralph Long	CC 68	Limestone	slave/ black	1843 Tennessee	——/ farmer		
Lloyd H. McCabe	CC 75	Fort Bend	free	1847 New York	——/ teacher	common	
James McWashington	CC 68	Montgomery	slave/ black	1840/ Alabama	——/ farmer		$500
Elias [Elius] Mayes	SR 79,89	Grimes Brazos	slave	1831 Alabama	farmer/ farmer, minister	common	

(continued)

TABLE 10.1. *Continued*

Name	Offices, dates	County of residence	Prewar status/color	Year and place of birth	Occupation: prewar/postwar	Education	Wealth
David Medlock	SR 70	Limestone	slave/black	1824 Georgia	minister	illiterate	$250
John Mitchell	SR 70 CC 75	Burleson	slave	[1837] Tennessee	farmer/blacksmith farmer		$3,750
Henry Moore	SR 70,73	Harrison	slave (bought freedom)	[1816] Alabama	farmer, managerial/farmer	illiterate	$3,000
R. J. Moore	SR 83,85 87	Washington	mulatto	Texas	—/teacher	literate	
Sheppard Mullins	CC 68 SR 70	McLennan	slave/black	1829 Alabama	blacksmith/blacksmith	literate	5 lots
Edward A. Patton	SR 91	San Jacinto		[1859] Texas	—/teacher, farmer		

Name	Refs	County	Status	Birth	Occupation	Education	Property
Henry Phelps	SR 73	Fort Bend	slave	[1830] Virginia	—— / farmer	literate	
William Reynolds	CC 75 DD 72	Waller	free	[?] Maryland	—— / teacher	college	
Walter Ripetoe	SS 76,79	Harrison		1838 Alabama	—— / teacher		
Shack R. Roberts	SR 73,74 76	Harrison	slave/ black	[1821] Arkansas	—— / minister		
George T. Ruby	CC 68 SS 70,73 ALD 68, 72	Galveston	free/ black	1841 New York	reporter editor, teacher	common	1 lot
Andrew L. Sledge	SR 79	Washington	slave	1854 Texas	—— / minister		
Robert L. Smith	SR 95,97 ALAD 96	Colorado	free/ black	1861 South Carolina	—— / principal, agrarian leader	Atlanta University	
Henry Sneed	SR 76	Waller		[1849] Texas	—— / farmer		

(continued)

TABLE 10.1. *Continued*

Name	Offices, dates	County of residence	Prewar status/ color	Year and place of birth	Occupation: prewar/ postwar	Education	Wealth
James H. Stewart	SR 85	Robertson	slave	1857 Louisiana	——/ teacher, principal	Yale, Prairie View	
Jams H. Washington	SR 73 ALAD 72	Grimes Galveston	free	[?] Virginia	——/ teacher, principal	Oberlin	
Benjamin O. Watrous	CC 68	Washington	slave/ black	1831 Tennessee	——/ minister, wheelwright	literate	$600
Allen M. Wilder	SR 73	Washington	slave	[1843] North Carolina	engineer/ teacher, lawyer		
Benjamin F. Williams	CC 68 SR 78 DD 72	Colorado	slave/ black	[1825] Alabama [Virginia]	merchant/ barber, minister, mechanic	literate	4 lots

| Richard Williams | SR 70,73 | Walker | slave | 1823 South Carolina | blacksmith/ minister, mechanic | illiterate | $1,000 |
| George W. Wyatt | SR 83 | Waller | | [1848] Texas | ——/ teacher | common | |

Abbreviations:

CC: delegate to state constitutional convention

SR: state representative

SS: state senator

ALD: at-large delegate, Republican National Convention

AD: alternate delegate, Republican National Convention

ALAD: at-large alternate delegate, Republican National Convention

DD: district delegate, Republican National Convention

NOTES

1. James A. Michener, *Texas* (New York: Random House, 1985), 1–9.

2. Alwyn Barr, "Black Texans," in *A Guide to the History of Texas,* ed. Light Townsend Cummins and Alvin R. Bailey, Jr. (Westport, Conn.: Greenwood Press, 1988), 107, 120; Barr, *Black Texans: A History of Negroes in Texas, 1528–1971* (Austin: Jenkins, 1973). Barr is overly optimistic about the "quantity and quality" of writings dealing with black Texans.

3. Barr, "Black Texans," 120–121.

4. Carl M. Moneyhon, *Republicanism in Reconstruction Texas* (Austin: Univ. of Texas Press, 1980); Ronald N. Gray, "Edmund J. Davis: Radical Republican and Reconstruction Governor of Texas" (PhD diss., Texas Tech Univ., 1976); Roger Griffin, "Connecticut Yankee in Texas: A Biography of Elisha Marshall Pease" (PhD diss., Univ. of Texas at Austin, 1973); Merline Pitre, "A Note on the Historiography of Blacks in the Reconstruction of Texas," *Journal of Negro History* 66 (Winter 1981–1982): 340–348; Pitre, "The Evolution of Black Political Participation in Reconstruction Texas," *East Texas Historical Journal* 26 (1988): 36–45; Lamar L. Kirven, "A Century of Warfare: Black Texans" (PhD diss., Indiana Univ., 1974), 1–37.

5. John Pressley Carrier, "A Political History of Texas during the Reconstruction, 1865–1874" (PhD diss., Vanderbilt Univ., 1971); Barr, *Black Texans;* Lawrence D. Rice, *The Negro in Texas, 1874–1900* (Baton Rouge: Louisiana State Univ. Press, 1971); James M. Smallwood, *Time of Hope, Time of Despair: Black Texans during Reconstruction* (Port Washington, N.Y.: Kennikat Press, 1981); Merline Pitre, *Through Many Dangers, Toils and Snares: The Black Leadership of Texas, 1868–1900* (Austin: Eakin, 1985); Alwyn Barr and Robert A. Calvert, eds., *Black Leaders: Texans for Their Times* (Austin: Texas State Historical Association, 1981). Texas is in dire need of a book on the war, slavery, and its ramifications. Ralph Wooster remarks that "although there are numerous specialized studies of Texas blacks after the war, the role of blacks during the war has scarcely been touched" ("The Civil War and Reconstruction in Texas," in *Guide to the History of Texas,* 50). This has been remedied partially in Randolph B. Campbell, *An Empire for Slavery: The Peculiar Institution in Texas, 1821–1865* (Baton Rouge: Louisiana State Univ. Press, 1989), 231–251; Campbell, "The End of Slavery in Texas: A Research Note," *Southwestern Historical Quarterly* 88 (July 1984): 71–80; Armstead L. Robinson, "'Day of Jubilo': Civil War and the Demise of Slavery in the Mississippi Valley, 1861–1865" (PhD diss., Univ. of Texas, 1977).

6. James A. Baggett, "The Rise and Fall of the Texas Radicals, 1867–1883" (PhD diss., North Texas State Univ., 1972); Baggett, "Beginnings of Radical Rule in Texas: The Special Legislative Session of 1870," *Southwestern Journal of Social Education* 2 (Spring–Summer 1972): 28–39; Baggett, "Birth of the Texas Republican Party," *Southwestern Historical Quarterly* 78 (July 1974): 1–20; Baggett, "Origins

of Early Texas Republican Party Leadership," *Journal of Southern History* 40 (Aug. 1974): 441–454.

7. One example which has no pretensions to professional scholarship is Rev. Jacob Fontaine, III, with Gene Burd, *Jacob Fontaine: From Slavery to the Greatness of the Pulpit, the Press, and Public Service . . . A Legacy of Church, Campus and Community* (Austin: Eakin, 1983). Fontaine's name appears in the Austin Freedmen's Bureau files. For new perspectives on county officials, see Randolph B. Campbell, "Grassroots Reconstruction: The Personnel of County Government in Texas, 1865–1876" (paper presented to Southern Historical Association meeting, New Orleans, November 1987).

8. Donald G. Nieman, "Black Political Power and Criminal Justice: Washington County, Texas, 1865–1884," *Journal of Southern History* 55 (Aug. 1989): 393, 395–396.

9. Pitre, *Through Many Dangers,* 4.

10. U.S. Bureau of the Census, *Statistics of the Population of the United States, Ninth Census* [1870], (Washington, D.C., 1872), 63–67; David G. McComb, *Galveston: A History* (Austin: Univ. of Texas Press, 1986), 66.

11. Robert E. Moran believes Pitre's book "makes its most distinctive contribution in the concluding part, with its illustrations of five types of leaders found among black Texans" (*Journal of American History* 73 [Mar. 1987]: 1045). See also Carl Moneyhon's assessment in *Journal of Southern History* 53 (May 1987): 340–341.

12. Carl Moneyhon, "George T. Ruby and the Politics of Expediency in Texas," in *Southern Black Leaders of the Reconstruction Era,* ed. Howard N. Rabinowitz (Urbana: Univ. of Illinois Press, 1982), 363–392; Randall B. Woods, "George T. Ruby: A Black Militant in the White Business Community," *Red River Valley Historical Review* 1 (Autumn 1974): 269–280; James M. Smallwood, "G. T. Ruby: Galveston's Black Carpetbagger in Reconstruction Texas," *Houston Review* 5 (Winter 1983): 24–33. For Ruby's bureau background, see Crouch, "Self-Determination and Local Black Leaders in Texas," *Phylon* 39 (Dec. 1978): 346–349, 354.

13. Ann Patton Malone, "Matt Gaines: Reconstruction Politician," in Barr and Calvert, *Black Leaders,* 50–81; Pitre, *Through Many Dangers,* 157–165.

14. On Smith, see Pitre, *Through Many Dangers,* 179–187; Pitre, "Robert Lloyd Smith: A Black Lawmaker in the Shadow of Booker T. Washington," *Phylon* 46 (Sept. 1985): 262–268. The fullest study of Smith to date is Robert Carroll, "Robert L. Smith and the Farmer's Improvement Society of Texas" (master's thesis, Baylor Univ., 1974). Very brief is Purvis M. Carter, "Robert Lloyd Smith and the Farmer's Improvement Society, a Self-Help Movement in Texas," *Negro History Bulletin* 29 (Fall 1966): 175–176, 190–191; Monroe N. Work, comp., "Some Negro Members of Reconstruction Conventions and Legislatures and of Congress," *Journal of Negro History* 5 (Jan. 1920): 112–113. For black populism, see

Gregg Cantrell and D. Scott Barton, "Texas Populists and the Failure of Biracial Politics," *Journal of Southern History* 55 (Nov. 1989): 659–692.

15. Pitre, *Through Many Dangers,* 87.

16. Ibid., 5, 192–193.

17. Virginia Neal Hinze, "Norris Wright Cuney" (master's thesis, Rice Univ., 1965). See also C. G. Woodson, "The Cuney Family," *Negro History Bulletin* 11 (Mar. 1948): 123–125, 143; Alwyn Barr, *Reconstruction to Reform: Texas Politics, 1876–1906* (Austin: Univ. of Texas Press, 1971), 26, 71, 92–93, 131–141, 177–189, 244; Paul D. Casdorph, "Norris Wright Cuney and Texas Republican Politics, 1883–1896," *Southwestern Historical Quarterly* 68 (Apr. 1965): 455–464; Casdorph, *The Republican Party in Texas, 1865–1965* (Austin: Pemberton Press, 1965); Robert C. Cotner, *James Stephen Hogg: A Biography* (Austin: Univ. of Texas Press, 1959), 218, 261, 267, 270–271, 277–278, 306, 313–315, 359, 371. An older but still useful study is Maude Cuney Hare, *Norris Wright Cuney: A Tribune of the Black People* (New York: Crisis Publishing Co., 1913 [reprint; Austin: Steck-Vaughn, 1968]). The reprint has an introduction by Cotner.

18. Alwyn Barr, "Black Legislators of Reconstruction Texas," *Civil War History* 32 (Dec. 1986): 342–346, 348–350; Pitre, *Through Many Dangers,* 174–178; Pitre, "Richard Allen: The Chequered Career of Houston's First Black State Legislator," *Houston Review* 8 (1986): 79–88.

19. Pitre, *Through Many Dangers,* 199–200.

20. Thomas Holt, *Black over White: Negro Political Leadership in South Carolina during Reconstruction* (Urbana: Univ. of Illinois Press, 1977).

21. Charles Vincent, *Black Legislators in Louisiana during Reconstruction* (Baton Rouge: Louisiana State Univ. Press, 1976); Edmund L. Drago, *Black Politicians and Reconstruction in Georgia: A Splendid Failure* (Baton Rouge: Louisiana State Univ. Press, 1982). An outstanding recent overview of Southern local black leaders and state legislators during Reconstruction is Eric Foner, *Reconstruction: America's Unfinished Revolution, 1863–1877* (New York: Harper and Row, 1988).

22. Barr, "Black Legislators," 342–346.

23. Ibid., 341–342, 347–350.

24. Ibid., 340, 350; Holt, *Black over White,* 3, 4, 38–39, 229–241; Vincent, *Black Legislators in Louisiana,* 223–225. On free blacks (a work for Texas is sorely needed), see the trenchant comments by Campbell, *Empire for Slavery,* 112–113.

25. Barr, "Black Legislators," 350–351; Holt, *Black over White,* 123–170; Vincent, *Black Legislators in Louisiana,* 71–112; Drago, *Black Politicians in Georgia,* 160–171.

Eleven

SELF-DETERMINATION AND
LOCAL BLACK LEADERS
IN TEXAS

In a recent article on the origins of early Texas Republican leadership James Alex Baggett correctly contends that in the Lone
Star state a

> few Negroes held local offices of responsibility in predomi-
> nantly black counties during and following Reconstruction.
> At the state level nine Negroes served in the 90-man consti-
> tutional convention of 1868–1869, eleven were legislators in
> the 120-man legislature of 1871, and thereafter the number of
> Negro legislators diminished.

Unlike the experience of other Southern states during this era, "not a single
Negro occupied an important executive or judicial post in Texas."[1] With
the exception of the Populist movement in the 1890s, black participation
in the political process reached its heights during the years following the
Civil War. Though not elected to the upper echelons of state government,
black politicians were active in their local communities, attempting to in-
sulate their constituents against the onslaughts of racism and violence and
organizing them in the direction of self-determination.

In the two years before the elections for the 1868 constitutional convention, when black males were first allowed to vote, Texas freedpeople
were outside the mainstream of politics. In many respects, these thirty-one
months were of critical importance to Texas's black communities. The disruption brought by the war and the tremendous influx of Negroes taken
into the Lone Star state for safekeeping had, at least according to some
accounts, more than doubled the black population residing in the state.[2]
In addition, blacks' search for better economic opportunities and their attempts to stabilize black family life strengthened the cohesiveness of black
communities. Without these efforts, the residents of black enclaves around

the state would never have been in a position to assert any of their newly won rights. Realizing this, many local black leaders attempted to work with local black citizens, white politicians, and the Freedmen's Bureau to ensure that upon entering the political arena, they would be able to exert as much pressure as possible within the confines of white Texas society and the law.[3]

There were, however, other barriers to the unity and cultural autonomy of Texas blacks. Of particular note are the geography and the utter vastness of the eastern portion of the state, where most blacks were concentrated. These factors hampered, and at times made impossible, communication between rural and urban areas, affecting not only elections and politics, but also the course followed by community leaders and their adherents. Even when the Freedmen's Bureau and the army were part of the Reconstruction entanglement, they were scattered so widely and thinly that they were often of little help in rural blacks' pursuit of freedom. This meant that blacks in outlying areas either had to conform to the system imposed upon them or attempt to combat it with the limited resources at hand. In short, this dictated a policy whereby each leader along with his followers had to make immediate and far-reaching decisions based solely upon their own needs, interests, and safety.

During the Reconstruction years in Texas, 1865–1873, when blacks began to organize and assert their independence (and this same pattern was to emerge in the 1890s), the social sanctions surrounding a frontier society were largely nonexistent. In the extreme rural areas, black leaders, their white sympathizers, and the black community itself more often than not faced the constant threat of death or disruption by violence, especially when state or national elections drew near. This state of affairs was also recognized by many black urban dwellers, who previously had suffered through some of the same vicissitudes. In Texas, the political base of an emerging black politician was of prime importance, but whether rural or urban, he still had to demonstrate to those he was serving, through policy and deeds, that he was alert to their needs, interests, and future situation. Several black leaders in Texas exhibited these very qualities, and at least one was in the forefront during and after the Civil War. Because of his background and previous experience, it was natural that he would establish his roots in an urban setting.

Undoubtedly the most prominent black politician and community organizer was George T. Ruby of Galveston. Ruby was not a native Texan, but because of his previous experience he was well aware of the aspirations of the Lone Star State's black populace. He was born in New York in 1841, and his family eventually moved to Portland, Maine, where he received a solid education. Before entering the Texas political arena, Ruby had worked with James Redpath, editor of a Boston newspaper, the *Pine and Palm*, and visited Haiti to collect information for United States blacks who might want to emigrate. When the war came, Ruby "entered at once, with zeal and energy, into the work of educating the freedpeople." In 1864 he went to New Orleans, where he became the principal of an eight-hundred-pupil elementary school, and was later appointed school agent for the entire state. In the fall of 1866, while trying to establish a school at Jackson, Ruby was almost beaten to death by a white mob. He then secured an appointment through the Texas Freedmen's Bureau as a teacher in the Galveston schools.[4] The fact that both Galveston and the surrounding county had a large black population—and the city was the headquarters of the bureau—may have influenced his decision to relocate there.

From October 15, 1866, to May 31, 1867, the black Galvestonian taught at School No. 2 at the Methodist Episcopal Church. While Ruby was a teacher, his school grew in numbers each month, so that by the time he resigned he had one of the largest schools in the city. But Ruby worked at more than educational concerns. He cultivated close ties with the city's black community and helped them at the grass roots level wherever he could. For example, when it became "utterly impossible" for the freedpeople to "obtain letters or papers" sent to Galveston because of the "inattentiveness of the Post Office Clerks," they took their complaints to Ruby, who immediately relayed them to the proper authorities. Ruby told Major General Abner Doubleday that the matter had "become so intolerable" that the blacks were appealing to the government "for redress." Doubleday recommended that new clerks, "who will attend to their duties properly," be appointed to the post office.[5]

Ruby was shrewd enough to realize that although he needed a strong political base in Galveston, he also had to become aware of the achievements of other black communities across the state. Thus, Ruby resigned his teaching position and became a traveling agent for the Texas Freedmen's Bureau. In the course of his numerous trips, he visited many areas in East Texas, and because he evaluated the performance of bureau agents, he also was in a position to influence the direction of bureau policy toward blacks. Charles Griffin, assistant commissioner for Texas, was most impressed with Ruby. "He is an energetic man," Griffin wrote Oliver Otis Howard (the national commissioner), "and has great influence among his people." The head of the Texas bureau particularly wanted Ruby as a traveling agent because in that "capacity many freedpeople may be reached and much good accomplished, which cannot be by others." Ruby served in this capacity until October 1867, when he accepted a civil office.[6]

One of Ruby's primary aims as he sojourned over the state was to establish Union Leagues for blacks so they could participate fully in politics. He had joined the league in 1866 and had begun promoting the organization while still a teacher. Now with his circle of contacts widened, he was able to help the agency expand to encompass blacks throughout the state. Because of Ruby, leagues were constituted in Marlin in Falls County and in Millican in Brazos County. Undoubtedly, he encouraged the formation of others. But Ruby also realized the tremendous obstacles that rural blacks had to overcome for everyday survival, let alone when dabbling in politics. In Millican, for example, the black leaders complained that "murder was so rampant" that the bureau agent "dared not act as he should." Moreover, the area was "an exceedingly rough one and nearly as bad" as Ruby found in Robertson County. Ruby concluded that the white "people need a little rough handling."[7] The black agent's assessment of conditions in Millican and Brazos County was indeed perceptive, for next year a major confrontation between the two races occurred there.

In addition to Ruby, two other blacks traversed the state as Union League organizers. Richard Allen, who later served in the statehouse in the Twelfth and Thirteenth Legislatures from Harris and Montgomery counties (in the Houston vicinity), was active when Ruby was performing his bureau duties. Allen, born a slave in Virginia, was eventually brought to Brazoria County. Freed along with all other Texas slaves on June 19, 1865, Allen, a skilled craftsman, settled in the Houston area. He became a contractor and bridge builder and also served as customs collector for the Port of Houston, city alderman, and city scavenger. Backed by Houston's large black constituency, Allen became a presidential elector and notable local figure for a number of years during and after Reconstruction.[8]

Along with Ruby and Allen, C. W. Bryant, also from Houston, was instrumental in a general effort to organize rural blacks for the Republican Party. Bryant was a strong advocate of freedpeople's right to vote, asserting in a reply to the *Houston Telegraph:* "give us the ballot and give it to us for all time, and if [whites] can outrun us in the race of life, all is well."[9]

Throughout 1867, freedmen, with urban black spokesmen like Ruby, Allen and Bryant leading the way, began to assert themselves and to pressure white Texas society for political and civil rights. Union Leagues were started in Austin, San Antonio, and Galveston, and in the rural areas where the three organizers had visited. Other community leaders had also taken it upon themselves to become part of the electorate. In a prelude to the state gathering, local sessions convened to choose delegates to the upcoming Republican meeting and passed resolutions supporting congressional legislation, the military, and full political and civil equality.[10]

When Republicans held their first state convention in Houston in July 1867, blacks formed a majority of the delegates and Ruby served as vice president. The black majority clearly indicated their priorities when they called for free schools and homesteads and support for Congressional Reconstruction. In February 1868, when Texas voted for a new constitutional convention, nine blacks were elected as delegates.[11] Now the long and difficult struggle for political survival and self-determination was beginning in earnest.

Although the unity of the urban blacks was often tenuous, as Ruby was later to realize, especially if one did not fulfill the expectations of the community, achieving group cohesion was an even more herculean task in rural areas. A close examination of one black community during this period can provide insight into the problems local black leaders encountered and how they attempted to protect their communities against violence and political reprisals. The following incident was somewhat atypical, but similar ones occurred in other Texas towns, though without as much terror.

Millican is in Brazos County, eighty miles northwest of Houston. The terminus of the Houston and Texas Central Railroad, it had three hundred or so inhabitants in 1860. After the war, however, Millican became the shipping center for all the cotton grown in the contiguous counties and in those northward, for "hundreds of miles." In the spring of 1867, when Congressional Reconstruction was just getting underway, a transformation seemed to take place among the whites in Millican and the surrounding area. One bureau agent declared that a "complete change seems to have come over the [white] people since the new military bill has become law, and they promise to do anything, if they will be saved from confiscation." This brief time of amicable race relations was soon to be destroyed by nature and politics. During the summer and fall an epidemic of yellow fever and cholera ravaged the black and white communities. Added to this was extensive damage to the cotton crop by armyworms. Moreover, many planters complained that the freedmen were "inclined to confound freedom with independence, and they leave plantations and stop work, to attend to their own business whenever they please."[12] Blacks, on the other hand, believed that some distinction had to be defined between the employers' time and the workers' time, and with their new sense of freedom, they were not reluctant to make sure that their employers knew this.

George T. Ruby's visit to Millican in mid-1867 apparently aroused the

black populace's political awareness. The blacks had established their community on the outskirts of the small town and had begun to form community institutions, and a leader had emerged. George E. Brooks—a minister, an election registrar, and a member of the Union League—became
the acknowledged spokesman for Millican blacks. There is no definite
evidence that he consulted with Ruby when he came through the town,
but just a month later a Union League was organized, and it was predominantly black. Brooks seems to have realized that he was in a precarious
position, for he directly antagonized no one. During the 1867 epidemic
he attended to the medical needs of both blacks and whites.[13] Politics and
resentment, in the final analysis, however, proved too strong for Brooks
and his followers to overcome.

As the elections for the constitutional convention approached, the
whites grew more "hostile and bitter" toward the blacks. Brooks and his
constituency had done their work well, and one black delegate, Stephen
Curtis, who had been born in Virginia, was elected to the convention.
The hostile attitudes of the whites persisted, especially against those Millican blacks who had actively participated in the election. The Millican
freedmen, for their part, were also starting to become uneasy; threats by
the Ku Klux Klan contributed to this uneasiness. The "considerable ill
feeling" that whites were manifesting toward blacks, as one bureau agent
phrased it, was about to erupt into open violence.[14]

From 1865 to July 1868, when the major confrontation between blacks
and whites occurred, violence was a way of life. The civil authorities
were "entirely nerveless" and ignored criminal offenses committed against
the freedpeople. But the Millican black community was not quiescent
throughout this time of unrest. After a black man was murdered within
five miles of the sheriff's residence and the murderer was permitted to stay
home for two days before being arrested, and then released on his own
recognizance, the blacks arose en masse. They demanded that the accused
be taken into custody until a trial took place; but instead, they were arrested by the sheriff as rioters.[15] This was at least an indication that Millican blacks were becoming aware of a group consciousness: they realized
they would have to band together if they expected to protect their lives,
property, and community.

On June 7, 1868, while the blacks were congregated at their church,
a party of about fifteen persons dressed as Klansmen marched through
the freedpeople's village in an attempt to frighten them. The blacks, apparently under Brooks's leadership, quickly rallied and commenced firing
with muskets and pistols at their white-draped tormentors. The Klansmen

immediately dispersed, leaving the ground littered with masks, winding sheets, other apparel, and two revolvers. Shortly after, the Millican blacks armed themselves and began drilling; the whites charged them with forming a "military organization" and requested the local bureau agent to forbid the freedpeople from bearing arms. The tentative compromise stated that if Klan depredations ceased, then "any warlike preparations" would be forbidden among the freedmen. An order proscribing any "armed band, organization or secret society not authorized by law" was issued.[16]

There were no more Klan raids into the black community, but race relations remained tense. Finally, the two races clashed in open violence. On July 15, 1868, it was rumored that a black man had been hanged. The Millican freedpeople mobilized, and in the ensuing confrontation between whites and blacks, a black leader, Harry Thomas, was killed, as was another black man. However, the initial confrontation was only part of the story. George E. Brooks had remained behind, and after the "riot," he attempted, along with the mayor of Millican, to reach a compromise. These efforts failed; Brooks began to express concern for his life and asked the bureau agent for protection. Brooks's fear was justified: on July 25 his decomposed body was found by a black man hunting for livestock.[17]

The total number of casualties, all black, in the Millican confrontation was recorded as follows: Harry Thomas, who led the freedmen in the initial firing, Dan Idle, Moses Hardy, and Brooks were killed; King Holiday was wounded and died on July 17; Dan Zephner, apparently one of those who tried to enter the town after the whites had established guards, was shot on July 16; a Mr. Moore received a slight wound in the right shoulder; and a man identified as Robert was wounded and missing. In sum, six killed and two wounded.[18]

Probably most important to the whites was that, in killing the two leaders, Brooks and Thomas, they created disorganization and disorder in the Millican black community. With these two important men out of the way, the blacks would not be the threat they had been when directed by effective leadership, nor would their institutions be quite as secure. Thus, most Millican whites were of the opinion that any change in blacks' status, and in race relations in general, would take place only at a tremendous price to blacks.

Millican blacks were struggling to establish viable community organizations. They accepted freedom at face value and attempted to put into practice all the rights and privileges that it supposedly brought. These encompassed some social issues, but involved political and economic concerns above all. The right to bear arms without interference from whites and to protect their village against depredations by masked raiders was important in stabilizing blacks' sense of community.

But the sight of blacks drilling and bearing arms in some form of military organization, no matter how justifiable, was simply abhorrent to the whites. Even groups of blacks gathering for meetings in their own churches made whites uneasy. Such a demonstration of solidarity was more than the Klan could tolerate. Foolish rumors adrift in the community and in the county press, particularly among the whites, added fuel to the conflict. Black leaders knew that without community stability, they would continue to be pawns of the white establishment.[19]

The racial violence in Millican and in other areas across the Lone Star State may have discouraged blacks briefly in their political activities, but it did not deter them permanently from continuing to engage in local and state elections. The victory of Edmund J. Davis in the gubernatorial contest of 1869 is evidence of this. From 1870 to 1873, when Davis was chief executive, black participation in local and state politics attained a higher level than at any time until the 1950s. Wherever Texas Republicans were able to maintain a semblance of power, blacks were generally part of the ruling structure and they strove for political removals and appointments on their own or with whites.

In Corpus Christi, for example, several blacks petitioned Governor Davis to appoint their "old friend Henry W. Berry" sheriff. And Shep Mullens, who had been elected to the Twelfth Legislature, apparently spoke for the Waco black citizenry in recommending a certain individual for sheriff. John L. King, a black schoolteacher in Hearne, Robinson County, requested that the city officers be removed and that he be appointed to the board of aldermen. King asserted that the present officials had "not improved[d] the City one atom" and had left it $5,000 in debt. Peter Hill, one of the leading black men in Jefferson, and "an uncompromising Republican," was supported for a post on the board of aldermen by W. G. Robinson, a state representative from that district.[20] Whether by their own initiative, like John L. King; by mass petition, as in Corpus Christi; or by way of support of whites such as Peter Hill, blacks all over the state attempted through whatever legal devices they could wield to promote their interests in a white society.

There were, however, times when the political struggle created splits in the black community that weakened its solidarity. A conflict for a board of aldermen position in Corsicana, in Navarro County, is one example. Two black men, Sandy Lewis and Frank Flint, were involved in this political appointment. On July 6, 1871, Flint received his commission as alderman, but almost immediately there were difficulties. Those supporting Lewis were distraught by Flint's becoming a member of the city government. One backer of Lewis wrote the governor that Flint was a "drunken worthless Freedman and without character among his own race while Sandy Lewis the Freedman recommended by your friends here is a man of high character—much respected by every one and a most efficient Republican worker."[21]

The objection to Flint was that he was a "man of such disreputable character" that he had "no respect or influence among his own people." On the other hand, Lewis was a desirable choice to be the one black member of the board, for he did have "influence" and could "control his own people." For the white community these were important considerations, but it may have also made it possible for Lewis to wring more concessions for the freedpeople. In order to placate both factions, in August Davis approved of Lewis's selection as alderman.[22] Divisiveness in the Republican Party obviously created factions in the black community and sometimes weakened the base of local black politicians.

In Clarksville, in the far northeastern part of the state in Red River County, blacks were able to win the battle in their choice for mayor. The Union League, whose officers were predominantly black, petitioned Davis for the removal of the incumbent mayor, whom, they felt, was "not doing the Colored people justice." Shortly after their petition reached the governor, the mayor was removed, although the white citizens reacted vehemently and induced a few blacks to support his reinstatement. Democrats used common tactics to influence the black community to support their candidate. In this case their maneuvering failed, and the blacks were able, through the strong organization of the Union League, to forestall defeat for a time.[23]

Politics were not the only area in which black leaders sought to promote community aspirations. In Cotton Gin, as in many other small areas, education was something that blacks were willing to protect at great length. A major part of this control was to have black trustees help oversee the education of black schoolchildren. In Cotton Gin the black community became aroused when the whites were determined to have an all-white board; the freedpeople had built their own school and owned the property on which the school was built. They believed quite strongly, as they indicated to the governor, that this type of interference in their community affairs was unwarranted and that they should be able to determine for themselves who should serve as trustees for their school.[24] Whether they were successful is not known, but it was illustrative of the lengths a black community was willing to go to in order to protect its cultural autonomy.

Blacks' rise to power in Texas was relatively short-lived, just as it was in other southern states. From 1871 until the Democrats won the governorship and other major posts in 1873, blacks were intimidated and forcibly removed from positions of authority. In Rusk County, the blacks expressed concerns about "being waylaid and shot" and "being driven from their homes." The intimidation was subtle, however, and "said and done in such a way that the law has no chance to get hold of the parties." Even with the state police present, an officer complained that if a "freedman is seen coming in town he is immediately surrounded by people and by the time he gets a chance to see me he is so confused or scared that he is unable to say anything to me."[25]

Some black politicians, however, succumbed, in one way or another, to extrapolitical needs and left office. Here, as earlier, George T. Ruby serves as the prime example. Although Ruby supported free public education for all and civil rights, he became so deeply intertwined with the white business community of Galveston that he neglected the needs of his black constituents. Moreover, the growing power of the Democrats dictated Ruby's decision not to stand for reelection in the fall of 1873. One disappointed black office seeker probably expressed it best when he asserted to the governor that Ruby was "not the favorite of the Colored people of Galveston."[26]

The urban-rural dichotomy for black political leaders and organizations occurred once again after Reconstruction—during the Populist movement of the 1880s and 1890s. As Lawrence C. Goodwyn has pointed out, the beginnings of a biracial coalition were also destroyed in this later period. During Reconstruction, he writes, blacks in Grimes County "had achieved a remarkably stable local Republican organization, headed by a number of resourceful black leaders." Although the Democrats regained power, "Grimes County blacks retained local power and sent a succession of black legislators to Austin for the next decade." But the black leadership of the People's Party, the populist organization, was decimated by assassination, with two of the major black leaders being killed. This same pattern was followed throughout the Reconstruction.[27]

After failing to destroy the third-party coalition in Grimes County through various tactics of "mild intimidation, petty bribery, campaign assertions that the Democrats were the Negroes' 'best friends,' or a combination of all three," the Democrats, according to Goodwyn, "decided upon an overt campaign of terrorism," and the politicians "they went after first were the leading black spokesmen of Populism in the county rather than the third party's white leadership." And as in Reconstruction, when blacks "retained the right to cast ballots in proportion to their numbers[,] they possessed bargaining power that became particularly meaningful on all occasions when whites divided their votes over economic issues." Moreover, the "fluence men" and "owl meetings" that have been derided by certain scholars surely were present during the years from 1868 to 1873.[28] In fact, George E. Brooks was a typical "fluence man," and he suffered the same fate as those black leaders in Grimes County during the Populist era.

During Reconstruction in Texas, there were attempts, some successful, others not, by both urban and rural black leaders to establish a semblance of self-determination for their communities and protection against the white establishment. Many factors were influential in determining whether black communities were able to build and maintain viable institutions and numerous forms of cultural autonomy. It is significant that no major black urban leader was killed in Texas during Reconstruction. The pattern of violence for rural areas and later for the Populist years of black leadership was the same. Whether in Brazos County during Reconstruction or Grimes County in the Populist era, whites knew whom to crush in order to maintain their hegemony. Recently, a former black Alabama sharecropper succinctly expressed what blacks faced every day of their lives: "all God's dangers aint a white man."[29] Perhaps not, but for blacks in Reconstruction Texas, they surely were at the top of a long list.

NOTES

1. James Alex Baggett, "Origins of Early Texas Republican Party Leadership," *Journal of Southern History* 40 (Aug. 1974): 442, note 3; Baggett, "Birth of the Texas Republican Party," *Southwestern Historical Quarterly* 78 (1974): 1–20; Baggett, "The Rise and Fall of the Texas Radicals, 1867–1883" (PhD diss., North Texas State Univ., 1972). See also Edward Magdol, "Local Black Leaders in the South, 1867–1875: An Essay toward the Reconstruction of Reconstruction History," *Societas: A Review of Social History* 4 (1974): 81–110.

2. In early 1866, Edgar M. Gregory, assistant commissioner of the Freedmen's Bureau, estimated there were about 400,000 blacks in Texas and that 20,000 to 50,000 laborers could be absorbed at once because of a worker shortage (Gregory to Oliver Otis Howard, national commissioner, Jan. 31, 1866, Assistant Commissioner, Letters Sent (ACLS), Texas, 4:123, Bureau of Refugees, Freedmen, and Abandoned Lands, Record Group 105, National Archives, Washington, D.C.). Unless otherwise indicated, all references will be to the Texas Freedmen's Bu-

reau records. *U.S. Bureau of the Census, Compendium to the Federal Population Census Schedule* [1870] (Washington, D.C., 1872), 65–66, enumerated only 253,475 blacks in Texas. For omissions and undercounting in the 1870 census in Harrison County, which had the second-largest black population in the state, see James Tunner (Marshall) to E. J. Davis, Jan. 6, 1871, Governor's Papers, E. J. Davis (Texas State Library, Austin). Hereafter these manuscripts will be referred to as the Davis Papers. An idea of the number of slaves brought into Texas during the Civil War may be gleaned from James Arthur Lyon Fremantle, *Three Months in the Southern States: April–June, 1863* (New York: John Bradburn, 1864); John Q. Anderson, ed., *Brokenburn: The Journal of Kate Stone, 1861–1868* (Baton Rouge: Louisiana State Univ. Press, 1955); J. Thomas May, "The Medical Care of Blacks in Louisiana during Occupation and Reconstruction, 1862–1868: Its Social and Political Background" (PhD diss., Tulane Univ., 1970).

3. Barry A. Crouch, "Black Dreams and White Justice," *Prologue: Journal of the National Archives* 6 (1974): 255–265. See also Donald G. Nieman, "'A Temporary Antagonism of Military Power': The Freedmen's Bureau and the Legal Rights of Blacks in 1865" (paper presented to the Missouri Valley History Conference, Omaha, 1972); Nieman, "Law, Politics and the Freedmen's Bureau, 1865–1868" (PhD diss., Rice Univ., 1975); Nieman, "The Freedmen's Bureau, Southern State Courts, and the Legal Rights of Blacks, 1865–1868" (paper presented to the Organization of American Historians, 1975); Daniel J. Flanigan, "The Criminal Law of Slavery and Freedom, 1800–1868" (PhD diss., Rice Univ., 1973); Harold M. Hyman, *A More Perfect Union: The Impact of the Civil War and Reconstruction on the Constitution* (New York: Knopf, 1973).

4. George T. Ruby (bureau inspector) to Charles Garretson (acting assistant adjutant general [AAAG]), Sept. 14 and Oct. 14, 1867, R-86, Box 9; Charles Griffin (AC, Texas) to O. O. Howard, May 24, 1867, ACLS, 5:55–56; *Austin Weekly State Journal,* July 28, 1870; Randall B. Woods, "George Ruby: A Black Militant in the White Business Community," *Red River Valley Historical Review* 1 (1974): 269–270.

5. Office of Superintendent of Education, Record of Teachers, 1869, 19:166–167; Office of Superintendent of Education, School Record, 1866–1867, 12:4; Office of Superintendent of Education, Record of Schools etc., 1867–1869, 23:68, 23:70–75; G. T. Ruby to Abner Doubleday (agent, Galveston), Mar. 27, 1867, R-1, Box 42; Endorsement, Doubleday, Mar. 30, 1867.

6. C. Griffin to O. O. Howard, May 24, 1867, ACLS, 5:55–56. See also note 4 above.

7. G. T. Ruby to Joel T. Kirkman (AAAG), June 23, 1867, Assistant Commissioner, Letters Received (ACLR), R-186, Box 4; Ruby to Kirkman, July 26, 1867, ACLR, R-186, Box 4; Woods, "George T. Ruby," 270.

8. Thomas H. Stribling to Whom It May Concern, Apr. 18, 1867, Calendar of James Pearson Newcomb Papers (Eugene C. Barker Texas History Center, University of Texas, Austin); Baggett, "Texas Republican Party," 14; Baggett, "Texas

Republican Leadership," 451; J. Mason Brewer, *Negro Legislators of Texas and Their Descendants* (Dallas: Mathis, 1935; 2nd ed., Austin: Jenkins, 1970), 53; Arthur Z. Brown, "The Participation of Negroes in the Reconstruction Legislatures of Texas," *Negro History Bulletin* 20 (1957): 87; Dale A. Somers, "James P. Newcomb: The Making of a Radical," *Southwestern Historical Quarterly* 72 (1969): 449–469.

9. C. W. Bryant quoted in Brewer, *Negro Legislators of Texas,* 23–24; Baggett, "Texas Republican Party," 14–15; John Pressley Carrier, "A Political History of Texas during the Reconstruction, 1865–1874" (PhD diss., Vanderbilt Univ., 1971).

10. Alwyn Barr, *Black Texans: A History of Negroes in Texas, 1528–1971* (Austin: Jenkins, 1973), 44; W. C. Nunn, *Texas under the Carpetbaggers* (Austin: Univ. of Texas Press, 1962); Lawrence D. Rice, *The Negro in Texas, 1874–1900* (Baton Rouge: Louisiana State Univ. Press, 1971), 34, 55, 129.

11. Barr, *Black Texans,* 46; Baggett, "Texas Republican Party," 16; Carrier, "Texas during Reconstruction"; Charles William Ramsdell, *Reconstruction in Texas* (New York: Columbia Univ. Press, 1910), 166–167; Philip J. Avillo, Jr., "Phantom Radicals: Texas Republicans in Congress, 1870–1873," *Southwestern Historical Quarterly* 77 (1974): 431–444.

12. Walter Prescott Webb and H. Bailey Carroll, eds., *The Handbook of Texas,* 2 vols. (Austin: Texas State Historical Association, 1952), 2:199; *Lippincott's Gazetteer of the World,* rev. and enlarged ed., 2 vols. (Philadelphia: Lippincott, 1883), 2:1422; William H. Sinclair (bureau inspector) to J. B. Kiddoo (AC, Texas), Dec. 23, 1866, ACLR, S-136, Box 4; Edward Miller (agent, Millican) to J. T. Kirkman, Mar. 2 and 31, July 1, 1867, Assistant Commissioner, Operations Reports (ACOR), Box 13. See also Thomas Wagstaff, "Call Your Old Master—'Master': Southern Political Leaders and Negro Labor During Presidential Reconstruction," *Labor History* 10 (Summer 1969): 323–345, especially 333.

13. Nathan H. Randlett (agent, Millican) to Charles A. Vernou (AAAG), July 23, 1868, ACLR, R-178, Box 9; E. Miller to J. T. Kirkman, July 29, 1867, ACOR, Box 14; *Daily Austin Republican,* July 28, 1868.

14. N. H. Randlett to J. P. Richardson (AAAG), Feb. 6, 1868, ACOR, Box 16; Randlett to C. A. Vernou, July 9, 1868, ACOR, Box 18; Brewer, *Negro Legislators of Texas,* 20, 115, 125.

15. Samuel C. Sloan (agent, Millican) to J. B. Kiddoo, Aug. 9, 1866, ACLR, S-71, Box 4; Sloan to Kiddoo, Jan. 1, 1867, ACOR, Box 13; E. Miller to J. T. Kirkman, Mar. 31, 1867, ACOR, Box 13.

16. N. H. Randlett to C. A. Vernou, July 9, 1868, ACOR, Box 18; Randlett to Vernou, July 23, 1868, ACLR, R-178, Box 9.

17. N. H. Randlett to C. A. Vernou, July 23, 1868, ACLR, R-178, Box 9. The bureau agent stated that the "deliberate murder" of Brooks was of a "most outrageous character."

18. Ibid. *Criminal Offenses Committed in the State of Texas,* AC, Austin, 13:156, case nos. 1954–1961.

19. N. H. Randlett to C. A. Vernou, July 23, 1868, ACLR, R-178, Box 9.

20. Freedpeople of Corpus Christi to Governor E. J. Davis, July 14, 1870; Shep Mullens et al. to Davis, Feb. 6, 1871; John L. King to Davis, Apr. 6, 1871; W. G. Robinson to Davis, May 8, 1871, all in Davis Papers; Lelia M. Batte, *History of Milam County, Texas* (San Antonio: Naylor, 1956), 64.

21. F. P. Wood to E. J. Davis, June 4, July 15 and 27, 1871, Davis Papers; *Election Register, 1870–1873,* Town of Corsicana, 132–133 (Texas State Library).

22. F. P. Wood to E. J. Davis, July 27, 1871; Ira B. Taylor and H. V. Hurlock to Davis, Aug. 8, 1871, Davis Papers; *Election Register,* Corsicana, 132–133.

23. John A. Bagly to E. J. Davis, Feb. 12 and Aug. 3, 1871; Andrew Sandy (marshall, Clarksville Union League) et al. to Davis, July 22, 1871; J. P. Dale, Andy Thompson, G. K. Cheatham, G. Silberberg (Board of Aldermen, Clarksville) et al. to Davis, Aug. 1, 1871: all in Davis Papers.

24. George P. Jackson to E. J. Davis, Jan. 25, 1871; Edgar Ennul, Ralph Busby, Sid Deams, George Jackson, and Robert Busby to Davis, Jan. 28, 1871; Jack Carter to Davis, n.d. [1871]: all in Davis Papers; Maud Cuney Hare, *Norris Wright Cuney: A Tribune of the Black People* (New York: Crisis, 1913; rept., Austin: Steck-Vaughn, 1968), 11–15.

25. Thomas Sheriff (lieutenant, state police) to E. J. Davis, Jan. 21, 1871, Davis Papers; Ann Patton Baenziger, "The Texas State Police during Reconstruction: A Reexamination," *Southwestern Historical Quarterly* 72 (1969): 470–491.

26. Silas Blonover to E. J. Davis, Jan. 18, 1870, Davis Papers; Woods, "George T. Ruby," 278. The Davis Papers have a number of letters from Ruby, as well as his endorsement on other applications, in which he supported only white office seekers. See also, Brown, "Negroes in Reconstruction Legislatures," 88.

27. Lawrence C. Goodwyn, "Populist Dreams and Negro Rights: East Texas as a Case Study," *American Historical Review* 76 (1971): 1437. There are strong indications in the Texas Freedmen's Bureau Records that the local Republican organization was not as cohesive as Goodwyn asserts. See also Jack Abramowitz, "The Negro in the Agrarian Revolt," *Agricultural History* 24 (1950): 89–95; Abramowitz, "The Negro in the Populist Movement," *Journal of Negro History* 38 (1953): 257–289; Martin Dann, "Black Populism: A Study of the Colored Farmers' Alliance through 1891," *Journal of Ethnic Studies* 2 (1974): 58–71; William F. Holmes, "The Demise of the Colored Farmers' Alliance," *Journal of Southern History* 41 (May, 1975): 187–200.

28. Goodwyn, "Populist Dreams," 1448, 1449–1450.

29. Theodore Rosengarten, *All God's Dangers: The Life of Nate Shaw* (New York: Knopf, 1974), 223.

Twelve

A POLITICAL EDUCATION

George T. Ruby and the Texas Freedmen's Bureau

George T. Ruby, one of two black state senators who
served during Reconstruction in Texas, has received considerable attention
from historians of the post–Civil War Lone Star State. Much of the focus
has been upon Ruby's political career, the characteristics that brought him
to the attention of the Republican Party, and his background. His performance in the Louisiana and Texas Freedmen's Bureaus has been ignored,
but this interlude in Ruby's life prepared him for his entrance into local
and state politics. Ruby's sojourn in the Texas Freedmen's Bureau provided
the foundation for his later prominence in state Republican circles.[1]

As a Galveston teacher, Ruby became well known in the city and to
the bureau. He brought considerable expertise with him from Louisiana,
where he had been employed as a teacher, a principal, and a traveling agent
for the Freedmen's Bureau, charged with identifying convenient locations
for the establishment of new schools. In both states, Ruby made tours that
allowed him to present his ideas about black freedom and to meet important local leaders of black and white communities. This knowledge of education and organization, along with his acquaintance with the condition of
Texas blacks, assisted Ruby in his future endeavors.[2]

Moreover, Ruby evaluated other bureau agents, judging their fitness for
their positions and their effectiveness at dealing with local black communities. Ruby, one of the few black agents in the entire South, evaluated the
strengths and weaknesses of white agents, informing headquarters whether
they were, in fact, serving the black communities in their subdistricts in a
manner that would promote economic well-being and civil rights. Southern blacks had now been enfranchised, so it was important that they understand the significance of their political power and how to use it. In
short, Ruby used his bureau position to further black equality.

Much has been written about Ruby's later political tenure in the state
senate and of his influence and power in Galveston. However, his early

years, when he was establishing himself, setting up a political base, and be-coming better known throughout the Texas black community, have been largely neglected. The focus in this essay is on Ruby's connection with the bureau as an educator and a traveling agent and how he used the agency as a springboard for his election to the state legislature. Without this initial acquaintance with the bureau's activities and its problems in dealing with postwar race relations, it would have been difficult for Ruby to make such dramatic strides in the political arena. The bureau provided a necessary platform to launch that career.

Testifying in March 1880 before a United States Senate select commit-tee on black migration to Kansas, Ruby declared that his occupation had been that "of journalist as well as that of an educationalist." Queried on whether he had "given special attention to the condition and wants and treatment" of southern blacks, Ruby claimed that he had had "intimate relations with them" and had become acquainted with their social, civil, and political situation during and after the war. Throughout his testimony, Ruby said little about his Texas political experience. He did suggest, how-ever, that it was his bureau activities that had prepared him for an entry into the new atmosphere of black political equality surrounding Recon-struction.[3]

Born in New York City two decades before the outbreak of the Civil War, Ruby later moved to Maine with his family. Almost nothing is known about his formative years, but in 1861 Ruby became involved with James Redpath's Haitian project, traveling to the island as a journalist to observe conditions and promote immigration by United States blacks as an alternative to slavery and restrictions on personal freedom. Redpath's scheme collapsed, and Ruby eventually found his way to Louisiana. Ex-actly when he arrived in Union-occupied New Orleans is unknown, but it may have been at the beginning of 1864. For the next two years he taught school, served as a principal, and sought out new sites for schools for black children.[4]

From 1865 until 1867, Ruby labored much of the time for the govern-ment organization commonly known as the Freedmen's Bureau. Officially entitled the Bureau of Refugees, Freedmen, and Abandoned Lands, the agency had been created by Congress in March 1865 to assist the former slaves in their transition to freedom. A national commissioner directed the bureau, and assistant commissioners supervised each of the former Con-federate states. Field agents served in cities, towns, and villages across the South. A major responsibility was the encouragement of schools for blacks.

Well-educated and highly literate, Ruby was well suited to become involved in the advancement of black education.[5]

The specific event that compelled Ruby to migrate to Texas occurred in September 1866 in Jackson, Louisiana. A few months before the incident, Ruby, as a traveling school agent for the Freedmen's Bureau, had visited East Feliciana Parish to evaluate schools and teachers and search for locations for new schools. After he completed his tenure with the bureau, Ruby returned to Jackson as a teacher and immediately encountered white opposition to the renewal of a school for blacks. Ruby proceeded to teach classes where he boarded. One day a group of whites appeared, seized Ruby, "belabored" him with the "muzzles of their revolvers," and threw him in a creek. It was time to leave Louisiana.[6]

Although their influence is not clearly documented, two men from Ruby's days at the Louisiana bureau may have promoted his budding political career. They were Edwin M. Wheelock and B. Rush Plumley. Both would become somewhat important figures in the Texas political arena. Wheelock was superintendent of education in 1866 and earned a reputation for being disputatious and more concerned about religious ideas than promoting black education. Texas Assistant Commissioner Charles Griffin removed him from his post. Plumley had initially been employed by the bureau in the education department in Louisiana, but, like Ruby, moved to Texas. He later served as a representative from Galveston in the Twelfth Legislature.[7]

It is not known precisely when Ruby arrived in Texas, but it appears to have been in the fall of 1866. It did not take him long to secure a teaching position with the Freedmen's Bureau in Galveston, since he was helped by his old acquaintances from Louisiana, Wheelock and Plumley. On October 15, 1866, Ruby began teaching at School No. 2; classes were held in the Methodist Episcopal Church. He started with a "small attendance," but by the end of the month he had admitted ten boys and twenty-one girls into the day school, two boys and three girls into the night school, and twenty adults and forty children into his Sunday classes. The majority of students paid tuition, of which he received $37.54. Ruby believed that prospects were good for increased attendance.[8]

During the period Ruby taught school in Galveston, he instructed over 1,900 students in his day, night, and Sunday school classes. Ruby must have been a particularly effective teacher, since the night school demonstrated spectacular growth in the early months of his tenure. Student tuition became the major source of Ruby's income, which amounted to

$359.19, or an average of about $44.90 a month. In January 1867, Ruby informed the superintendent that "for the first time since my labors here as a teacher I hope to pay my expense from money received for my duties as such." In his last report, Ruby believed that the "general progress" of the school had been "commendable and highly creditable to the pupils."[9]

On May 31, 1867, Ruby resigned his position as principal of the freedmen's school at the Colored Methodist Church. His resignation coincided with his appointment by Assistant Commissioner Griffin as an agent in the bureau itself, at a salary of $1,200 a year. Griffin, in urging Ruby's selection, stated that the black Galvestonian was "a very intelligent mulatto" and had been engaged in freedpeople's education in Louisiana and Texas since June 1864. "He is an energetic man," Griffin informed National Commissioner O. O. Howard, "and has great influence among his people."[10]

In June, before Ruby joined the bureau, he briefly assumed a position with the Texas State Council of the Union League. Although roundly condemned for a host of unverified sins, the Union League of America (ULA) was the institutional structure through which the Republican Party organized the Texas black community. Ruby was prominent in establishing various chapters throughout the state and later became president of the ULA. Although the League is often described as a secret society, in fact its major purpose was to imbue black Texans with the Republican philosophy of legal and political equality. Unlike its adversary, the Ku Klux Klan, the League rarely resorted to midnight assassinations and violence.[11] In Ruby's initial foray into the internal affairs of the League, he found himself embroiled in controversy. One of the council's agents, the Reverend H. Reedy, encountered "serious opposition" from Brazoria County blacks, who spread what Ruby styled as "malignant falsehoods" (namely, that Reedy was an "emissary of the rebels"). Opponents subsequently threatened Reedy's life. Ruby attempted to mediate the dispute, but with little success. He partially convinced the freedmen of Reedy's "good intentions," but the damage had been irreparable, and Reedy failed to establish a league chapter. Highly disappointed over Reedy's failure, Ruby wrote that it had retarded the "growth of so important a movement for our people."[12]

In July 1867, Ruby received a promotion from agent to Texas Freedmen's Bureau official. Assigned to tour the various bureau subdistricts, Ruby set out to evaluate the bureau's performance. First, he would determine how effectively a local bureau agent was conducting his responsibilities. Second, he was to observe how the black communities in the agent's region responded to the bureau's administration. Third, Ruby was to report on the status of race relations wherever he visited and determine how they influenced the work of the bureau agent—in short, how Reconstruction was progressing at the local level.

Initially, Ruby traveled to Brazos, Robertson, Falls, and Bell counties. At Millican, in Brazos County, his first destination, which was headquarters for the bureau's Twentieth Subdistrict, Ruby discovered serious problems. The bureau agent, Edward Miller, suffered from "bilious fever." Afflicted with chronic rheumatism, nephritis, and acute uremia, Miller was in such poor health that he was in no condition to fulfill his responsibilities; plus, he had lost an arm and received other serious wounds in the war. In addition, he was almost forty years old, whereas most other agents were in their mid- to late twenties.

Miller, who may have also been infected with yellow fever, complained to Ruby of the "multiplicity of his duties" and wished to be transferred to a position that had "less labor and care." Ruby observed Miller transact business: the agent impressed Ruby "as an earnest officer who would do all he could but who rather lacks the 'savoir faire' in execution." The more "thoughtful" freedmen, Ruby wrote, complained that Miller simply was not active enough in performing his job. This resulted in murder being so "rampant" that he "dared not act as he should." Actually, despite his limitations, Miller had investigated several killings and discovered that some federal soldiers had been paid to "stir up" black laborers.[13]

Ruby believed that Miller's subdistrict was "an exceedingly rough one" and nearly as bad as what he later found in Robertson County. He felt that the "people need a little rough handling." Since Miller was physically incapable of such activity, Ruby suggested that the area needed "an *energetic faithful* officer who can and will materially aid in the work of 'Reconstruction.'" But Miller was not totally inactive. With Ruby's assistance, he apparently formed a Union League chapter in Millican, as Ruby rather cryptically notes in a letter dated July 26, 1887.[14]

Nevertheless, Ruby's evaluation of Miller suggested that a change in the field officer for the subdistrict was required. Ruby had spoken with the freedpeople about their feelings regarding the agent, and they admitted they had little confidence in his ability. He learned that they did not feel Miller protected their rights to the fullest, and that someone should be appointed who did not suffer from the disabilities that affected him. Ruby concluded that the bureau was "not happy here in its appointment," the complaint being "'want of activity and energy' in the *administration of duties* in a subdistrict notorious for the general lawlessness of its rebel inhabitants."[15] Records do not provide evidence of Miller's fate.

In Robertson County, Ruby visited the town of Sterling, bureau head-quarters for that subdistrict. Here he encountered a "terrible state of affairs" involving freedmen and planters. Ruby believed the agent, Joshua L. Randall, to be "on the right side and determined to do his duty," but the rebels avowed their intention of "shooting the 'Bureau.'" Randall had been trained as a lawyer, so he was legally equipped to challenge the planter elite on behalf of freedmen who had been cheated out of their wages. The planters attempted to intimidate Randall with violence and even established a reward on his life. Randall, however, would not be deterred. Popular with the black community, he even went so far as to form a posse of blacks as a military escort.[16]

When Ruby arrived, Randall was "just up" from a severe attack of "bilious fever." While sick, the agent had "sent repeatedly for the doctors, [but] *not one would come near him.*" Ruby was impressed with Randall's efforts and declared that the bureau field officer was "active and true in the discharge of his duties and exceedingly popular among the freedmen and to the only Union white man known to live in the county," a Mr. Thompson, a bookkeeper for Ranger and Company. Being a Unionist, Thompson was in a precarious political position and could therefore offer no significant assistance to Randall. Ruby left Robertson County believing race and political relations were so disruptive that he feared for the future of long-term progress for the freedmen.[17]

Ruby could breathe a sigh of relief when he left Brazos and Robertson counties and moved into Falls and Bell counties. Ruby felt comfortable in Falls County and commented that "everything is quiet and orderly." But this was only on the surface. In fact, tensions were mounting in the county because of the antiblack actions of a previous bureau agent. Ruby contended that in the appointment of agent F. B. Sturgis, the Bureau gained "a judicious firm officer who endeavors to do his duty despite reports to the contrary." But Ruby soon discovered that the freedpeople and the Unionists were not pleased with Sturgis.[18]

Sturgis, who was from Pennsylvania, had a lengthy tenure in the Texas Freedmen's Bureau at various stations. In his initial efforts at LaGrange, Sturgis so pleased the white community that even conservative Governor James W. Throckmorton wrote a letter of praise to General J. B. Kiddoo, the second assistant commissioner of the Texas Bureau. But when Sturgis replaced A. P. Delano at Marlin, in Falls County, trouble ensued. Delano, whom a bureau inspector described as a "general overseer for the planters," had allowed employers to physically abuse their laborers and engage in assorted unlawful pursuits. Sturgis, who by now had observed Delano's activities somewhat, participated in Delano's indictment, which turned many whites against Sturgis.[19]

The leading Union men complained to Ruby that on "several occasions" Sturgis, in denouncing Delano's policies, had been guilty of refusing to listen to freedmen's complaints about planters' use of physical abuse ("blows and sticks") to discipline the laborers. Ruby asked the complainants if their county was quiet and did the agent "really do all he can?" After some investigation, Ruby concluded that it was in Sturgis's favor that under him the subdistrict had been "quiet and orderly when disorder and murder have stalked rampant all about him." Nevertheless, there was evidence that during Sturgis's tenure the freedmen were being "unfairly treated." The belief prevailed that violence would soon increase, since registration for the fall election had commenced and whites were expected to use intimidation to prevent black registration. Considering the circumstances, only military intervention could preserve the peace.[20]

Ruby attempted to negotiate some kind of compromise between the loyalists and Sturgis. Ruby asked the Unionists why they did not confront the bureau agent and inform him in unambiguous terms that he was "unwittingly perhaps frightening the freedmen from any action in the work of Reconstruction." The Unionists quickly responded that they had approached Sturgis once to no avail, but that they were willing to try again. Ruby also spoke with Sturgis about how matters stood. Sturgis, Ruby reported, expressed a "warm desire to act in harmony with the party," and Ruby discovered him to be a "very affable courteous gentleman," whom he hoped would settle his differences with the black and white Union men.[21] Once again, Ruby moved on before a resolution could be reached.

After completing his evaluation tour, Ruby took to the road once again, in August, to organize temperance societies and establish schools among the freedpeople throughout Brazos, Robertson, Falls, McLennan, Hill, Ellis, Navarro, Leon, Freestone, Bosque, and Bell counties. In Millican, Ruby found the school suspended (probably because of the yellow fever epidemic), but the freedmen expressed an eagerness to revive it. Millican blacks met with Ruby and pledged themselves to maintain 100 or more pupils. The instructor would be Kelsey, the registrar, who was also a "competent teacher." When voter registration ended, the school would open.[22]

As Ruby traveled about, observing the workings of the bureau and the black communities' responses to the agents, he learned of seemingly small matters that in reality were not insignificant. The bureau did not have an enviable record of paying its obligations quickly. For example, in Millican it came to Ruby's attention that Mary and Ella Smith, two teachers, owed a Mr. I. Myers, a freedman, and other black citizens, $50 for board. Miller, the bureau agent, had been requested to receive the various vouchers for the amount due. Trying to expedite payment, Ruby told headquarters that Myers was a "hard working man" and in need of the money.[23] Such matters were numerous and time-consuming, and in the end it was impossible even for a man of Ruby's energy and interest to settle them all.

For example, Ruby found the educational situation in Robertson County to be almost hopeless. He emphasized that no freedmen's school could be established where the freed people did not demonstrate a strong unity. The "fiendish lawlessness of the whites who murder and outrage the free people with the same indifference as displayed in the killing of snakes or other venomous reptiles" would prevent such an undertaking. Local blacks, however, refused to concede total defeat and continued to make plans to educate their children. Such was the case when Ruby visited the Ranger plantation, where he was told by the laborers that regardless of the opposition, they intended to open a school about the beginning of October.[24]

As another part of his assignment, Ruby focused upon the subject of temperance, or encouraging people not to drink alcohol. This was a favorite theme of Commissioner Howard and also of the missionary associations that sent teachers to Texas. The Texas bureau rarely required its agents to stress the importance of temperance; after all, they had enough other responsibilities. Perhaps being black and educated gave Ruby an advantage in speaking to a black audience, and he felt that he spoke to the freedmen with a "great deal of success on the importance of Temperance." They manifested much interest in the subject, and Ruby obtained in Brazos County 200 signers to the "pledge" to abstain from drinking.[25]

Ruby deemed it neither "wise" nor "expedient" to remain too long in Robertson County. After he induced more than fifty to sign temperance pledges, Ruby quickly moved on to Falls County. The school had been suspended for the summer. In Marlin, the county seat, Ruby proposed that a school be opened, since enough freedmen lived in this section to fully warrant its establishment. He thought it might attract thirty or forty pupils. In addition, there were several large plantations where schools might be opened. On the Stallworth place, Ruby found the owner favorable to the "school movement" and disposed to facilitate its organization, promising that by October a school would be in operation.[26]

At a "camp meeting," Ruby addressed a large number of laborers and planters, stressing the twin themes of temperance and education. He was "listened to with a great deal of attention." The 100 people who signed the temperance pledge also agreed to prominently display the certificate in their homes. Others promised to practice temperance in the future and to conduct themselves in a manner befitting "their new condition as citizens." Although some Sunday schools were in operation on area plantations, the local freedpeople needed the bureau's assistance to establish regular schools.[27]

At Waco, in McLennan County, a "prosperous inland town," a school with over 100 pupils had been organized under the direction of a principal and an assistant teacher. At a meeting, 300 freedpeople signed temperance pledges and listened attentively to speeches on education and abstinence. In east Waco, freedmen maintained a small private school, but Ruby was unable to gather any additional information. On the Downs plantation, nine miles below Waco, Downs indicated a willingness to educate the freedchildren, who numbered about thirty, and promised to give aid and provide a building if a male teacher could be sent. Other black settlements in the county required schools that Ruby thought could be used to "good advantage."[28]

Ruby found Hill County sparsely settled and the town of Hillsborough (present-day Hillsboro) a "squalid affair of a few tumble down houses." There were fifty or sixty black children in the area, and the freedmen were desirous to establish a school. One or two Union men privately told Ruby that they would contribute "their *moral* support," no "mean thing," Ruby remarked, "in a rebel community." In Ellis County, the bureau agent was hampered in his effort to maintain schools by the vast amount of violence aimed at black institutions. In Dresden (Navarro County), fifty children awaited a school, but again the "terrorism engendered by the brutal and murderous acts of the inhabitants, mostly rebels," wrote Ruby, prevented a school from being established anywhere.[29]

Moving on to Spring Hill, also in Navarro County, Ruby characterized the town as "a miserable rebel hole" and a "community of unreconstructed rebels." Despite the prevailing attitude, a Unionist by the name of Richy donated a large lot upon which could be erected a building for a school and church. Black and white loyalists agreed to cooperate in organizing a school, and another "unflinching Unionist" named Charles Winn agreed to be the teacher. To Ruby, this demonstrated "how *much* and *how deeply* the Union men of this section feel the importance of education for the freed and newly enfranchised people." He did not visit Leon, Freestone, and Bosque counties because of the numerous outrages that continued to be committed in those sections.[30]

According to Ruby, Bell County had been noted for its lack of murders and "grave outrages" during the war. In the aftermath, though, the freedmen were abused and the Union cause suffered. "Ultra secessionists" and outlaws who promoted constant turmoil had plagued the subdistrict, but by the time of Ruby's arrival, affairs had quieted somewhat. At Belton, the county seat, a "poor struggling village rough and uncouth in looks," as were its inhabitants, a freedman had begun a school with about sixty children.

In Salado (in southern Bell County), Ruby visited the bureau agent, Matthew Young. Young had assumed his position only about a month before Ruby arrived.[31] Apparently, the opposition to the bureau in this area had not yet marshaled its forces, because when Ruby visited the county, Young told him that all was "generally quiet." One of the major reasons for this peacefulness, Ruby soon discovered, was that only a few freedpeople lived in this vicinity. Ruby found their community "an extremely moral one for this county and Texas." They sold no whiskey, so no temperance lecture was necessary. Perhaps because of the community's moral and temperate tone, violence had rarely occurred. Ruby considered it a success that "but one freedman" had been "taken out and hung within a year." As political tensions began to increase, so did the number of outrages, but Ruby was gone by then.[32]

Ruby stopped at Georgetown, in Williamson County, on his return trip to Galveston. The freedpeople had purchased a lot upon which stood a house measuring twenty by thirty feet, to be used for school purposes. Unfortunately, the building required $250 of repairs to make it usable. Local blacks did not possess this amount. They requested the bureau's financial assistance, since approximately fifty children in the area were anxious to attend school. Even the white former rebels—Ruby called them "unreconstructed"—appeared to be "friendly to the proposed school." The freedpeople manifested "much anxiety" about their school, Ruby wrote, and the bureau agent had "promised to represent them and their wants."[33]

Although Ruby never specifically stated his precise educational philosophy, he did think it significant as a community endeavor, as evident from the number of speeches he gave on the subject. Ruby obviously understood the importance of an education, particularly for a largely illiterate people and the challenges that awaited them in a new society. But he also thought schooling valuable for loyal whites as well. Ruby believed that "schools ought to be established in every interior county of the State" to benefit both the freedpeople and the Unionist whites, who would also send their children. Ruby emphasized that this class of whites, who supported the Republican Party, was "socially ostracized and debarred even from school privileges by their rebel neighbors." [34]

Ruby remained with the bureau through September 1867, but he had begun to focus his energies upon political organization and the Union League. In late August, Governor E. M. Pease appointed him a notary public for Galveston County, which gave him an official position from which to expand his activities. Active in the Republican Party since early in the year, Ruby had served in a series of minor offices while performing his bureau duties. This heralded his entrance into the Texas political scramble, and he was elected a delegate to the constitutional convention that met in 1868 – 1869.

His Louisiana and Texas Bureau experience was an excellent training ground for the political machinations he would encounter. [35] Ruby had learned firsthand in his county visits the seriousness of the problems that freedmen and their families faced when trying to secure an education for their children and fair labor treatment, not to mention political rights.

As a northern-born black man and a mulatto, Ruby needed familiarity with southern mores and white attitudes in order to launch a successful political career. His tours of duty with the bureau in Louisiana and Texas gave him the opportunity to observe, evaluate, and respond to the condition of southern blacks at the close of the war and during Reconstruction. In educational settings or as a traveling agent and organizer, whether for schools, temperance societies, or the Union League, Ruby gained invaluable experience and cemented his ties with the former slaves. He worked long and hard, and suffered indignities, to promote the ideas of the Republican Party and the betterment of his race.

Ruby was one of a handful of black bureau agents in the entire South. Given the responsibility to evaluate and determine the future status of white agents in both Louisiana and Texas, Ruby received an insider's view into organizational politics and the tenor of the times. In addition, he came to understand the attitudes and hopes of both urban and rural former slaves. Working among them for three years, Ruby learned a great deal about their commitment to education and civil rights, often in the face of overwhelming odds. Ruby's bureau experience gave him the knowledge, the contacts, and the organizational base to enhance his future as a skillful politician.

NOTES

1. The best account of Ruby's career is Carl H. Moneyhon, "George T. Ruby and the Politics of Expediency in Texas," in *Southern Black Leaders of the Reconstruction Era,* ed. Howard N. Rabinowitz, 363–392 (Urbana: Univ. of Illinois Press, 1982). Other essays worth consulting are J. Mason Brewer, *Negro Legislators of Texas and Their Descendants* (Dallas: Mathis, 1935; 2nd ed., Austin: Jenkins, 1970), 20, 23–30, 53, 55–57, 61, 63, 75, 81, 115, 125–126; Randall B. Woods, "George T. Ruby: A Black Militant in the White Business Community," *Red River Valley Historical Review* 1 (Autumn 1974): 269–280; Barry A. Crouch, "Self-Determination and Local Black Leaders in Texas," *Phylon* 39 (Dec. 1978): 346–348, 354; James Smallwood, "G. T. Ruby: Galveston's Black Carpetbagger in Reconstruction Texas, *Houston Review* 5 (Winter 1983): 24–33; Merline Pitre, "George T. Ruby: The Party Loyalist," in *Through Many Dangers, Toils, and Snares: The Black Leadership of Texas, 1868–1900,* 166–173 (Austin: Eakin, 1985); Pitre, "The Evolution of Black Political Participation in Reconstruction Texas," *East Texas Historical Journal* 26 (1988): 36–45. Two brief sketches are *The Handbook of Texas* (Austin: Texas State Historical Association, 1952), s.v. "G. T. Ruby," 2:513; and Eric Foner, *Freedom's Lawmakers: A Directory of Black Officeholders during Reconstruction* (New York: Oxford Univ. Press, 1993), 187. Two surveys of black Texas legislators during this era, with attendant background information, are Alwyn Barr, "Black Legislators of Reconstruction Texas," *Civil War History* 32 (Dec. 1986): 340–352; and Crouch, "Hesitant Recognition: Texas Black Politicians, 1865–1900," *East Texas Historical Journal* 31 (Spring 1993): 13–34. It is unfortunate that no Ruby papers exist, because he does merit a full-scale biography.

2. For Ruby's Louisiana activities, see Barry A. Crouch, "Black Education in Civil War and Reconstruction Louisiana: George T. Ruby, the Army, and the Freedmen's Bureau," *Louisiana History* 38 (Summer 1997): 287–308

3. *Report and Testimony of the Select Committee of the United States Senate to Investigate the Causes of the Removal of the Negroes from the Southern States to the Northern States,* 26th Congress, 2nd sess., Sen. Report 693, serial 1899 (Washington, D.C.: Government Printing Office, 1880), Part II, 37–38. Ruby's involvement in the Kansas exodus is briefly discussed in Nell Irvin Painter, *Exodusters: Black Migration to Kansas after Reconstruction* (New York: Knopf, 1977), 213, 215–216, 245–246, 254.

4. Rodney Carlisle, *The Roots of Black Nationalism* (Port Washington, N.Y.: Kennikat Press, 1975), 75–76; Willis B. Boyd, "James Redpath and American Negro Colonization in Haiti, 1860–1862," *Americas* 12 (Dec. 1955): 169–182.

5. There is no satisfactory account of the bureau, but in general see George R. Bentley, *A History of the Freedmen's Bureau* (Philadelphia: Univ. of Pennsylvania Press, 1955); William S. McFeely, *Yankee Stepfather: General O. O. Howard and the Freedmen* (New Haven, Conn.: Yale Univ. Press, 1968); Donald G. Nieman, *To Set the Law in Motion: The Freedmen's Bureau and the Legal Rights of Blacks, 1865–1868* (Millwood, N.Y.: KTO Press, 1979). On the Texas bureau, see two widely di-

vergent studies: William L. Richter, *Overreached on All Sides: The Freedmen's Bureau Administrators in Texas, 1865–1868* (College Station: Texas A&M Univ. Press, 1991); and Barry A. Crouch, *The Freedmen's Bureau and Black Texans* (Austin: Univ. of Texas Press, 1992).

6. *Removal of the Negroes*, Sen. Report 693, 55; *Austin Weekly State Journal*, July 28, 1870; George T. Ruby (traveling agent, Texas) to Charles Garretson (acting assistant adjutant general [AAAG]), Assistant Commissioner, Letters Received (ACLR), R-26, Texas, Bureau of Refugees, Freedmen, and Abandoned Lands, Record Group 105, National Archives. Hereafter "George T. Ruby" will be abbreviated "GTR," and unless otherwise indicated, all citations will be to the Texas Bureau records in RG 105.

7. Richter, *Overreached on All Sides*, 212–213.

8. GTR, School Report for October 1866, Texas, Superintendent of Education (SOE). For background on Galveston during the immediate postwar years, see Stephen Franklin Shannon, "Galvestonians and Military Reconstruction, 1865–1867" (master's thesis, Rice Univ., 1975).

9. GTR School Reports, October 1866–May 1867; School Record, 21:4; Records of Schools, Vol. 23, 178, 181, 184, 187, 190, 194, 197; Records of Schools, Vol. 23, 68–75, all in Texas, SOE. Ruby did not explain how he paid the expenses from October to January. The general status of black education after the war can be followed in Alton Hornsby, Jr., "The Freedmen's Bureau Schools in Texas, 1865–1870," *Southwestern Historical Quarterly* 76 (Apr. 1973): 397–417. It is not based upon manuscript sources, which are voluminous for the Texas bureau.

10. GTR (Galveston) to J. T. Kirkman (AAAG), May 25, 1867, ACLR, R-25; Charles Griffin (AC, Texas) to Oliver Otis Howard (national commissioner), May 24, 1867, ACLR, 5:55; Griffin to Howard, May 24, 1867, ACLR, 5:55–56.

11. For general background, see Clement Mario Silvestro, "None but Patriots: The Union Leagues in Civil War and Reconstruction" (PhD diss., Univ. of Wisconsin, 1959).

12. GTR (Galveston) to C. Griffin, Apr. 10, 1867, ACLR, R-96; *General Orders, Special Orders, Circulars, and Rosters*, AC, Texas, 1865–1869, 9:374–375, 380–383. On the Union Leagues, see Carl Moneyhon, *Republicanism in Reconstruction Texas* (Austin: Univ. of Texas Press, 1980).

13. GTR (Marlin) to J. T. Kirkman, July 26, 1867, Texas, ACLR, R-186; Richter, *Overreached on All Sides*, 241.

14. GTR to Kirkman, July 26, 1867; Ruby also observed that few Union men lived in the county. Ruby's habit of not fully identifying people—either using only their last names or simply referring to their occupation—makes it difficult at times to follow his activities.

15. GTR (Galveston) to J. T. Kirkman, Aug. 12, 1867, Texas, SOE, LR, R-49.

16. Ibid.; Richter, *Overreached on All Sides*, 256–257.

17. GTR to Kirkman, Aug. 12, 1867; GTR (Marlin) to Kirkman, July 27, 1867, Texas, ACLR, R-187.

18. Ibid.

19. Richter, *Overreached On All Sides,* 180–182.

20. GTR to Kirkman, July 27, 1867.

21. Ibid. Ruby told headquarters that he wrote on the subject "as the matter may assume proportion." In sum, the political situation and violence could become serious and require attention.

22. GTR to Kirkman, Aug. 12, 1867; GTR (Millican) to SOE, July 21, 1867, SOE, LR, R-44; Robert C. Morris, *Reading, 'Riting, and Reconstruction: The Education of the Freedmen in the South, 1861–1870* (Chicago: Univ. of Chicago Press, 1981), 143.

23. GTR to SOE, July 21, 1867.

24. Ibid.; GTR (Galveston) to SOE, July 28, 1867, SOE, LR, R-44.

25. Ibid.; GTR to Kirkman, Aug. 12, 1867.

26. Ibid.

27. Ibid. Close to the Robertson plantation was a Sunday school with forty or fifty pupils, taught by a former bureau agent. Problems had arisen, however, because of a misunderstanding between the Union men and the agent, who had elicited "considerable feeling" among the loyalists.

28. Ibid.

29. Ibid.

30. Ibid. Ruby also claimed that Winn was an "educated talented gentleman." He further asserted that Charles E. Culver, the bureau agent, was "winning high encomiums from the Union people," who were pleased with his "efficiency and energy." On Culver, who was later assassinated, see James M. Smallwood, "Charles E. Culver, a Reconstruction Agent in Texas: The Work of Local Freedmen's Bureau Agents and the Black Community," *Civil War History* 27 (Dec. 1981): 350–361.

31. Ibid.; GTR to Kirkman, July 27, 1867; Richter, *Overreached on All Sides,* 174–175.

32. GTR to Kirkman, Aug. 12, 1867; GTR (Galveston) to J. T. Kirkman, Aug. 17, 1867, ACLR.

33. Ibid.

34. Ibid.

35. *General Orders, Special Orders, Circulars, and Rosters,* Sept. 1867, 9:403; GTR (Galveston) to E. M. Pease, Aug. 16, 1867, Governor's Letters (Pease), Texas State Library, Austin; Pease to GTR, Aug. 22, 1867, Executive Record Book, Governor's Papers (Pease), 28; Moneyhon, "Ruby and the Politics of Expediency," 364–368. Ruby's application for the notary-public position had endorsements from Charles Griffin, assistant commissioner of the Freedmen's Bureau, as well as B. Rush Plumley (Ruby's old Louisiana contact) and Oscar F. Hunsaker, who were prominent in the Galveston and Austin political arenas, respectively.

POSTSCRIPT TO PART IV

Crouch believed that the Freedmen's Bureau agents dispensed justice fairly. They treated the newly freed blacks with respect, and the former Confederates without arrogance or ill will. Working against nineteenth-century beliefs in limited government and the hostility whites felt toward their former slaves, a small number of Texas bureau agents nevertheless successfully administered the nation's first antipoverty program. Crouch's *Freedmen's Bureau and Black Texans* (Univ. of Texas Press, 1992) takes issue with the more critical and institutional approach of William L. Richter, who sees the army and the bureau agents acting in an imperious and authoritarian manner; for Richter's views, see *The Army in Texas during Reconstruction, 1865–1870* (Texas A&M Univ. Press, 1987) and *Overreached on All Sides: The Freedmen's Bureau Administrators in Texas, 1865–1868* (Texas A&M Univ. Press, 1991). Crouch's view in 1990 that a full-scale modern history of the Freedmen's Bureau needs to be written remains true today. Good starting points are the essays edited by Paul A. Cimbala and Randall M. Miller in *The Freedmen's Bureau and Reconstruction: Reconsiderations* (Fordham Univ. Press, 1999).

Crouch's most sophisticated analysis of Texas Reconstruction politics is his critical review essay of Merline Pitre's *Through Many Dangers, Toils, and Snares: The Black Leadership of Texas, 1868–1900* (Univ. of Texas Press, 1985). Here he calls for a prosopographical, or collective biographical, analysis of black Texas legislators and suggests models for analyzing the backgrounds and voting patterns of black Texas politicians and comparing them to those of their counterparts in other states. Carl H. Moneyhon's *Republicanism in Reconstruction Texas* (Univ. of Texas Press, 1980; reprint, Texas A&M Univ. Press, 2001) remains the best political monograph on the subject. The most recent study is *The Shattering of Texas Unionism: Politics in the Lone Star State during the Civil War Era* (Louisiana State Univ. Press, 1998) by Dale Baum, which combines thirty-nine tables and nine electoral maps with an array of literary sources, but goes only through the gubernatorial election of 1869. Baum emphasizes the reluctance of white Texans to accept African Americans as equal citizens. Other important essays include Alwyn Barr, "Black Legislators of Reconstruction Texas," *Civil War History* (1986); Donald G. Nieman, "Black Political Power and Criminal Justice: Washington County, Texas, 1868–1885," *Journal of Southern History* (1989); Randolph B. Campbell, "Grass Roots Reconstruction: The Personnel of County Government in Texas, 1865–1876," *Journal of Southern History* (1992); Campbell, "Carpetbagger Rule in Reconstruction Texas: An Enduring Myth," *Southwestern Historical Quarterly* (1994).

George Ruby, the best-known African American politician of Reconstruction Texas, has been the subject of a number of articles, as indicated in the footnotes of Crouch's essay. See in particular Carl H. Moneyhon's essay "George T. Ruby and the Politics of Expediency in Texas" (collected in *Southern Black Leaders of the Reconstruction Era,* edited by Howard N. Rabinowitz [Univ. of Illinois Press, 1982]), which also provides a nice short summary of Texas Reconstruction politics. A prosopographical study that could be a model for a study of black Texas politicians is Thomas Holt's *Black over White: Negro Political Leadership in South Carolina during Reconstruction* (Univ. of Illinois Press, 1977). For other, less sophisticated studies of local black politicians in Louisiana, Georgia, and other southern states, see note 21 to Chapter 10. Ken Howell has written an up-to-date, critical, yet nuanced biography of Governor Throckmorton: "James Webb Throckmorton: The Life and Career of a Southern Politician, 1825–1894" (PhD diss., Texas A&M Univ., 2005).

BIBLIOGRAPHY OF WORKS
BY BARRY A. CROUCH

BOOKS

(with John Vickrey Van Cleve). *A Place of Their Own: Creating the Deaf Community in America* (Gallaudet Univ. Press, 1982).

The Freedmen's Bureau and Black Texans (Univ. of Texas Press, 1992).

(with Donaly E. Brice). *Cullen Montgomery Baker: Reconstruction Desperado* (Louisiana State Univ. Press, 1997).

(with James M. Smallwood and Larry Peacock). *Murder and Mayhem: The War of Reconstruction in Texas* (Texas A&M Univ. Press, 2003).

(with Donaly E. Brice). *"The Governor's Hounds": The Texas State Police, 1870–1873* (to be published by the Univ. of Texas Press).

ARTICLES AND REVIEW ESSAYS (ESSAYS REPRINTED IN THIS BOOK ARE MARKED WITH AN ASTERISK [★].)

1967

"Dennis Chavez and FDR's 'Court-Packing' Plan." *New Mexico Historical Review* 42 (Oct.): 261–280.

1969

★(with L. J. Schulz). "Crisis in Color: Racial Separation in Texas during Reconstruction." *Civil War History* 16 (Mar.): 37–49.

1972

"The Freedmen's Bureau and the 30th Sub-District in Texas: Smith County and Its Environs during Reconstruction." *Chronicles of Smith County, Texas* 11 (Spring): 15–30.

"Rusticated Rebel: Amos A. Lawrence and His Harvard Years." *Harvard Library Bulletin* 20 (Jan.): 69–83.

258   *The Dance of Freedom*

1973
(ed.). "View from Within: Letters of Gregory Barrett, Freedmen's Bureau Agent." *Chronicles of Smith County, Texas* 12 (Winter): 13–26.
1974
★"Black Dreams and White Justice." *Prologue: Journal of the National Archives* 6 (Winter): 255–265.
"The Merchant and the Senator: An Attempt to Save East Tennessee for the Union." *East Tennessee Historical Society Publications* 46: 53–75. (Winner, Mc-Clung Award).
1975
"Postbellum Violence, 1871." In *Congress Investigates: A Documented History, 1792–1974,* edited by Arthur M. Schlesinger, Jr., and Roger Burns, 3:1689–1846. 5 vols. New York: Chelsea House.
1978
★"Self-Determination and Local Black Leaders in Texas." *Phylon* 39 (Dec.): 344–355.
1980
"Amos A. Lawrence and the Formation of the Constitutional Union Party: The Conservative Failure in 1860." *Historical Journal of Massachusetts* 8 (June): 46–58.
"Hidden Sources of Black History: The Texas Freedmen's Bureau Records as a Case Study." *Southwestern Historical Quarterly* 83 (Jan.): 211–226.
1981
"Freedmen's Bureau Records: Texas, a Case Study." In *Afro-American History: Sources for Research,* edited by Robert L. Clarke, 74–94. Washington, D.C.: Howard Univ. Press.
1984
★"A Spirit of Lawlessness: White Violence, Texas Blacks, 1865–1868." *Journal of Social History* 18 (Dec.): 217–232.
1985
" 'Booty Capitalism' and Capitalism's Booty: Slaves and Slavery in Ancient Rome and the American South." *Slavery and Abolition* 6 (May): 3–24.
1986
"Alienation and the Mid-Nineteenth-Century American Deaf Community: A Response." *American Annals of the Deaf* 131 (Dec.): 322–324.
"A Deaf Commonwealth," "Jay C. Howard," and "Anson Spear." In *Gallaudet Encyclopedia of Deaf People and Deafness,* edited by John V. Van Cleve. 3 vols. New York: McGraw-Hill.
"A Deaf Utopia? Martha's Vineyard, 1700–1900." *Sign Language Studies* 53 (Winter): 381–387.
★(with Larry Madaras). "Reconstructing Black Families: Perspectives from the Texas Freedmen's Bureau Records." *Prologue: Journal of the National Archives* 18

(Summer): 109–122. Reprinted in Timothy Walch, comp., *Our Family, Our Town: Essays on Family and Local History Sources in the National Archives,* 156–167. Washington, D.C.: National Archives and Records Administration, 1987. Also reprinted in Foundation for the National Archives, *The Road to Freedom: The Freedmen's Bureau Records* (Washington, D.C.: National Archives, 2006), a publication marking the completion of a five-year effort by the National Archives to preserve the Freedmen's Bureau Records.

1988

(with Patricia A. Mulvey). "Black Solidarity: A Comparative Perspective on Slave Sodalities in Latin America." In *Manipulating the Saints: Religious Brotherhoods and Social Integration in Postconquest Latin America,* edited by Albert Meyers and Diane Elizabeth Hopkins, 51–65. Hamburg, Germany: Wayasbah.

1989

"Gallaudet, Bell and the Sign Language Controversy." *Sign Language Studies* 62 (Spring): 71–80.

1990

★"'Unmanacling' Texas Reconstruction: A Twenty-Year Perspective." *Southwestern Historical Quarterly* 93 (Jan.): 275–302.

1992

"The Freedmen's Bureau in Beaumont." Pts. 1 and 2. *Texas Gulf Historical and Biographical Record* 28: 8–27; 29 (1993): 8–29.

★"Guardian of the Freedpeople: Texas Freedmen's Bureau Agents and the Black Community." *Southern Studies* 3, no. 3 (Fall): 185–201.

★"Seeking Equality: Houston Black Women during Reconstruction." In *Black Dixie: Afro-Texan History and Culture in Houston,* edited by Howard Beeth and Cary D. Wintz, 54–73. College Station: Texas A&M Univ. Press.

1993

★"'All the Vile Passions': The Texas Black Code of 1866." *Southwestern Historical Quarterly* 97 (July): 13–34.

★"Hesitant Recognition: Texas Black Politicians, 1865–1900." *East Texas Historical Journal* 31 (Spring): 41–58.

"'Magnificent Barbarian': Sam Houston Revisited." *Houston Review* 15: 3–30.

1994

"The 'Chords of Love': Legalizing Black Marital and Family Rights in Postwar Texas." *Journal of Negro History* 79 (Fall): 334–351.

"The Freedmen's Bureau in Colorado County, Texas, 1865–1868." Pts. 1 and 2. *Nesbitt Memorial Library Journal* 5 (May): 71–104; 7 (Sept. 1997): 147–175.

1996

★"The Fetters of Justice: Black Texans and the Penitentiary during Reconstruction." *Prologue: Journal of the National Archives* 28 (Fall): 183–193.

★"A Political Education: George T. Ruby and the Texas Freedmen's Bureau." *Houston Review* 18: 144–156.

1997

"Black Education in Civil War and Reconstruction Louisiana: George T. Ruby, the Army, and the Freedmen's Bureau." *Louisiana History* 38 (Summer): 287–308.

1998

"The People of the Eye." *Reviews in American History* 26 (June): 402–407.

1999

(with Donaly E. Brice). "Dastardly Scoundrels: The State Police and the Linn Flat Affair." *East Texas Historical Journal* 37: 29–38.

"A 'Fiend in Human Shape'? William Clarke Quantrill and His Biographers." *Kansas History* 22 (Summer): 143–149.

"'That Good Citizens Ask for It': The Pardon of John Wesley Hardin." *Quarterly of the National Association for Outlaw and Lawmen History* (July–Sept.): 10–23.

"'To Enslave the Rising Generation': The Freedmen's Bureau and the Texas Black Code." In *The Freedmen's Bureau and Reconstruction: Reconsiderations*, edited by Paul A. Cimbala and Randall M. Miller. New York: Fordham Univ. Press.

2001

"Captain Thomas Williams: The Path of Duty." In *The Human Tradition in Texas*, edited by Ty Cashion and Jesus F. de la Teja. Wilmington, Del.: Scholarly Resources.

INDEX

Ab initio controversy, 9. *See also*
    Pease, E. M.
African Americans. *See* Blacks
Agriculture, crimes concerning,
    166–170
Alamo City. *See* San Antonio
Albert (freedman), 103
Albrecht, Winnell, 136
Allen, Richard, 208–209, 230
Anderson, Thomas, 63
Apprentice law, provisions of, 143–144
Apprenticeship: black concerns over,
    44; and courts, 59; description of,
    44–45; legal cases involving, 58
Apprenticing law, and courts in
    Texas, 73
Apprenticing of children, 46
Apprenticing Statute of 1866, 45
Archer, John H., 188
Austin, Texas, 123–124
Austin Democratic Statesman
    (newspaper), 122

Baggett, James Alex, 4, 9, 227
Baker, Cullen, 108
Barnett, George, 170
Barns, Levi, 168
Barr, Alwyn, 14, 137, 203, 210–211
Bayou City. *See* Houston
Beath, David S., 189
Bell County, 195, 250

Belz, Herman, 199
Bickerstaff, Ben, 108
Bird, Luke, 168
Black Code of 1866: and blacks, 141;
    historians' views on, 134
Black codes: arguments for, 135, 138;
    and blacks, 119–120; enactment of,
    135, 148–150; historiography of,
    134–150; in southern states, 147; in
    Texas, 134–150
Black politicians: assessment of by
    historians, 251; comparison of black
    politicians in the South, 212; need for
    further study of, 213; needs of, 236
Blacks: and agricultural crime, 166,
    168; and apprenticing, 44–45,
    59–61; barriers to unity of, 228; and
    children, 43, 46–47, 71, 73; com-
    munity life of, 4, 15, 41, 107, 122,
    231, 234–235; concern for morality,
    60; and contract law, 141–143; and
    courts, 47, 59, 64–65; and education,
    7, 120, 235; and 1868 constitutional
    convention, 227; family life of, 39,
    42, 48, 58, 71, 75; and field agents,
    188–189; and Freedmen's Bureau, 46,
    48, 63, 65; in historiography, 4, 13,
    15, 203; and law, 54–63, 139–140,
    162, 191; limitations upon, 141,
    145; major concerns of, 211; and
    marriage, 62; and orphans, 44, 48;

Frigg, Campbell, 61
Furra, William, 189

Gaines, Matt, 13, 207
Galveston, Texas, 207, 241
Gender, 77–78
Geography, 228
Georgetown, Texas, 250
Gillespie, James, 161–162
Goodwyn, Lawrence C., 236–237
Goree, Thomas J., 159
Granger, Maj. Gen. Gordon, 55
Gregory, Edgar M., 55
Gregory Institute, 209
Griffin, Charles, 164, 229–230
Griffin, Roger Allen, 9
Griffith, Benjamin F., 108
Guns, legislation of, 145

Hamilton, Andrew Jackson, 8–9, 139
Harper, Jr., Cecil, 6–7, 186
Harriet Lane (U.S. steamer), 160
Harris, Virginia (of Harrisburg,
    Texas), 73
Harris County, 74, 77
Harrison County, 17–18
Hartsfield, Emma, 63
Haynes, John L., 149
Heath, R. B., 56
Hillsboro, Texas, 249
Historians: schools of, 204; views on
    Texas black code, 135
Historiography, 36, 90–91, 181–182,
    255–256; of Texas, 214. *See also*
    Blacks; Dunning school; Reconstruc-
    tion; Violence
Hogg, James Stephen, 208
Holt, Thomas, 210
Hooks, Wyatt, 103
Hornsby, Alton S., 7
Houston, Texas: black women in,
    69–83; and orphans, 73–74; racial
    violence in, 80–81

Houston and Texas Central Railroad,
    terminus in Millican, 231
Houston Massacre, 127
Howard, Gen. Oliver O., 123
Huntsville Prison, 159–160, 162–163.
    See also Prisons; Texas

Jenkins, Nesbit, B., 192
Johnson, Andrew, 40, 138
Johnson, Guy, 59–60
Johnson, Hiram S., 187
Johnson, P. T., 59–60
Johnson, Richard, 168
Jones, Lewis, 56
Jones, Thomas, 63
Jordan, Winthrop D., 118, 126

Kelley, James, 42
Kiddoo, J. B., 164
Kirk, Neil, 189
Klutz, George, 58
Ku Klux Klan, 100, 102, 232–233

Labor: and apprentice law, 143; and con-
    tract law, 141–143; and field agents,
    190; and Freedmen's Bureau, 149;
    and violence, 104–105, 109
Labor contracts, 56
Law: in antebellum period, 54; black
    acculturation to American values of,
    65; and blacks, 145, 162, 191; and
    children, 58; and civil authorities,
    191–192
Lewis, Gabriel, 46
Lewis, Lew, 46
Lewis, Sandy, 234–235
Liberty, Texas, 187
Lien laws, 143
Linney, Michael, 80
Litwack, Leon, 95, 100
Livestock: as commodities, 167; focus
    of penal code, 145–146; theft of,
    167–168

of black deficiencies, 187; to control blacks, 161; obligations imposed on whites, 173

Smallwood, James M., 7, 15, 137

Smiley, Fred, 190

Smith, Ashbel, 13

Smith, Robert L., 207

Sneed, Edgar P., 4, 137

Social code, guarded by whites, 105

South, definition of former slaves in, 138–139

Southern Intelligencer (newspaper), 125. *See also* Newspapers

Southern Methodist Church, 121

Special Committee on Lawlessness and Violence, 97

Spencer, Samuel, 60

Spencer-Dikes Case, 60–61

Spring Hill, Texas, 249

Sterling, Texas, 246

Stewart, Charles, 135

Stewart, John, 57

Sturgis, F. B., 246

Sturgis, R. B., 195

Sub-assistant commissioners, 6–7, 186. *See also* Field agents

Swayne, Wager, 172

Swine, theft of, 168–169

Taxation, 10. *See also* Republican Party

Taylor, Buck, 108

Tejanos, 20

Temperance, 248–249. *See also* Education; Ruby, George T.

Texas: apprenticing law in, 73; army of occupation in, 4; and black codes, 134–150; and blacks, 13, 59, 121, 125; and 1868 constitutional convention, 9–10; Freedmen's Bureau in, 6, 186; Freedmen's Bureau violence register, 96; racial separation in, 127; Reconstruction historiography of, 3–4, 6, 19, 198; Reconstruction

politics in, 8, 11; rural vs. urban areas in, 206; size of as issue, 100; and state historiography, 214; state penitentiary system in, 159–174; and state police, 11; vagrancy law in, 123; and violence, 100, 109. *See also* Black codes; Blacks, Freedmen's Bureau; Historiography; Prisons; Violence

Texas Constitutional Convention (1868), 96, 139

Texas State Council of the Union League, 244

Texas State Educational Convention, 121

Thirteenth Amendment, 64, 118

Thomas, Harry, 233

Thompson, Isaac, 42

Throckmorton, James W., 8, 140, 171–172

Timsy, Sarah, 43

Twelfth Texas Legislature (1870), 14, 210–211

Unionists, 247

Union League, 194, 230; and Republican Party, 244

Union League of America, 244

United States, as a rural society, 161

United States Army: and black codes, 134–150; and field agents, 195–196; and protection of blacks, 100; in Reconstruction historiography, 4; in Reconstruction politics, 5

Urban areas, 122

Urbanization, 20

Urban studies, 4

Vagrancy law, 123–124, 144–145

Vagrant, defined, 144

Vandal, Gilles, 167

Vick, Mary, 78

Vigilantes, 63, 166

Violence: and blacks, 104, 127, 166; towards black women, 80–82;